Approaches to Peace

~~~

A Reader in Peace Studies

Edited by

David P. Barash
University of Washington

New York   Oxford

OXFORD UNIVERSITY PRESS

2000

Oxford University Press

Oxford New York
Athens Auckland Bangkok Bogotá Buenos Aires Calcutta
Cape Town Chennai Dar es Salaam Delhi Florence Hong Kong Istanbul
Karachi Kuala Lumpur Madrid Melbourne Mexico City Mumbai
Nairobi Paris São Paulo Singapore Taipei Tokyo Toronto Warsaw

and associated companies in
Berlin Ibadan

Published by Oxford University Press, Inc.,
198 Madison Avenue, New York, New York 10016

Oxford is a registered trademark of Oxford University Press

Library of Congress Cataloging-in-Publication Data

Approaches to peace : a reader in peace studies/edited
  by David P. Barash.
      p.   cm.
    Includes bibliographical references.
    ISBN-13 978-0-19-512386-9 (pbk.)

    1. Peace. 2. International relations. 1. Barash,
David P.
JZ5538.A67 2000
327.1'72—dc21   98-27847
                                            CIP

20 19 18 17 16 15 14 13 12 11

Printed in the United States of America
on acid-free paper

Contents

Approaches to Peace

Introduction:
Approaches to *Approaches to Peace*

~~~

"There is no way to peace," wrote theologian and antiwar activist A. J. Muste. "Peace is the way." Maybe so, but there are, at least, ways of *approaching* peace, and this book will investigate some of them.

Rephrasing Muste, we might say that peace is never fully achieved; it can only be approached. Mathematicians call something "asymptotic" if it can be infinitely (or rather, infinitesimally) approached, but never quite reached. Peace, then, may be an asymptote. Unfortunately, we do not yet have the luxury of bemoaning a "near miss," regretting that although we approach peace very closely, it continues to elude us, remaining just beyond our grasp. The hard reality is that peace can barely be glimpsed, never mind grasped; what is frustrating, therefore, is not that peace is so close, but that it remains so far away.

Yet there is cause for hope. The Cold War is over. From Berlin to Johannesburg, seemingly intractable systems of oppression have collapsed, with remarkably little overt violence, and, in at least some cases, with the beginning of genuine reconciliation. More people—especially in Latin America—live under democracy than ever before. Environmental consciousness is widespread and increasingly acknowledged, along with the importance of human rights. Nonetheless, human beings are faced with many problems: a polluted and otherwise threatened planet composed of resources that are finite and whose limits may soon be reached (or may in many cases have already been exceeded); gross maldistribution of wealth, as a result of which the great majority of human beings are unable to realize their potential and vast numbers die prematurely; persistent patterns of social and political injustice, in which racism, sexism, and other forms of unfairness abound, and in which representative government is relatively rare, and torture and other forms of oppression are distressingly common. And this is only a partial list.

Despite all of these difficulties, daunting enough even if the world was to cooperate actively in their solution, the remarkable fact is that enormous sums of money and vast reserves of material, time, and energy are expended, not in solving what we might call the "problems of peace," but rather, in threatening and actually making war on one another. If it wasn't so tragic, the situation would be so absurd as to be high comedy. It seems unlikely that human beings will ever achieve anything approaching heaven on earth; however, it also seems reasonable to hope—and perhaps even to demand—that we will someday behave far more responsibly and establish a society based on the needs of the entire planet and the beings that inhabit it, a society that is just and sustainable, and one that is not characterized by major outbreaks of self-defeating violence.

In this book, we'll explore some of the prospects of, and the obstacles to, achieving such a world. We shall do so by sampling an array of classic, near-classic, and potentially "future classic" readings. My hope is that *Approaches to Peace* will serve as a kind of core curriculum around which courses in peace studies can cohere. This book, then, will have been successful if it proves to be a convenient source of certain essential and provocative writings, a useful touchstone from which students and instructors can voyage out into the important and exciting field of peace studies, defining it for themselves as they go.

A quick explanation and apology is therefore called for: assembling a collection of such readings is unavoidably arbitrary. Different editors would doubtless come up with different selections, particularly as the field of peace studies is itself a "work in progress." There is no shortage of suitable readings, however, and it has been painful to omit so many excellent candidates. Similarly, it has been difficult—and a bit arrogant—to abridge many of them. But to some extent, *Approaches to Peace* may be useful insofar as it doesn't go too far in indulging anyone's preference, even its editor's! So if this book whets the appetite but doesn't entirely satisfy, if it leaves the reader wanting more, then so much the better.

Students of peace are, ironically, a feisty and even occasionally combative lot . . . perhaps because their enterprise is especially likely to attract its share of dissidents. Different instructors may therefore want to branch out from this book and devote special attention to those topics of special concern to them: feminism and women's rights, for example, or specific regions of current violence and war, the history of recent conflicts, detailed proposals for a peaceful future, ideas of environmental and economic amelioration, exposé of egregious human rights abuses, additional sources of religious and/or ethical inspiration, case studies of particular crusaders for peace, human rights, nonviolence, and so forth.

Approaches to Peace reflects the assumption—characteristic of peace studies—that peace can and must include not only the absence of war ("negative peace") but also the establishment of life-affirming and life-enhancing values and structures ("positive peace"). Thus, an important concept in peace studies is that, as logicians might put it, negative peace is a necessary but not sufficient condition for positive peace. This book also assumes that there are no simple solutions to the problems of either peace or war; the war–peace dilemma is complex, interconnected, and often poorly understood. On the other hand, there is much to be gained by exploring the various dimensions of war and peace, including the prospects of achieving a just, sustainable world: in short, a way of living that will nurture life itself, and of which its citizens can be proud. A degree of optimism seems warranted, not simply as an article of faith, but based on the realistic premise that once human beings understand the situation and their own best interests, they can behave rationally, creatively, and with compassion. As we shall see, there are positive steps to be taken that will diminish humanity's reliance on organized violence to settle conflicts, and that will begin the construction of a better, more truly peaceful world.

To some scholars, peace studies may appear redundant, since most of its subject matter can legitimately be covered in various other academic disciplines, nearly all of which are better established: history, psychology, anthropology, sociology, literature, political science, economics, and so forth. But the reality is that students are unable to take courses in all of these fields, and if they wanted to cover the peace-related material, they would have to pick and choose, like a gourmet eating just a couple of shrimp from one casserole, picking out a few candied raisins from the dessert, and so on. Peace studies offers, instead, a unique focus on peace, just as women's studies selects material from traditional disciplines that relate specifically to women, or environmental studies focuses on the environment.

There is another way in which peace studies is special. Unlike the usual social science approach, which prides itself on being "value free," peace studies unblushingly acknowledges biases and preferences. It is scholarly, but not disinterested. It does not simply encourage the study of peace, but is in *favor* of peace: peace, we proclaim, is better than war, just as social justice is better than injustice, environmental integrity is better than destruction, and so forth. Peace studies is thus similar to medical science, which freely admits to a preference for health over disease. (Think of it as offering a kind of "planetary medicine.")

Despite the enormous ills of our planet, there is reason to believe that our most pressing problem is not hunger, disease, poverty, social inequity, overpopulation, or environmental degradation, but rather the violence that human beings commit and threaten to commit against others. This is especially true in modern times, with the invention of nuclear weapons, but is valid, too, in a world of "merely" conventional arms. Consider the deep irony of a planet, beset with desperate crises, whose inhabitants nonetheless spend their time and energies fighting with each other, thereby making things even worse: imagine a small, overcrowded lifeboat facing severe shortages of food and water, springing leaks, tossed about in stormy seas, and facing a long trip to safe harbor. Imagine further that within this lifeboat there are sufficient resources to patch the leaks,[1] keep everyone nourished, build adequate oars and makeshift sails so as to complete the voyage safely (maybe even enjoyably) . . . but squabbling breaks out among the occupants. Precious supplies, including the compass, get thrown overboard, and the boat itself is in danger of capsizing.

Perhaps try a different image. Imagine that a space probe headed for Mars has run into serious technical difficulties: the air supply is endangered, the energy source has begun to fail, and the craft has entered an unexpected metcor shower . . . whereupon the astronauts, instead of dealing with their problems, begin a fist fight among themselves!

It is indeed paradoxical that in a time of unique danger and difficulty, the inhabitants of planet Earth waste their time, resources, and energy—as well as their lives— fighting among themselves and/or preparing to do so. Sadly, there is nothing new in the human experience about recourse to war. What is new, however, is its profound inappropriateness: with the wolf at the door, we leap to our feet, grab a gun . . . and begin shooting each other!

It is also noteworthy that after decades on the brink of nuclear annihilation, the world situation has changed dramatically, notably with the dissolution of the former

---

[1] Or for an even more disquieting scenario, imagine that resources are *not* sufficient.

Soviet Union and the widespread disavowal of communism. This has deprived many of the most war-prone individuals of a feared (or favorite) enemy. And yet, such extraordinary reworking of the global map has not resulted in a comparable reworking of military expenditures, at least on the part of the United States. This may be because there has not been a comparable restructuring of the intellectual and emotional map, or of social relationships based on power, violence, or the threat of violence.

Any attempt to approach peace, if it is to be meaningful, must also approach this problem of redrawing the "conceptual cartography" through which most people structure their view of the world and their place in it. *Approaches to Peace* is perhaps best approached this way: as an offering to help its readers make some progress in approaching peace, in as many ways as possible, and regardless of whether—or even, where—they eventually arrive.

David P. Barash

Redmond, Washington

1

~~~

Approaches to War

It may seem perverse to begin our survey of "approaches to peace" by looking at the causes of war. But it can't be helped. War is humanity's most inhumane and destructive endeavor. Destroying not only lives, property, the environment, hopes, and dreams, it also wreaks havoc with any prospects for "positive peace," the goal for which most workers in peace studies strive. Accordingly, we must understand some of the causes of war. And this, alas, is easier said than done.

Mark Twain is reputed to have said that it was easy to stop smoking; he had done it hundreds of times! Similarly, it is easy to identify the causes of war: it seems there are hundreds of them.

"War" does not exist as a generality. There are, instead, individual wars, just as there are individual human beings. And just as every person is unique (not only genetically, but also in the private trajectory of his or her experience), it can be argued that the causes of *each* war require detailed study. The danger thus exists that in attempting to unravel the causes of war, or even of a particular war, we will fall into the error portrayed by poet John Saxe, when he depicted the blind men and the elephant:

> It was six men from Industan, to learning much inclined,
> Who went to see the elephant (though all of them were blind),
> that each by observation might satisfy his mind . . .

Each felt a different part of the elephant, and so the one touching the legs thought it was a tree, the one touching the tail thought it was a snake, and so forth. As it turned out, the blind men

> disputed loud and long, each in his opinion stiff and strong,
> though each was partly in the right, and all of them were wrong.

Trying to comprehend the cause(s) of war, each of the efforts presented in this chapter is similarly "wrong." But if we put them all together—and add a number of others, which considerations of space have prevented inclusion in this book—it is possible to get a comprehensive view of the peculiar, complex elephant that is war. Despite the fact that every person is unique, it is also true that useful generalizations can be made about

Homo sapiens. Similar generalizations can be made about that "species" of human behavior known as war.

It goes almost without saying that—at least from the Western perspective—every effect must have a pre-existing cause, and war should be no exception, even though there has been vigorous debate as to how best to categorize these causative factors. Not surprisingly, and not inappropriately, the search for war's causes has often become an effort to finger a limited number of identifiable culprits, or villains:

> In the eighteenth century, many philosophers thought that the ambitions of absolute monarchs were the main cause of war; pull down the mighty, and wars would become rare. Another theory contended that many wars came from the Anglo-French rivalry for colonies and commerce: restrain that quest, and peace would be more easily preserved. The wars following the French Revolution fostered an idea that popular revolutions were becoming the main cause of international war. In the nineteenth century, monarchs who sought to unite their troubled country by a glorious foreign war were widely seen as culprits. At the end of that century the capitalists' chase for markets or investment outlets became a popular villain. The First World War convinced many writers that armaments races and arms salesmen had become the villains, and both world wars fostered the idea that militarist regimes were the main disturbers of the peace.[1]

Circumstances thus do not only influence events, but also the interpretation of events. During the United States–Soviet Cold War, for example (not a direct shooting war, but a period of heightened tensions, characterized by a vigorous nuclear arms race, in addition to many "proxy wars," as in Korea, Vietnam, and Afghanistan), peace researchers tended to emphasize the clash of ideologies, the role of misunderstandings and misperceptions, as well as the potential danger of false alarms, while attributing roughly equal blame to expansionist tendencies on the part of the United States and the Soviet Union. Much attention was also given to the dynamics of arms races and the dangers of crisis decision-making. With the Cold War gone—but with war and warlike situations continuing—emphasis has shifted to nationalist passions, as well as to religious and ethnic conflicts.

Some researchers, attempting a more detached perspective, have looked to possible causes that are less situation linked, in the process coming up with theories connecting the onset of wars to factors as diverse as grand cycles of history and sunspots, population pressure, sexual competition and frustration, early childhood experiences, protein shortage, even the existence of pure, unmitigated Evil.

Preferred explanations are also influenced by political orientation. Thus, capitalism is often blamed by leftists, communism by conservatives. Progressive and left-leaning thinkers are generally more likely to attribute war to misunderstandings and other psychological factors, whereas those of the political right are generally more comfortable identifying what they see as innate human depravity. Nor is professional orientation irrelevant: biologists, for example, are prone to suggest that insight into the causes of war can be derived from consulting the human gene pool, as well as by examining aggressive behavior in animals. Psychologists are likely to emphasize the importance of

---

[1]Geoffrey Blainey. 1973. *The Causes of War.* New York: Free Press.

individual experience, whether early in life or as a result of learning and social conditioning, perceptions, and misperceptions. For many anthropologists, nontechnological war among "primitive" people can provide models for the more elaborate war of modern nation–states. Sociologists are inclined toward explanations that involve complex group processes, such as stability, national image, and the dynamics of industrialization or militarization. For political scientists, war-proneness cannot be meaningfully separated from the governmental systems involved, nor from reigning political ideologies. Economists, not surprisingly, are struck not only by the economic consequences of war and preparation for war, but also by the role of markets, competition, and economic systems in predisposing a country toward war. Mathematically inclined analysts examine quantitative models, including the so-called Prisoner's Dilemma, while theologians, psychiatrists, lawyers, and military specialists all have their own favored interpretations of why and under what conditions people are likely to resort to war.

This diversity should be seen as a source of hope, not discouragement. After all, it would be absurd to think that anything as complex as war could be "explained" in a single, simple way. (If it could, then the problem of war would probably have been solved long ago, and this book would be concerned only with "positive peace!") When it comes to understanding the causes of war, diversity is not only a source of strength, it is also more likely to yield answers.

In attempting to assess the causes of any war, or of war in general, it is important to distinguish between the announced reason(s) for its outbreak, which are often excuses concocted as public justification, and the actual, underlying causes, which may not even be accessible to the participants. One must also identify not only immediate precipitating factors (often military, political, or economic), but also pre-existing historical antecedents, as well as any other causes that may lie deeper yet, within the specific individuals involved, and also, perhaps, within human beings generally.

Take a recent undeclared war, the so-called Gulf War of 1991, in which the United States mobilized and led a multinational, United Nations coalition that drove Iraqi forces out of Kuwait. What was its cause? Here are just a few possibilities.

1. The role of leaders: The Iraqi leader, Saddam Hussein, was a violent, aggressive dictator, who took an opportunity to invade his defenseless neighbor, hoping to enhance his political prestige; and/or, United States president George Bush was largely responsible, because he felt personally challenged and perceived a need to banish his "wimp" image before the next presidential election.
2. Economic factors: Iraq sought to gain the economic benefits that would come from capturing Kuwaiti oil fields, and/or United States economic dependence on Middle Eastern oil made it willing to "trade blood for oil."
3. Psychological decision-making factors: Saddam Hussein misunderstood the position of the United States, when the U.S. ambassador indicated that Iraq's border dispute with Kuwait was an Iraqi–Kuwaiti matter and not one that the United States considered vital to its "national interest," and/or the American public's fears and hatreds were aroused by reports of Iraqi brutality toward Kuwaitis, and/or the Iraqi public was envious of the ostentatious wealth of the neighboring Kuwaitis, and/or Arab people, frustrated by their inability to defeat Israel, were eager to vent their rage against other enemies.
4. Historical factors: British colonialism actually caused the war, for when the British withdrew from the area, they created an artificial border between Iraq and Kuwait, because the British wanted to establish a pliant sheikdom that would permit Western oil companies to dominate

the extraction of petroleum from the region; and/or the U.S. military and political leadership wanted to prove that it had outgrown the "Vietnam syndrome," a supposed hesitatancy in the aftermath of the U.S. military debacle in Vietnam.

5. The Military-Industrial Complex: The U.S. military wanted to test an array of newly developed weapons, and also to demonstrate its importance since, with the ending of the Cold War, people had begun to question the value of maintaining a huge military establishment; and/or the U.S. "military-industrial complex" was eager for a war, so it could profit from greater demand for new weapons systems.

6. International Politics: Iraq's invasion of Kuwait was a clear invasion of international law, such that the maintenance of long-term peace and stability required a clear and vigorous response; and/or with the end of the Cold War, the United States no longer felt constrained by the prospect that the Soviet Union (previously Iraq's ally) would support Iraq.

For better or worse, a different list—similar in its complexity, unique in its specifics—can be constructed for every war. It would be a useful exercise, in fact, to select a few wars and do just that. The fact that the causes of war are often complex, diffuse, and multidimensional does not mean that searching for them is a waste of time. Out of that search can come a deeper understanding of the dilemma that is war; moreover, our insights into the causes of war will have great influence on methods of preventing specific ones, as well as on the prospects for eliminating war altogether.

Why War?

Psychiatric theories of war emphasize the role of individuals, both as leaders and as personal participants. Carl G. Jung, for example, attached special importance to the existence of a "dark side" within human nature. For Jungian analysts, this dark side, unacceptable to one's consciousness, is "projected" onto an Other, who becomes the Enemy, imbued with an array of hateful traits ... which actually originate within one's self. Jung was impressed with what he considered to be the human "collective unconscious," including powerful images such as those of heroes and enemies. Alfred Adler attributed great importance to interpersonal struggles for social dominance and to the "inferiority complex."

The American psychiatrist Harry Stack Sullivan felt that human fears and anxieties derived from inhibited communication, which in turn gave rise to terror-ridden distortions, which in their turn produce a tendency to strike out at those one does not understand and who are different. For Erik Erikson, personal wholeness and healthy integration can be threatened by confusing social ambiguity, both at home and in the society; as a result, according to Erikson, the confused individual may seek refuge in "totalism," which leads to unquestioning identification of the Self with the State, along with equally total rejection of the selfhood of others. Another important psychiatric theorist of war was Erich Fromm, who examined the formation of various "malignant," pathological personalities, especially among despotic, violence-prone leaders such as Hitler and Stalin.

The towering figure among psychiatrists looking for the causes of war, however, was Sigmund Freud, founder of psychoanalysis. For Freud, there is a direct link between aggression—a behavior of individuals—and the social phenomenon that is war, in that both are manifestations of the same underlying drive system. He believed that much "inhumane" behavior was in fact all too human, deriving from the operation of "Thanatos," or the death instinct, which he saw as opposed to "Eros," the life instinct. Although many of Freud's notions appear quaint today, and some of them could be seen as downright crackpot, his identification of the unconscious remains central to nearly all efforts to explain war (and most other behavior) at the level of the individual.

In 1932, Albert Einstein was invited by the League of Nations to initiate an exchange of views with another renowned person on a subject of Einstein's choosing. Einstein selected the question, "Is there any way of delivering mankind from the menace of war?" and his chosen correspondent was Sigmund Freud. Freud's response is reprinted below.

... Conflicts of interest between man and man are resolved, in principle, by the recourse to violence. It is the same in the animal kingdom, from which man cannot claim exclusion; nevertheless, men are also prone to conflicts of opinion, touching, on occasion, the loftiest peaks of abstract thought, which seem to call for settlement by quite another method. This refinement is, however, a late development. To start with, brute force was the factor which, in

"Why War" from *The Collected Papers*, Vol. 5, by Sigmund Freud. 1959. Edited by James Strachey. Published by Basic Books by arrangement with The Hogarth Press and the Institute of Psycho-Analysis, London. Reprinted by permission of Basic Books, a subsidiary of Perseus Books Group.

small communities, decided points of ownership and the question which man's will was to
prevail. Very soon physical force was implemented, then replaced, by the use of various
adjuncts; he proved the victor whose weapon
was the better or handled the more skillfully.
Now, for the first time, with the coming of
weapons, superior brains began to oust brute
force, but the object of the conflict remained
the same: one party was to be constrained, by
the injury done him or impairment of his
strength, to retract a claim or a refusal. This
end is most effectively gained when the opponent is definitively put out of action—in other
words, is killed. This procedure has two advantages; the enemy cannot renew hostilities,
and, second, his fate deters others from following his example. Moreover, the slaughter
of a foe gratifies an instinctive craving—a
point to which we shall revert hereafter. However, another consideration may be set off
against this will to kill: the possibility of using
an enemy for servile tasks if his spirit be broken and his life spared. Here violence finds an
outlet not in slaughter but in subjugation.
Hence springs the practice of giving quarter;
but the victor, having from now on to reckon
with the craving for revenge that rankles in his
victim, forfeits to some extent his personal
security.

Thus, under primitive conditions, it is
superior force—brute violence or violence
backed by arms—that lords it everywhere. We
know that in the course of evolution this state
of things was modified, a path was traced that
led away from violence to law. But what was
this path? Surely it issued from a single ver-
ity: that the superiority of one strong man can
be overborne by an alliance of many weaklings, that *l'union fait la force*. Brute force is
overcome by union, the allied might of scattered units makes good its right against the
isolated giant. Thus we may define "right"
(i.e., law) as the might of a community. Yet it,
too, is nothing else than violence, quick to
attack whatever individual stands in its path,
and it employs the selfsame methods, follows
like ends, with but one difference; it is the communal, not individual, violence that has its
way. But, for the transition from crude violence to the reign of law, a certain psychological condition must first obtain. The union of
the majority must be stable and enduring. If
its sole *raison d'être* be the discomfiture of some

overweening individual and, after his down-
fall, it be dissolved, it leads to nothing. Some
other man, trusting to his superior power, will
seek to reinstate the rule of violence, and the
cycle will repeat itself unendingly. Thus the
union of the people must be permanent and
well organized; it must enact rules to meet the
risk of possible revolts, must set up machinery
ensuring that its rules—the laws—are
observed and that such acts of violence as the
laws demand are duly carried out. This recognition of a community of interests engenders
among the members of the group a sentiment
of unity and fraternal solidarity which constitutes its real strength.

So far I have set out what seems to me the
kernel of the matter: the suppression of brute
force by the transfer of power to a larger combination, founded on the community of sentiments linking up its members. All the rest is
mere tautology and glosses. Now, the position
is simple enough so long as the community
consists of a number of equipollent individuals. The laws of such a group can determine to
what extent the individual must forfeit his personal freedom, the right of using personal
force as an instrument of violence, to ensure
the safety of the group. But such a combination is only theoretically possible; in practice
the situation is always complicated by the fact
that, from the outset, the group includes elements of unequal power, men and women,
elders and children, and, very soon, as a result
of war and conquest, victors and the vanquished—that is, masters and slaves—as well.
From this time on the common law takes
notice of these inequalities of power, laws are
made by and for the rulers, giving the servile
classes fewer rights. . . .

Thus we see that, even within the group
itself, the exercise of violence cannot be
avoided when conflicting interests are at stake.
But the common needs and habits of men who
live in fellowship under the same sky favor a
speedy issue of such conflicts and, this being
so, the possibilities of peaceful solutions make
steady progress. Yet the most casual glance at
world history will show an unending series of
conflicts between one community and another
or a group of others, between large and smaller
units, between cities, countries, races, tribes
and kingdoms, almost all of which were settled
by the ordeal of war. Such wars end either in
pillage or in conquest and its fruits, the down-

fall of the loser. No single all-embracing judgment can be passed on these wars of aggrandizement. Some, like the war between the Mongols and the Turks, have led to unmitigated misery; others, however, have furthered the transition from violence to law, since they brought larger units into being, within whose limits a recourse to violence was banned and a new regime determined all disputes. Thus the Roman conquests brought that boon, the *Pax Romana*, to the Mediterranean lands. The French kings' lust for aggrandizement created a new France, flourishing in peace and unity. Paradoxical as it sounds, we must admit that warfare well might serve to pave the way to that unbroken peace we so desire, for it is war that brings vast empires into being, within whose frontiers all warfare is proscribed by a strong central power. In practice, however, this end is not attained, for as a rule the fruits of victory are but short-lived, the new-created unit falls asunder once again, generally because there can be no true cohesion between the parts that violence has welded. Hitherto, moreover, such conquests have only led to aggregations which, for all their magnitude, had limits, and disputes between these units could be resolved only by recourse to arms. For humanity at large the sole result of all these military enterprises was that, instead of frequent not to say incessant little wars, they had now to face great wars which, for all they came less often, were so much the more destructive. . . .

I now can comment on another of your statements. You are amazed that it is so easy to infect men with the war fever, and you surmise that man has in him an active instinct for hatred and destruction, amenable to such stimulations. I entirely agree with you. I believe in the existence of this instinct and have been recently at pains to study its manifestations. In this connection may I set out a fragment of that knowledge of the instincts, which we psychoanalysts, after so many tentative essays and gropings in the dark, have compassed? We assume that human instincts are of two kinds: those that conserve and unify, which we call "erotic" (in the meaning Plato gives to *eros* in his *Symposium*) or else "sexual" (explicitly extending the popular connotation of "sex"); and, second, the instincts to destroy and kill, which we assimilate as the aggressive or destructive instincts. These are, as you perceive, the well-known opposites, love and hate, transformed into the-

oretical entities; they are, perhaps, another aspect of those eternal polarities, attraction and repulsion, which fall within your province. But we must be chary of passing overhastily to the notions of good and evil. Each of these instincts is every whit as indispensable as its opposite, and all the phenomena of life derive from their activity, whether they work in concert or in opposition. It seems that an instinct of either category can operate but rarely in isolation; it is always blended ("alloyed," as we say) with a certain dosage of its opposite, which modifies its aim or even, in certain circumstances, is a prime condition of its attainment. Thus the instinct of self-preservation is certainly of an erotic nature, but to gain its ends this very instinct necessitates aggressive action. In the same way the love instinct, when directed to a specific object, calls for an admixture of the acquisitive instinct if it is to enter into effective possession of that object. It is the difficulty of isolating the two kinds of instinct in their manifestations that has so long prevented us from recognizing them.

If you travel with me a little further on this road, you will find that human affairs are complicated in yet another way. Only exceptionally does an action follow on the stimulus of a single instinct, which is per se a blend of *eros* and destructiveness. . . . Thus, when a nation is summoned to engage in war, a whole gamut of human motives may respond to this appeal; high and low motives, some openly avowed, others slurred over. The lust for aggression and destruction is certainly included; the innumerable cruelties of history and man's daily life confirm its prevalence and strength. The stimulation of these destructive impulses by appeals to idealism and the erotic instinct naturally facilitates their release. Musing on the atrocities recorded on history's page, we feel that the ideal motive has often served as a camouflage for the lust of destruction; sometimes, as with the cruelties of the Inquisition, it seems that, while the ideal motives occupied the foreground of consciousness, they drew their strength from the destructive instincts submerged in the unconscious. Both interpretations are feasible.

You are interested, I know, in the prevention of war, not in our theories, and I keep this fact in mind. Yet I would like to dwell a little longer on this destructive instinct which is seldom given the attention that its importance warrants. With the least of speculative efforts we are led to conclude that this instinct functions in every living being, striving to work its ruin and reduce life to its primal state of inert matter. Indeed it might well be called the "death instinct," whereas the erotic instincts vouch for the struggle to live on. The death instinct becomes an impulse to destruction when, with the aid of certain organs, it directs its action outward, against external objects. The living being, that is to say, defends its own existence by destroying foreign bodies. But, in one of its activities, the death instinct is operative *within* the living being, and we have sought to trace back a number of normal and pathological phenomena to this *introversion* of the destructive instinct. We have even committed the heresy of explaining the origin of human conscience by some such "turning inward" of the aggressive impulse. Obviously when this internal tendency operates on too large a scale, it is no trivial matter, rather a positively morbid state of things; whereas the diversion of the destructive impulse toward the external world must have beneficial effects. Here is then the biological justification for all those vile, pernicious propensities which we now are combating. We can but own that they are really more akin to nature than this our stand against them, which, in fact, remains to be accounted for. . . .

The upshot of these observations, as bearing on the subject in hand, is that there is no likelihood of our being able to suppress humanity's aggressive tendencies. In some happy corners of the earth, they say, where nature brings forth abundantly whatever man desires, there flourish races whose lives go gently by, unknowing of aggression or constraint. This I can hardly credit; I would like further details about these happy folk. The Bolshevists, too, aspire to do away with human aggressiveness by ensuring the satisfaction of material needs and enforcing equality between man and man. To me this hope seems vain. Meanwhile they busily perfect their armaments, and their hatred of outsiders is not the least of the factors of cohesion amongst themselves. In any case, as you too have observed, complete suppression of man's aggressive tendencies is not in issue; what we may try is to divert it into a channel other than that of warfare.

From our "mythology" of the instincts, we may easily deduce a formula for an indirect method of eliminating war. If the propensity

for war be due to the destructive instinct, we have always its counteragent, *eros,* to our hand. All that produces ties of sentiment between man and man must serve us as war's antidote. These ties are of two kinds. First, such relations as those toward a beloved object, void though they be of sexual intent. The psychoanalyst need feel no compunction in mentioning "love" in this connection; religion uses the same language: Love thy neighbor as thyself. A pious injunction easy to enounce, but hard to carry out! The other bond of sentiment is by way of identification. All that brings out the significant resemblances between men calls into play this feeling of community, identification, whereon is founded, in large measure, the whole edifice of human society.

. . . The ideal conditions would obviously be found in a community where every man subordinated his instinctive life to the dictates of reason. Nothing less than this could bring about so thorough and so durable a union between men, even if this involved the severance of mutual ties of sentiment. But surely such a hope is utterly Utopian, as things are. The other indirect methods of preventing war are certainly more feasible, but entail no quick results. They conjure up an ugly picture of mills which grind so slowly that, before the flour is ready, men are dead of hunger.

As you see, little good comes of consulting a theoretician, aloof from worldly contacts, on practical and urgent problems! Better it were to tackle each successive crisis with means that we have ready to our hands. However, I would like to deal with a question which, though it is not mooted in your letter, interests me greatly. Why do we, you and I and many another, protest so vehemently against war, instead of just accepting it as another of life's odious importunities? For it seems a natural thing enough, biologically sound and practically unavoidable. I trust you will not be shocked by my raising such a question. For the better conduct of an inquiry it may be well to don a mask of feigned aloofness. The answer to my query may run as follows: Because every man has a right over his own life, and war destroys lives that were full of promise; it forces the individual into situations that shame his manhood, obliging him to murder fellow men, against his will; it ravages material amenities, the fruits of human toil, and much besides. Moreover, wars, as now conducted, afford no scope for acts of heroism according to the old ideals, and, given the high perfection of modern arms, war today would mean the sheer extermination of one of the combatants, if not of both. This is so true, so obvious, that we can but wonder why the conduct of war is not banned by general consent. Doubtless either of the points I have just made is open to debate. It may be asked if the community, in its turn, cannot claim a right over the individual lives of its members. Moreover, all forms of war cannot be indiscriminately condemned; so long as there are nations and empires, each prepared callously to exterminate its rival, all alike must be equipped for war. But we will not dwell on any of these problems; they lie outside the debate to which you have invited me. I pass on to another point, the basis, as it strikes me, of our common hatred of war. It is this: we cannot do otherwise than hate it. Pacifists we are, since our organic nature wills us thus to be. Hence it comes easy to us to find arguments that justify our standpoint.

This point, however, calls for elucidation. Here is the way in which I see it. The cultural development of mankind (some, I know, prefer to call it civilization) has been in progress since immemorial antiquity. . . . It well may lead to the extinction of mankind, for it impairs the sexual function in more than one respect, and even today the uncivilized races and the backward classes of all nations are multiplying more rapidly than the cultured elements. This process may, perhaps, be likened to the effect of domestication on certain animals—it clearly involves physical changes of structure—but the view that cultural development is an organic process of this order has not yet become generally familiar. The psychic changes which accompany this process of cultural change are striking and not to be gainsaid. They consist in the progressive rejection of instinctive ends and a scaling down of instinctive reactions. Sensations which delighted our forefathers have become neutral or unbearable to us; and, if our ethical and aesthetic ideals have undergone a change, the causes of this are ultimately organic. On the psychological side two of the most important phenomena of culture are, first, a strengthening of the intellect, which tends to master our instinctive life, and, second, an introversion of the aggressive impulse, with all its consequent benefits and perils. Now war runs most emphatically counter to the psychic disposition imposed on us by the growth of culture; we are therefore bound to resent war, to find it utterly intolerable. With pacifists like us it is not merely an intellectual and affective repulsion, but a constitutional intolerance, an idiosyncrasy in its most drastic form. And it would seem that the aesthetic ignominies of warfare play almost as large a part in this repugnance as war's atrocities.

How long have we to wait before the rest of men turn pacifist? Impossible to say, and yet perhaps our hope that these two factors—man's cultural disposition and a well-founded dread of the form future wars will take—may serve to put an end to war in the future.

KONRAD Z. LORENZ

On Aggression

Maybe human beings are "instinctively" aggressive. Not surprisingly, this approach has been especially prominent among biologists, themselves strongly influenced by a Darwinian approach to human nature. Of these, perhaps the most influential has been the Austrian ethologist Konrad Z. Lorenz, who shared a Nobel Prize in 1973 for his research on animal behavior. According to his thinking, there are a variety of positive, adaptive advantages to animal—and human—aggression. This is not to say that Lorenz extolled human aggressiveness; rather, he sought to understand its origin, pointing out that with the advent of modern technology, the human penchant for violence has become *Homo sapiens'* greatest danger, especially in conjunction with "militant enthusiasm" and, ironically, a *lack* of human instincts when it comes to restraints on violence.

In recent years, a more sophisticated version of instinctivism has gained currency. Known as "sociobiology," this approach is even more avowedly evolutionary, emphasizing that the capacity for aggressiveness is within the biological repertoire of human beings, just as it is for many living things. But so is cooperation and altruism. The key, then, is to identify circumstances in which people are predisposed to one behavior pattern or the other. Although biologists no longer accept "good of the species" arguments, we have chosen the following selection because the writings of Konrad Lorenz have been so influential.

What is the value of all this fighting? In nature, fighting is such an ever-present process, its behavior mechanisms and weapons are so highly developed and have so obviously arisen under the selection pressure of a species-preserving function, that it is our duty to ask this Darwinian question.

The layman, misguided by sensationalism in press and film, imagines the relationship between the various "wild beasts of the jungle" to be a bloodthirsty struggle, all against all. In a widely shown film, a Bengal tiger was seen fighting with a python, and immediately afterward the python with a crocodile. With a clear conscience I can assert that such things never occur under natural conditions. What advantage would one of these animals gain from exterminating the other? Neither of them interferes with the other's vital interests.

Darwin's expression, "the struggle for existence," is sometimes erroneously interpreted as the struggle between different species. In reality, the struggle Darwin was thinking of and which drives evolution forward is the competition between near relations. What causes a species to disappear or become transformed into a different species is the profitable "invention" that falls by chance to one or a few of its members in the everlasting gamble of hereditary change. The descendants of these lucky ones gradually outstrip all others until the particular species consists only of individuals who possess the new "invention."

There are, however, fightlike contests between members of different species: at night an owl kills and eats even well-armed birds of prey, in spite of their vigorous defense, and when these birds meet the owl by day they attack it ferociously. Almost every animal capable of self-defense, from the smallest rodent upward, fights furiously when it is cornered and has no means of escape. Besides these three particular types of inter-specific fighting, there are other, less typical cases; for instance, two cave-nesting birds of different species may fight for a nesting cavity. Something must be said here about these three types of inter-specific fighting in order to explain their peculiarity and to distinguish them from the *intra*-specific aggression which is really the subject of this book.

The survival value of inter-specific fights is much more evident than that of intra-specific contests. The way in which a predatory animal and its prey influence each other's evolution is a classical example of how the selection pressure of a certain function causes corresponding adaptations. The swiftness of the hunted ungulate forces its feline pursuers to evolve enormous leaping power and sharply armed toes. Paleontological discoveries have shown impressive examples of such evolutionary competition between weapons of attack and those of defense. The teeth of grazing animals have achieved better and better grinding power, while, in their parallel evolution, nutritional plants have devised means of protecting themselves against being eaten, as by the storage of silicates and the development of hard, wooden thorns. This kind of "fight" between the eater and the eaten never goes so far that the predator causes extinction of the prey: a state of equilibrium is always established between them, endurable by both species. The last lions would have died of hunger long before they had killed the last pair of antelopes or zebras; . . .

The opposite process, the "counteroffensive" of the prey against the predator, is more nearly related to genuine aggression. Social animals in particular take every possible chance to attack the "eating enemy" that threatens their safety. This process is called "mobbing." Crows or other birds "mob" a cat or any other nocturnal predator, if they catch sight of it by day. . . .

All the cases described above, in which animals of different species fight against each other, have one thing in common: every one of the fighters gains an obvious advantage by its behavior or, at least, in the interests of preserving the species it "ought to" gain one. But intra-specific aggression, aggression in the proper and narrower sense of the word, also fulfills a species-preserving function. Here, too, the Darwinian question "What for?" may and must be asked. Many people will not see the obvious justification for this question, and those accustomed to the classical psychoanalytical way of thinking will probably regard it as a frivolous attempt to vindicate the life-destroying principle or, purely and simply, evil. The average normal civilized human being witnesses aggression only when two of his fellow citizens or two of his domestic animals fight, and therefore sees only its evil effects. In addition there is the alarming progression of aggressive actions ranging from cocks fighting in the barnyard to dogs biting each other, boys thrashing each other, young men throwing beer mugs at each other's heads, and so on to bar-room brawls about politics, and finally to wars and atom bombs.

With humanity in its present cultural and technological situation, we have good reason to consider intra-specific aggression the greatest of all dangers. We shall not improve our chances of counteracting it if we accept it as something metaphysical and inevitable, but on the other hand, we shall perhaps succeed in finding remedies if we investigate the chain of its natural causation. Wherever man has achieved the power of voluntarily guiding a natural phenomenon in a certain direction, he has owed it to his understanding of the chain of causes which formed it. Physiology, the science concerned with the normal life processes and how they fulfill their species-preserving function, forms the essential foundation for pathology, the science investigating their disturbances. Let us forget for a moment that the aggression drive has become derailed under conditions of civilization, and let us inquire impartially into its natural causes. For the reasons already given, as good Darwinians we must inquire into the species-preserving function which, under natural—or rather precultural—conditions, is fulfilled by fights within the species, and which by the process of selection has caused the advanced development of intra-specific fighting behavior in so many higher animals. It is not only fishes that fight their own species: the majority of vertebrates do so too, man included.

Darwin had already raised the question of the survival value of fighting, and he has given us an enlightening answer: It is always favorable to the future of a species if the stronger of two rivals takes possession either of the territory or of the desired female. . . .

Unless the special interests of a social organization demand close aggregation of its members, it is obviously most expedient to spread the individuals of an animal species as evenly as possible over the available habitat. To use a human analogy: if, in a certain area, a larger number of doctors, builders, and mechanics want to exist, the representatives of these professions will do well to settle as far away from each other as possible.

The danger of too dense a population of an animal species settling in one part of the available biotope and exhausting all its sources of nutrition and so starving can be obviated by a mutual repulsion acting on the animals of the same species, effecting their regular spacing out, in much the same manner as electrical charges are regularly distributed all over the surface of a spherical conductor. This, in plain terms, is the most important survival value of intra-specific aggression. . . .

I think it has been adequately shown that the aggression of so many animals toward members of their own species is in no way detrimental to the species but, on the contrary, is essential for its preservation. However, this must not raise false hopes about the present situation of mankind. Innate behavior mechanisms can be thrown completely out of balance by small, apparently insignificant changes of environmental conditions. Inability to adapt quickly to such changes may bring about the destruction of a species, and the changes which man has wrought in his environment are by no means insignificant. An unprejudiced observer from another planet, looking upon man as he is today, in his hand the atom bomb, the product of his intelligence, in his heart the aggression drive inherited from his anthropoid ancestors, which this same intelligence cannot control, would not prophesy long life for the species. Looking at the situation as a human being whom it personally concerns, it seems like a bad dream, and it is hard to believe that aggression is anything but the pathological product of our disjointed cultural and social life.

And one could only wish it were no more than that! Knowledge of the fact that the aggression drive is a true, primarily species-preserving instinct enables us to recognize its full danger: it is the spontaneity of the instinct that makes it so dangerous. If it were merely a reaction to certain external factors, as many sociologists and psychologists maintain, the state of mankind would not be as perilous as it really is, for, in that case, the reaction-eliciting factors could be eliminated with some hope of success. It was Freud who first pointed out the essential spontaneity of instincts, though he recognized that of aggression only rather late. He also showed that lack of social contact, and above all deprivation of it (Liebesverlust), were among the factors strongly predisposing to facilitate aggression. However, the conclusions which many American psychologists drew from this correct surmise were erroneous. It was supposed that children would grow up less neurotic, better adapted to their social environment, and less aggressive if they were spared all disappointments and indulged in every way. An American method of education, based on these surmises, only showed that the aggressive drive, like many other instincts, springs "spontaneously" from the inner human being, and the results of this method of upbringing were countless unbearably rude children who were anything but nonaggressive. . . .

It is a curious paradox that the greatest gifts of man, the unique faculties of conceptual thought and verbal speech which have raised him to a level high above all other creatures and given him mastery over the globe, are not altogether blessings, or at least are blessings that have to be paid for very dearly indeed. All the great dangers threatening humanity with extinction are direct consequences of conceptual thought and verbal speech. They drove man out of the paradise in which he could follow his instincts with impunity and do or not do whatever he pleased. There is much truth in the parable of the tree of knowledge and its fruit, though I want to make an addition to it to make it fit into my own picture of Adam: that apple was thoroughly unripe! Knowledge springing from conceptual thought robbed man of the security provided by his well-adapted instincts long, long before it was sufficient to provide him with an equally safe adaptation. Man is, as Arnold Gehlen has so truly said, by nature a jeopardized creature. . . .

I have spoken of the inhibitions controlling aggression in various social animals, preventing it from injuring or killing fellow members of the species. As I explained, these inhibitions are most important and consequently most highly differentiated in those animals which are capable of killing living creatures of about their own size. A raven can peck out the eye of another with one thrust of its beak, a wolf can rip the jugular vein of another with a single bite. There would be no more ravens and no more wolves if reliable inhibitions did not prevent such actions. Neither a dove nor a hare nor even a chimpanzee is able to kill its own kind with a single peck or bite; in addition, animals with relatively poor defense weapons have a correspondingly great ability to escape quickly, even from specially armed predators which are more efficient in chasing, catching, and killing than even the strongest of their own species. Since there rarely is, in nature, the possibility of such an animal's seriously injuring one of its own kind, there is no selection pressure at work here to breed in killing inhibitions. The absence of such inhibitions is apparent to the animal keeper, to his own and to his animals' disadvantage, if he does not take seriously the intra-specific fights of completely "harmless" animals. Under the unnatural conditions of captivity, where a defeated animal cannot escape from its victor, it may be killed slowly and cruelly. In my book King Solomon's Ring, I have described in the chapter "Morals and Weapons" how the symbol of peace, the dove, can torture one of its own kind to death, without the arousal of any inhibition.

Anthropologists concerned with the habits of Australopithecus have repeatedly stressed that these hunting progenitors of man have left humanity with the dangerous heritage of what they term "carnivorous mentality." This statement confuses the concepts of the carnivore and the cannibal, which are to a large extent, mutually exclusive. One can only deplore the fact that man has definitely not got a carnivorous mentality! All his trouble arises from his being a basically harmless, omnivorous creature, lacking in natural weapons with which to kill big prey, and, therefore, also devoid of the built-in safety devices which prevent "professional" carnivores from abusing their killing power to destroy fellow members of their own species. A lion or a wolf may, on extremely rare occasions, kill another by one angry stroke, but, all heavily armed carnivores possess sufficiently reliable inhibitions which prevent the self-destruction of the species.

In human evolution, no inhibitory mechanisms preventing sudden manslaughter were necessary, because quick killing was impossible anyhow; the potential victim had plenty of opportunity to elicit the pity of the aggressor by submissive gestures and appeasing attitudes. No selection pressure arose in the prehistory of mankind to breed inhibitory mechanisms preventing the killing of conspecifics until, all of a sudden, the invention of artificial weapons upset the equilibrium of killing potential and social inhibitions. When it did, man's position was very nearly that of a dove which, by some unnatural trick of nature, has suddenly acquired the beak of a raven. One shudders at the thought of a creature as irascible as all prehuman primates are, swinging a well-sharpened handax. Humanity would indeed have destroyed itself by its first inventions, were it not for the very wonderful fact that inventions and responsibility are both the achievements of the same specifically human faculty of asking questions.

Not that our prehuman ancestor, even at a stage as yet devoid of moral responsibility, was a fiend incarnate; he was by no means poorer in social instincts and inhibitions than a chimpanzee, which, after all, is—his irascibility not withstanding—a social and friendly creature. But whatever his innate norms of social behavior may have been, they were bound to be thrown out of gear by the invention of weapons. If humanity survived, as, after all, it did, it never achieved security from the danger of self-destruction. If moral responsibility and unwillingness to kill have indubitably increased, the ease and emotional impunity of killing have increased at the same rate. The distance at which all shooting weapons take effect screens the killer against the stimulus situation which would otherwise activate his killing inhibitions. The deep, emotional layers of our personality simply do not register the fact that the crooking of the forefinger to release a shot tears the entrails of another man. No sane man would even go rabbit hunting for pleasure if the necessity of killing his prey with his natural weapons brought home to him the full, emotional realization of what he is actually doing.

The same principle applies, to an even greater degree, to the use of modern remote-control weapons. The man who presses the releasing button is so completely screened against seeing, hearing, or otherwise emotionally realizing the consequences of his action, that he can commit it with impunity—even if he is burdened with the power of imagination. Only thus can it be explained that perfectly good-natured men, who would not even smack a naughty child, proved to be perfectly able to release rockets or to lay carpets of incendiary bombs on sleeping cities, thereby committing hundreds and thousands of children to a horrible death in the flames. The fact that it is good, normal men who did this, is as eerie as any fiendish atrocity of war! . . .

Militant enthusiasm is particularly suited for the paradigmatic illustration of the manner in which a phylogenetically evolved pattern of behavior interacts with culturally ritualized social norms and rites, and in which, though absolutely indispensable to the function of the compound system, it is prone to miscarry most tragically if not strictly controlled by rational responsibility based on causal insight. The Greek word *enthousiasmos* implies that a person is possessed by a god; the German *Begeisterung* means that he is controlled by a spirit, a *Geist*, more or less holy.

In reality, militant enthusiasm is a specialized form of communal aggression, clearly distinct from and yet functionally related to the more primitive forms of petty individual aggression. Every man of normally strong emotions knows, from his own experience, the subjective phenomena that go hand in hand with the response of militant enthusiasm. A shiver runs down the back and, as more exact observation shows, along the outside of both arms.

One soars elated, above all the ties of everyday life, one is ready to abandon all for the call of what, in the moment of this specific emotion, seems to be a sacred duty. All obstacles in its path become unimportant; the instinctive inhibitions against hurting or killing one's fellows lose, unfortunately, much of their power. Rational considerations, criticisms, and all reasonable arguments against the behavior dictated by militant enthusiasm are silenced by an amazing reversal of all values, making them appear not only untenable but base and dishonorable. Men may enjoy the feeling of absolute righteousness even while they commit atrocities. Conceptual thought and moral responsibility are at their lowest ebb. As a Ukrainian proverb says: "When the banner is unfurled, all reason is in the trumpet." . . .

Anybody who has ever seen the corresponding behavior of the male chimpanzee defending his band or family with self-sacrificing courage will doubt the purely spiritual character of human enthusiasm. The chimp, too, sticks out his chin, stiffens his body, and raises his elbows; his hair stands on end, producing a terrifying magnification of his body contours as seen from the front. The inward rotation of his arms obviously has the purpose of turning the longest-haired side outward to enhance the effect. The whole combination of body attitude and hair-raising constitutes a bluff. This is also seen when a cat humps its back, and is calculated to make the animal appear bigger and more dangerous than it really is. Our shiver, which in German poetry is called a "*heiliger Schauer*," a "holy" shiver, turns out to be the vestige of a prehuman vegetative response of making a fur bristle which we no longer have.

To the humble seeker of biological truth there cannot be the slightest doubt that human militant enthusiasm evolved out of a communal defense response of our prehuman ancestors. The unthinking single-mindedness of the response must have been of high survival value even in a tribe of fully evolved human beings. It was necessary for the individual male to forget all his other allegiances in order to be able to dedicate himself, body and soul, to the cause of the communal battle. . . .

The object which militant enthusiasm tends to defend has changed with cultural development. Originally it was certainly the community of concrete, individually known members of a group, held together by the bond of personal love and friendship. With the growth of the social unit, the social norms and rites held in common by all its members became the main factor holding it together as an entity, and therewith they became automatically the symbol of the unit. . . .

Like the triumph ceremony of the greylag goose, militant enthusiasm in man is a true autonomous instinct: it has its own appetitive behavior, its own releasing mechanisms, and, like the sexual urge or any other strong instinct, it engenders a specific feeling of intense satisfaction. The strength of its seductive lure explains why intelligent men may behave as irrationally and immorally in their political as in their sexual lives. Like the triumph ceremony, it has an essential influence on the social structure of the species. Humanity is not enthusiastically combative because it is split into political parties, but it is divided into opposing camps because this is the adequate stimulus situation to arouse militant enthusiasm in a satisfying manner. . . .

The first prerequisite for rational control of an instinctive behavior pattern is the knowledge of the stimulus situation which releases it. Militant enthusiasm can be elicited with the predictability of a reflex when the following environmental situations arise. First of all, a social unit with which the subject identifies himself must appear to be threatened by some danger from outside. That which is threatened may be a concrete group of people, the family or a little community of close friends, or else it may be a larger social unit held together and symbolized by its own specific social norms and rites. . . .

A second key stimulus which contributes enormously to the releasing of intense militant enthusiasm is the presence of a hated enemy from whom the threat to the above "values" emanates. This enemy, too, can be of a concrete or of an abstract nature. It can be "the" Jews, Huns, Boches, tyrants, etc., or abstract concepts like world capitalism, Bolshevism, fascism, and any other kind of ism; it can be heresy, dogmatism, scientific fallacy, or what not. Just as in the case of the object to be defended, the enemy against whom to defend it is extremely variable, and demagogues are well versed in the dangerous art of producing supranormal dummies to release a very dangerous form of militant enthusiasm.

A third factor contributing to the environmental situation eliciting the response is an inspiring leader figure. Even the most emphatically antifascistic ideologies apparently cannot do without it, as the giant pictures of leaders displayed by all kinds of political parties prove clearly enough. . . .

A fourth, and perhaps the most important, prerequisite for the full eliciting of militant enthusiasm is the presence of many other individuals, all agitated by the same emotion. Their absolute number has a certain influence on the quality of the response. Smaller numbers at issue with a large majority tend to obstinate defense with the emotional value of "making a last stand," while very large numbers inspired by the same enthusiasm feel the urge to conquer the whole world in the name of their sacred cause. Here . . . the excitation grows in proportion, perhaps even in geometrical progression, with the increasing number of individuals. This is exactly what makes militant mass enthusiasm so dangerous.

MARGARET MEAD

Warfare Is Only an Invention—Not a Biological Necessity

Instinctivist theories of human aggressiveness have been criticized, especially because such views seem to promote the notion that warfare is "in our genes" and, hence, cannot be prevented. There is, indeed, some evidence that people who are politically conservative and typically pro-military disproportionately tend to believe that human beings are "naturally" aggressive, untrustworthy, and incapable of changing. In any event, the prevailing view among social scientists is that there is no "war instinct," even though aggressiveness may sometimes be readily evoked.

Anthropologists concern themselves largely with the activities of non-Western, typically nontechnological societies. There is legitimate debate about whether such study casts valuable light on modern, technological war-making. Some emphasize that the two situations are quite different, while others argue that examination of "primitive" war might help illuminate the conditions under which group violence has evolved. Some anthropologists, for example, claim that the capacity for warfare developed along with adaptations for hunting large game; others have emphasized competition for mates, for social prestige, or between rival bands.

A cross-cultural perspective on war reveals, among other things, a widespread tendency to dehumanize members of other tribes, often using literally animalizing terms to describe strangers and enemies. War-making is also typically associated with an array of rituals, with the enhancement of group cohesion, as well as with ritual purification connected with the taking of human life. A schism of sorts also exists among anthropologists, with some convinced that "primitive war" is functional (although not necessarily good) in meeting various ecological and social needs, while others claim that it is essentially dysfunctional, a social pathology.

In general, however, anthropologists have contributed less heavily to the study of war than might be expected. An exception is Margaret Mead, whose brief essay, reprinted below, has become a classic statement of the anti-instinctivist school.

From "Warfare is Only an Invention—not a Biological Necessity," by Margaret Mead. 1940. *Asia*, XL: 402–5.

Is war a biological necessity, a sociological inevitability, or just a bad invention? Those who argue for the first view endow man with such pugnacious instincts that some outlet in aggressive behavior is necessary if man is to reach full human stature. . . . A basic, competitive, aggressive, warring human nature is assumed, and those who wish to outlaw war or outlaw competitiveness merely try to find new and less socially destructive ways in which these biologically given aspects of man's nature can find expression. Then there are those who take the second view: warfare is the inevitable concomitant of the development of the state, the struggle for land and natural resources of class societies springing not from the nature of man, but from the nature of history. War is nevertheless inevitable unless we change our social system and outlaw classes, the struggle for power, and possessions; and in the event of our success warfare would disappear, as a symptom vanishes when the disease is cured.

One may hold a sort of compromise position between these two extremes; one may claim that all aggression springs from the frustration of man's biologically determined drives and that, since all forms of culture are frustrating, it is certain each new generation will be aggressive and the aggression will find its natural and inevitable expression in race war, class war, nationalistic war, and so on. All three of these positions are very popular today among those who think seriously about the problems of war and its possible prevention, but I wish to urge another point of view, less defeatist, perhaps, than the first and third and more accurate than the second: that is, that warfare, by which I mean recognized conflict between two groups *as groups,* in which each group puts an army (even if the army is only fifteen pygmies) into the field to fight and kill, if possible, some of the members of the army of the other group—that warfare of this sort is an invention like any other of the inventions in terms of which we order our lives, such as writing, marriage, cooking our food instead of eating it raw, trial by jury, or burial of the dead, and so on. Some of this list anyone will grant are inventions: trial by jury is confined to very limited portions of the globe; we know that there are tribes that do not bury their dead but instead expose or cremate them; and we know that only part of the human race has had the

knowledge of writing as its cultural inheritance. But, whenever a way of doing things is found universally, such as the use of fire or the practice of some form of marriage, we tend to think at once that it is not an invention at all but an attribute of humanity itself. And yet even such universals as marriage and the use of fire are inventions like the rest, very basic ones, inventions which were, perhaps, necessary if human history was to take the turn that it has taken, but nevertheless inventions. At some point in his social development man was undoubtedly without the institution of marriage or the knowledge of the use of fire.

The case for warfare is much clearer because there are peoples even today who have no warfare. Of these the Eskimos are perhaps the most conspicuous examples, but the Lepchas of Sikkim described by Geoffrey Gorer in *Himalayan Village* are as good.[2] Neither of these peoples understands war, not even defensive warfare. The idea of warfare is lacking, and this idea is as essential to really carrying on war as an alphabet or a syllabary is to writing. But, whereas the Lepchas are a gentle, unquarrelsome people, and the advocates of other points of view might argue that they are not full human beings or that they had never been frustrated and so had no aggression to expand in warfare, the Eskimo case gives no such possibility of interpretation. The Eskimos are not a mild and meek people; many of them are turbulent and troublesome. Fights, theft of wives, murder, cannibalism, occur among them—all outbursts of passionate men goaded by desire or intolerable circumstance. Here are men faced with hunger, men faced with loss of their wives, men faced with the threat of extermination by other men, and here are orphan children, growing up miserably with no one to care for them, mocked and neglected by those about them. The personality necessary for war, the circumstances necessary to goad men to desperation are present, but there is no war. When a traveling Eskimo entered a settlement, he might have to fight the strongest man in the settlement to establish his position among them, but this was a test of strength and bravery, not war. The idea of warfare, of one *group* organizing against another *group* to maim and wound

---

[2]G. Gorer, *Himalayan Village* (London: M. Joseph, 1938).

and kill them was absent. And, without that idea, passions might rage but there was no war.

But, it may be argued, is not this because the Eskimos have such a low and undeveloped form of social organization? They own no land, they move from place to place, camping, it is true, season after season on the same site, but this is not something to fight for as the modern nations of the world fight for land and raw materials. They have no permanent possessions that can be looted, no towns that can be burned. They have no social classes to produce stress and strains within the society which might force it to go to war outside. Does not the absence of war among the Eskimos, while disproving the biological necessity of war, just go to confirm the point that it is the state of development of the society which accounts for war and nothing else?

We find the answer among the pygmy peoples of the Andaman Islands in the Bay of Bengal. The Andamans also represent an exceedingly low level of society; they are a hunting and food-gathering people; they live in tiny hordes without any class stratification; their houses are simpler than the snow houses of the Eskimo. But they knew about warfare. The army might contain only fifteen determined pygmies marching in a straight line, but it was the real thing none the less. Tiny army met tiny army in open battle, blows were exchanged, casualties suffered, and the state of warfare could only be concluded by a peacemaking ceremony.

Similarly, among the Australian aborigines, who built no permanent dwellings but wandered from water hole to water hole over their almost desert country, warfare—and rules of "international law"—were highly developed. The student of social evolution will seek in vain for his obvious causes of war, struggle for lands, struggle for power of one group over another, expansion of population, need to divert the minds of a populace restive under tyranny, or even the ambition of a successful leader to enhance his own prestige. All are absent, but warfare as a practice remained, and men engaged in it and killed one another in the course of a war because killing is what is done in wars.

From instances like these it becomes apparent that an inquiry into the causes of war misses the fundamental point as completely as does an insistence upon the biological neces-

sity of war. If a people have an idea of going to war and the idea that war is the way in which certain situations, defined within their society, are to be handled, they will sometimes go to war. If they are a mild and unaggressive people, like the Pueblo Indians, they may limit themselves to defensive warfare, but they will be forced to think in terms of war because there are peoples near them who have warfare as a pattern, and offensive, raiding, pillaging warfare at that. When the pattern of warfare is known, people like the Pueblo Indians will defend themselves, taking advantage of their natural defenses, the mesa village site, and people like the Lepchas, having no natural defenses and no idea of warfare, will merely submit to the invader. But the essential point remains the same. There is a way of behaving which is known to a given people and labeled as an appropriate form of behavior; a bold and warlike people like the Sioux or the Maori may label warfare as desirable as well as possible, a mild people like the Pueblo Indians may label warfare as undesirable, but to the minds of both peoples the possibility of warfare is present. Their thoughts, their hopes, their plans are oriented about this idea—that warfare may be selected as the way to meet some situation.

So simple peoples and civilized peoples, mild peoples and violent, assertive peoples, will all go to war if they have the invention, just as those peoples who have the custom of dueling will have duels and peoples who have the pattern of vendetta will indulge in vendetta. And, conversely, peoples who do not know of dueling will not fight duels, even though their wives are seduced and their daughters ravished; they may on occasion commit murder but they will not fight duels. Cultures which lack the idea of the vendetta will not meet every quarrel in this way. A people can use only the forms it has. So the Balinese have their special way of dealing with a quarrel between two individuals: if the two feel that the causes of quarrel are heavy, they may go and register their quarrel in the temple before the gods, and, making offerings, they may swear never to have anything to do with each other again. . . . But in other societies, although individuals might feel as full of animosity and as unwilling to have any further contact as do the Balinese, they cannot register their quarrel with the gods and go on

quietly about their business because registering quarrels with the gods is not an invention
of which they know. . . .

In many parts of the world, war is a game
in which the individual can win counters—
counters which bring him prestige in the eyes
of his own sex or of the opposite sex; he plays
for these counters as he might, in our society,
strive for a tennis championship. Warfare is a
frame for such prestige-seeking merely
because it calls for the display of certain skills
and certain virtues; all of these skills—riding
straight, shooting straight, dodging the missiles of the enemy and sending one's own
straight to the mark—can be equally well exercised in some other framework and, equally,
the virtues—endurance, bravery, loyalty,
steadfastness—can be displayed in other contexts. The tie-up between proving oneself a
man and proving this by a success in organized
killing is due to a definition which many societies have made of manliness. And often, even
in those societies which counted success in
warfare a proof of human worth, strange turns
were given to the idea, as when the plains Indians gave their highest awards to the man who
touched a live enemy rather than to the man
who brought in a scalp—from a dead enemy—
because the latter was less risky. Warfare is just
an invention known to the majority of human
societies by which they permit their young
men either to accumulate prestige or avenge
their honor or acquire loot or wives or slaves or
sago lands or cattle or appease the blood lust of
their godsor the restless souls of the recently
dead. It is just an invention, older and more
widespread than the jury system, but none the
less an invention.

. . . Grant that war is an invention, that it
is not a biological necessity nor the outcome of
certain special types of social forms, still, once
the invention is made, what are we to do about
it? . . . Warfare is here, as part of our thought;
the deeds of warriors are immortalized in the
words of our poets, the toys of our children are
modeled upon the weapons of the soldier, the
frame of reference within which our statesmen
and our diplomats work always contains war.

If we know that it is not inevitable, that it is due
to historical accident that warfare is one of the
ways in which we think of behaving, are we
given any hope by that? What hope is there of
persuading nations to abandon war, nations so
thoroughly imbued with the idea that resort to
war is, if not actually desirable and noble, at
least inevitable whenever certain defined circumstances arise?

In answer to this question I think we might
turn to the history of other social inventions,
and inventions which must once have seemed
as firmly entrenched as warfare. Take the
methods of trial which preceded the jury system: ordeal and trial by combat. Unfair, capricious, alien as they are to our feeling today,
they were once the only methods open to individuals accused of some offense. The invention
of trial by jury gradually replaced these methods until only witches, and finally not even
witches, had to resort to the ordeal. . . . In each
case the old method was replaced by a new
social invention. The ordeal did not go out
because people thought it unjust or wrong; it
went out because a method more congruent
with the institutions and feelings of the period
was invented. And, if we despair over the way
in which war seems such an ingrained habit of
most of the human race, we can take comfort
from the fact that a poor invention will usually
give place to a better invention.

For this, two conditions, at least, are necessary. The people must recognize the defects of
the old invention, and someone must make a
new one. Propaganda against warfare, docu-
mentation of its terrible cost in human suffering
and social waste, these prepare the ground by
teaching people to feel that warfare is a defective social institution. There is further needed a
belief that social invention is possible and the
invention of new methods which will render
warfare as out of date as the tractor is making
the plow, or the motor car the horse and buggy.
A form of behavior becomes out of date only
when something else takes its place, and, in
order to invent forms of behavior which will
make war obsolete, it is a first requirement to
believe that an invention is possible.

War and Other Essays

Sociological perspectives on war tend to fall into two camps. A German school, under the influence of the philosopher Georg Hegel, and later, sociologists such as von Bernhardi, Gumplowicz, and Ranzenhofer, developed a "sociology of conflict," which saw warfare as necessary and desirable for the evolution of society. "War," wrote Hegel, in *Philosophy of Right*, "has the higher meaning that through it ... the ethical health of nations is maintained; ... war prevents a corruption of nations which a perpetual peace would produce."

By contrast, an Anglo-French-American tradition, represented initially by John Stuart Mill, Auguste Comte, and Emile Durkheim, focused on the differentiation and integration of social groups, the role of group consensus, and what they saw as the problem of "in-group amity, out-group enmity." They were interested in the role of war in the development of the nation-state, and they treated national competition less as a desired outcome than as an objective fact of life to be analyzed and understood.

Others have sought to understand the relationship between industrialization and war, as well as the powerful and complex phenomenon of nationalism. The following selection is by William Graham Sumner, one of the founders of American sociology.

We have heard our political leaders say from time to time that, "War is necessary," "War is a good thing." They were trying to establish a major premise which would suggest the conclusion, "Therefore let us have a little war now," or "It is wise, on general principles, to have a war once in a while." That argument may be taken as the text of the present essay. It has seemed to me worth while to show from the history of civilization just what war has done and has not done for the welfare of mankind.

In the eighteenth century it was assumed that the primitive state of mankind was one of Arcadian peace, joy, and contentment. In the nineteenth century the assumption went over to the other extreme—that the primitive state was one of universal warfare. This, like the former notion, is a great exaggeration. Man in the most primitive and uncivilized state known to us does not practice war all the time; he dreads it. He might rather be described as a peaceful animal. Real warfare comes with the collisions of more developed societies. . . .

War arises from the competition of life, not from the struggle for existence. In the struggle for existence a man is wrestling with nature to extort from her the means of subsistence. It is when two men are striving side by side in the struggle for existence to extort from nature the supplies they need that they come into rivalry, and a collision of interest with each other takes place. This collision may be light and unimportant, if the supplies are large and the number of men small, or it may be harsh and violent, if there are many men striving for a small supply. This collision we call the competition of life. Of course, men are in the competition of life with beasts, reptiles, insects, and plants—in short, with all organic forms; we will, however, confine our attention to men. The greater or less intensity of the competition of life is a fundamental condition of human existence ... The members of the unit group work together. The Australian or Bushman hunter goes abroad to seek meat food, while the woman stays by the fire at a trysting place with the children and collects

From *War and Other Essays*. by Graham Sumner. 1911. New Haven, Conn: Yale University Press.

plant food. They cooperate in the struggle for existence, and the size of the group is fixed by the number who can work, together to the greatest advantage under their mode of life. Such a group, therefore, has a common interest. It must have control of a certain area of land; hence it comes into collision of interest with every other group. The competition of life, therefore, arises between groups not between individuals, and we see that the members of the ingroup are allies and joint partners in one interest while they are brought into antagonism of interest with all outsiders. . . .

Each group must regard every other as a possible enemy on account of the antagonism of interests, and so it views every other group with suspicion and distrust, although actual hostilities occur only on specific occasion. Every member of another group is a stranger; he may be admitted as a guest, in which case rights and security are granted him, but, if not so admitted, he is an enemy. We can now see why the sentiments of peace and cooperation inside are complementary to sentiments of hostility outside. It is because any group, in order to be strong against an outside enemy, must be well disciplined, harmonious, and peaceful inside; in other words, because discord inside would cause defeat in battle with another group. Therefore the same conditions which made men warlike against outsiders made them yield to the control of chiefs, submit to discipline, obey law, cultivate peace, and create institutions inside. The notion of rights grows up in the ingroup from the usages established there securing peace. There was a double education, at the same time, out of the same facts and relations. It is no paradox at all to say that peace makes war and that war makes peace. There are two codes of morals and two sets of mores, one for comrades inside and the other for strangers outside, and they arise from the same interests. Against outsiders it was meritorious to kill, plunder, practice blood revenge, and to steal women and slaves, but inside none of these things could be allowed because they would produce discord and weakness. Hence, in the ingroup, law (under the forms of custom and taboo) and institutions had to take the place of force. Every group was a peace group inside, and the peace was sanctioned by the ghosts of the ancestors who had handed down the customs and taboos. Against outsiders religion sanctioned and encouraged

war, for the ghosts of the ancestors, or the gods, would rejoice to see their posterity and worshipers once more defeat, slay, plunder, and enslave the ancient enemy.

. . . A peaceful society must be industrial because it must produce instead of plundering; it is for this reason that the industrial type of society is the opposite of the militant type. In any state on the continent of Europe today these two types of societal organization may be seen interwoven with each other and fighting each other. Industrialism builds up; militancy wastes. If a railroad is built, trade and intercourse indicate a line on which it ought to run; military strategy, however, overrules this and requires that it run otherwise. Then all the interests of trade and intercourse must be subjected to constant delay and expense because the line does not conform to them. Not a discovery or invention is made but the war and navy bureaus of all the great nations seize it to see what use can be made of it in war. It is evident that men love war; when two hundred thousand men in the United States volunteer in a month for a war with Spain which appeals to no sense of wrong against their country and to no other strong sentiment of human nature, when their lives are by no means monotonous or destitute of interest, and where life offers chances of wealth and prosperity, the pure love of adventure and war must be strong in our population. Europeans who have to do military service have no such enthusiasm for war as war. The presence of such a sentiment in the midst of the most purely industrial state in the world is a wonderful phenomenon. At the same time the social philosophy of the modern civilized world is saturated with humanitarianism and flabby sentimentalism. The humanitarianism is in the literature; by it the reading public is led to suppose that the world is advancing along some line which they call "progress" toward peace and brotherly love. Nothing could be more mistaken. We read of fist law and constant war in the Middle Ages and think that life must have been full of conflicts and bloodshed then, but modern warfare bears down on the whole population with a frightful weight through all the years of peace. Never, from the day of barbarism down to our own time, has every man in a society been a soldier until now, and the armaments of today are immensely more costly than ever before. There is only one limit possible to the war preparations of a modern European state; that is, the last man and the last dollar it can control. What will come of the mixture of sentimental social philosophy and warlike policy? There is only one thing rationally to be expected, and that is a frightful effusion of blood in revolution and war during the century now opening.

It is said that there are important offsets to all the burden and harm of this exaggerated militancy. That is true. Institutions and customs in human society are never either all good or all bad. We cannot adopt either peacefulness or warlikeness as a sole true philosophy. Military discipline educates; military interest awakens all the powers of men, so that they are eager to win and their ingenuity is quickened to invent new and better weapons. In history the military inventions have led the way and have been afterward applied to industry. Chemical inventions were made in the attempt to produce combinations which would be destructive in war; we owe some of our most useful substances to discoveries which were made in this effort. The skill of artisans has been developed in making weapons, and then that skill has been available for industry. The only big machines which the ancients ever made were battering rams, catapults, and other engines of war. The construction of these things familiarized men with mechanical devices which were capable of universal application. Gunpowder was discovered in the attempt to rediscover Greek fire; it was a grand invention in military art, but we should never have had our canals, railroads, and other great works without such explosives. Again, we are indebted to the chemical experiments in search of military agents for our friction matches. . . . We find, then, that in the past, war has played a great part in the irrational nature process by which things have come to pass. But the nature processes are frightful; they contain no allowance for the feelings and interests of individuals—for it is only individuals who have feelings and interests. The nature elements never suffer, and they never pity. If we are terrified at the nature processes, there is only one way to escape them; it is the way by which men have always evaded them to some extent; it is by knowledge, by rational methods, and by the arts. The facts which have been presented about the functions of war in the past are not flattering to the human reason or conscience. They seem to show that we are as much indebted for our welfare to base passion as to noble and intelligent endeavor. At the present moment things do not look much better. We talk of civilizing lower races, but we never have done it yet; we have exterminated them. Our devices for civilizing them have been as disastrous to them as our firearms. At the beginning of the twentieth century the great civilized nations are making haste, in the utmost jealousy of each other, to seize upon all the outlying parts of the globe; they are vying with each other in the construction of navies by which each may defend its share against the others. What will happen? As they are preparing for war, they certainly will have war, and their methods of colonization and exploitation will destroy the aborigines. In this way the human race will be civilized—but by the extermination of the uncivilized—unless the men of the twentieth century can devise plans for dealing with aborigines which are better than any which have yet been devised. No one has yet found any way in which two races, far apart in blood and culture, can be amalgamated into one society with satisfaction to both. Plainly, in this matter which lies in the immediate future, the only alternatives to force and bloodshed are more knowledge and more reason. . . .

Can peace be universal? There is no reason to believe it. It is a fallacy to suppose that, by widening the peace group more and more, it can at last embrace all mankind. What happens is that, as it grows bigger, differences, discords, antagonisms, and war begin inside of it on account of the divergence of interests. Since evil passions are a part of human nature and are in all societies all the time, a part of the energy of the society is constantly spent in repressing them. If all nations should resolve to have no armed ships any more, pirates would reappear upon the ocean; the police of the seas must be maintained. We could not dispense with our militia; we have too frequent need of it now. But police defense is not war in the sense in which I have been discussing it. War in the future will be the clash of policies of national vanity and selfishness when they cross each other's path.

If you want war, nourish a doctrine. Doctrines are the most frightful tyrants to which men ever are subject, because doctrines get inside of a man's own reason and betray him against himself. Civilized men have done their fiercest fighting for doctrines. The reconquest of the Holy Sepulcher, "the balance of power," "no universal dominion," "trade follows the flag," "he who holds the land will hold the sea," "the throne and the altar," the revolution, the faith—these are the things for which men have given their lives. What are they all? Nothing but rhetoric and phantasms. Doctrines are always vague; it would ruin a doctrine to define it, because then it could be analyzed, tested, criticized, and verified; but nothing ought to be tolerated which cannot be so tested. Somebody asks you with astonishment and horror whether you do not believe in the Monroe Doctrine. You do not know whether you do or not because you do not know what it is, but you do not dare to say that you do not because you understand that it is one of the things which every good American is bound to believe in. Now when any doctrine arrives at that degree of authority, the name of it is a club which any demagogue may swing over you at any time and apropos of anything. In order to describe a doctrine, we must have recourse to theological language. A doctrine is an article of faith. It is something which you are bound to believe not because you have some rational grounds for believing it true, but because you belong to such and such a church or denomination. The nearest parallel to it in politics is the "reason of state." The most frightful injustice and cruelty which has ever been perpetrated on earth has been due to the reason of state. . . .

What has just been said suggests a consideration of the popular saying, "In time of peace prepare for war." If you prepare a big army and navy and are all ready for war, it will be easy to go to war; the military and naval men will have a lot of new machines, and they will be eager to see what they can do with them. There is no such thing nowadays as a state of readiness for war. It is a chimera, and the nations which pursue it are falling into an abyss of wasted energy and wealth. When the army is supplied with the latest and best rifles, someone invents a new field gun; then the artillery must be provided with that before we are ready. By the time we get the new gun, somebody has invented a new rifle, and our rival nation is getting that; therefore we must have it—or one a little better. It takes two or three years and several millions to do that. In the meantime somebody proposes a more effective organization which must be introduced; signals, balloons, dogs, bicycles, and every other device and invention must be added, and men must be trained to use them all. There is no state of readiness for war; the notion calls for never-ending sacrifices. It is a fallacy. It is evident that to pursue such a notion with any idea of realizing it would absorb all the resources and activity of the state; this the great European states are now proving by experiment. A wiser rule would be to make up your mind soberly what you want, peace or war, and then to get ready for what you want; for what we prepare for is what we shall get.

BARBARA TUCHMAN

The Guns of August

In searching for the causes of war, many historians, and psychologists as well, emphasize the importance of crisis decision-making, the particular circumstances as well as the personalities of those (relatively few) individuals in power whose decisions shape the course of world events. In some cases—Attila, Tamerlaine, Hitler—such leaders are considered especially villainous. In others, the *absence* of strong, far-sighted leaders has been cited.

Situations of extreme tension lead to limitations in cognitive function, a tendency to consider only a restricted range of options, intolerance of ambiguity, a tendency to engage in wishful or grandiose thinking, and seeing the opponent as motivated by more animosity than is often in fact the case. Faulty communication is more likely, notably a tendency to misinterpret the other side's statements and actions. In addition, with modern war so tightly bound to technology, and with leaders often obligated by connections to their allies and fearful of appearing weak in front of their opponents (as well as their own populace), politicians—especially in the twentieth century—have often felt themselves tragically constrained in their range of possible actions. Perhaps the most well-studied example of inflexibility combined with weak leadership took place in the days leading up to World War I, as memorably portrayed by popular historian Barbara Tuchman, in this selection from her book, *The Guns of August.*

"Some damned foolish thing in the Balkans," Bismarck had predicted, would ignite the next war. The assassination of the Austrian heir apparent, Archduke Franz Ferdinand, by Serbian nationalists on June 28, 1914, satisfied his condition. Austria-Hungary, with the bellicose frivolity of senile empires, determined to use the occasion to absorb Serbia as she had absorbed Bosnia and Herzegovina in 1909. Russia on that occasion, weakened by the war with Japan, had been forced to acquiesce by a German ultimatum followed by the Kaiser's appearance in "shining armor," as he put it, at the side of his ally, Austria. To avenge that humiliation and for the sake of her prestige as the major Slav power, Russia was now prepared to put on the shining armor herself. On July 5 Germany assured Austria that she could count on Germany's "faithful support" if whatever punitive action she took against Serbia brought her into conflict with Russia. This was the signal that let loose the irresistible onrush of events. On July 23 Austria delivered an ultimatum to Serbia, on July 26 rejected the Serbian reply (although the Kaiser, now nervous, admitted that it "dissipates every reason for war"), on July 28 declared war on Serbia, on July 29 bombarded Belgrade. On that day Russia mobilized along her Austrian frontier and on July 30 both Austria and Russia ordered general mobilization. On July 31 Germany issued an ultimatum to Russia to demobilize within twelve hours and "make us a distinct declaration to that effect."

War pressed against every frontier. Suddenly dismayed, governments struggled and twisted to fend it off. It was no use. Agents at frontiers were reporting every cavalry patrol as a deployment to beat the mobilization gun. General staffs, goaded by their relentless timetables, were pounding the table for the signal to move lest their opponents gain an hour's head start. Appalled upon the brink, the chiefs of state who would be ultimately responsible for their country's fate attempted to back away but the pull of military schedules dragged them forward. . . .

At noon on Saturday, August 1, the German ultimatum to Russia expired without a Russian reply. Within an hour a telegram went out to the German ambassador in St. Petersburg instructing him to declare war by five o'clock that afternoon. At five o'clock the Kaiser decreed general mobilization, some preliminaries having already got off to a head start under the declaration of *Kriegesgefahr* (Danger of War) the day before. At five-thirty Chancellor Bethmann-Hollweg, absorbed in a document he was holding in his hand and accompanied by little Jagow, the Foreign Minister, hurried down the steps of the Foreign Office, hailed an ordinary taxi, and sped off to the palace. Shortly afterward General von Moltke, the gloomy Chief of the General Staff, was pulled up short as he was driving back to his office with the mobilization order signed by the Kaiser in his pocket. A messenger in another car overtook him with an urgent summons from the palace. He returned to hear a last-minute, desperate proposal from the Kaiser that reduced Moltke to tears and could have changed the history of the twentieth century. . . .

In Berlin on August 1, the crowds milling in the streets and massed in thousands in front of the palace were tense and heavy with anxiety. Socialism, which most of Berlin's workers professed, did not run so deep as their instinctive fear and hatred of the Slavic hordes. Although they had been told by the Kaiser, in his speech from the balcony announcing *Kriegesgefahr* the evening before, that the "sword has been forced into our hand," they still waited in the ultimate dim hope of a Russian reply. The hour of the ultimatum passed. A journalist in the crowd felt the air "electric with rumor. People told each other Russia had asked for an extension of time. The Bourse writhed in panic. The afternoon passed in almost insufferable anxiety." Bethmann-Hollweg issued a statement ending, "If the iron dice roll, may God help us." At five o'clock a policeman appeared at the palace gate and announced mobilization to the crowd, which obediently struck up the national hymn, "Now thank we all our God." Cars raced down Unter den Linden with officers standing up in them, waving handkerchiefs and shouting, "Mobilization!" Instantly converted from Marx to Mars, people cheered wildly and rushed off to vent their feelings on suspected Russian spies, several of whom were pummeled or trampled to death in the course of the next few days.

Once the mobilization button was pushed, the whole vast machinery for calling up, equipping, and transporting two million men began turning automatically. Reservists went to their designated depots, were issued uniforms, equipment, and arms, formed into companies and companies into battalions, were joined by cavalry, cyclists, artillery, medical units, cook wagons, blacksmith wagons, even postal wagons, moved according to prepared railway timetables to concentration points near the frontier where they would be formed into divisions, divisions into corps, and corps into armies ready to advance and fight. One army corps alone—out of the total of 40 in the German forces—required 170 railway cars for officers, 965 for infantry, 2,960 for cavalry, 1,915 for artillery and supply wagons, 6,010 in all, grouped in 140 trains and an equal number again for their supplies. From the moment the order was given, everything was to move at fixed times according to a schedule precise down to the number of train axles that would pass over a given bridge within a given time.

. . . More cosmopolitan and more timid than the archetype Prussian, the Kaiser had never actually wanted a general war. He wanted greater power, greater prestige, above all more authority in the world's affairs for Germany but he preferred to obtain them by frightening rather than by fighting other nations. He wanted the gladiator's rewards without the battle, and whenever the prospect of battle came too close, as at Algeciras and Agadir, he shrank.

. . . The Kaiser would have welcomed any way out of the commitment to fight both Russia and France and, behind France, the looming figure of still-undeclared England.

At the last moment one was offered. A colleague of Bethmann's came to beg him to do anything he could to save Germany from a two-front war and suggested a means. For years a possible solution for Alsace had been discussed in terms of autonomy as a Federal State within the German Empire. If offered and accepted by the Alsatians, this solution would have deprived France of any reason to liberate the lost provinces. As recently as July 16, the French Socialist Congress had gone on record in favor of it. But the German military had always insisted that the provinces must remain garrisoned and their political rights subordinated to "military necessity." Until 1911 no constitution had ever been granted and autonomy never. Bethmann's colleague now urged him to make an immediate, public, and official offer for a conference on autonomy for Alsace. This could be allowed to drag on without result, while its moral effect would force France to refrain from attack while at least considering the offer. Time would be gained for Germany to turn her forces against Russia while remaining stationary in the West, thus keeping England out.

The author of this proposal remains anonymous, and it may be apocryphal. It does not matter. The opportunity was there, and the Chancellor could have thought of it for himself. But to seize it required boldness, and Bethmann, behind his distinguished facade of great height, somber eyes, and well-trimmed imperial, was a man, as Theodore Roosevelt said of Taft, "who means well feebly." Instead of offering France an inducement to stay neutral, the German government sent her an ultimatum at the same time as the ultimatum to Russia. . . .

In Berlin just after five o'clock a telephone rang in the Foreign Office. Under-Secretary Zimmermann, who answered it, turned to the editor of the *Berliner Tageblatt* sitting by his desk and said, "Moltke wants to know whether things can start." At that moment a telegram from London, just decoded, broke in upon the planned proceedings. It offered hope that if the movement against France could be instantly stopped Germany might safely fight a one-front war after all. Carrying it with them, Bethmann and Jagow dashed off on their taxi trip to the palace.

The telegram, from Prince Lichnowsky, ambassador in London, reported an English offer, as Lichnowsky understood it, "that in case we did not attack France, England would remain neutral and would guarantee France's neutrality." . . .

When the Foreign Secretary, Sir Edward Grey, telephoned him that morning, in the interval of a Cabinet meeting, Lichnowsky, out of his own anxiety, interpreted what Grey said to him as an offer by England to stay neutral and to keep France neutral in a Russo-German war, if, in return, Germany would promise not to attack France.

Actually, Grey had not said quite that. What, in his elliptical way, he offered was a promise to keep France neutral if Germany would promise to stay neutral as against France *and* Russia, in other words, not go to war against either, pending the result of efforts to settle the Serbian affair. . . .

The Kaiser clutched at Lichnowsky's passport to a one-front war. Minutes counted. Already mobilization was rolling inexorably toward the French frontier. The first hostile act, seizure of a railway junction in Luxembourg, whose neutrality the five Great Powers, including Germany, had guaranteed, was scheduled within an hour. It must be stopped, stopped at once. But how? Where was Moltke? Moltke had left the palace. An aide was sent off, with siren screaming, to intercept him. He was brought back.

The Kaiser was himself again, the All-Highest, the War Lord, blazing with a new idea, planning, proposing, disposing. He read

Moltke the telegram and said in triumph: "Now we can go to war against Russia only. We simply march the whole of our Army to the East!"

Aghast at the thought of his marvelous machinery of mobilization wrenched into reverse, Moltke refused pointblank. For the past ten years, first as assistant to Schlieffen, then as his successor, Moltke's job had been planning for this day, The Day, *Der Tag,* for which all Germany's energies were gathered, on which the march to final mastery of Europe would begin. It weighed upon him with an oppressive, almost unbearable responsibility. . . .

Now, on the climactic night of August 1, Moltke was in no mood for any more of the Kaiser's meddling with serious military matters, or with meddling of any kind with the fixed arrangements. To turn around the deployment of a million men from west to east at the very moment of departure would have taken a more iron nerve than Moltke disposed of. He saw a vision of the deployment crumbling apart in confusion, supplies here, soldiers there, ammunition lost in the middle, companies without officers, divisions without staffs, and those 11,000 trains, each exquisitely scheduled to click over specified tracks at specified intervals of ten minutes, tangled in a grotesque ruin of the most perfectly planned military movement in history.

"Your Majesty," Moltke said to him now, "it cannot be done. The deployment of millions cannot be improvised. If Your Majesty insists on leading the whole army to the East it will not be an army ready for battle but a disorganized mob of armed men with no arrangements for supply. Those arrangements took a whole year of intricate labor to complete"— and Moltke closed upon that rigid phrase, the basis for every major German mistake, the phrase that launched the invasion of Belgium and the submarine war against the United States, the inevitable phrase when military plans dictate policy—"and once settled, it cannot be altered."

IRVING JANIS

Victims of Groupthink

The preamble to the UNESCO Constitution states that "Since wars begin in the minds of men, it is in the minds of men that the defenses of peace must be constructed." This is generally interpreted to mean that all individuals (of both sexes!) are crucial to preventing war. However, some students of peace and war would amend the above sentence to begin "Since wars begin in the minds of the crucial, decision-making elite of each country ..." It is widely acknowledged that the psychology of decision-making plays a key role in influencing the immediate outcome (although this is not to deny the importance of other factors—historical, economic, sociological, etc.—in setting the stage).

Psychologically minded researchers have identified a number of factors involved in going to war, decisions that have often proved ill-advised not only on moral grounds, but also based on their immediate, practical outcomes. Here is but a sample: Robert Jervis has inquired into various patterns of misperception, by which decision-makers labor under inaccurate views of reality. Ole Holsti has investigated the costly consequences of stress during decision-making under crisis conditions. Morton Deutsch analyzed the process of hostile interactions, by which the mutually reinforcing impressions of adversaries can spiral out of control. Ralph White has pointed out the role of fear and of such "motivated misperceptions" as the "diabolical enemy image" combined with a self-righteous "moral self-image."

Irving Janis, a social psychologist, has provided a great service by identifying an important syndrome, which he calls "groupthink," whereby small groups tend to be vulnerable to a dangerous psychological process. In the following selection, from his book, *Victims of Groupthink,* Janis examines the ill-conceived and ill-fated Bay of Pigs invasion during 1961. It is also rewarding to compare this experience with the Cuban Missile Crisis of 1962, widely hailed as a U.S. triumph, yet also acknowledged to be the closest the world has even come to all-out nuclear war.

Nobody Is Perfect

Year after year newscasts and newspapers inform us of collective miscalculations—companies that have unexpectedly gone bankrupt because of misjudging their market, federal agencies that have mistakenly authorized the use of chemical insecticides that poison our environment, and White House executive committees that have made ill-conceived foreign policy decisions that inadvertently bring the major powers to the brink of war. Most people, when they hear about such fiascoes, simply remind themselves that, after all, "organizations are run by human beings," "to err is human," and "nobody is perfect." But platitudinous thoughts about human nature do not help us to understand how and why avoidable miscalculations are made.

Fiasco watchers who are unwilling to set the problem aside in this easy fashion will find that contemporary psychology has something to say (unfortunately not very much) about distortions of thinking and other sources of human error. The deficiencies about which we know the most pertain to disturbances in the behavior of each individual in a decision-making group—temporary states of elation, fear, or anger that reduce a person's mental efficiency; chronic blind spots arising from a person's social prejudices; shortcomings in information-processing that prevent a person from comprehending the complex consequences of a seemingly simple policy decision. One psychologist has suggested that because the information-processing capabilities of every individual are limited, no responsible leader of a large organization ought to make a policy decision without using a computer that is programmed to spell out all the probable benefits and costs of each alternative under consideration. The usual way of trying to counteract the limitations of individuals' mental functioning, however, is to relegate important decisions to groups.

Imperfections of Group Decisions

Groups, like individuals, have shortcomings. Groups can bring out the worst as well as the best in man. Nietzsche went so far as to say that madness is the exception in individuals but the rule in groups. A considerable amount of social science literature shows that in circumstances of extreme crisis, group contagion occasionally gives rise to collective panic, violent acts of scapegoating, and other forms of what could be called group madness. Much more frequent, however, are instances of mindless conformity and collective misjudgment of serious risks, which are collectively laughed off in a clubby atmosphere of relaxed conviviality. . . .

Lack of vigilance and excessive risk-taking are forms of temporary group derangement to which decision-making groups made up of responsible executives are not at all immune. Sometimes the main trouble is that the chief executive manipulates his advisers to rubber-stamp his own ill-conceived proposals. . . . I shall be dealing mainly with a different source of defective decision-making, which often involves a much more subtle form of faulty leadership: During the group's deliberations, the leader does not deliberately try to get the group to tell him what he wants to hear but is quite sincere in asking for honest opinions. The group members are not transformed into sycophants. They are not afraid to speak

their minds. Nevertheless, subtle constraints, which the leader may reinforce inadvertently, prevent a member from fully exercising his critical powers and from openly expressing doubts when most others in the group appear to have reached a consensus. . . .

I use the term "groupthink" as a quick and easy way to refer to a mode of thinking that people engage in when they are deeply involved in a cohesive in-group, when the members' strivings for unanimity override their motivation to realistically appraise alternative courses of action. "Groupthink" is a term of the same order as the words in the newspeak vocabulary George Orwell presents in his dismaying *1984*—a vocabulary with terms such as "doublethink" and "crimethink." By putting groupthink with those Orwellian words, I realize that groupthink takes on an invidious connotation. The invidiousness is intentional: Groupthink refers to a deterioration of mental efficiency, reality testing, and moral judgment that results from in-group pressures. . . .

At least six major defects in decision-making contribute to failures to solve problems adequately. First, the group's discussions are limited to a few alternative courses of action (often only two) without a survey of the full range of alternatives. Second, the group fails to reexamine the course of action initially preferred by the majority of members from the standpoint of nonobvious risks and drawbacks that had not been considered when it was originally evaluated. Third, the members neglect courses of action initially evaluated as unsatisfactory by the majority of the group: They spend little or no time discussing whether they have overlooked nonobvious gains or whether there are ways of reducing the seemingly prohibitive costs that had made the alternatives seem undesirable. Fourth, members make little or no attempt to obtain information from experts who can supply sound estimates of losses and gains to be expected from alternative courses of actions. Fifth, selective bias is shown in the way the group reacts to factual information and relevant judgments from experts, the mass media, and outside critics. The members show interest in facts and opinions that support their initially preferred policy and take up time in their meetings to discuss them, but they tend to ignore facts and opinions that do not support their initially preferred policy. Sixth, the members spend little time deliberating about how the chosen policy might be hindered by bureaucratic inertia, sabotaged by political opponents, or temporarily derailed by the common accidents that happen to the best of well-laid plans. Consequently, they fail to work out contingency plans to cope with foreseeable setbacks that could endanger the overall success of the chosen course of action.

I assume that these six defects and some related features of inadequate decision-making result from groupthink. But, of course, each of the six can arise from other common causes of human stupidity as well—erroneous intelligence, information overload, fatigue, blinding prejudice, and ignorance. Whether produced by groupthink or by other causes, a decision suffering from most of these defects has relatively little chance of success. . . .

At first I was surprised by the extent to which the groups in the fiascoes I have examined adhered to group norms and pressures toward uniformity. Just as in groups of ordinary citizens, a dominant characteristic appears to be remaining loyal to the group by sticking with the decisions to which the group has committed itself, even when the policy is working badly and has unintended consequences that disturb the conscience of the members. In a sense, members consider loyalty to the group the highest form of morality. That loyalty requires each member to avoid raising controversial issues, questioning weak arguments, or calling a halt to softheaded thinking.

Paradoxically, softheaded groups are likely to be extremely hardhearted toward outgroups and enemies. In dealing with a rival nation, policy-makers comprising an amiable group find it relatively easy to authorize dehumanizing solutions such as large-scale bombings. An affable group of government officials is unlikely to pursue the difficult and controversial issues that arise when alternatives to a harsh military solution come up for discussion. Nor are the members inclined to raise ethical issues that imply that this "fine group of ours, with its humanitarianism and its high-minded principles, might be capable of adopting a course of action that is inhumane and immoral."

Many other sources of human error can prevent government leaders from arriving at well worked out decisions, resulting in failures to achieve their practical objectives and violations of their own standards of ethical conduct. But, unlike groupthink, these other sources of error do not typically entail increases in hardheartedness along with softheadedness. Some errors involve blind spots that stem from the personality of the decision-makers. Special circumstances produce unusual fatigue and emotional stresses that interfere with efficient decision-making. Numerous institutional features of the social structure in which the group is located may also cause inefficiency and prevent adequate communication with experts. In addition, well-known interferences with sound thinking arise when the decision-makers comprise a noncohesive group. For example, when the members have no sense of loyalty to the group and regard themselves merely as representatives of different departments, with clashing interests, the meetings may become bitter power struggles, at the expense of effective decision-making.

The concept of groupthink pinpoints an entirely different source of trouble, residing neither in the individual nor in the organizational setting. Over and beyond all the familiar sources of human error is a powerful source of defective judgment that arises in cohesive groups—the concurrence-seeking tendency, which fosters overoptimism, lack of vigilance, and sloganistic thinking about the weakness and immorality of out-groups. This tendency can take its toll even when the decision-makers are conscientious statesmen trying to make the best possible decisions for their country and for all mankind.

I do not mean to imply that all cohesive groups suffer from groupthink, though all may display its symptoms from time to time. Nor should we infer from the term "groupthink" that group decisions are typically inefficient or harmful. On the contrary, a group whose members have properly defined roles, with traditions and standard operating procedures that facilitate critical inquiry, is probably capable of making better decisions than any individual in the group who works on the problem alone. And yet the advantages of having decisions made by groups are often lost because of psychological pressures that arise when the members work closely together, share the same values, and above all face a crisis situation in which everyone is subjected to stresses that generate a strong need for affiliation. In these circumstances, as conformity pressures begin to dominate, groupthink and the attendant deterioration of decision-making set in.

The central theme of my analysis can be summarized in this generalization, which I offer in the spirit of Parkinson's laws: *The more amiability and esprit de corps among the members of a policy-making in-group, the greater is the danger that independent critical thinking will be replaced by groupthink, which is likely to result in irrational and dehumanizing actions directed against out-groups.* . . .

The Kennedy administration's Bay of Pigs decision ranks among the worst fiascoes ever perpetrated by a responsible government. Planned by an over-ambitious, eager group of American intelligence officers who had little background or experience in military matters, the attempt to place a small brigade of Cuban exiles secretly on a beachhead in Cuba with the ultimate aim of overthrowing the government of Fidel Castro proved to be a "perfect failure." The group that made the basic decision to approve the invasion plan included some of the most intelligent men ever to participate in the councils of government. Yet all the major assumptions supporting the plan were so completely wrong that the venture began to founder at the outset and failed in its earliest stages.

The "Ill-Starred Adventure"

Ironically, the idea for the invasion was first suggested by John F. Kennedy's main political opponent, Richard M. Nixon. As Vice President during the Eisenhower administration, Nixon had proposed that the United States government secretly send a trained group of Cuban exiles to Cuba to fight against Castro. In March 1960, acting on Nixon's suggestion, President Dwight D. Eisenhower directed the Central Intelligence Agency to organize Cuban exiles in the United States into a unified political movement against the Castro regime and to give military training to those who were willing to return to their homeland to engage in guerrilla warfare. The CIA put a large number of its agents to work on this clandestine operation, and they soon evolved an elaborate plan for a military invasion. Apparently without informing President Eisenhower, the CIA began to assume in late 1960 that they could

land a brigade of Cuban exiles not as a band of guerrilla infiltrators but as an armed force to carry out a full-scale invasion.

Two days after the inauguration in January 1961, President John F. Kennedy and several leading members of his new administration were given a detailed briefing about the proposed invasion by Allen Dulles, head of the CIA, and General Lyman Lemnitzer, chairman of the Joint Chiefs of Staff. During the next eighty days, a core group of presidential advisers repeatedly discussed this inherited plan informally and in the meetings of an advisory committee that included three Joint Chiefs of Staff. In early April 1961, at one of the meetings with the President, all the key advisers gave their approval to the CIA's invasion plan. Their deliberations led to a few modifications of details, such as the choice of the invasion site.

On April 17, 1961, the brigade of about fourteen hundred Cuban exiles, aided by the United States Navy, Air Force, and the CIA, invaded the swampy coast of Cuba at the Bay of Pigs. Nothing went as planned. On the first day, not one of the four ships containing reserve ammunition and supplies arrived; the first two were sunk by a few planes in Castro's air force, and the other two promptly fled. By the second day, the brigade was completely surrounded by twenty thousand troops of Castro's well-equipped army. By the third day, about twelve hundred members of the brigade, comprising almost all who had not been killed, were captured and ignominiously led off to prison camps. . . .

An important symptom of groupthink is the illusion of being invulnerable to the main dangers that might arise from a risky action in which the group is strongly tempted to engage. Essentially, the notion is that "If our leader and everyone else in our group decides that it is okay, the plan is bound to succeed. Even if it is quite risky, luck will be on our side." A sense of "unlimited confidence" was widespread among the "New Frontiersmen" as soon as they took over their high government posts, according to a Justice Department confidant, with whom Robert Kennedy discussed the secret CIA plan on the day it was launched:

> It seemed that, with John Kennedy leading us and with all the talent he had

assembled, *nothing could stop us.* We believed that if we faced up to the nation's problems and applied bold, new ideas with common sense and hard work, we would overcome whatever challenged us. . . .

Once this euphoric phase takes hold, decision-making for everyday activities, as well as long-range planning, is likely to be seriously impaired. The members of a cohesive group become very reluctant to carry out the unpleasant task of critically assessing the limits of their power and the real losses that could arise if their luck does not hold. They tend to examine each risk in black and white terms. If it does not seem overwhelmingly dangerous, they are inclined simply to forget about it, instead of developing contingency plans in case it materializes. The group members know that no one among them is a superman, but they feel that somehow the group is a super-group, capable of surmounting all risks that stand in the way of carrying out any desired course of action: "Nothing can stop us!" Athletic teams and military combat units may often benefit from members' enthusiastic confidence in the power and luck of their group. But policy-making committees usually do not.

We would not expect sober government officials to experience such exuberant esprit de corps, but a subdued form of the same tendency may have been operating—inclining the President's advisers to become reluctant about examining the drawbacks of the invasion plan. In group meetings, this groupthink tendency can operate like a low-level noise that prevents warning signals from being heeded. Everyone becomes somewhat biased in the direction of selectively attending to the messages that feed into the members' shared feelings of confidence and optimism, disregarding those that do not. . . .

In a concurrence-seeking group, there is relatively little healthy skepticism of the glib ideological formulas on which rational policy-makers, like many other people who share their nationalistic goals, generally rely in order to maintain self-confidence and cognitive mastery over the complexities of international politics. One of the symptoms of groupthink is the members' persistence in conveying to each other the cliché and oversimplified images of political enemies embodied in long-standing ideological stereotypes. Throughout their deliberations they use the same old stereotypes, instead of developing differentiated concepts derived from an openminded inquiry enabling them to discern which of their original ideological assumptions, if any, apply to the foreign policy issue at hand. Except in unusual circumstances of crisis, the members of a concurrence-seeking group tend to view any antagonistic out-group against whom they are plotting not only as immoral but also as weak and stupid. These wishful beliefs continue to dominate their thinking until an unequivocal defeat proves otherwise, whereupon—like Kennedy and his advisers—they are shocked at the discrepancy between their stereotyped conceptions and actuality. . . .

The sense of group unity concerning the advisability of going ahead with the CIA's invasion plan appears to have been based on superficial appearances of complete concurrence, achieved at the cost of self-censorship of misgivings by several of the members. From post-mortem discussions with participants, Sorensen concluded that among the men in the State Department, as well as those on the White House staff, "doubts were entertained but never pressed, partly out of a fear of being labelled 'soft' or undaring in the eyes of their colleagues." Schlesinger was not at all hesitant about presenting his strong objections in a memorandum he gave to the President and the Secretary of State. But he became keenly aware of his tendency to suppress objections when he attended the White House meetings of the Kennedy team, with their atmosphere of assumed consensus:

> In the months after the Bay of Pigs I bitterly reproached myself for having kept so silent during those crucial discussions in the Cabinet Room, though my feelings of guilt were tempered by the knowledge that a course of objection would have accomplished little save to *gain me a name as a nuisance.* . . .

Schlesinger says that when the Cuban invasion plan was being presented to the group, "virile poses" were conveyed in the rhetoric used by the representatives of the CIA and the Joint Chiefs of Staff. He thought the State Department representatives and others responded by becoming anxious to show that they were not softheaded idealists but really were just as tough as the military men. Schlesinger's references to the "virile" stance of the militant advocates of the invasion plan suggest that the members of Kennedy's in-group may have been concerned about protecting the leader from being embarrassed by their voicing "unvirile" concerns about the high risks of the venture. . . .

At a large birthday party for his wife, Robert Kennedy, who had been constantly informed about the Cuban invasion plan, took Schlesinger aside and asked him why he was opposed. The President's brother listened coldly and then said, "You may be right or you may be wrong, but the President has made his mind up. Don't push it any further. Now is the time for everyone to help him all they can." Here is another symptom of groupthink, displayed by a highly intelligent man whose ethical code committed him to freedom of dissent. What he was saying, in effect, was, "You may well be right about the dangerous risks, but I don't give a damn about that; all of us should help our leader right now by not sounding any discordant notes that would interfere with the harmonious support he should have."

When Robert Kennedy told Schlesinger to lay off, he was functioning in a self-appointed role that I call being a "mindguard." Just as a body guard protects the President and other high officials from injurious physical assaults, a mindguard protects them from thoughts that might damage their confidence in the soundness of the policies to which they are committed or to which they are about to commit themselves. . . .

The group pressures that help to maintain a group's illusions are sometimes fostered by various leadership practices, some of which involve subtle ways of making it difficult for those who question the initial consensus to suggest alternatives and to raise critical issues. The group's agenda can readily be manipulated by a suave leader, often with the tacit approval of the members, so that there is simply no opportunity to discuss the drawbacks of a seemingly satisfactory plan of action. This is one of the conditions that fosters groupthink.

President Kennedy, as leader at the meetings in the White House, was probably more active than anyone else in raising skeptical questions; yet he seems to have encouraged the group's docility and uncritical acceptance of the defective arguments in favor of the CIA's plan. At each meeting, instead of opening up the agenda to permit a full airing of the opposing considerations, he allowed the CIA representatives to dominate the entire discussion. The President permitted them to refute immediately each tentative doubt that one of the others might express, instead of asking whether anyone else had the same doubt or wanted to pursue the implications of the new worrisome issue that had been raised. . . .

Although the available evidence consists of fragmentary and somewhat biased accounts of the deliberations of the White House group, it nevertheless reveals gross miscalculations and converges on the symptoms of groupthink. My tentative conclusion is that President Kennedy and the policy advisers who decided to accept the CIA's plan were victims of groupthink. If the facts I have culled from the accounts given by Schlesinger, Sorensen, and other observers are essentially accurate, the groupthink hypothesis makes more understandable the deficiencies in the government's decision-making that led to the enormous gap between conception and actuality.

The failure of Kennedy's inner circle to detect any of the false assumptions behind the Bay of Pigs invasion plan can be at least partially accounted for by the group's tendency to seek concurrence at the expense of seeking information, critical appraisal, and debate. The concurrence-seeking tendency was manifested by shared illusions and other symptoms, which helped the members to maintain a sense of group solidarity. Most crucial were the symptoms that contributed to complacent overconfidence in the face of vague uncertainties and explicit warnings that should have alerted the members to the risks of the clandestine military operation—an operation so ill conceived that among literate people all over the world the name of the invasion site has become the very symbol of perfect failure.

The Causes of War

The defining quality of war is violence: organized, armed violence on the part of large groups of people. Yet, war does not always involve strong, out-of-control emotion. For soldiers, boredom (either repetitive drill, or prolonged periods of inaction) is typically more prominent than "action," such that actual combat is sometimes seen as a relief. It has also been argued that for political and military elites as well, war-making is more likely to involve a reasoned decision than a spasm of aggressiveness.

Deterrence—whether nuclear or non-nuclear—is supposed to rely on such a careful, rational calculus, in which a would-be aggressor is expected to be "deterred" by recognizing that the cost of launching a war will be greater than any potential benefits that might accrue. The thinking is similar to the so-called "rational actor" model used by economists, in which consumers are expected to get the maximum value for their money, and businesses are predicted to behave in a way that (rationally) maximizes their profits. It is, of course, debatable whether human beings limit their motivations to such dry and reasoned decisions, especially when issues of pride, prestige, fear, hope, revenge, anger, etc.—not to mention life and death!—are involved. There is also the fact that whatever their "best judgment," people are prone to making mistakes. Among other things, since most wars do not end in a tie, roughly half the participants were incorrect if they assumed they would win. Further, wars may begin in the reasoned hope of generating greater political support and internal cohesiveness within a country, although as they drag on, they often become destabilizing instead.

In any event, historians and political scientists in particular have been partial to emphasizing the role of coolly reasoned, hard-headed "realpolitik," or "power politics," in the causation of war. In his book *On War,* Carl von Clausewitz, Prussian spokesperson for the military aspects of realpolitik, made the renowned observation that war is "the continuation of politics by other means." For Clausewitz, war, although often brutal, should not be senseless, but rather "an act of violence to compel the enemy to fulfill our will."

In this view, war is merely one of many tools employed by politicians and strategists. This is essentially the perspective of most conservative students of war, including British military historian Michael Howard.

It is true, and it is important to bear in mind . . . that before 1914 war was almost universally considered an acceptable, perhaps an inevitable and for many people a desirable, way of settling international differences, and that the war generally foreseen was expected to be, if not exactly brisk and cheerful, then certainly brief; no longer, certainly, than the war of 1870 between France and Prussia that was consciously or unconsciously taken by that generation as a model. Had it not been so generally felt that war was an acceptable and

From *The Causes of War* by Michael Howard. Copyright © 1984. Reprinted by permission of Harvard University Press, Cambridge, Mass.

tolerable way of solving international disputes, statesmen and soldiers would no doubt have approached the crisis of 1914 in a very different fashion.

But there was nothing new about this attitude to war. Statesmen had always been able to assume that war would be acceptable at least to those sections of their populations whose opinion mattered to them, and in this respect the decision to go to war in 1914—for continental statesmen at least—in no way differed from those taken by their predecessors of earlier generations. The causes of the Great War are thus in essence no more complex or profound than those of any previous European war, or indeed than those described by Thucydides as underlying the Peloponnesian War: "What made war inevitable was the growth of Athenian power and the fear this caused in Sparta." In Central Europe, there was the German fear that the disintegration of the Habsburg Empire would result in an enormous enhancement of Russian power—power already becoming formidable as French-financed industries and railways put Russian manpower at the service of her military machine. In Western Europe, there was the traditional British fear that Germany might establish a hegemony over Europe which, even more than that of Napoleon, would place at risk the security of Britain and her own possessions, a fear fueled by the knowledge that there was within Germany a widespread determination to achieve a world status comparable with her latent power. Considerations of this kind had caused wars in Europe often enough before. Was there really anything different about 1914?

∽

Ever since the eighteenth century, war had been blamed by intellectuals upon the stupidity or the self-interest of governing elites (as it is now blamed upon "military-industrial complexes"), with the implicit or explicit assumption that if the control of state affairs were in the hands of sensible men—businessmen, as Richard Cobden thought, the workers, as Jean Jaurès thought—then wars would be no more.

By the twentieth century, the growth of the social and biological sciences was producing alternative explanations. As Quincy Wright expressed it in his massive *A Study of War* (1942), "Scientific investigators . . . tended to attribute war to immaturities in social knowledge and control, as one might attribute epidemics to insufficient medical knowledge or to inadequate public health services." The Social Darwinian acceptance of the inevitability of struggle, indeed of its desirability if mankind was to progress, the view, expressed by the elder Moltke but very widely shared at the turn of the century, that perpetual peace was a dream and not even a beautiful dream, did not survive the Great War in those countries where the bourgeois-liberal culture was dominant, Britain and the United States. The failure of these nations to appreciate that such bellicist views, or variants of them, were still widespread in other areas of the world, those dominated by Fascism and by Marxism-Leninism, was to cause embarrassing misunderstandings, and possibly still does.

For liberal intellectuals, war was self-evidently a pathological aberration from the norm, at best a ghastly mistake, at worst a crime. Those who initiated wars must in their view have been criminal, or sick, or the victims of forces beyond their power to control. Those who were so accused disclaimed responsibility for the events of 1914, throwing it on others or saying the whole thing was a terrible mistake for which no one was to blame. None of them, with their societies in ruins around them and tens of millions dead, were prepared to say courageously: "We only acted as statesmen always have in the past. In the circumstances then prevailing, war seemed to us to be the best way of protecting or forwarding the national interests for which we were responsible. There was an element of risk, certainly, but the risk might have been greater had we postponed the issue. Our real guilt does not lie in the fact that we started the war. It lies in our mistaken belief that we could win it."

∽

The trouble is that if we are to regard war as pathological and abnormal, then all conflict must be similarly regarded; for war is only a particular kind of conflict between a particular category of social groups: sovereign states. It is, as Clausewitz put it, "a clash between major interests that is resolved by bloodshed—that is the only way in which it differs from other conflicts." If one had no sovereign states, one would have no wars, as Rousseau rightly pointed out—but, as Hobbes equally rightly pointed out, we would probably have no peace either. As states acquire a monopoly of violence, war becomes the only remaining form of conflict that may legitimately be settled by physical force. The mechanism of legitimization of authority and of social control that makes it possible for a state to moderate or eliminate conflicts within its borders or at very least to ensure that these are not conducted by competitive violence—the mechanism to the study of which historians have quite properly devoted so much attention—makes possible the conduct of armed conflict with other states, and on occasion—if the state is to survive—makes it necessary.

These conflicts arise from conflicting claims, or interests, or ideologies, or perceptions; and these perceptions may indeed be fueled by social or psychological drives that we do not fully understand and that one day we may learn rather better how to control. But the problem is the control of social conflict *as such,* not simply of war. However inchoate or disreputable the motives for war may be, its initiation is almost by definition a deliberate and carefully considered act and its conduct, at least at the more advanced levels of social development, a matter of very precise central control. If history shows any record of "accidental" wars, I have yet to find them. Certainly statesmen have sometimes been surprised by the nature of the war they have unleashed, and it is reasonable to assume that in at least 50 percent of the cases they got a result they did not expect. But that is not the same as a war begun by mistake and continued with no political purpose.

∾

Statesmen in fact go to war to achieve very specific ends, and the reasons for which states have fought one another have been categorized and recategorized innumerable times. Vattel, the Swiss lawyer, divided them into the necessary, the customary, the rational, and the capricious. Jomini, the Swiss strategist, identified ideological, economic, and popular wars, wars to defend the balance of power, wars to assist allies, wars to assert or to defend rights. Quincy Wright, the American political scientist, divided them into the idealistic, the psy-

chological, the political, and the juridical. Bernard Brodie in our own times has refused to discriminate: "Any theory of the causes of war in general or any war in particular that is not inherently eclectic and comprehensive," he stated," . . . is bound for that very reason to be wrong." Another contemporary analyst, Geoffrey Blainey, is on the contrary unashamedly reductionist. All war aims, he wrote, "are simply varieties of power. The vanity of nationalism, the will to spread an ideology, the protection of kinsmen in an adjacent land, the desire for more territory . . . all these represent power in different wrappings. The conflicting aims of rival nations are always conflicts of power."

In principle, I am sure that Bernard Brodie was right: No single explanation for conflict between states, any more than for conflict between any other social groups, is likely to stand up to critical examination. But Blainey is right as well. Quincy Wright provided us with a useful indicator when he suggested that "while animal war is a function of instinct and primitive war of the mores, civilized war is primarily a function of state politics."

Medievalists will perhaps bridle at the application of the term "primitive" to the sophisticated and subtle societies of the Middle Ages, for whom war was also a "function of the mores," a way of life that often demanded only the most banal of justifications. As a way of life, it persisted in Europe well into the seventeenth century, if no later. For Louis XIV and his court war was, in the early years at least, little more than a seasonal variation on hunting. But by the eighteenth century, the mood had changed. For Frederick the Great, war was to be pre-eminently a function of *Staatspolitik,* and so it has remained ever since. And although statesmen can be as emotional or as prejudiced in their judgments as any other group of human beings, it is very seldom that their attitudes, their perceptions, and their decisions are not related, however remotely, to the fundamental issues of *power,* that capacity to control their environment on which the independent existence of their states and often the cultural values of their societies depend.

∾

And here perhaps we do find a factor that sets interstate conflict somewhat apart from other forms of social rivalry. States may fight—indeed as often as not they do fight—not over any specific issue such as might otherwise have been resolved by peaceful means, but in order to acquire, to enhance, or to preserve their capacity to function as independent actors in the international system at all. "The stakes of war," as Raymond Aron has reminded us, "are the existence, the creation, or the elimination of States." It is a somber analysis, but one which the historical record very amply bears out.

It is here that those analysts who come to the study of war from the disciplines of the natural sciences, particularly the biological sciences, tend, it seems to me, to go astray. The conflicts between states which have usually led to war have normally arisen, not from any irrational and emotive drives, but from almost a superabundance of analytic rationality. Sophisticated communities (one hesitates to apply to them Quincy Wright's word, "civilized") do not react simply to immediate threats. Their intelligence (and I use the term in its double sense) enables them to assess the implications that any event taking place anywhere in the world, however remote, may have for their own capacity, immediately to exert influence, ultimately perhaps to survive. In the later Middle Ages and the early Modern period, every child born to every prince anywhere in Europe was registered on the delicate seismographs that monitored the shifts in dynastic power. Every marriage was a diplomatic triumph or disaster. Every stillbirth, as Henry VIII knew, could presage political catastrophe.

Today, the key events may be different. The pattern remains the same. A malfunction in the political mechanism of some remote African community, a coup d'état in a minuscule Caribbean republic, an insurrection deep in the hinterland of Southeast Asia, an assassination in some emirate in the Middle East—all these will be subjected to the kind of anxious examination and calculation that was devoted a hundred years ago to the news of comparable events in the Balkans: an insurrection in Philippopoli, a coup d'état in Constantinople, an assassination in Belgrade. To whose advantage will this ultimately redound, asked the worried diplomats, ours or *theirs*? Little enough in itself, perhaps, but will it not precipitate or strengthen a trend, set in motion a tide whose melancholy withdrawing roar will strip us of our friends and influence and leave us isolated in a world dominated by adversaries deeply hostile to us and all that we stand for?

There have certainly been occasions when states have gone to war in a mood of ideological fervor like the French republican armies in 1792; or of swaggering aggression like the Americans against Spain in 1898 or the British against the Boers a year later; or to make more money, as did the British in the War of Jenkins' Ear in 1739; or in a generous desire to help peoples of similar creed or race, as perhaps the Russians did in helping the Bulgarians fight the Turks in 1877 and the British dominions certainly did in 1914 and 1939. But, in general, men have fought during the past two hundred years neither because they are aggressive nor because they are acquisitive animals, but because they are reasoning ones: because they discern, or believe that they can discern, dangers before they become immediate, the possibility of threats before they are made.

But be this as it may, in 1914 many of the German people, and in 1939 nearly all of the British, felt justified in going to war, not over any specific issue that could have been settled by negotiation, but *to maintain their power*; and to do so while it was still possible, before they found themselves so isolated, so impotent, that they had no power left to maintain and had to accept a subordinate position within an international system dominated by their adversaries. "What made war inevitable was the growth of Athenian power and the fear this caused in Sparta." Or, to quote another grimly apt passage from Thucydides:

> The Athenians made their Empire more and more strong . . . [until] finally the point was reached when Athenian strength attained a peak plain for all to see and the Athenians began to encroach upon Sparta's allies. It was at this point that Sparta felt the position to be no longer tolerable and decided by starting the present war to employ all her energies in attacking and if possible destroying the power of Athens.

You can vary the names of the actors, but the model remains a valid one for the purposes of our analysis. I am rather afraid that it still does.

Something that has changed since the time of Thucydides, however, is the nature of the power that appears so threatening. From the time of Thucydides until that of Louis XIV, there was basically only one source of political and military power—control of territory, with all the resources in wealth and manpower that this provided. This control might come through conquest, or through alliance, or through marriage, or through purchase, but the power of princes could be very exactly computed in terms of the extent of their territories and the number of men they could put under arms.

In seventeenth-century Europe, this began to change. Extent of territory remained important, but no less important was the effectiveness with which the resources of that territory could be exploited. Initially there were the bureaucratic and fiscal mechanisms that transformed loose bonds of territorial authority into highly structured centralized states whose armed forces, though not necessarily large, were permanent, disciplined, and paid.

~

Then came the political transformations of the revolutionary era that made available to these state systems the entire manpower of their country, or at least as much of it as the administrators were able to handle. And finally came the revolution in transport, the railways of the nineteenth century that turned the revolutionary ideal of the "Nation in Arms" into a reality. By the early twentieth century, military power—on the continent of Europe, at least—was seen as a simple combination of military manpower and railways. The quality of armaments was of secondary importance, and political intentions were virtually excluded from account. The growth of power was measured in terms of the growth of populations and of communications; of the number of men who could be put under arms and transported to the battlefield to make their weight felt in the initial and presumably decisive battles. It was the mutual perception of threat in those terms that turned Europe before 1914 into an armed camp, and it was their calculations within this framework that reduced German staff officers increasingly to despair and launched their leaders on their catastrophic gamble in 1914, which started the First World War.

But already the development of weapons technology had introduced yet another element into the international power calculus, one that has in our own age become dominant. It was only in the course of the nineteenth century that technology began to produce weapons systems—initially in the form of naval vessels—that could be seen as likely in themselves to prove decisive, through their qualitative and quantitative superiority, in the event of conflict. But as war became increasingly a matter of competing technologies rather than competing armies, so there developed that escalatory process known as the "arms race." As a title, the phrase, like so many coined by journalists to catch the eye, is misleading.

~

"Arms races" are in fact continuing and open-ended attempts to match power for power. They are as much means of achieving stable or, if possible, favorable power balances as were the dynastic marriage policies of Valois and Habsburg. To suggest that they in themselves are causes of war implies a naive if not totally mistaken view of the relationship between the two phenomena. The causes of war remain rooted, as much as they were in the preindustrial age, in perceptions by statesmen of the growth of hostile power and the fears for the restriction, if not the extinction, of their own. The threat, or rather the fear, has not changed, whether it comes from aggregations of territory or from dreadnoughts, from the numbers of men under arms or from missile systems. The means that states employ to sustain or to extend their power may have been transformed, but their objectives and preoccupations remain the same.

"Arms races" can no more be isolated than wars themselves from the political circumstances that give rise to them, and like wars they will take as many different forms as political circumstances dictate. They may be no more than a process of competitive modernization, of maintaining a status quo that commands general support but in which no participant wishes, whether from reasons of pride or of prudence, to fall behind in keeping his armory up to date. If there are no political causes for fear or rivalry, this process need not in itself be a destabilizing factor in international relations. But arms races may, on the other hand, be the result of a quite deliberate assertion of an intention to *change* the status quo, as was, for example, the German naval challenge to Britain at the beginning of this century.

This challenge was an explicit attempt by Admiral Alfred von Tirpitz and his associates to destroy the hegemonic position at sea which Britain saw as essential to her security, and, not inconceivably, to replace it with one of their own. As British and indeed German diplomats repeatedly explained to the German government, it was not the German naval program in itself that gave rise to so much alarm in Britain. It was the intention that lay behind it. If the status quo was to be maintained, the German challenge had to be met.

∽

The naval race could quite easily have been ended on one of two conditions. Either the Germans could have abandoned their challenge, as had the French in the previous century, and acquiesced in British naval supremacy; or the British could have yielded as gracefully as they did, a decade or so later, to the United States and abandoned a status they no longer had the capacity, or the will, to maintain. As it was, they saw the German challenge as one to which they could and should respond, and their power position as one which they were prepared, if necessary, to use force to preserve. The British naval program was thus, like that of the Germans, a signal of political intent; and that intent, that refusal to acquiesce in a fundamental transformation of the power balance, was indeed a major element among the causes of the war. The naval competition provided a very accurate indication and measurement of political rivalries and tensions, but it did not cause them; nor could it have been abated unless the rivalries themselves had been abandoned.

It was the general perception of the growth of German power that was awakened by the naval challenge, and the fear that a German hegemony on the Continent would be the first step to a challenge to her own hegemony on the oceans, that led Britain to involve herself in the continental conflict in 1914 on the side of France and Russia. "What made war inevitable was the growth of *Spartan* power," to reword Thucydides, "and the fear which this caused in

Athens." In the Great War that followed, Germany was defeated, but survived with none of her latent power destroyed. A "false hegemony" of Britain and France was established in Europe that could last only so long as Germany did not again mobilize her resources to challenge it. German rearmament in the 1930s did not of itself mean that Hitler wanted war (though one has to ignore his entire philosophy if one is to believe that he did not); but it did mean that he was determined, with a great deal of popular support, to obtain a free hand on the international scene.

With that free hand, he intended to establish German power on an irreversible basis; this was the message conveyed by his armament program. The armament program that the British reluctantly adopted in reply was intended to show that, rather than submit to the hegemonic aspirations they feared from such a revival of German power, they would fight to preserve their own freedom of action. Once again to recast Thucydides:

> Finally the point was reached when German strength attained a peak plain for all to see, and the Germans began to encroach upon Britain's allies. It was at this point that Britain felt the position to be no longer tolerable and decided by starting this present war to employ all her energies in attacking and if possible destroying the power of Germany.

What the Second World War established was not a new British hegemony, but a Soviet hegemony over the Euro-Asian land mass from the Elbe to Vladivostok; and that was seen, at least from Moscow, as an American hegemony over the rest of the world; one freely accepted in Western Europe as a preferable alternative to being absorbed by the rival hegemony. Rival armaments were developed to define and preserve the new territorial boundaries, and . . . arms competition began. . . .

∽

The trouble is that what is seen by one party as the breaking of an alien hegemony and the establishment of equal status will be seen by the incumbent powers as a striving for the establishment of an alternate hegemony, and they are not necessarily wrong. In international politics, the appetite often comes with eating; and there really may be no way to check an aspiring rival except by the mobilization of stronger military power. An arms race then becomes almost a necessary surrogate for war, a test of national will and strength; and arms control becomes possible only when the underlying power balance has been mutually agreed.

We would be blind, therefore, if we did not recognize that the causes which have produced war in the past are operating in our own day as powerfully as at any time in history. . . .

But times *have* changed since Thucydides. They have changed even since 1914. These were, as we have seen, bellicist societies in which war was a normal, acceptable, even a desirable way of settling differences. The question that arises today is, how widely and evenly spread is that intense revulsion against war that at present characterizes our own soci-

ety? For if war is indeed now *universally* seen as being unacceptable as an instrument of policy, then all analogies drawn from the past are misleading, and although power struggles may continue, they will be diverted into other channels. But if that revulsion is not evenly spread, societies which continue to see armed force as an acceptable means for attaining their political ends are likely to establish a dominance over those which do not. Indeed, they will not necessarily have to fight for it.

My second and concluding point is this: whatever may be the underlying causes of international conflict, even if we accept the role of atavistic militarism or of military-industrial complexes or of sociobiological drives or of domestic tensions in fueling it, wars begin with conscious and reasoned decisions based on the calculation, made by *both* parties, that they can achieve more by going to war than by remaining at peace.

JOHAN GALTUNG

A Structural Theory of Imperialism

What about social and economic factors? It seems likely that poverty, for example, can lead to anger, desperation, and willingness to go to war. However, poor countries are not especially likely to make war on richer countries, seeking their wealth; if anything, national poverty may be a restraint on war-making, since military forces require expensive high-tech weaponry. The opposite is more likely: wealthy countries attacking poorer ones, not only because they feel that they can get away with it, but also out of fear that nearby "hungry" states are ultimately threatening to their security.

At the same time, poverty, and being exploited and oppressed generally, appears to predispose to civil wars and revolutionary unrest. (This, in turn, poses an important question: What about wars of national liberation or those to end oppression and exploitation?) Traditional Marxist—especially Leninist—doctrine states that imperialism drives capitalist states to make war on each other when their extraterritorial ambitions collide. Another perspective emphasizes the role of a promilitary elite, later extended to include military-industrial complexes, in which professional soldiers, politicians, and industrialists promote antagonism among states to enhance their own careers and profits.

From "A Structural Theory of Imperialism" by Johan Galtung, *Journal of Peace Research* 8: 81–117. Copyright © 1971. Reprinted by permission of *Journal of Peace Research*.

In the following excerpt, famed peace researcher Johan Galtung addresses traditional concerns about imperialism and colonialism. His analysis applies more broadly, however, to economic underdevelopment and inequality in general.

This theory takes as its point of departure two of the most glaring facts about this world: the tremendous inequality, within and between nations, in almost all aspects of human living conditions, including the power to decide over those living conditions; *and* the resistance of this inequality to change. The world consists of Center and Periphery nations; and each nation, in turn, has its centers and periphery. Hence, our concern is with the mechanism underlying this discrepancy, particularly between the center in the Center, and the periphery in the Periphery. In other words, how to conceive of, how to explain, and how to counteract inequality as one of the major forms of *structural violence*. Any theory of liberation from structural violence presupposes theoretically and practically adequate ideas of the dominance system against which the liberation is directed; and the special type of dominance system to be discussed here is *imperialism*.

Imperialism will be conceived of as a dominance relation between collectivities, particularly between nations. It is a sophisticated type of dominance relation which cuts across nations, basing itself on a bridgehead which the center in the Center nation establishes in the center of the Periphery nation, for the joint benefit of both. It should not be confused with other ways in which one collectivity can dominate another in the sense of exercising power over it. Thus, a military occupation of B by A may seriously curtail B's freedom of action, but is not for that reason an imperialist relationship unless it is set up in a special way. The same applies to the *threat* of conquest and possible occupation, as in a balance of power relationship. Moreover, *subversive* activities may also be brought to a stage where a nation is dominated by the pinpricks exercised against it from below, but this is clearly different from imperialism.

Thus, imperialism is a species in a genus of dominance and power relationships. It is a subtype of something and has itself subtypes to be explored later. Dominance relations between nations and other collectivities will not disappear with the disappearance of imperialism; nor will the end to one type of imperialism (e.g.,

political or economic) guarantee the end to another type of imperialism (e.g., economic or cultural). Our view is not reductionist in the traditional sense pursued in Marxist-Leninist theory, which conceives of imperialism as an economic relationship under private capitalism, motivated by the need for expanding markets, and which bases the theory of dominance on a theory of imperialism. According to this view, imperialism and dominance will fall like dominoes when the capitalistic conditions for economic imperialism no longer obtain. According to the view we develop here, imperialism is a more general structural relationship between two collectivities and has to be understood at a general level in order to be understood and counteracted in its more specific manifestations—just like smallpox is better understood in a context of a theory of epidemic diseases, and these diseases better understood in a context of general pathology.

Briefly stated, imperialism is a system that splits up collectivities and relates some of the parts to each other in relations of *harmony of interest*, and other parts in relations of *disharmony of interest*, or *conflict of interest*. . . .

"Conflict of interest" is a special case of conflict in general, defined as a situation where parties are pursuing incompatible goals. In our special case, these goals are stipulated by an outsider as the "true" interests of the parties, disregarding wholly or completely what the parties themselves say explicitly are the values they pursue. . . .

Let us conclude this discussion by pointing out that a gap in living condition, or at least one important kind, is a necessary, if not sufficient, condition for conflict or disharmony of interest. If in addition the gap can be observed over time, a more satisfactory basis for a diagnosis in terms of imperialism may emerge.

. . . In our two-nation world, imperialism can be defined as one way in which the Center nation has power over the Periphery nation, so as to bring about a condition of disharmony of interest between them. Concretely, *Imperialism* is a relation between a Center and a Periphery nation so that

1. there is *harmony of interest* between the *center in the Center* nation and the *center in the Periphery* nation,
2. there is more *disharmony of interest* within the Periphery nation than within the Center nations,
3. there is *disharmony of interest* between the *periphery in the Center* nation and the *periphery in the Periphery* nation.

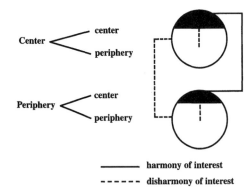

Figure 1 The Structure of Imperialism.

Diagrammatically it looks something like Figure 1. This complex definition, borrowing largely from Lenin, needs spelling out. The basic idea is, as mentioned, that the center in the Center nation has a bridgehead in the Periphery nation, and a well-chosen one: the center in the Periphery nation. This is established such that the Periphery center is tied to the Center center with the best possible tie: the tie of harmony of interest. They are linked so that they go up together and down, even under, together. How this is done in concrete terms will be explored in the subsequent sections.

Inside the two nations there is disharmony of interest. . . . Moreover, the gap is not decreasing, but is at best constant. But the basic idea, absolutely fundamental for the whole theory to be developed, is that *there is more disharmony in the Periphery nation than in the Center nation*. At the simplest static level of description this means there is more inequality in the Periphery than in the Center. At the more complex level we might talk in terms of the gap opening more quickly in the Periphery than in the Center, where it might even remain constant. Through welfare state activities, redistribution takes place and disharmony is reduced for at least some dimensions, including income, but usually excluding power.

If we now would capture in a few sentences what imperialism is about, we might perhaps say something like this:

In the Periphery nation, the center grows more than the periphery, due partly to how interaction between center and periphery is organized. Without necessarily thinking of economic interaction, the center is more enriched than the periphery—in ways to be explored below. However, for part of this enrichment, the center in the Periphery only serves as a transmission belt (e.g., as commercial firms, trading companies) for value (e.g., raw materi-

als) forwarded to the Center nation. This value enters the Center in the center, with some of it drizzling down to the periphery in the Center. Importantly, there is less disharmony of interest in the Center than in the Periphery, so that *the total arrangement is largely in the interest of the periphery in the Center*. Within the Center the two parties may be opposed to each other. But in the total game, the periphery see themselves more as the partners of the center in the Center than as the partners of the periphery in the Periphery—and this is the essential trick of that game. Alliance formation between the two peripheries is avoided, while the Center nation becomes more and the Periphery nation less cohesive—and hence less able to develop long-term strategies.

Actually, concerning the three criteria in the definition of imperialism as given above it is clear that no. 3 is implied by nos. 1 and 2. The two centers are tied together and the Center periphery is tied to its center: that is the whole essence of the situation. If we now presuppose that the center in the Periphery is a smaller proportion of that nation than the center in the Center, we can also draw one more implication: *there is disharmony of interest between the Center nation as a whole and the Periphery nation as a whole*. But that type of finding, frequently referred to, is highly misleading because it blurs the harmony of interest between the two centers and leads to the belief that imperialism is merely an international relationship, *not a combination of intra- and international relations*.

However, even if the definition given above purports to define the pure case of imperialism, we may nevertheless fruitfully think in terms of degenerate cases. Thus, the first point in the definition about harmony between the two centers is obviously the most important one. If the second point does not hold, and consequently not the third point either, it may still be fruitful to talk about imperialism. But in this degenerate case the two peripheries may more easily find each other, since they are now only kept apart by geographical distance (assuming that the two nations are nation-states, often even located far apart), not in addition by disharmony of interest. Thus, if the relationship between the two peripheries and their centers should become more similar, periphery alliance formation might easily be the result, and the two centers would have to resort to more direct means of violence rather than, or in addition to, the delicate type of structural violence that characterizes the pure type of imperialistic relationship.

But what if there is no distinction between center and periphery in the two nations; what if they are completely horizontal societies? In that case, we should not talk about the dominance relationship whereby the Center nation extracts something from the Periphery nation as an imperialistic one, but rather as something else—looting, stealing, etc. Where there is no bridgehead from the Center nation in the center of the Periphery nation, there cannot be any imperialism by this definition.

KENNETH BOULDING

National Images and International Systems

Nationalism is one of the most powerful forces of modern times. It can be beautiful, reflecting the yearning of people to associate themselves with others, evoking compassion, love, respect for one's past, one's culture, even the natural environment. In offering perhaps its most famous definition, French philosopher and historian J. Ernest Renan suggested that nationalism is

> a grand solidarity constituted by the sentiment of sacrifices which one has made and those that time is disposed to make again. . . . The existence of a nation is an everyday plebiscite.[3]

At the same time, nationalism can become malevolent, fostering chauvinism, group intolerance, and violent divisions between people, which threaten to destroy the values it claims to venerate. "By nationalism," wrote George Orwell,

> I mean first of all the habit of assuming that human beings can be classified like insects and that whole blocks of millions or tens of millions of people can be confidently labeled "good" or "bad." But secondly—and this is much more important—I mean the habit of identifying oneself with a single nation or other unit, placing it beyond good or evil and recognizing no other duty than that of advancing its own interests.[4]

From "National Images and International Systems" by Kenneth Boulding, *Journal of Conflict Resolution* 3: 120–31. Copyright © 1959. Reprinted by permission of Sage Publications, Newbury Park, Calif.

---

[3] J. Ernest Renan. 1882. *What Is a Nation?* Calmann-Levy: Paris.

---

[4] George Orwell. 1953. *Such, Such Were the Joys.* Harcourt, Brace: New York

Here, Kenneth Boulding—one of the founders of peace studies—discusses the phenomenon of national "images."

We must recognize that the people whose decisions determine the policies and actions of nations do not respond to the "objective" facts of the situation, whatever that may mean, but to their "image" of the situation. It is what we think the world is like, not what it is really like, that determines our behavior. If our image of the world is in some sense "wrong," of course, we may be disappointed in our expectations, and we may therefore revise our image; if this revision is in the direction of the "truth" there is presumably a long-run tendency for the "image" and the "truth" to coincide. Whether this is so or not, it is always the image, not the truth, that immediately determines behavior. We act according to the way the world appears to us, not necessarily according to the way it "is." Thus ... it is one nation's image of the hostility of another, not the "real" hostility, which determines its reaction. The "image," then, must be thought of as the total cognitive, affective, and evaluative structure of the behavior unit, or its internal view of itself and its universe.

Generally speaking, the behavior of complex organizations can be regarded as determined by *decisions,* and a decision involves the selection of the most preferred position in a contemplated field of choice. Both the field of choice and the ordering of this field by which the preferred position is identified lie in the image of the decisionmaker. Therefore, in a system in which decisionmakers are an essential element, the study of the ways in which the image grows and changes, both of the field of choice and of the valuational ordering of this field, is of prime importance. The image is always in some sense a product of messages received in the past. It is not, however, a simple inventory or "pile" of such messages but a highly structured piece of information capital, developed partly by its inputs and outputs of information and partly by internal messages and its own laws of growth and stability.

The images which are important in international systems are those which a nation has of itself and of those other bodies in the system which constitute its international environment. At once a major complication suggests itself. A nation is some complex of the images of the persons who contemplate it, and as there are many different persons, so there are many different images. The complexity is increased by the necessity for inclusion, in the image of each person or at least of many persons, his image of the image of others. This complexity, however, is a property of the real world, not to be evaded or glossed over. It can be reduced to simpler terms if we distinguish between two types of persons in a nation—the powerful, on the one hand, and the ordinary, on the other. This is not, of course, a sharp distinction. The power of a decisionmaker may be measured roughly by the number of people which his decisions potentially affect, weighted by some measure of the effect itself. Thus the head of a state is powerful, meaning that his decisions affect the lives of millions of people; the ordinary person is not powerful, for his decisions affect only himself and the lives of a few people around him. There is usually a continuum of power among the persons of a society: thus in international relations there are usually a few very powerful individuals in a state—the chief executive, the prime minister, the secretary of state or minister of foreign affairs, the chiefs of staff of the armed forces. There will be some who are less powerful but still influential—members of the legislature, of the civil service, even journalists, newspaper owners, prominent businessmen, grading by imperceptible degrees down to the common soldier, who has no power of decision even over his own life. For purposes of the model, however, let us compress this continuum into two boxes, labeled the "powerful" and the "ordinary," and leave the refinements of power and influence for later studies.

We deal, therefore, with two representative images, (1) the image of the small group of powerful people who make the actual decisions which lead to war or peace, the making or breaking of treaties, the invasions or withdrawals, alliances, and enmities which make up the major events of international relations, and (2) the image of the mass of ordinary people who are deeply affected by these decisions but who take little or no direct part in making them. The tacit support of the mass, however, is of vital importance to the powerful. The powerful are always under some obligation to represent the mass, even under dictatorial regimes. In democratic societies the aggregate influence of the images of ordinary people is very great; the image of the powerful cannot diverge too greatly from the image of the mass without the powerful losing power. On the other hand, the powerful also have some ability to manipulate the images of the mass toward those of the powerful. This is an important object of instruments as diverse as the public education system, the public relations departments of the armed services, the Russian "agitprop," and the Nazi propaganda ministry.

In the formation of the national images, however, it must be emphasized that impressions of nationality are formed mostly in childhood and usually in the family group. It would be quite fallacious to think of the images as being cleverly imposed on the mass by the powerful. If anything, the reverse is the case: the image is essentially a mass image, or what might be called a "folk image," transmitted through the family and the intimate face-to-face group, both in the case of the powerful and in the case of ordinary persons. Especially in the case of the old, long-established nations, the powerful share the mass image rather than impose it; it is passed on from the value systems of the parents to those of the children, and agencies of public instruction and propaganda merely reinforce the images which derived essentially from the family culture. This is much less true in new nations which are striving to achieve nationality, where the family culture frequently does not include strong elements of national allegiance but rather stresses allegiance to religious ideals or to the family as such. Here the powerful are frequently inspired by a national image derived not from family tradition but from a desire to imitate other nations, and here they frequently try to impose their images on the mass of people. Imposed images, however, are fragile by comparison with those which are deeply internalized and transmitted through family and other intimate sources.

Whether transmitted orally and informally through the family or more formally through schooling and the written word, the national image is essentially a *historical* image—that is, an image which extends through time, back-

ward into a supposedly recorded or perhaps mythological past and forward into an imagined future. The more conscious a people is of its history, the stronger the national image is likely to be. To be an Englishman is to be conscious of "1066 and All That" rather than of "Constantine and All That," or "1776 and All That." A nation is the creation of its historians, formal and informal. The written word and public education contribute enormously to the stability and persistence of the national images. The Jews, for instance, are a creation of the Bible and the Talmud, but every nation has its bible, whether formed into a cannon or not—noble words like the Declaration of Independence and the Gettysburg Address—which crystallize the national image in a form that can be transmitted almost unchanged from generation to generation. It is no exaggeration to say that the function of the historian is to pervert the truth in directions favorable to the images of his readers or hearers. Both history and geography as taught in national schools are devised to give "perspective" rather than truth: that is to say, they present the world as seen from the vantage point of the nation. The national geography is learned in great detail, and the rest of the world is a fuzzy outline; the national history is emphasized and exalted; the history of the rest of the world is neglected or even falsified to the glory of the national image.

It is this fact that the national image is basically a lie, or at least a perspective distortion of the truth, which perhaps accounts for the ease with which it can be perverted to justify monstrous cruelties and wickednesses. There is much that is noble in the national image. It has lifted man out of the narrow cage of self-centeredness, or even family-centeredness, and has forced him to accept responsibility, in some sense, for people and events far beyond his face-to-face cognizance and immediate experience. It is a window of some sort on both space and time and extends a man's concern far beyond his own little lifetime and petty interests. Nevertheless, it achieves these virtues usually only at the cost of untruth, and this fatal flaw constantly betrays it. Love of country is perverted into hatred of the foreigner, and peace, order, and justice at home are paid for by war, cruelty, and injustice abroad.

In the formation of the national image the consciousness of great *shared* events and experiences is of the utmost importance. A nation is a body of people who are conscious of having "gone through something" together. Without the shared experience, the national image itself would not be shared, and it is of vital importance that the national image be highly similar. The sharing may be quite vicarious; it may be an experience shared long ago but constantly renewed by the ritual observances and historical memory of the people, like the Passover and the Captivity in the case of the Jews. Without the sharing, however, there is no nation. It is for this reason that war has been such a tragically important element in the creation and sustenance of the national image. There is hardly a nation that has not been cradled in violence and nourished by further violence. This is not, I think, a necessary property of war itself. It is rather that, especially in more primitive societies, war is the one experience which is dramatic, obviously important, and shared by everybody....

We now come to the central problem, which is that of the impact of national images on the relations among states, that is, on the course of events in international relations. The relations among states can be described in terms of a number of different dimensions. There is, first of all, the dimension of simple geographical space. It is perhaps the most striking single characteristic of the national state as an organization, by contrast with organizations such as firms or churches, that it thinks of itself as occupying, in a "dense" and exclusive fashion, a certain area of the globe. The schoolroom maps which divide the world into colored shapes which are identified as nations have a profound effect on the national image. Apart from the very occasional condominium, it is impossible for a given plot of land on the globe to be associated with two nations at the same time. The territories of nations are divided sharply by frontiers carefully surveyed and frequently delineated by a chain of customs houses, immigration stations, and military installations. We are so accustomed to this arrangement that we think of it as "natural" and take it completely for granted. It is by no means the only conceivable arrangement, however. In primitive societies the geographical image is not sharp enough to define clear frontiers; there may be a notion of the rough territory of a tribe, but, especially among nomadic peoples, there is no clear concept of a frontier and no notion of a

nation as something that has a shape on a map. In our own society the shape on the map that symbolizes the nation is constantly drilled into the minds of both young and old, both through formal teaching in schools and through constant repetition in newspapers, advertisements, cartoons, and so on. A society is not inconceivable, however, and might even be desirable, in which nations governed people but not territories and claimed jurisdiction over a defined set of citizens, no matter where on the earth's surface they happened to live.

The territorial aspect of the national state is important in the dynamics of international relations because of the *exclusiveness* of territorial occupation. This means that one nation can generally expand only at the expense of another; an increase in the territory of one is achieved only at the expense of a decrease in the territory of another. This makes for a potential conflict situation. This characteristic of the nation does not make conflict inevitable, but it does make it likely and is at least one of the reasons why the history of international relations is a history of perpetual conflict.

The territorial aspect of international relations is complicated by the fact that in many cases the territories of nations are not homogeneous but are composed of "empires," in which the populations do not identify themselves with the national image of the dominant group. Thus when one nation conquers another and absorbs the conquered territory into an empire, it does not thereby automatically change the culture and allegiances of the conquered nation. The Poles remained Polish for a hundred and twenty-five years of partition between Germany, Austria, and Russia. The Finns retained their nationality through eight hundred years of foreign rule and the Jews, through nearly two thousand years of dispersion. If a nation loses territory occupied by disaffected people, this is much less damaging than the loss of territory inhabited by a well-disposed and loyal population. Thus Turkey, which was the "sick man of Europe" as long as it retained its heterogeneous empire, enjoyed a substantial renewal of national health when stripped of its empire and pushed back to the relatively homogeneous heartland of Anatolia. In this case the loss of a disaffected empire actually strengthened the national unit.

The image of the map shape of the nations may be an important factor affecting the general frame of mind of the nation. There is a tendency for nations to be uneasy with strong irregularities, enclaves, detached portions, and protuberances or hollows. The ideal shape is at least a convex set, and there is some tendency for nations to be more satisfied if they have regularly round or rectangular outlines. Thus the detachment of East Prussia from the body of Germany by the Treaty of Versailles was an important factor in creating the fanatical discontent of the Nazis.

A second important dimension of the national image is that of hostility or friendliness. At any one time a particular national image includes a rough scale of the friendliness or hostility of, or toward, other nations. The relationship is not necessarily either consistent or reciprocal—in nation A the prevailing image may be that B is friendly, whereas in nation B itself the prevailing image may be one of hostility toward A; or again in both nations there may be an image of friendliness of A toward B but of hostility of B toward A. On the whole, however, there is a tendency toward both consistency and reciprocation—if a nation A pictures itself as hostile toward B, it usually also pictures B as hostile toward it, and the image is likely to be repeated in B. One exception to this rule seems to be observable: most nations seem to feel that their enemies are more hostile toward them than they are toward their enemies. This is a typical paranoid reaction; the nation visualizes itself as surrounded by hostile nations toward which it has only the nicest and friendliest of intentions.

An important subdimension of the hostility-friendliness image is that of the stability or security of the relationship. A friendly relationship is frequently formalized as an alliance. Alliances, however, are shifting; some friendly relations are fairly permanent, others change as the world kaleidoscope changes, as new enemies arise, or as governments change. Thus . . . most people in the United States visualized Germany and Japan, even before the outbreak of the war, as enemies, and after Hitler's invasion of Russia, Russia was for a while regarded as a valuable friend and ally. . . . We can roughly classify the reciprocal relations of nations along some scale of friendliness-hostility. At one extreme we have stable friendliness, such as between Britain and Portugal or between Britain and the Commonwealth countries. At the other extreme we have stable hostility—the "traditional enemies" such as France and Germany. Between these extremes we have a great many pairs characterized by shifting alliances. On the whole, stable friendly relations seem to exist mainly between strong nations and weaker nations which they have an interest in preserving and stable hostile relations between adjacent nations each of which has played a large part in the formation of the other.

Glamorized Nationalism: Some Examples in Poetry

In his essay "Christianity and Patriotism," Leo Tolstoy pitied "the good-natured foolish people, who, showing their healthy white teeth as they smile, gape like children, naively delighted at the dressed-up admirals and presidents, at the flags waving above them, and at the fireworks, and the playing bands." Most wars begin with similar bursts of nationalistic enthusiasm. Tolstoy warned, however, that such euphoria is typically short-lived, with the flags, bands, and glowing sense of being part of a glorious enterprise, greater than one's self being replaced by

> only the desolate wet plain, cold, hunger, misery—in front of them the slaughterous enemy, behind them the relentless government, blood, wounds, agonies, rotting corpses and a senseless, useless death.

In the aftermath of war, military exploits are often celebrated and dramatized, in the process generating a powerful blend of emotion and nationalism. Virtually no society is immune from this tendency to glamorize and thus legitimize acts of violent heroism, which are often taught to children, thereby becoming part of the national mythology. In turn, such images are available not only to support ongoing wars, but also to fuel enthusiasm for future ones. Here are three examples.

The Defense of the Alamo:
Joaquin Miller

SANTA ANNA came storming, as a storm
might come;
    There was rumble of cannon; there was rattle
of blade;
    There was cavalry, infantry, bugle and
drum—
    Full seven proud thousand in pomp and
parade,

    The chivalry, flower of all Mexico;
    And a gaunt two hundred in the Alamo!

    And thirty lay sick, and some were shot
through;
    For the siege had been bitter, and bloody and
long.
    "Surrender, or die"—"Men, what will you
do?"
    And Travis, great Travis, drew sword, quick
and strong;
    Drew a line at his feet . . . Will you come?
Will you go?
    I die with my wounded, in the Alamo."

    Then Bowie gasped, "Guide me over that
line!"
    Then Crockett, one hand to the sick, one
hand to his gun,
    Crossed with him; then never a word or a
sign,
    Till all, sick or well, all, all, save but one,
    One man. Then a woman stopped praying
and slow
    Across, to die with the heroes of the Alamo.

    Then that one coward fled, in the night, in
that night
    When all men silently prayed and thought
Of home; of tomorrow; of God and the right,
    Till dawn; then Travis sent his single last can-
non-shot,
    In answer to insolent Mexico,
    From the old bell-tower of the Alamo.

    Then came Santa Anna; a crescent of flame!
    Then the red escalade; then the fight hand to
hand;
    Such an unequal fight as never had name
    Since the Persian hordes butchered that
doomed Spartan band.
    All day—all day and all night, and the morn-
ing, so slow,
    Through the battle smoke mantling the
Alamo.

    Then silence! Such silence! Two thousand lay
dead
    In a crescent outside! And within? Not a
breath
    Save the gasp of a woman, with gory, gashed
head,
    All alone, with her dead there, waiting for
death;
    And she but a nurse. Yet when shall we
know
    Another like this of the Alamo?

    Shout "Victory, victory, victory ho!"
    I say, 'tis not always with the hosts that win:
    I say that the victory, high or low,
    Is given the hero who grapples with sin,
    Or legion or single; just asking to know
    When duty fronts death in his Alamo.

The Charge of the Light Brigade:
Alfred Tennyson

HALF a league, half a league,
Half a league onward,
All in the valley of Death
Rode the six hundred.
"Forward, the Light Brigade!
Charge for the guns!" he said:
Into the valley of Death
Rode the six hundred.

"Forward, the Light Brigade!"
Was there a man dismay'd?
Not though the soldier knew

Some one had blunder'd:
Their's not to make reply,
Their's not to reason why,
Their's but to do and die:
Into the valley of Death
Rode the six hundred.

Cannon to right of them,
Cannon to left of them,
Cannon in front of them
Volley'd and thunder'd;
Storm'd at with shot and shell,
Boldly they rode and well,
Into the jaws of Death,
Into the mouth of Hell
Rode the six hundred:

Flash'd all their sabres bare,
Flash'd as they turn'd in air,
Sabring the gunners there,
Charging an army, while
All the world wonder'd:
Plunged in the battery-smoke,
Right through the line they broke;
Cossack and Russian
Reel'd from the sabre-stroke
Shatter'd and sunder'd.
Then they rode back, but not—
Not the six hundred.

Cannon to right of them,
Cannon to left of them,
Cannon behind them
Volley'd and thunder'd;
Storm'd at with shot and shell,
While horse and hero fell,
They that had fought so well
Came through the jaws of Death
Back from the mouth of Hell,
All that was left of them,
Left of six hundred.

When can their glory fade?
Oh, the wild charge they made!
All the world wonder'd.
Honor the charge they made!
Honor the Light Brigade,
Noble six hundred!

Battle-Hymn of the Republic: Julia Wand Howe

MINE EYES have seen the glory of the coming
of the Lord:
He is trampling out the vintage where the
grapes of wrath are stored;
He hath loosed the fateful lightning of his terrible swift sword:
His truth is marching on.

I have seen him in the watch-fires of a hundred circling camps;
They have builded him an altar in the
evening dews and damps;
I can read his righteous sentence by the dim
and flaring lamps:
His day is marching on.

I have read a fiery gospel, writ in burnished
rows of steel:
"As ye deal with my contemners, so with you
my grace shall deal;
Let the Hero, born of woman, crush the ser-
pent with his heel,
Since God is marching on."

He has sounded forth the trumpet that shall
never call retreat;
He is sifting out the hearts of men before his
judgment-seat:
O, be swift, my soul, to answer him! be jubi-
lant, my feet!
Our God is marching on.

In the beauty of the lilies Christ was born
across the sea,
With a glory in his bosom that transfigures
you and me;
As he died to make men holy, let us die to
make men free,
While God is marching on.

He is coming like the glory of the morning on
the wave,
He is wisdom to the mighty, he is honor to
the brave,
So the world shall be his footstool, and the
soul of wrong his slave,
Our God is marching on!

MICHAEL T. KLARE

Redefining Security: The New Global Schisms

It is sometimes said that generals are always prepared to refight the last war. Similarly, it is possible that in focusing on explanations for past wars, we give insufficient attention to the causes of future conflicts. (On the other hand, it seems likely that certain fundamental characteristics—of "human nature," social systems, etc.—are likely to be relatively unchanged from one time to the next.) In the last selection of this chapter, we present an effort by a noted peace researcher to look ahead and anticipate "new global schisms" that may characterize violent conflict in the twenty-first century. Note especially the suggestion that interstate wars have been and will be replaced by intrastate conflicts.

Geopolitical boundaries—notably those separating rival powers and major military blocs—have constituted the principal "fault lines" of international politics during much of the twentieth century. Throughout the cold war, the world's greatest concentrations of military strength were to be found along such key dividing lines as the Iron Curtain between East and West in Europe and the demilitarized zone between North and South Korea.

When the cold war ended, many of these boundaries quickly lost their geopolitical significance. With the reunification of Germany and the breakup of the Soviet Union, the divide between East and West in Europe ceased to have any meaning. Other key boundaries—for example, the demilitarized zone in Korea—retained their strategic importance, but elsewhere thousands of miles of previously fortified frontier became open borders with a minimal military presence. The strategic alliances associated with these divisions also lost much of their prominence: the Warsaw Treaty Organization was eliminated altogether, while NATO was given new roles and missions in order to forestall a similar fate.

Battle Lines of the Future

The changes associated with the cold war's end have been so dramatic and profound that it is reasonable to question whether traditional assumptions regarding the nature of global conflict will continue to prove reliable in the new, post–cold war era. In particular, one could question whether conflicts between states (or groups of states) will remain the principal form of international strife, and whether the boundaries between them will continue to constitute the world's major fault lines. Certainly the outbreak of ethnonationalist conflict in the former Yugoslavia and several other former communist states has focused fresh attention on internal warfare, as has the persistence of tribal and religious strife in such countries as Afghanistan, Burundi, Liberia, Rwanda, Somalia, Sri Lanka, and Sudan.

Nevertheless, traditional concepts retain great currency among security analysts. Although the Iron Curtain has disappeared, it is argued, similar schisms of a geographic or territorial nature will arise to take its place. Indeed, several theories have been advanced positing the likely location of these schisms.

Some analysts contend that the territorial schisms of earlier periods—notably those produced by military competition among the major powers—will be revived in the years ahead. Professor Kenneth Waltz of the University of California at Berkeley suggests that such competition will eventually reappear, with Germany, Japan, or some other rising power such as China building its military strength in

From "Redefining Security: The New Global Schisms" by Michael T. Klare, *Current History* 95:353–58. Copyright © 1996. Reprinted by permission of *Current History*.

order to contest America's global paramountcy. "Countries have always competed for wealth and security, and the competition has often led to conflict," he wrote in *International Security's* summer 1993 issue. "Why should the future be different from the past?"

More novel, perhaps, is the suggestion that the principal schisms of the post–cold war era are to be found along the peripheries of the world's great civilizations: Western (including Europe and North America), Slavic-Orthodox (including Russia, Ukraine, and Serbia), Japanese, Islamic, Confucian (China), Latin American, and African. First propounded by Harvard's Samuel Huntington in the summer 1993 issue of *Foreign Affairs,* this argument holds that the economic and ideological antagonisms of the nineteenth and twentieth centuries will be superseded in the twenty-first by antagonisms over culture and cultural identity. "Nation-states will remain the most powerful actors in world affairs," Huntington wrote, "but the principal conflicts of global politics will occur between nations and groups of different civilizations." Although the boundaries between civilizations are not as precise as those between sovereign states, he noted, these loose frontiers will be the site of major conflict. "The clash of civilizations will dominate global politics. The fault lines between civilizations will be the battle lines of the future."

Others have argued that the world's future fault lines will fall not between the major states or civilizations, but between the growing nexus of democratic, market-oriented societies and those "holdout" states that have eschewed democracy or defied the world community in other ways. Such "pariah" states or "rogue" powers are said to harbor aggressive inclinations, to support terrorism, and to seek the production of nuclear or chemical weapons. "[We] must face the reality of recalcitrant and outlaw states that not only choose to remain outside the family [of nations] but also to assault its basic values," wrote President Clinton's national security adviser, Anthony Lake, in the March–April 1994 *Foreign Affairs.* Lake placed several nations in this category—Cuba, North Korea, Iran, Iraq, and Libya—and other writers have added Sudan and Syria. But while there is disagreement about which of these states might actually fall into the "outlaw" category, Lake and other proponents of this analysis hold that the United States and its allies must work

together to "contain" the rogue states and frustrate their aggressive designs.

While these assessments of the world security environment differ in many of their particulars, they share a common belief that the "battle lines of the future" (to use Huntington's expression) will fall along geographically defined boundaries, with the contending powers (and their friends and allies) arrayed on opposite sides. This, in turn, leads to similar policy recommendations that generally entail the maintenance of sufficient military strength by the United States of defeat any potential adversary or combination of adversaries.

It is certainly understandable that many analysts have proceeded from traditional assumptions regarding the nature of conflict when constructing models of future international relations, but it is not at all apparent that such assessments will prove reliable. While a number of crises since the end of the cold war appear to have followed one of the three models described, many have not. Indeed, the most intense conflicts of the current period—including those in Algeria, Angola, Bosnia, Burma, Burundi, Haiti, Kashmir, Liberia, Rwanda, Somalia, Sri Lanka, and Sudan—cannot be fully explained using these models. Moreover, other forms of contemporary violence—terrorism, racial and religious strife, gang warfare, violence against women, and criminal violence—have shown no respect for geography or civilizational identity whatsoever, erupting in virtually every corner of the world.

The Threat from Within

A fresh assessment of the world security environment suggests that the major international schisms of the twenty-first century will not always be definable in geographic terms. Many of the most severe and persistent threats to global peace and stability are arising not from conflicts between major political entities but from increased discord within states, societies, and civilizations along ethnic, racial, religious, linguistic, caste, or class lines.

The intensification and spread of internal discord is a product of powerful stresses on human communities everywhere. These stresses—economic, demographic, sociological, and environmental—are exacerbating the existing divisions within societies and creating entirely new ones. As a result, we are seeing the emergence of new or deepened fissures across international society, producing multiple outbreaks of intergroup hostility and violence. These cleavages cannot be plotted on a normal map, but can be correlated with other forms of data: economic performance, class stratification, population growth, ethnic and religious composition, environmental deterioration, and so on. Where certain conditions prevail—a widening gulf between rich and poor, severe economic competition between neighboring ethnic and religious communities, the declining habitability of marginal lands—internal conflict is likely to erupt.

This is not to say that traditional geopolitical divisions no longer play a role in world security affairs. But it does suggest that such divisions may have been superseded in importance by the new global schisms.

For Richer and Poorer: The Widening Gap

The world has grown much richer over the past 25 years. According to the Worldwatch Institute, the world's total annual income rose from $10.1 trillion in 1970 to approximately $20 trillion in 1994 (in constant 1987 dollars). This increase has been accompanied by an improved standard of living for many of the world's peoples. But not all nations, and not all people in the richer nations, have benefited from the global increase in wealth: some countries, mostly concentrated in Africa and Latin America, have experienced a net decline in gross domestic product over the past few decades, while many of the countries that have achieved a higher GDP have experienced an increase in the number of people living in extreme poverty. Furthermore, the gap in national income between the richest and the poorest nations continues to increase, as does the gap between rich and poor people within most societies.

These differentials in economic growth rates, along with the widening gap between rich and poor, are producing dangerous fissures in many societies. As the masses of poor see their chances of escaping acute poverty diminish, they are likely to become increasingly resentful of those whose growing wealth is evident. This resentment is especially pro-

Sources of Human Insecurity

Income	1.3 billion people in developing countries live in poverty; 200 million people live below the poverty line in industrial countries.
Clean Water	1.3 billion people in developing countries do not have access to safe water.
Literacy	900 million adults worldwide are illiterate.
Food	800 million people in developing countries have inadequate food supplies; 500 million of this number are chronically malnourished, and 175 million are under the age of five.
Housing	500 million urban dwellers worldwide are homeless or do not have adequate housing; 100 million young people are homeless.
Preventable Death	Between 15 million and 20 million people die annually because of starvation or disease aggravated by malnutrition; 10 million people die each year because of substandard housing, unsafe water, or poor sanitation in densely populated cities.

Source: Adapted from Michael Renner, *Fighting for Survival: Environmental Decline, Social Conflict, and the New Age of Insecurity* (New York: Norton, 1996), p. 81.

nounced in the impoverished shantytowns that surround many of the seemingly prosperous cities of the third world. In these inhospitable surroundings, large numbers of people—especially among the growing legions of unemployed youth—are being attracted to extremist political movements like the Shining Path of Peru and the Islamic Salvation Front of Algeria, or to street gangs and drug-trafficking syndicates. The result is an increase in urban crime and violence.

Deep economic cleavages are also emerging in China and the postcommunist states of Eastern Europe and the former Soviet Union. Until the recent introduction of market reforms in these countries, the financial gap between rich and poor was kept relatively narrow by state policy, and such wealth as did exist among the bureaucratic elite was kept well hidden from public view. With the onset of capitalism the economic plight of the lowest strata of these societies has become considerably worse, while the newly formed entrepreneurial class has been able to accumulate considerable wealth—and to display it in highly conspicuous ways. This has generated new class tensions and provided ammunition for those who, like Gennadi Zyuganov of Russia's reorganized Communist Party, seek the restoration of the old, state-dominated system.

Equally worrisome is the impact of growing income differentials on intergroup relations in multiethnic societies. In most countries the divide between rich and poor is not the only schism that matters: of far greater significance are the divisions between various strata of the poor and lower middle class. When such divisions coincide with ethnic or religious differences—that is, when one group of poor people finds itself to be making less economic progress than a similar group of a different ethnic composition—the result is likely to be increased ethnic antagonisms and, at the extreme, increased intergroup violence. This is evident in Pakistan, where violent gang warfare in Karachi has been fueled by economic competition between the indigenous inhabitants of the surrounding region and several waves of Muslim immigrants from India and Bangladesh; it is also evident in Sri Lanka, where efforts by the Sinhalese to deny employment opportunities to the Tamils helped spark a deadly civil war.

Kindling Ethnic Strife

According to information assembled by the Stockholm International Peace Research Institute (SIPRI), ethnic and religious strife figured prominently in all but 3 of the 31 major armed conflicts underway in 1994. And while several long-running ethnic and sectarian conflicts have subsided in recent years, most analysts believe that such strife is likely to erupt repeatedly in the years ahead.

It is true that many recent ethnic and religious conflicts have their roots in clashes or invasions that occurred years ago. It is also true that the violent upheavals that broke out in the former Yugoslavia and the former Soviet Union drew upon deep-seated ethnic hostilities, even if these cleavages were not generally visible during much of the communist era (when overt displays of ethnic antagonism were prohibited by government decree). In this sense, the ethnic fissures that are now receiving close attention from international policymakers are not really new phenomena. Nevertheless, many of these schisms have become more pronounced since the end of the Cold War, or have exhibited characteristics that are unique to the current era.

Greatly contributing to the intensity of recent ethnic and religious strife is the erosion or even disappearance of central state authority in poor third world countries experiencing extreme economic, political, and environmental stress. In such countries—especially Burundi, Liberia, Rwanda, Somalia, and Zaire—the flimsy state structures established after independence are simply unable to cope with the demands of housing and feeding their growing populations with the meager resources at hand. In such circumstances people lose all confidence in the state's ability to meet their basic needs and turn instead to more traditional, kinship-based forms of association for help in getting by—a process that often results in competition and conflict among groups over what remains of the nation's scarce resources. This shift in loyalty from the state to group identity is also evident in Bosnia and parts of the former Soviet Union, where various ethnic factions have attempted to seize or divide up the infrastructure (and in some cases the territory) left behind by the communist regime.

Also contributing to the intensity of intergroup conflict in the current era is the spread of mass communications and other instruments of popular mobilization. These advances have contributed to what Professor James Rosenau of George Washington University calls a "skill revolution" in which individual citizens "have become increasingly competent in assessing where they fit in international affairs and how their behavior can be aggregated into significant collective outcomes." This competence can lead to calls for greater personal freedom and democracy. But it can also lead to increased popular mobilization along ethnic, religious, caste, and linguistic lines, often producing great friction and disorder within heteroge-

neous societies. An important case in point is
India, where Hindu nationalists have proved
adept at employing modern means of communication and political organization—while
retaining traditional symbols and motifs—to
encourage anti-Muslim sentiment and thereby
erode the authority of India's largely secular
government.

Demographic Schisms

According to the most recent UN estimates, total
world population is expected to soar from
approximately 5.6 billion people in 1994 to
somewhere between 8 billion and 12 billion by
the year 2050—an increase that will undoubtedly place great strain on the earth's food production and environmental capacity. But the
threat to the world's environment and food
supply is not all that we have to worry about.
Because population growth is occurring
unevenly in different areas, with some of the
highest rates of growth to be found in countries
with the slowest rates of economic growth,
future population increases could combine
with other factors to exacerbate existing cleavages along ethnic, religious, and class lines.

Overall, the populations of the less-devel-
oped countries (LDCs) are growing at a much
faster rate than those of the advanced industrial nations. As a result, the share of world
population accounted for by the LDCs rose from
69 percent in 1960 to 74 percent in 1980, and
is expected to jump to nearly 80 percent in the
year 2000. Among third world countries,
moreover, there have been marked variations
in the rate of population growth: while the
newly industrialized nations of East Asia have
experienced a sharp decline in the rate of
growth, Africa and parts of the Middle East
have experienced an increase. If these trends
persist, the global distribution of population
will change dramatically over the next few
decades, with some areas experiencing a substantial increase in total population and others
moderate or even negligible growth.

This is where other factors enter the picture. If the largest increases in population were
occurring in areas of rapid economic growth,
the many young adults entering the job market each year would be able to find productive
employment and would thus be able to feed
and house their families. In many cases, how-

ever, large increases in population are coin-
ciding with low or stagnant economic growth,
meaning that future job-seekers are not likely
to find adequate employment. This will have
a considerable impact on the world security
environment. At the very least, it is likely to
produce increased human migration from
rural areas (where population growth tends to
be greatest) to urban centers (where most new
jobs are to be found), and from poor and low-
growth countries to more affluent ones. The
former process is resulting in the rapid expansion of many third world cities, with an attendant increase in urban crime and intergroup
friction (especially where the new urban dwellers are of a different ethnic or tribal group
from the original settlers); the latter is producing huge numbers of new immigrants in
the developed and high-growth countries,
often sparking hostility and sometimes violence from the indigenous populations.

Rapid population growth in poor countries with slow or stagnant economic growth
has other implications for world security. In
many societies it is leading to the hyperutiliza-
tion of natural resources, particularly arable
soil, grazing lands, forests, and fisheries, a
process that severely complicates future economic growth (as vital raw materials are
depleted) and accelerates the pace of environmental decline. It can also overwhelm the
capacity of weak or divided governments to
satisfy their citizens' basic needs, leading eventually to the collapse of states and to the intergroup competition and conflict described
earlier. Finally, it could generate fresh international conflicts when states with slow population growth employ stringent measures to
exclude immigrants from nearby countries
with high rates of growth. While some of this
is speculative, early signs of many of these phenomena have been detected. The 1994 United
States intervention in Haiti, for instance, was
partly motivated by a desire on Washington's
part to curb the flow of Haitian "boat people"
to the United States.

Endangered by Environment

As with massive population growth, the world
has been bombarded in recent years with dire
predictions about the consequences of further
deterioration in the global environment. The

continuing build-up of industrial gases in the earth's outer atmosphere, for example, is thought to be impeding the natural radiation of heat from the planet and thereby producing a gradual increase in global temperatures—a process known as "greenhouse warming." If such warming continues, global sea levels will rise, deserts will grow, and severe drought could afflict many important agricultural zones. Other forms of environmental degradation—the thinning of the earth's outer ozone layer, the depletion of arable soil through overcultivation, the persistence of acid rain caused by industrial emissions—could endanger human health and survival in other ways. As with population growth, these environmental effects will not be felt uniformly around the world but will threaten some states and groups more than others, producing new cleavages in human society.

The uneven impact of global environmental decline is being seen in many areas. The first to suffer are invariably those living in marginally habitable areas—arid grazing lands, coastal lowlands, tropical rainforests. As annual rainfall declines, sea levels rise, and forests are harvested, these lands become uninhabitable. The choice, for those living in such areas, is often grim: to migrate to the cities, with all of their attendant problems, or to move onto the lands of neighboring peoples (who may be of a different ethnicity or religion), producing new outbreaks of inter-group violence. This grim choice has fallen with particular severity on indigenous peoples, who in many cases were originally driven into these marginal habitats by more powerful groups. A conspicuous case in point is the Amazon region of Brazil, where systematic deforestation is destroying the habitat and lifestyle of the indigenous peoples and producing death, illness, and unwelcome migration to the cities.

States also vary in their capacity to cope with environmental crisis and the depletion of natural resources. While the wealthier countries can rebuild areas damaged by flooding or other disasters, relocate displaced citizens to safer regions, and import food and other commodities no longer produced locally, the poorer countries are much less capable of doing these things. As noted by Professor Thomas Homer-Dixon of the University of Toronto, "Environmental scarcity sharply raises financial and political demands on government by

requiring huge spending on new infrastructure." Because many third world countries cannot sustain such expenditures, he notes, "we have . . . the potential for a widening gap between demands on the state and its financial ability to meet these demands"—a gap that could lead to internal conflict between competing ethnic groups, or significant out-migration to countries better able to cope with environmental stresses.

Finally, there is a danger that acute environmental scarcities will lead to armed interstate conflict over such vital resources as water, forests, and energy supplies. Some believe that the era of "resource wars" has already occurred in the form of recurring conflict over the Middle East's oil supplies and that similar conflicts will arise over control of major sources of water, such as the Nile, Euphrates, and Ganges Rivers.

The New Cartography

These new and growing schisms are creating a map of international security that is based on economic, demographic, and environmental factors. If this map could be represented in graphic terms, it would show an elaborate network of fissures stretching across human society in all directions—producing large concentrations of rifts in some areas and smaller clusters in others, but leaving no area entirely untouched. Each line would represent a cleavage in the human community, dividing one group (however defined) from another; the deeper and wider clefts, and those composed of many fault lines, would indicate the site of current or potential conflict.

These schisms, and their continued growth, will force policymakers to rethink their approach to international security. It is no longer possible to rely on strategies of defense and diplomacy that assume a flat, two-dimensional world of contending geopolitical actors. While such units still play a significant role in world security affairs, they are not the only actors that matter; nor is their interaction the only significant threat to peace and stability. Other actors, and other modes of interaction, are equally important. Only by considering the full range of security threats will it be possible for policymakers to design effective strategies for peace.

When the principal fault lines of international security coincided with the boundaries between countries, it was always possible for individual states to attempt to solve their security problems by fortifying their borders or by joining with other nations in regional defense systems like NATO and the Warsaw Pact. When the fault lines fall *within* societies, however, there are no clear boundaries to be defended and no role for traditional alliance systems. Indeed, it is questionable whether there is a role for military power at all: any use of force by one side in these disputes, however successful, will inevitably cause damage to the body politic as a whole, eroding its capacity to overcome the problems involved and to provide for its long-term stability. Rather than fortifying and defending borders, a successful quest for peace must entail strategies for easing and erasing the rifts in society, by eliminating the causes of dissension or finding ways to peacefully bridge the gap between mutually antagonistic groups.

The new map of international security will not replace older, traditional types. The relations between states will still matter in world affairs, and their interactions may lead, as they have in the past, to major armed conflicts. But it will not be possible to promote international peace and stability without using the new map as well, and dealing with the effects of the new global schisms. Should we fail to do so, the world of the next century could prove as violent as the present one.

STUDY QUESTIONS

1. Can you identify and describe an important cause of war that is not represented in this chapter?

2. Is there any fundamental sense in which the causes of war in the twenty-first century are likely to be different from those earlier in history?

3. Compare "war" among animals with war among human beings. Comment on both the advantages and dangers of looking at human war as a special case of a more general phenomenon, found in other species.

4. Discuss the advantages and disadvantages of looking for the causes of "war" as opposed to looking for the causes of specific wars.

5. Is there any evidence for a *dis*inclination to kill? If people are "naturally" inclined to be peaceful, why are there so many wars? If people are "naturally" inclined to be warlike, is the hope for peace unrealistic and doomed to failure?

6. Compare the basic attitudes of the political "left" and "right" with respect to war.

7. Make an argument that students of peace studies should know more about the anthropology of war; make an argument that it is not terribly relevant.

8. During the nineteenth century, many people felt that nationalism could be a potent force for peace. Was it? Could it still be?

9. Make a case for (or against) the proposition that poverty is a major cause of war; similarly for population pressure, for military spending and preparation, for the role of leaders, and for technology.

10. In what ways is nuclear war likely to be different from (and similar to) conventional war, with respect to possible causes?

SUGGESTIONS FOR FURTHER READING

Bell, P. M. H. 1997. *The Origins of the Second World War in Europe.* New York: Longman.

Blainey, Geoffrey. 1973. *The Causes of War.* London: Macmillan.

Bramson, Leon and George W. Goethals. eds. 1964. *War: Studies from Psychology, Sociology, Anthropology.* New York: Basic Books.

Brown, Seyom. 1987. *The Causes and Prevention of War.* New York: St. Martin's Press.

Ferguson, R. Brian. ed. 1984. *Warfare, Culture, and Environment.* Orlando, Fla: Academic Press.

Frank, Jerome. 1982. *Sanity and Survival in the Nuclear Age.* New York: Random House.

Geva, Nehemia and Alex Mintz. eds. 1997. *Decisionmaking on War and Peace: The Cognitive-rational Debate.* Boulder, Colo: L. Rienner Publishers.

Groebel, Jo and Robert A. Hinde. eds. 1989. *Aggression and War: Their Biological and Social Bases.* Cambridge, UK: Cambridge University Press:

Pick, Daniel. 1993. *War Machine: The Rationalisation of Slaughter in the Modern Age.* New Haven, Conn: Yale University Press.

Scheff, Thomas J. 1994. *Bloody Revenge: Emotions, Nationalism, and War.* Boulder, Co: Westview Press.

Suganami, Hidemi. 1996. *On the Causes of War.* New York: Oxford University Press.

2

~~~

Preventing War: Building "Negative Peace"

We have looked briefly at some of the outstanding approaches to the causes of war. Now we turn to prevention.

It has often been said that war is too important to be left to the generals. By the same token, the prevention of war is too important to be left to the politicians. Similarly, study of war's prevention is too important to be left to specialists in international relations, political science, or experts in "strategic studies," especially since many of these scholars tend to be apologists for the "war system" as it has operated for centuries.

And yet, most of the world's religious and ethical traditions deplore war and profess a desire for peace. "My peace I give unto you," offers Jesus (John 14:27), along with "the peace of God, which passeth all understanding" (Phil. 4:7). The Indian leader Gandhi, a devout Hindu, became perhaps the world's greatest crusader for nonviolence. The Chinese philosopher Lao Tse, founder of Taoism, emphasized that the way of war is not the "Tao," or the "Way" that human beings ought to follow.

Tennyson (who also wrote the pro-military ode, "The Charge of the Light Brigade"!) expressed what is nonetheless a worldwide yearning:

> Ring out the old, ring in the new. Ring out the false, ring in the true . . .
> Ring out old shapes of foul disease, ring out the narrowing lust of gold.
> Ring out the thousand wars of old, ring in the thousand years of peace.[1]

Considering the positive connotations of "peace" as opposed to "war," it is only fair to ask why peace—even in its inadequate and negative form as the mere absence of war—has not yet been attained. After all, longing for a thousand years of peace when nothing like it has every been experienced, seems a bit like someone who has never attended a concert looking forward to a paradise in which he or she will spend eternity listening to some heavenly choir! Most people readily give lip service to peace, but perhaps at some level, they haven't really desired it as fervently as they claim.

For one thing, maybe peace is boring. There are lots of war movies, but precious few "peace movies"; lots of martial music but only a handful of peace songs, etc. As with rubber-necking at the scene of a traffic accident, people's attention is drawn to

---

[1]"In Memoriam."

61

extreme situations of violence, in which exciting things happen. Those who complain, for example, about a tendency for the news media to focus only on "bad news," must confront the fact that whereas people are likely to pay attention to a war or even a border clash between contending forces, they would be less than fascinated by a headline blaring "France and Germany did not go to war today."

For another thing, many people—despite their announced abhorrence of war—make exceptions in particular cases, especially in the interest of a "greater good." Thomas Jefferson once wrote of the United States that "peace is our passion," yet he also suggested that "the tree of liberty must be refreshed from time to time with the blood of patriots and tyrants." Similarly, Benjamin Franklin wrote that "there never was a good war, or a bad peace." But Franklin also warned that "even peace can be purchased at too high a price." For all its protestations on behalf of peace, the truth is that the United States has not been especially peaceful, having intervened militarily in other countries more than a hundred times.

Theodore Roosevelt urged his fellow citizens to cherish "the great fighting masterful virtues," and to accept imperial responsibilities in Hawaii, Puerto Rico, the Philippines, and Cuba:

> I preach to you, then, my countrymen, that our country calls not for the life of ease but for the life of strenuous endeavor. . . . If we stand idly by, if we seek merely swollen, slothful ease and ignoble peace, if we shrink from the hard contests where men must win at hazard of their lives and at the risk of all they hold dear, then the bolder and stronger peoples will pass us by, and will win for themselves the domination of the world.[2]

It is interesting that an acknowledged embracing of war is rare in modern thinking . . . although war itself is not rare at all. Departments of War, common until the 1940s, have universally been replaced by Departments or Ministries of "Defense." Only ideological devotees on either extreme have embraced war as virtuous and desirable, with Chinese revolutionary leader Mao Ze-Dong, for example, having spoken for the far left when he announced that "Political power grows out of the barrel of a gun . . . All things grow out of the barrel of a gun . . ." and fascist Italian dictator Benito Mussolini, for the far right:

> War alone brings up to their highest tension all human energies and puts a stamp of nobility upon the people who have the courage to meet it. . . . A doctrine, therefore, which begins with a prejudice in favor of peace is foreign to Fascism.

Many have extolled the sheer intensity of confronting basic issues of life and death, exploring the boundaries of one's capacities, and often reveling in the bonding that is involved. Shakespeare's Henry V rhapsodizes about the joy a forthcoming battle holds for "We few, we happy few, we band of brothers; For he today that sheds his blood with me shall be my brother." And a combat veteran from World War II wrote

> We are liberated from our individual impotence and are drunk with the power that union with our fellows brings. In moments like these many have a vague awareness of how isolated and separate their lives have hitherto been.[3]

---

[2]Theodore Roosevelt. 1910. *The Strenuous Life and Other Essays*. New York: Review of Reviews Co.

---

[3]Glen Gray. 1967. *The Warriors: Reflections on Men in Battle*. New York: Harper & Row.

It is said that the Inuit ("Eskimos") have about a dozen words for "snow" (distinguishing between wet, powder, icy, etc.) and that among the Bedouin there are more than a hundred words for "camel" (ornery, easy-to-ride, etc.). Similarly, in English—and most other languages—there are numerous terms referring to specific wars: the Vietnam War, Korean War, World War II, etc. By contrast, there is only one word for "peace." Although the peace that obtained, say, between World Wars I and II was quite different from that between the Franco-Prussian War and World War I, we do not identify distinct "peaces." Maybe when—or if—peace becomes as important to English-speaking people as snow is to the Inuit or camels are to the Bedouin, we will distinguish as carefully among the different varieties of peace, as we now do about different wars. For now, it must be concluded that war—for all its horrors—holds a particular interest, and even a special appeal. Hence, the need for organized opposition and for "positive approaches to negative peace."

Based on the number of national states that have existed since 1815, there have been approximately 16,000 nation-years, and during this time, war has occupied "only" 600 of these nation-years, or somewhat less that 4% of the possible total. The twentieth century was a comparatively warlike one, and yet modern warfare, even with its enormous capacity for devastation, was directly responsible for fewer than about 2% of all human deaths occurring during that time. Note, however, that there have also been many indirect casualties of war, since war and preparation for war divert resources that might be directed against other causes of death, such as disease and starvation. In addition, war itself typically retards economic development, destroys existing infrastructure, devastates natural environments, renders agriculture dangerous or impossible, displaces huge numbers of people who become homeless and desperate refugees, and also creates long-lasting psychological and social wounds.

Between the years 1500 and 1942 there was an average of nearly one formally declared war per year, not including armed revolutions, yet between 1900 and 1965 there were approximately 350, for an average of more than five per year. According to peace researcher Lewis Richardson, there were at least 59 million deaths from human violence between 1820 and 1946, of which fewer than 10 million were attributable to individual and small-group violence; the remainder were due to war.[4] It is also noteworthy that historically, deaths directly attributable to disease (notably influenza, cholera, and pneumonia) as well as exposure have exceeded battle losses. In 1632, during the Thirty Years' War, the armies of Gustavus and Wallenstein faced each other outside Nuremberg, losing 18,000 men to typhus and scurvy, before separating without a shot having been fired!

The sheer wastefulness of war has been appalling, even with non-nuclear weapons. During the Battle of the Somme (1916) in World War I, for example, the British gained a mere 120 square miles at a cost of 420,000 men (3,500 deaths per square mile), while the Germans lost 445,000. During World War I alone, Europe lost virtually an entire generation of young men. Here is F. Scott Fitzgerald's description of the Somme battlefield, after the war:

---

[4]Lewis Richardson. 1960. *Statistics of Deadly Quarrels*. Pittsburg: Boxwood Press.

See that little stream—we could walk to it in two minutes. It took the British a month to walk to it—a whole empire walking very slowly, dying in front and pushing forward behind. And another empire walked very slowly backward, a few inches a day, leaving the dead like a million bloody rugs.[5]

Of the 2,900,000 men who served in the U.S. armed forces in Vietnam (average age, 19), 300,000 were wounded and 55,000 were killed, along with an unknown number of Vietnamese (estimated at about 2 million). Yet these figures convey very little of the Vietnam War's significance, destructiveness, or horror. Numbers can be numbing.

There is no shortage of proposed solutions to the problem of war. Perhaps the simplest can be derived from the so-called "war on drugs," or efforts to promote celibacy: "Just say NO." But once again, this turns out to be no solution at all. "What if they had a war," goes the perennial question, "and no one came?" The problem, however, is that "they" have had many a war, and nearly always, lots of people show up. Simple condemnation of war, and/or moral exhortation for peace do not, by themselves, do the job.

Fortunately, there have been voices of sanity . . . indeed, many of them. Perhaps these voices, and the suggestions they give, have not been sufficiently innovative, forward-thinking or—that bugaboo of attempts to move beyond the war consensus—"realistic." Perhaps the problem is that no one solution has been pushed hard or far enough, or perhaps war is still with us because these various solutions have not been attempted in the right combination or with the right nuance. Perhaps war—like Jesus' observation about the poor—will always be with us. Perhaps, instead, the eventual prevention of war is already en route, so that peace (or rather, "negative peace") is—like Herbert Hoover's claim about prosperity during the Great Depression—just around the corner. Or perhaps something altogether new and different is needed. In any event, perhaps by reviewing some of the distilled wisdom of humanity's efforts to prevent war, we can help peacemakers of the future avoid repeating the errors of the past. And, maybe, we can inspire greater efforts and achieve greater success in the days to come.

"War is waged," wrote St. Augustine, "so that peace may prevail. . . . But it is a greater glory to slay war with a word than people with a sword, and to gain peace by means of peace and not by means of war." In the following chapter, we shall examine efforts to gain peace by means of peace instead of by war or by threatening war. It is no easy quest, and there may be many routes, some of them blind alleys, others leading into thickets of maze-like complexity, while others may be downright dangerous. But in the interest of "realism," it should be noted that war itself is downright dangerous, too.

---

[5]F. Scott Fitzgerald. 1934. *Tender is the Night.* New York. Scribner's.

The Moral Equivalent of War

Famed historian Will Durant was once asked if he could summarize the history of the world in about five minutes. Responding that he could do so in even less time, he then said,

> History books describe the history of the world as a river red with blood. Running fast, it is filled with the men and events that cause bloodshed: kings and princes, diplomats and politicians. They cause revolutions and wars, violations of territory and rights. But the real history of the world takes place on the riverbanks where ordinary people dwell. They are loving one another, bearing children, and providing homes, all the while trying to remain untouched by the swiftly flowing river.[6]

Much of peace studies is concerned with efforts to build dikes—or at least, place sandbags—to channel the warlike river and keep it from peoples homes; eventually, perhaps, to dry it up altogether.

But Durant's vision may be a bit romantic; after all, even though human beings have long yearned for peace, on many occasions they have also jumped rather enthusiastically into the river of war. If, as some suggest, this is at least in part because war meets certain deep-seated human needs, then it seems only reasonable to seek other, less destructive ways of satisfying those needs. If war represents what psychologist Abraham Maslow called a "peak experience," then it should be possible to achieve such experience without killing. Probably the most famous attempt to come to terms with this problem occurred in the following essay by psychologist and philosopher William James. James' suggestion has its modern counterpart in such endeavors as the Peace Corps, VISTA, and other national service programs, although its basic thrust is directed less toward social betterment per se than toward a peaceful rechanneling of human energy.

The war against war is going to be no holiday excursion or camping party. The military feelings are too deeply grounded to abdicate their place among our ideals until better substitutes are offered than the glory and shame that come to nations as well as to individuals from the ups and downs of politics and the vicissitudes of trade. There is something highly paradoxical in the modern man's relation to war. Ask all our millions, north and south, whether they would vote now (were such a thing possible) to have our war for the Union expunged from history and the record of a peaceful transition to the present time substituted for that of its marches and battles, and probably hardly a handful of eccentrics would say yes. Those ancestors, those efforts, those memories and legends, are the most ideal part of what we now own together, a sacred spiritual possession worth more than all the blood poured out. Yet ask those same people whether they would be willing in cold blood to start another civil war now to gain another similar possession, and not one man or woman would vote for the proposition. In modern eyes, precious though wars may be, they must not be waged solely for the sake of the ideal harvest. Only when forced upon one, only when an enemy's injustice leaves us no alternative, is a war now thought permissible.

From "The Moral Equivalent of War" by William James, *McClure's Magazine,* August, 1910.

---

[6]quoted in Kermit Johnson. 1988. *Realism and Hope in a Nuclear Age.* Atlanta, GA: John Kow Press.

It was not thus in ancient times. The earlier men were hunting men, and to hunt a neighboring tribe, kill the males, loot the village, and possess the females was the most profitable, as well as the most exciting, way of living. Thus were the more martial tribes selected, and in chiefs and peoples a pure pugnacity and love of glory came to mingle with the more fundamental appetite for plunder.

Modern war is so expensive that we feel trade to be a better avenue to plunder, but modern man inherits all the innate pugnacity and all the love of glory of his ancestors. Showing war's irrationality and horror is of no effect upon him. The horrors make the fascination. War is the *strong* life; it is life *in extremis; war* taxes are the only ones men never hesitate to pay, as the budgets of all nations show us.

History is a bath of blood. The *Iliad* is one long recital of how Diomedes and Ajax, Sarpedon and Hector, *killed.* No detail of the wounds they made is spared us, and the Greek mind fed upon the story. Greek history is a panorama of jingoism and imperialism—war for war's sake, all the citizens being warriors. It is horrible reading, because of the irrationality of it all—save for the purpose of making history—and the history is that of the utter ruin of a civilization in intellectual respects perhaps the highest the earth has ever seen. . . .

Alexander's career was piracy pure and simple, nothing but an orgy of power and plunder made romantic by the character of the hero. There was no rational principle in it, and the moment he died his generals and governors attacked one another. The cruelty of those times is incredible. When Rome finally conquered Greece, Paulus Aemilius was told by the Roman Senate to reward his soldiers for their toil by "giving" them the old kingdom of Epirus. They sacked seventy cities and carried off one hundred and fifty thousand inhabitants as slaves. How many they killed I know not, but in Aetolia they killed all the senators, five hundred and fifty in number. Brutus was "the noblest Roman of them all," but, to reanimate his soldiers on the eve of Philippi, he similarly promises to give them the cities of Sparta and Thessalonica to ravage if they win the fight.

Such was the gory nurse that trained societies to cohesiveness. We inherit the warlike type, and, for most of the capacities of heroism that the human race is full of, we have to thank this cruel history. Dead men tell no tales, and, if there were any tribes of other type than this,

they have left no survivors. Our ancestors have bred pugnacity into our bone and marrow, and thousands of years of peace won't breed it out of us. The popular imagination fairly fattens on the thought of wars. Let public opinion once reach a certain fighting pitch, and no ruler can withstand it. In the Boer War both governments began with bluff but couldn't stay there; the military tension was too much for them. In 1898 our people had read the word "war" in letters three inches high for three months in every newspaper. The pliant politician McKinley was swept away by their eagerness, and our squalid war with Spain became a necessity.

At the present day, civilized opinion is a curious mental mixture. The military instincts and ideals are as strong as ever, but are confronted by reflective criticisms which sorely curb their ancient freedom. Innumerable writers are showing up the bestial side of military service. Pure loot and mastery seem no longer morally avowable motives, and pretexts must be found for attributing them solely to the enemy. England and we, our army and navy authorities repeat without ceasing, arm solely for "peace"; Germany and Japan it is who are bent on loot and glory. "Peace" in military mouths today is a synonym for "war expected." The word has become a pure provocative, and no government wishing peace sincerely should allow it ever to be printed in a newspaper. Every up-to-date dictionary should say that "peace" and "war" mean the same thing, now *in posse,* now *in actu.* It may even reasonably be said that the intensely sharp competitive *preparation* for war by the nations *is the real war,* permanent, unceasing, and that the battles are only a sort of public verification of the mastery gained during the "peace" interval.

It is plain that on this subject civilized man has developed a sort of double personality. If we take European nations, no legitimate interest of any one of them would seem to justify the tremendous destructions which a war to compass it would necessarily entail. It would seem as though common sense and reason ought to find a way to reach agreement in every conflict of honest interests. I myself think it our bounden duty to believe in such international rationality as possible. But, as things stand, I see how desperately hard it is to bring the peace party and the war party together, and I believe that the difficulty is due to certain deficiencies in the program of pacifism which set the militarist imagination strongly, and, to a certain extent, justifiably, against it. In the whole discussion both sides are on imaginative and sentimental ground. It is but one Utopia against another, and everything one says must be abstract and hypothetical. Subject to this criticism and caution, I will try to characterize in abstract strokes the opposite imaginative forces and point out what to my own very fallible mind seems the best utopian hypothesis, the most promising line of conciliation.

In my remarks, pacificist though I am, I will refuse to speak of the bestial side of the war regime (already done justice to by many writers) and consider only the higher aspects of militaristic sentiment. Patriotism no one thinks discreditable, nor does anyone deny that war is the romance of history. But inordinate ambitions are the soul of every patriotism, and the possibility of violent death the soul of all romance. The militarily patriotic and romantic-minded everywhere, and especially the professional military class, refuse to admit for a moment that war may be a transitory phenomenon in social evolution. The notion of a sheep's paradise like that revolts, they say, our higher imagination. Where then would be the steeps of life? If war had ever stopped, we should have to reinvent it, on this view, to redeem life from flat degeneration.

Reflective apologists for war at the present day all take it religiously. It is a sort of sacrament. Its profits are to the vanquished as well as to the victor, and, quite apart from any question of profit, it is an absolute good, we are told, for it is human nature at its highest dynamic. Its "horrors" are a cheap price to pay for rescue from the only alternative supposed, of a world of clerks and teachers, of coeducation and zoophily, of consumer's leagues and associated charities, of industrialism unlimited, and femininism unabashed. No scorn, no hardness, no valor any more! Fie upon such a cattleyard of a planet!

So far as the central essence of this feeling goes, no healthy-minded person, it seems to me, can help to some degree partaking of it. Militarism is the great preserver of our ideals of hardihood, and human life with no use for hardihood would be contemptible. Without risks or prizes for the darer, history would be insipid indeed, and there is a type of military character which everyone feels that the race should never cease to breed, for everyone is sensitive to its superiority. The duty is incumbent on mankind of keeping military characters

in stock—of keeping them, if not for use, then as ends in themselves and as pure pieces of perfection—so that Roosevelt's weaklings and mollycoddles may not end by making everything else disappear from the face of nature. . . .

The virtues that prevail, it must be noted, are virtues anyhow, superiorities that count in peaceful as well as in military competition; but the strain on them, being infinitely intenser in the latter case, makes war infinitely more searching as a trial. No ordeal is comparable to its winnowings. Its dread hammer is the welder of men into cohesive states, and nowhere but in such states can human nature adequately develop its capacity. The only alternative is degeneration.

. . . Mankind was nursed in pain and fear and that the transition to a pleasure economy may be fatal to a being wielding no powers of defense against its disintegrative influences. If we speak of the *fear of emancipation from the fear regime,* we put the whole situation into a single phrase, fear regarding ourselves now taking the place of the ancient fear of the enemy.

Turn the fear over as I will in my mind, it all seems to lead back to two unwillingnesses of the imagination, one aesthetic and the other moral; unwillingness, first, to envisage a future in which army life, with its many elements of charm, shall be forever impossible and in which the destinies of peoples shall nevermore be decided quickly, thrillingly, and tragically by force, but only gradually and insipidly by evolution; and, second, unwillingness to see the supreme theater of human strenuousness closed and the splendid military aptitudes of men doomed to keep always in a state of latency and never show themselves in action. These insistent unwillingnesses, no less than other aesthetic and ethical insistencies, have, it seems to me, to be listened to and respected. One cannot meet them effectively by mere counterinsistency on war's expensiveness and horror. The horror makes the thrill, and, when the question is of getting the extremest and supremest out of human nature, talk of expense sounds ignominious. The weakness of so much merely negative criticism is evident— pacificism makes no converts from the military party. The military partly denies neither the bestiality nor the horror nor the expense; it only says that these things tell but half the story. It only says that war is *worth* them; that, taking human nature as a whole, its wars are its best protection against its weaker and more cowardly self and that mankind cannot *afford* to adopt a peace economy.

Pacificists ought to enter more deeply into the aesthetical and ethical point of view of their opponents. . . . So long as antimilitarists propose no substitute for war's disciplinary function, no *moral equivalent* of war, analogous, as one might say, to the mechanical equivalent of heat, so long they fail to realize the full inwardness of the situation. And as a rule they do fail. The duties, penalties, and sanctions pictured in the Utopias they paint are all too weak and tame to touch the military-minded. Tolstoi's pacificism is the only exception to this rule, for it is profoundly pessimistic as regards all this world's values and makes the fear of the Lord furnish the moral spur provided elsewhere by the fear of the enemy. But our socialistic peace advocates all believe absolutely in this world's values, and, instead of the fear of the Lord and the fear of the enemy, the only fear they reckon with is the fear of poverty if one be lazy. This weakness pervades all the socialistic literature with which I am acquainted. . . . Meanwhile men at large still live as they always have lived, under a pain-and-fear economy—for those of us who live in an ease economy are but an island in the stormy ocean—and the whole atmosphere of present-day Utopian literature tastes mawkish and dishwatery to people who still keep a sense for life's more bitter flavors. It suggests, in truth, ubiquitous inferiority.

Inferiority is always with us, and merciless scorn of it is the keynote of the military temper. "Dogs, would you live forever?" shouted Frederick the Great. "Yes," say our Utopians, "let us live forever and raise our level gradually." The best thing about our "inferiors" today is that they are as tough as nails and physically and morally almost as insensitive. Utopianism would see them soft and squeamish, while militarism would keep their callousness, but transfigure it into a meritorious characteristic, needed by "the service" and redeemed by that from the suspicion of inferiority. All the qualities of a man acquire dignity when he knows that the service of the collectivity that owns him needs them. If proud of the collectivity, his own pride rises in proportion. No collectivity is like an army for nourishing such pride, but it has to be confessed that the only sentiment which the image of pacific cosmopolitan industrialism is capable of arousing in countless worthy breasts is shame at the idea of belonging to *such* a collectivity. . . . Where is the sharpness and precipitousness, the contempt for life, whether one's own, or another's? Where is the savage yes and no, the unconditional duty? Where is the conscription? Where is the blood tax? Where is anything that one feels honored by belonging to?

Having said thus much in preparation, I will now confess my own Utopia. I devoutly believe in the reign of peace and in the gradual advent of some sort of a socialistic equilibrium. The fatalistic view of the war function is to me nonsense, for I know that war-making is due to definite motives and subject to prudential checks and reasonable criticisms, just like any other form of enterprise. And when whole nations are the armies and the science of destruction vies in intellectual refinement with the sciences of production, I see that war becomes absurd and impossible from its own monstrosity. Extravagant ambitions will have to be replaced by reasonable claims, and nations must make common cause against them. . . .

All these beliefs of mine put me squarely into the antimilitarist party. But I do not believe that peace either ought to be or will be permanent on this globe, unless the states pacifically organized preserve some of the old elements of army discipline. A permanently successful peace economy cannot be a simple pleasure economy. In the more-or-less socialistic future toward which mankind seems drifting, we must still subject ourselves collectively to those severities which answer to our real position upon this only partly hospitable globe. We must make new energies and hardihoods continue the manliness to which the military mind so faithfully clings. Martial virtues must be the enduring cement; intrepidity, contempt of softness, surrender of private interest, obedience to command must still remain the rock upon which states are built—unless, indeed, we wish for dangerous reactions against commonwealths fit only for contempt and liable to invite attack whenever a center of crystallization for military-minded enterprise gets formed anywhere in their neighborhood.

The war party is assuredly right in affirming and reaffirming that the martial virtues, although originally gained by the race through war, are absolute and permanent human goods. Patriotic pride and ambition in their military form are, after all, only specifications of a more general competitive passion. They are its first form, but that is no reason for supposing them to be its last form. Men now are proud of belonging to a conquering nation, and without a murmur they lay down their persons and their wealth, if by so doing they may fend off subjection. But who can be sure that *other aspects of one's country* may not, with time and education and suggestion enough, come to be regarded with similarly effective feelings of pride and shame? Why should men not someday feel that it is worth a blood tax to belong to a collectivity superior in *any* ideal respect? Why should they not blush with indignant shame if the community that owns them is vile in any way whatsoever? Individuals, daily more numerous, now feel this civic passion. It is only a question of blowing on the spark until the whole population gets incandescent and, on the ruins of the old morals of military honor, a stable system of morals of civic honor builds itself up. What the whole community comes to believe in grasps the individual as in a vise. The war function has grasped us so far, but constructive interests may someday seem no less imperative and impose on the individual a hardly lighter burden.

Let me illustrate my idea more concretely. There is nothing to make one indignant in the mere fact that life is hard, that men should toil and suffer pain. The planetary conditions once and for all are such, and we can stand it. But that so many men, by mere accidents of birth and opportunity, should have a life of *nothing else* but toil and pain and hardness and inferiority imposed upon them, should have *no* vacation, while others natively no more deserving never get any taste of this campaigning life at all—*this* is capable of arousing indignation in reflective minds. It may end by seeming shameful to all of us that some of us have nothing but campaigning and others nothing but unmanly ease. If now—and this is my idea—there were, instead of military conscription, a conscription of the whole youthful population to form for a certain number of years a part of the army enlisted against nature, the injustice would tend to be evened out, and numerous other goods to the commonwealth would follow. The military ideals of hardihood and discipline would be wrought into the growing fiber of the people; no one would remain blind, as the luxurious classes now are blind, to man's relations to the globe he lives on and to the permanently sour and hard foundations of his higher life. To coal and iron mines, to freight trains, to fishing fleets in December, to dishwashing, clothes-washing, and window-washing, to road-building and tunnel-making, to foundries and stokeholes, and to the frames of skyscrapers, would our gilded youths be drafted off, according to their choice, to get the childishness knocked out of them and to come back into society with healthier sympathies and soberer ideas. They would have paid their blood tax, done their own part in the immemorial human warfare against nature; they would tread the earth more proudly, the women would value them more highly, they would be better fathers and teachers of the following generation.

Such a conscription, with the state of public opinion that would have required it and the many moral fruits it would bear, would preserve in the midst of a pacific civilization the manly virtues which the military party is so afraid of seeing disappear in peace. We should get toughness without callousness, authority with as little criminal cruelty as possible, and painful work done cheerily because the duty is temporary and threatens not, as now, to degrade the whole remainder of one's life. I spoke of the moral equivalent of war. So far, war has been the only force that can discipline a whole community, and, until an equivalent discipline is organized, I believe that war must have its way. But I have no serious doubt that the ordinary prides and shames of social man, once developed to a certain intensity, are capable of organizing such a moral equivalent as I have sketched or some other just as effective for preserving manliness of type. It is but a question of time, of skillful propagandism, and of opinion-making men seizing historic opportunities.

The martial type of character can be bred without war. Strenuous honor and disinterestedness abound elsewhere. Priests and medical men are in a fashion educated to it, and we should all feel some degree of it imperative if we were conscious of our work as an obligatory service to the state. We should be *owned*, as soldiers are by the army, and our pride would rise accordingly. We could be poor, then, without humiliation, as army officers now are. The only thing needed henceforward is to inflame the civic temper as past history has inflamed the military temper.

Getting to YES

One way of gaining peace "by means of peace and not by means of war"is for the contending sides to reach a mutually acceptable agreement among themselves. Not surprisingly, it is easier said than done, although normal people negotiate their differences every day, typically without violence. One of the most pervasive and pernicious myths of our current culture of militarism is that war and preparation for war are natural and unavoidable, whereas peace and preparation for peace are hopelessly unrealistic activities. Peacemaking is represented as an impossible dream, the stuff of saints or the hopelessly deluded, whereas only the making of war—or at best, deterrence—is the reality. Hence, it is important to affirm and make visible the peacemaking that happens all around us, most of the time. The active field of nonviolent conflict resolution offers an interesting examples of applying peace studies to interpersonal behavior, as well as to international affairs.

Although ways of fighting have changed through history, the basic techniques of negotiation scarcely have. At their most contentious, negotiators have recourse only to threats or promises, and conflict resolution can be backed up by varying degrees of goodwill or ill will, and based on a continuum from blind trust to iron-clad verification and/or arm-twisting. Negotiations, however, can succeed only if there is a set of outcomes that each party prefers over reaching no agreement. Occasionally, participants in a dispute negotiate only to appear virtuous; but in most cases at least, it appears that a negotiated settlement is preferred over failure to agree or to using violence to force an outcome. The trick is to find a peaceful outcome that will be acceptable to all sides.

There are several ways to facilitate this "trick." One is by the involvement of highly trained Third Parties, who may arbitrate disputes (that is, lay down a judgment which the contenders have previously pledged to accept), or serve as mediators, whose role is to help the disputants clarify the issues and come to agreement. Third Parties can help resolve disputes in several ways. For example, they can make suggestions that both sides find acceptable, but which neither would be willing to offer, for fear of being seen as weak. They can also help disputants go beyond the traditional, adversarial procedure of "positional bargaining," to a more creative and mutually acceptable outcome, the result of so-called "integrative" or "principled" negotiations. The following selection discusses this new and forward-looking approach, in which solving a problem takes precedence over "winning"; it was written by a highly respected team of professional negotiators.

Like it or not, you are a negotiator. Negotiation is a fact of life. You discuss a raise with your boss. You try to agree with a stranger on a price for his house. Two lawyers try to settle a lawsuit arising from a car accident. A group of oil companies plan a joint venture

From *Getting to YES* by Roger Fisher and William Ury. 1981. Boston: Houghton Mifflin, Reprinted by permission of the author.

exploring for offshore oil. A city official meets with union leaders to avert a transit strike. The United States Secretary of State sits down with his Soviet counterpart to seek an agreement limiting nuclear arms. All these are negotiations.

Everyone negotiates something every day. Like Molière's Monsieur Jourdain, who was delighted to learn that he had been speaking prose all his life, people negotiate even when they don't think of themselves as doing so. A person negotiates with his spouse about where to go for dinner and with his child about when the lights go out. Negotiation is a basic means of getting what you want from others. It is back-and-forth communication designed to reach an agreement when you and the other side have some interests that are shared and others that are opposed.

More and more occasions require negotiation; conflict is a growth industry. Everyone wants to participate in decisions that affect them; fewer and fewer people will accept decisions dictated by someone else. People differ, and they use negotiation to handle their differences. Whether in business, government, or the family, people reach most decisions through negotiation. Even when they go to court, they almost always negotiate a settlement before trial.

Although negotiation takes place every day, it is not easy to do well. Standard strategies for negotiation often leave people dissatisfied, worn out, or alienated—and frequently all three.

People find themselves in a dilemma. They see two ways to negotiate: soft or hard. The soft negotiator wants to avoid personal conflict and so makes concessions readily in order to reach agreement. He wants an amicable resolution; yet he often ends up exploited and feeling bitter. The hard negotiator sees any situation as a contest of wills in which the side that takes the more extreme positions and holds out longer fares better. He wants to win; yet he often ends up producing an equally hard response which

exhausts him and his resources and harms his relationship with the other side. Other standard negotiating strategies fall between hard and soft, but each involves an attempted trade-off between getting what you want and getting along with people.

There is a third way to negotiate, a way neither hard nor soft, but rather both hard *and* soft. The method of *principled negotiation* . . . is to decide issues on their merits rather than through a haggling process focused on what each side says it will and won't do. It suggests that you look for mutual gains wherever possible, and that where your interests conflict, you should insist that the result be based on some fair standards independent of the will of either side. The method of principled negotiation is hard on the merits, soft on the people. It employs no tricks and no posturing. Principled negotiation shows you how to obtain what you are entitled to and still be decent. It enables you to be fair while protecting you against those who would take advantage of your fairness. . . .

Every negotiation is different, but the basic elements do not change. Principled negotiation can be used whether there is one issue or several; two parties or many; whether there is a prescribed ritual, as in collective bargaining, or an impromptu free-for-all, as in talking with hijackers. The method applies whether the other side is more experienced or less, a hard bargainer or a friendly one. Principled negotiation is an all-purpose strategy. Unlike almost all other strategies, if the other side learns this one, it does not become more difficult to use; it becomes easier. . . .

Whether a negotiation concerns a contract, a family quarrel, or a peace settlement among nations, people routinely engage in positional bargaining. Each side takes a position, argues for it, and makes concessions to reach a compromise. The classic example of this negotiating minuet is the haggling that takes place between a customer and the proprietor of a secondhand store:

Customer	*Shopkeeper*
How much do you want for this brass dish?	That is a beautiful antique, isn't it? I guess I could let it go for $75.
Oh come on, it's dented. I'll give you $15.	Really! I might consider a serious offer, but $15 certainly isn't serious.

(*Continued on next page*)

Customer	Shopkeeper
Well, I could go to $20, but I would never pay anything like $75. Quote me a realistic price.	You drive a hard bargain, young lady. $60 cash, right now.
$25.	It cost me a great deal more than that. Make me a serious offer.
$37.50. That's the highest I will go.	Have you noticed the engraving on that dish? Next year pieces like that will be worth twice what you pay today.

And so it goes, on and on. Perhaps they will reach agreement; perhaps not.

Any method of negotiation may be fairly judged by three criteria: It should produce a wise agreement if agreement is possible. It should be efficient. And it should improve or at least not damage the relationship between the parties. (A wise agreement can be defined as one which meets the legitimate interests of each side to the extent possible, resolves conflicting interests fairly, is durable, and takes community interests into account.)

The most common form of negotiation, illustrated by the above example, depends upon successively taking—and then giving up—a sequence of positions.

Taking positions, as the customer and storekeeper do, serves some useful purposes in a negotiation. It tells the other side what you want; it provides an anchor in an uncertain and pressured situation; and it can eventually produce the terms of an acceptable agreement. But those purposes can be served in other ways. And positional bargaining fails to meet the basic criteria of producing a wise agreement, efficiently and amicably.

Arguing over Positions Produces Unwise Agreements

When negotiators bargain over positions, they tend to lock themselves into those positions. The more you clarify your position and defend it against attack, the more committed you become to it. The more you try to convince the other side of the impossibility of changing your opening position, the more difficult it becomes to do so. Your ego becomes identified with your position. You now have a new interest in "saving face"—in reconciling future action with past positions—making it less and less likely that any agreement will wisely reconcile the parties' original interests.

The danger that positional bargaining will impede a negotiation was well illustrated by the breakdown of the talks under President Kennedy for a comprehensive ban on nuclear testing. A critical question arose: How many on-site inspections per year should the Soviet Union and the United States be permitted to make within the other's territory to investigate suspicious seismic events? The Soviet Union finally agreed to three inspections. The United States insisted on no less than ten. And there the talks broke down—over positions—despite the fact that no one understood whether an "inspection" would involve one person looking around for one day, or a hundred people prying indiscriminately for a month. The parties had made little attempt to design an inspection procedure that would reconcile the United States's interest in verification with the desire of both countries for minimal intrusion.

As more attention is paid to positions, less attention is devoted to meeting the underlying concerns of the parties. Agreement becomes less likely. Any agreement reached may reflect a mechanical splitting of the difference between final positions rather than a solution carefully crafted to meet the legitimate interests of the parties. The result is frequently an agreement less satisfactory to each side than it could have been.

Arguing over Positions Is Inefficient

The standard method of negotiation may produce either agreement, as with the price of a brass dish, or breakdown, as with the number of on-site inspections. In either event, the process takes a lot of time.

Bargaining over positions creates incentives that stall settlement. In positional bargaining you try to improve the chance that any settlement reached is favorable to you by starting with an extreme position, by stubbornly holding to it, by deceiving the other party as to your true views, and by making small concessions only as necessary to keep the negotiation going. The same is true for the other side. Each of those factors tends to interfere with reaching a settlement promptly. The more extreme the opening positions and the smaller the concessions, the more time and effort it will take to discover whether or not agreement is possible.

The standard minuet also requires a large number of individual decisions as each negotiator decides what to offer, what to reject, and how much of a concession to make. Decision-making is difficult and time-consuming at best. Where each decision not only involves yielding to the other side but will likely produce pressure to yield further, a negotiator has little incentive to move quickly. Dragging one's feet, threatening to walk out, stonewalling, and other such tactics become commonplace. They all increase the time and costs of reaching agreement as well as the risk that no agreement will be reached at all.

Arguing over Positions Endangers an Ongoing Relationship

Positional bargaining becomes a contest of will. Each negotiator asserts what he will and won't do. The task of jointly devising an acceptable solution tends to become a battle. Each side tries through sheer will power to force the other to change its position. "I'm not going to give in. If you want to go to the movies with me, it's *The Maltese Falcon* or nothing." Anger and resentment often result as one side sees itself bending to the rigid will of the other while its own legitimate concerns go unaddressed. Positional bargaining thus strains and sometimes shatters the relationship between the parties. Commercial enterprises that have been doing business together for years may part company. Neighbors may stop speaking to each other. Bitter feelings generated by one such encounter may last a lifetime. . . .

Being Nice Is no Answer

Many people recognize the high costs of hard positional bargaining, particularly on the par-

ties and their relationship. They hope to avoid them by following a more gentle style of negotiation. Instead of seeing the other side as adversaries, they prefer to see them as friends. Rather than emphasizing a goal of victory, they emphasize the necessity of reaching agreement. In a soft negotiating game the standard moves are to make offers and concessions, to trust the other side, to be friendly, and to yield as necessary to avoid confrontation.

The following table illustrates two styles of positional bargaining, soft and hard. Most people see their choice of negotiating strategies as

PROBLEM
Positional Bargaining: Which Game Should You Play?

SOFT	HARD
Participants are friends.	Participants are adversaries.
The goal is agreement.	The goal is victory.
Make concessions to cultivate the relationship.	Demand concessions as a condition of the relationship.
Be soft on the people and the problem.	Be hard on the problem and the people.
Trust others.	Distrust others.
Change your position easily.	Dig in to your position.
Make offers.	Make threats.
Disclose your bottom line.	Mislead as to your bottom line.
Accept one-sided losses to reach agreement.	Demand one-sided gains as the price of agreement.
Search for the single answer: the one *they* will accept.	Search for the single answer: the one *you* will accept.
Insist on agreement.	Insist on your position.
Try to avoid a contest of will.	Try to win a contest of will.
Yield to pressure.	Apply pressure.

between these two styles. Looking at the table as presenting a choice, should you be a soft or a hard positional bargainer? Or should you perhaps follow a strategy somewhere in between?

The soft negotiating game emphasizes the importance of building and maintaining a relationship. Within families and among friends much negotiation takes place in this way. The process tends to be efficient, at least to the extent of producing results quickly. As each party competes with the other in being more generous and more forthcoming, an agreement becomes highly likely. But it may not be a wise one. The results may not be as tragic as in the O. Henry story about an impoverished couple in which the loving wife sells her hair in order to buy a handsome chain for her husband's watch, and the unknowing husband sells his watch in order to buy beautiful combs for his wife's hair. However, any negotiation primarily concerned with the relationship runs the risk of producing a sloppy agreement.

More seriously, pursuing a soft and friendly form of positional bargaining makes you vulnerable to someone who plays a hard game of positional bargaining. In positional bargaining, a hard game dominates a soft one. If the hard bargainer insists on concessions and makes threats while the soft bargainer yields in order to avoid confrontation and insists on agreement, the negotiating game is biased in favor of the hard player. The process will produce an agreement, although it may not be a wise one. It will certainly be more favorable to the hard positional bargainer than to the soft one. If your response to sustained, hard positional bargaining is soft positional bargaining, you will probably lose your shirt.

There Is an Alternative

If you do not like the choice between hard and soft positional bargaining, you can change the game.

The game of negotiation takes place at two levels. At one level, negotiation addresses the substance; at another, it focuses—usually implicitly—on the procedure for dealing with the substance. The first negotiation may concern your salary, the terms of a lease, or a price to be paid. The second negotiation concerns how you will negotiate the substantive question: by soft positional bargaining, by hard

positional bargaining, or by some other method. This second negotiation is a game about a game—a "meta-game." Each move you make within a negotiation is not only a move that deals with rent, salary, or other substantive questions; it also helps structure the rules of the game you are playing. Your move may serve to keep the negotiations within an ongoing mode, or it may constitute a game-changing move.

This second negotiation by and large escapes notice because it seems to occur without conscious decision. Only when dealing with someone from another country, particularly someone with a markedly different cultural background, are you likely to see the necessity of establishing some accepted process for the substantive negotiations. But whether consciously or not, you are negotiating procedural rules with every move you make, even if those moves appear exclusively concerned with substance.

The answer to the question of whether to use soft positional bargaining or hard is "neither." Change the game. . . . We have been developing an alternative to positional bargaining: a method of negotiation explicitly designed to produce wise outcomes efficiently and amicably. This method, called *principled negotiation* or *negotiation on the merits*, can be boiled down to four basic points.

These four points define a straightforward method of negotiation that can be used under almost any circumstance. Each point deals with a basic element of negotiation, and suggests what you should do about it.

People: Separate the people from the problem.

Interests: Focus on interests, not positions.

Options: Generate a variety of possibilities before deciding what to do.

Criteria: Insist that the result be based on some objective standard.

The first point responds to the fact that human beings are not computers. We are creatures of strong emotions who often have radically different perceptions and have difficulty communicating clearly. Emotions typically become entangled with the objective merits of the problem. Taking positions just makes this worse because people's egos become identified with their positions. Hence, before working on the substantive problem, the "people problem" should be disentangled from it and dealt with separately. Figuratively if not literally, the participants should come to see themselves as working side by side, attacking the problem, not each other. Hence the first proposition: *Separate the people from the problem.*

The second point is designed to overcome the drawback of focusing on people's stated positions when the object of a negotiation is to satisfy their underlying interests. A negotiating position often obscures what you really want. Compromising between positions is not likely to produce an agreement which will effectively take care of the human needs that led people to adopt those positions. The second basic element of the method is: *Focus on interests, not positions.*

The third point responds to the difficulty of designing optimal solutions while under pressure. Trying to decide in the presence of an adversary narrows your vision. Having a lot at stake inhibits creativity. So does searching for the one right solution. You can offset these constraints by setting aside a designated time within which to think up a wide range of possible solutions that advance shared interests and creatively reconcile differing interests. Hence the third basic point: Before trying to reach agreement, *invent options for mutual gain.*

Where interests are directly opposed, a negotiator may be able to obtain a favorable result simply by being stubborn. That method tends to reward intransigence and produce arbitrary results. However, you can counter such a negotiator by insisting that his single say-so is not enough and that the agreement must reflect some fair standard independent of the naked will of either side. This does not mean insisting that the terms be based on the standard you select, but only that some fair standard such as market value, expert opinion, custom, or law determine the outcome. By discussing such criteria rather than what the parties are willing or unwilling to do, neither party need give in to the other; both can defer to a fair solution. Hence the fourth basic point: *Insist on objective criteria.*

The method of principled negotiation is contrasted with hard and soft positional bargaining in the table below, which shows the four basic points of the method in boldface type. . . .

PROBLEM
Positional Bargaining: Which Game Should You Play?

SOLUTION
Change the Game—Negotiate on the Merits

SOFT	*HARD*	*PRINCIPLED*
Participants are friends.	Participants are adversaries.	Participants are problem-solvers.
The goal is agreement.	The goal is victory.	The goal is a wise outcome reached efficiently and amicably.
Make concessions to cultivate the relationship.	Demand concessions as a condition of the relationship.	**Separate the people from the problem.**
Be soft on the people and the problem.	Be hard on the problem and the people.	Be soft on the people, hard on the problem.
Trust others.	Distrust others.	Proceed independent of trust.
Change your position easily.	Dig in to your position.	**Focus on interests, not positions.**
Make offers.	Make threats.	Explore interests.
Disclose your bottom line.	Mislead as to your bottom line.	Avoid having a bottom line.
Accept one-sided losses to reach agreement.	Demand one-sided gains as the price of agreement.	**Invent options for mutual gain.**
Search for the single answer: the one *they* will accept.	Search for the single answer: the one *you* will accept.	Develop multiple options to choose from; decide later.
Insist on agreement.	Insist on your position.	**Insist on objective criteria.**
Try to avoid a contest of will.	Try to win a contest of will.	Try to reach a result based on standards independent of will.
Yield to pressure.	Apply pressure.	Reason and be open to reasons; yield to principle, not pressure.

"Winning"

In 1964 an American father and his twelve-year-old son were enjoying a beautiful Saturday in Hyde Park, London, playing catch with a Frisbee. Few in England had seen a Frisbee at that time and a small group of strollers gathered to watch this strange sport. Finally, one Homburg-clad Britisher came over to the father: "Sorry to bother you. Been watching you a quarter of an hour. Who's *winning?*"

In most instances to ask a negotiator, "Who's winning?" is as inappropriate as to ask who's winning a marriage. If you ask that question about your marriage, you have already lost the more important negotiation—the one about what kind of game to play, about the way you deal with each other and your shared and differing interests.

... Both theory and experience suggest that the method of principled negotiation will produce over the long run substantive outcomes as good as or better than you are likely to obtain using any other negotiation strategy. In addition, it should prove more efficient and less costly to human relationships. We find the method comfortable to use and hope you will too.

That does not mean it is easy to change habits, to disentangle emotions from the merits, or to enlist others in the task of working out a wise solution to a shared problem. From time to time you may want to remind yourself that the first thing you are trying to win is a better way to negotiate—a way that avoids your having to choose between the satisfactions of getting what you deserve and of being decent. You can have both.

CHARLES OSGOOD

Disarmament Demands GRIT

All too often, when two parties disagree, their communication is limited to threats and—more rarely—promises. Moreover, if the situation deteriorates, there can be a rapid escalation of anger and distrust, as a result of which things can spiral out of control. But as social psychologist Charles Osgood points out, people also have other behaviors in their repertoire, by which tensions can be ratcheted down. Osgood's formulation calls for unilateral peace initiatives, encouraging the other side to reciprocate. Although it was especially developed with superpower tensions in mind, it is equally applicable to daily life, and to non-nuclear conflicts.

... The focus of my own long-term concern at the inter-nation level has been the rationalization of a strategy ... whose technical name is "Graduated and Reciprocated Initiatives in Tension-reduction." While doodling at a conference in the early 1960s, I discovered that the initials of this mind-boggling phrase spelled out GRIT, and although I generally take a dim view of acronyms, this one was not only easy

for people to remember, but also suggested the kind of determination and patience required to successfully apply it. One of the aims of GRIT is to reduce and control international tension levels. Another is to create an atmosphere of mutual trust within which negotiations on critical military and political issues can have a better chance of succeeding; in other words, GRIT is not a substitute for the

From "Disarmament Demands GRIT" by Charles Osgood. In E. Laszlo and D. Keys, eds., *Disarmament: The Human Factor*. 1981. New York: Pergamon Press.

more familiar process of negotiation, but rather a parallel process designed to enable a nation to take the initiative in a situation where a dangerous "balance" of mutual fear exists—and, to the degree successful, GRIT smooths the path of negotiation.

However, being unconventional in international affairs, the GRIT strategy is open to suspicion abroad and resistance at home. Therefore, it is necessary to spell out the ground rules under which this particular "game" should be played, to demonstrate how national security can be maintained during the process, how the likelihood of reciprocation can be maximized, and how the genuineness of initiations and reciprocations can be evaluated. These "rules" are spelled out in detail in my "basic" pocketbook, *An Alternative to War or Surrender.* . . .

Rules for Maintaining Security

RULE 1: *Unilateral initiatives must not reduce one's capacity to inflict unacceptable nuclear retaliation should one be attacked at that level.*

Nuclear capacity can serve rational foreign policy (a) if it is viewed not only as a deterrent, but also as a security base from which to take limited risks in the direction of reducing tensions; (b) if the retaliatory, second-strike nature of the capacity is made explicit; and (c) if only the minimum capacity required for effective deterrence is maintained and the arms race damped. Needless to say, none of these conditions have been met to date by the two nuclear superpowers. Not only are nuclear weapons ambiguous as to initiation or retaliation, but both strategic and tactical weapons are redundantly deployed and in oversupply as far as capacity for graded response to aggression is concerned. Therefore, at some stage in the GRIT process, graduated and reciprocated reductions in nuclear weapons, along with the men that are assigned to them, should be initiated.

RULE 2: *Unilateral initiatives must not cripple one's capacity to meet conventional aggression with appropriately graded conventional response.*

Conventional forces are the front line of deterrence, and they must be maintained at rough

parity in regions of confrontation. But the absolute level at which the balance is maintained is variable. The general rule would be to initiate unilateral moves in the regions of least tension and gradually extend them to what were originally the most tense regions.

RULE 3: *Unilateral initiatives must be graduated in risk according to the degree of reciprocation obtained from an opponent.*

This is the self-regulating characteristic of GRIT that keeps the process within reasonable limits of security. If bona fide reciprocations of appropriate magnitude are obtained, the magnitude and significance of subsequent steps can be increased; if not, then the process continues with a diversity of steps of about the same magnitude of risk. The relative risk thus remains roughly constant throughout the process.

RULE 4: *Unilateral initiatives should be diversified in nature, both as to sphere of action and as to geographical locus of application.*

The reason for diversification is twofold. First, in maintaining security, diversification minimizes weakening one's position in any one sphere (such as in combat troops) or any one geographical locus. Second, in inducing reciprocation, diversification keeps applying the pressure of initiatives having a common tension-reducing intent (and, hopefully, effect), but does not "threaten" the opponent by pushing steadily in the same sphere or locus and thereby limiting his options in reciprocating.

Rules for Inducing Reciprocation

RULE 5: *Unilateral initiatives must be designed and communicated so as to emphasize a sincere intent to reduce tensions.*

Escalation and de-escalation strategies cannot be "mixed" in the sense that military men talk about the "optimum mix" of weapon systems. The reason is psychological: reactions to threats (aggressive impulses) are incompatible with reactions to promises (conciliatory impulses); each strategy thus destroys the credibility of the other. It is therefore essential that a complete shift in basic policy be clearly signaled at the beginning. The top leadership of the initiating power must establish the right atmosphere by stating the overall nature of the new policy and by emphasizing its tension-reducing intent. Early initiatives must be clearly perceived as tension reducing by the opponents in conflict situations, must be of such significance that they cannot be easily discounted as "propaganda," and they must be readily verifiable. . . .

RULE 6: *Unilateral initiatives should be publicly announced at some reasonable interval prior to their execution and identified as part of a deliberate policy of reducing tensions.*

Prior announcements minimize the potentially unstabilizing effect of unilateral acts and their identification with total GRIT strategy helps shape the opponent's interpretation of them. However, the GRIT process cannot *begin* with a large, precipitate, and potentially destabilizing unilateral action. . . .

RULE 7: *Unilateral initiatives should include in their announcement an explicit invitation to reciprocation in some form.*

The purpose of this "rule" is to increase pressure on an opponent by making it clear that reciprocation of appropriate form and magnitude is essential to the momentum of GRIT, and to bring to bear pressures of world opinion. However, exactly specifying the form or magnitude of reciprocation has several drawbacks: having the tone of a demand rather than an invitation, it carries an implied threat of retaliation if the demand is not met; furthermore, the specific reciprocation requested may be based on faulty perceptions of the other's situation and this may be the reason for failure to get reciprocation. It is the occurrence of reciprocation in any form, yet having the same tension-reducing intent, that is critical. Again speaking psychologically, the greatest conciliatory impact on an opponent in a conflict situation is produced by his own, voluntary act of reciprocating. Such behavior is incompatible with his Neanderthal beliefs about the unalterable hostility and aggressiveness of the initiators, and once he *has* committed a reciprocating action, all of the cognitive pressure is on modifying these beliefs.

Rules for Demonstrating the Genuineness of Initiatives and Reciprocations

RULE 8: *Unilateral initiatives that have been announced must be executed on schedule regardless of any prior commitments to reciprocate by the opponent.*

This is the best indication of the firmness and bona fides of one's own intent to reduce tensions. The control over what and how much is committed is the graduated nature of the process; at the point when each initiative is announced, the calculation has been made in terms of prior-reciprocation history that this step can be taken within reasonable limits of security. Failure to execute an announced step, however, would be a clear sign of ambivalence in intent. This is particularly important in the early stages, when announced initiatives are liable to the charge of "propaganda."

RULE 9: *Unilateral initiatives should be continued over a considerable period, regardless of the degree or even absence of reciprocation.*

Like the steady pounding on a nail, pressure toward reciprocating builds up as one announced act follows another announced act of a tension-reducing nature, even though the individual acts may be small in significance. It is this characteristic of GRIT which at once justifies the use of the acronym and which raises the hackles of most military men. But the essence of this strategy is the calculated manipulation of the intent component of the "perceived-threat-equals-capability-times-intent" equation. It is always difficult to read the intentions of an opponent in a conflict situation and they are usually very complex. In such a situation, GRIT can be applied to consistently encourage conciliatory intents and interpretations at the expense of aggressive ones.

RULE 10: *Unilateral initiatives must be as unambiguous and as susceptible to verification as possible*

Although actions do speak louder than words, even overt deeds are liable to misinterpretation. Inviting opponent verification via direct, on-the-spot observation or via indirect media observation (such as televising the act in question), along with requested reciprocation in the verification of his actions, is ideal; what little might be lost in the way of secrecy by both sides might be more than made up in a reduced need for secrecy on both sides. . . . However, the strategy of GRIT can be directly applied to this problem. Particularly in the early stages, when the risk potentials are small, observers could be publicly invited to guarantee the verifiability of doing what was announced, and although entirely *without* explicit insistence on reciprocation by the opponent, the implication would be strong indeed. Initiatives whose validities are apparently very high should be designed (for example, initial pullbacks of forces from border confrontations), and they can operate to gradually reduce suspicion and resistance to verification procedures. This should accelerate as the GRIT process continues.

Applications of GRIT Strategy

Over the past fifteen years or so there has been considerable experimentation with the GRIT strategy, but mostly in the laboratory. There have been sporadic GRIT-like moves in the real world; for example, the graduated and reciprocated pullback of American and Soviet tanks that had been lined up practically snout-to-snout at the height of the Berlin Crisis. But for the most part in recent history, these have been one-shot affairs, always tentatively made and never reflecting any genuine change in basic strategy.

The one exception to this dictum was "the Kennedy experiment," as documented in a significant paper by Amitai Etzioni. The real-world test of a strategy of calculated de-escalation was conducted in the period from June [1962] to November of 1963. The first step was President Kennedy's speech at the American University on June 10, in which he outlined what he called "a strategy of peace," praised the Russians for their accomplishments, noted that "our problems are man-made . . . and can be solved by man," and then announced the first unilateral initiative: the United States was stopping all nuclear tests in the atmosphere, and would not resume them unless another country did. Kennedy's speech was published *in full* in both *Izvestia* and *Pravda*, with a combined circulation of 10 million. On June 15 Premier Khrushchev reciprocated with a speech welcoming the U.S. initiative, and he an-

nounced that he had ordered the production of strategic bombers to be halted.

The next step was a symbolic reduction in the trade barriers between East and West. On October 9, President Kennedy approved the sale of $250 million worth of wheat to the Soviet Union. Although the United States had proposed a direct America-Russia communication link (the "hot line") in 1962, it was not until June 20, 1963—after the "Kennedy experiment" had begun—that the Soviets agreed to this measure. Conclusion of a test-ban treaty, long stalled, was apparently the main goal of the experiment. Multilateral negotiators began in earnest in July, and on August 5, 1963, the test-ban treaty was signed. The Kennedy experiment slowed down with the deepened involvement in Vietnam, and it came to an abrupt end in Dallas.

Had this real-world experiment in calculated de-escalation been a success? To most of the initiatives taken by either side, the other reciprocated, and the reciprocations were roughly proportional in significance. What about psychological impact? I do not think that anyone who lived through that period will deny that there was a definite warming of American attitudes toward Russians, and the same is reported for Russian attitudes toward Americans. The Russians even coined their own name for the new strategy, "the policy of mutual example."

The novelty of GRIT raises shrieks of incredulity from hawks and clucks of worry even from doves. The question I am most often asked is this: Doesn't any novel approach like this involve too much risk? Anything we do in the nuclear age means taking risks. To escalate conflicts that involve another nuclear power unquestionably carries the greatest risk. Simply doing nothing—remaining frozen in a status quo that is already at much too high a level of force and tension—is certainly not without risk over the long run. GRIT also involves risk. But the risking comes in small packages. Looked at in a broad perspective, the superpower confrontation has many positive elements in it and many motivations on both sides that favor détente. It therefore offers itself as a potential proving ground for a strategy that is novel but yet appropriate to the nuclear age in which we are trying to survive. The assumption behind nuclear deterrence—that we can go spinning forever into eternity, poised for mutual annihilation and kept from it only by fragile bonds of mutual fear—is untenable. The ultimate goal must be to get out from under the nuclear sword of Damocles by eliminating such weapons from the human scene.

WILLIAM V. O'BRIEN

The Conduct of Just and Limited War

War involves killing, one of the most drastic actions that anyone can take. Killing another human being—except by accident, self-defense, or out of insanity—is universally condemned . . . except during war, in which time it is not only permitted, but applauded. Nonetheless, such applause is not universal, and even when it occurs, it is rarely unequivocal. Advocates of peace have often derived strength, inspiration, and even concrete assistance from moral and ethical teaching, although to be sure, such teachings have not been unilaterally antiwar. There have been concerted and influential efforts to support the ethical legitimacy of war under certain circumstances and, indeed, even though violence is perhaps the most frequent target of the world's moral systems, and although war in general is widely criticized, it is debatable whether such systems have been more likely to oppose or to support *specific* wars.

Perhaps it avails nothing if moralists condemn war in general but lend their approval to each particular war as it comes along. But this conclusion omits a potentially important characteristic of moral thought: a continuing predisposition *against* violence and killing. There is little room, after all, to criticize the horrors of Auschwitz or the bombing of Hiroshima from an engineering standpoint; these events were technological triumphs. It is only by applying moral judgments that outrage—and from such outrage, a determination to change—can be developed.

The most carefully enunciated and influential moral approach to war in the Western tradition, so-called "just war doctrine," is largely the result of Catholic teaching, derived especially from the writing of St. Augustine. This approach, sometimes called "Christian realism," can be criticized as unacceptably apologetic when it comes to warmaking. Certainly, it cannot by itself be counted on as a bulwark against war, if only because "just war doctrine" is specifically concerned with identifying circumstances under which war is permissible. But its approach is nuanced and, if anything, biased against war except under carefully defined conditions and in carefully restricted ways. Thus, it offers some potential assistance in preventing war . . . or at least, in making it less destructive, and possibly even less likely.

The original just-war doctrine of St. Augustine, St. Thomas, and other Scholastics emphasized the conditions for permissible recourse to war—the *jus ad bellum*. To this doctrine was added another branch of prescriptions regulating the conduct of war, the *jus in bello*.

From *The Conduct of Just and Limited War* by William V. O'Brien, 1981. New York: Praeger.

The *Jus Ad Bellum*

The *jus ad bellum* lays down conditions that must be met in order to have permissible recourse to armed coercion. They are conditions that should be viewed in the light of the fundamental tenet of just-war doctrine: the presumption is always against war. The taking of human life is not permitted to man unless there are exceptional justifications. Just-war doctrine provides those justifications, but they are in the nature of special pleadings to overcome the presumption against killing. The decision to invoke the exceptional rights of war must be based on the following criteria: there must be competent authority to order the war for a public purpose; there must be a just cause (it may be self-defense or the protection of rights by offensive war) and the means must be proportionate to the just cause and all peaceful alternatives must have been exhausted; and there must be right intention on the part of the just belligerent. Let us examine these criteria.

COMPETENT AUTHORITY

Insofar as large-scale, conventional war is concerned, the issue of competent authority is different in modern times than it was in the thirteenth century. The decentralized political system wherein public, private, and criminal violence overlapped, as well as the state of military art and science, permitted a variety of private wars. So it was important to insist that war—in which individuals would be called upon to take human lives—must be waged on the order of public authorities for public purposes. This is not a serious problem in most parts of the world today. Only states have the material capacity to wage large-scale, modern, conventional war. Two other problems do, however, exist in connection with the condition of competent authority. First, there may be disputes as to the constitutional competence of a particular official or organ of state to initiate war. Second, civil war and revolutionary terrorism are frequently initiated by persons and organizations claiming revolutionary rights.

Most states today, even totalitarian states, have specific constitutional provisions for the declaration and termination of war. If an official or state organ violates these provisions, there may not be a valid exercise of the sovereign right to declare and wage war. In such a case the first condition of the just war might not

be met. This was the charge, implicitly or explicitly, against President Johnson in the Vietnam War. Johnson never requested a declaration of war from Congress with which he shared war-making powers. War critics asserted that the undeclared war was illegal. A sufficient answer to this charge is to be found in congressional cooperation in the war effort and in the refusal of the courts to declare the war unconstitutional.

In this connection a word should be said about declaring wars. Any examination of modern wars will show that the importance of a declaration of war has diminished greatly in international practice. Because of the split-second timing of modern war, it is often undesirable to warn the enemy by way of a formal declaration. Defense measures are geared to react to hostile behavior, not declarations. When war is declared it is often an announcement confirming a condition that has already been established. Nevertheless, if a particular state's constitution does require a formal declaration of war and one is not forthcoming, the issue of competence is raised. If a public official exceeds his authority in mobilizing the people and conducting war, there is a lack of competent authority.

The second problem, however, is by far the greatest. Today, rights of revolution are frequently invoked by organizations and individuals. They clearly do not have the authority and capacity to wage war in the conventional sense. However, they do wage revolutionary war, often on an international scale. Indeed, international terrorism is one of the most pervasive and difficult problems facing the international community. . . .

JUST CAUSE

Authorities vary in their presentation of just cause, but it seems to break down into four subdivisions: the substance of the just cause, the forms of pursuing just cause, the requirement of proportionality of ends and means, and the requirement of exhaustion of peaceful remedies.

The substance of the just cause must, . . . be sufficiently "serious and weighty" to overcome the presumption against killing in general and war in particular . . . (1) "to protect the innocent from unjust attack," (2) "to restore rights wrongfully denied," (3) "to re-establish a just order." . . .

The forms of pursuing just cause are defensive and offensive wars. The justice of self-defense is generally considered to be axiomatic. Just-war doctrine, following Aristotle and St. Thomas as well as the later Scholastics, places great importance on the state as a natural institution essential for man's development. Defense of the state is prima facie defense of an essential social institution. So strong is the presumption in favor of the right of self-defense that the requirement of probable success, to be discussed under proportionality, is usually waived.

Offensive wars raise more complications. In classical just-war doctrine, offensive wars were permitted to protect vital rights unjustly threatened or injured. Moreover, in a form now archaic, offensive wars of vindictive justice against infidels and heretics were once permitted. Such wars disappeared with the decline of the religious, holy-war element as a cause of and rationale for wars. Thus, the forms of permissible wars today are twofold: wars of self-defense and offensive wars to enforce justice for oneself. [Moreover,] the second is now seemingly prohibited by positive international law. . . .

Turning from the forms of just war we come to the heart of just cause—proportionality between the just ends and the means. This concerns the relationship between *raison d'état* (the high interests of state) and the use of the military instrument in war as the means to achieve these interests. This concept of proportionality at the level of *raison d'état* is multidimensional. To begin with, the ends held out as the just cause must be sufficiently good and important to warrant the extreme means of war, the arbitrament of arms. Beyond that, a projection of the outcome of the war is required in which the probable good expected to result from success is weighed against the probable evil that the war will cause.

The process of weighing probable good against probable evil is extremely complex. The balance sheet of good and evil must be estimated for each belligerent. Additionally, there should be a balancing of effects on individual third parties and on the international common good. International interpendence means that international conflicts are difficult to contain and that their shock waves affect third parties in a manner that must be accounted for in the calculus of probable good

and evil. Moreover, the international community as such has its international common good, which is necessarily affected by any war. Manifestly, the task of performing this calculus effectively is an awesome one. . . . They may need revision or replacement by completely new estimates. The *jus ad bellum* requirement of proportionality, then, includes these requirements:

There must be a just cause of sufficient importance to warrant its defense by recourse to armed coercion.

The probable good to be achieved by successful recourse to armed coercion in pursuit of the just cause must outweigh the probable evil that the war will produce.

The calculation of proportionality between probable good and evil must be made with respect to all belligerents, affected neutrals, and the international community as a whole before initiating a war and periodically throughout a war to reevaluate the balance of good and evil that is actually produced by the war.

These calculations must be made in the light of realistic estimates of the probability of success.

There is an important qualification to the requirement of probability of success. A war of self-defense may be engaged in irrespective of the prospects for success, particularly if there is a great threat to continued existence and to fundamental values.

The last component of the condition of just cause is that war be employed only as a last resort after the exhaustion of peaceful alternatives. To have legitimate recourse to war, it must be the *ultima ratio*, the arbitrament of arms. . . .

RIGHT INTENTION

Among the elements of the concept of right intention, several points may be distinguished. First, right intention limits the belligerent to the pursuit of the avowed just cause. That pursuit may not be turned into an excuse to pursue other causes that might not meet the conditions of just cause. Thus, if the just cause is to defend a nation's borders and protect them from future aggressions, but the fortunes of war place the just belligerent in the position to conquer the unjust nation, such a conquest might show a lack of right intention and change the just war into an unjust war. The just cause would have been realized by a war of limited objectives rather than a war of total conquest.

Second, right intention requires that the just belligerent have always in mind as the ultimate object of the war a just and lasting peace. There is an implicit requirement to prepare for reconciliation even as one wages war. This is a hard saying. It will often go against the grain of the belligerents' disposition, but pursuit of a just and lasting peace is an essential characteristic of the difference between just and unjust war. Accordingly, any belligerent acts that unnecessarily increase the destruction and bitterness of war and thereby endanger the prospects for true peace are liable to condemnation as violations of the condition of right intention.

Third, underlying the other requirements, right intention insists that charity and love exist even among enemies. Enemies must be treated as human beings with rights. The thrust of this requirement is twofold. Externally, belligerents must act with charity toward their enemies. Internally, belligerents must suppress natural animosity and hatred, which can be sinful and injurious to the moral and psychological health of those who fail in charity. Gratuitous cruelty may be as harmful to those who indulge in it as to their victims. . . .

The *Jus in Bello*

In the *jus in bello* that emerged rather late in the development of just-war doctrine, two basic limitations on the conduct of war were laid down. One was the principle of proportion requiring proportionality of military means to political and military ends. The other was the principle of discrimination prohibiting direct, intentional attacks on noncombatants and nonmilitary targets. These are the two categories of *jus in bello* limitations generally treated by modern works on just war.

THE PRINCIPLE OF PROPORTION

In the preceding [discussion] the principle of proportion was discussed at the level of *raison d'état*. One of the criteria of just-war *jus ad bellum* requires that the good to be achieved by the realization of the war aims be proportionate to the evil resulting from the war. When the principle of proportion is again raised in the *jus in bello*, the question immediately arises as to the referent of proportionality in judging the means of war. Are the means to be judged in relation to the end of the war, the ends being formulated in the highest *raison d'état* terms? Or are intermediate political/military goals, referred to in the law-of-war literature as *raison de guerre*, the more appropriate referents in the calculus of proportionality as regards the conduct of a war? . . .

Assuming that in World War II the Allied forces were fighting a just war, it is clear that some of the means they employed may have been unjust (for example, strategic bombing of cities and the two atomic bomb attacks). It is not difficult to assimilate these controversial means into the total Allied war effort and pronounce that total effort proportionate to the just cause of the war. It is much more difficult and quite a different calculation to justify these means as proportionate to discrete military ends. Even in the absence of war-crimes proceedings, a just belligerent ought to respect the *jus in bello* standards by meeting the requirement of proportionality of means to military ends. . . .

THE PRINCIPLE OF DISCRIMINATION

The principle of discrimination prohibits direct intentional attacks on noncombatants and nonmilitary targets. It holds out the potential for very great, specific limitations on the conduct of just war. Accordingly, debates over the meaning of the *principle of discrimination* have become increasingly complex and important as the character of war has become more total. It is in the nature of the principle of proportion to be elastic and to offer possibilities for justifications of means that are truly necessary for efficacious military action. However, it is in the nature of the principle of discrimination to remain rigidly opposed to various categories of means irrespective of their necessity to success in war. It is not surprising, then, that most debates about the morality of modern war have focused on the principle of discrimination.

Such debates are vastly complicated by the opportunities afforded in the definition of the principle of discrimination to expand or contract it by interpretations of its component elements. There are debates over the meaning of *direct intentional attack, noncombatants,* and *nonmilitary targets.*

In order to discuss the problem of interpreting the principle of discrimination, it is necessary to understand the origins of the principle. The most fundamental aspect of the principle of discrimination lies in its direct relation to the justification for killing in war. If the presumption against killing generally and war in particular is overcome (in the case of war by meeting the just-war conditions), the killing then permitted is limited to the enemy combatants, the aggressors. The exceptional right to take life in individual self-defense and in war is limited to the attacker in the individual case and the enemy's soldiers in the case of war. One may not attack innocent third parties as part of individual selfdefense. In war the only permissible objects of direct attack are the enemy's soldiers. In both cases, the overriding moral prescription is that evil must not be done to obtain a good object. . . .

However, it is important to recognize that the principle of discrimination did not find its historical origins solely or even primarily in the fundamental argument summarized above. As a matter of fact, the principle seems to have owed at least as much to codes of chivalry and to the subsequent development of positive customary laws of war. These chivalric codes and customary practices were grounded in the material characteristics of warfare during the medieval and Renaissance periods. During much of that time, the key to the conduct of war was combat between mounted knights and supporting infantry. Generally speaking, there was no military utility in attacking anyone other than the enemy knights and their armed retainers. Attacks on unarmed civilians, particularly women and children, would have been considered unchivalric, contrary to the customary law of war, and militarily gratuitous. . . .

It is often contended that there is an absolute principle of discrimination prohibiting any use of means that kill noncombatants. It is further contended that this absolute principle constitutes the central limitation of just war and that it is based on an immutable moral imperative that may never be broken no matter how just the cause. This is the moral axiom mentioned above, that evil may never be done in order to produce a good result. In this formulation, killing noncombatants intentionally is always an inadmissible evil.

These contentions have produced two principal reactions. The first is pacifism. Pacifists rightly argue that war inevitably involves violation of the absolute principle of discrimination. If that principle is unconditionally binding, a just war is difficult if not impossible to envisage. The second reaction to the claims of an absolute principle of discrimination is to modify the principle by some form of the principle of double effect whereby the counterforce component of a military means is held to represent the intent of the belligerent, whereas the countervalue, indiscriminate component of that means is explained as a tolerable, concomitant, unintended effect—collateral damage in contemporary strategic terms. . . .

As nations engaged in total mobilization, one society or system against another, it was no longer possible to distinguish sharply between the military forces and the home fronts that rightly held themselves out as critical to the war effort. By the American Civil War this modern phenomenon had assumed critical importance. The material means of supporting the Confederate war effort were attacked directly and intentionally by Union forces. War in the age of the Industrial Revolution was waged against the sources of war production. Moreover, the nature of the attacks on noncombatants was psychological as well as material. Military forces have always attempted to break the will of the opposing forces as well as to destroy or scatter them. It now became the avowed purpose of military forces to break the will of the home front as well as to destroy its resources for supporting the war. This, of course, was to become a major purpose of modern strategic aerial bombardment.

To be sure, attacks on the bases of military forces have historically often been an effective strategy. But in the simpler world before the Industrial Revolution, this was not such a prominent option. When the huge conscript armies began to fight for profound ideological causes with the means provided by modern industrial mobilization and technology, the home front and consequently the noncombatants became a critical target for direct intentional attack.

The question then arose whether a civilian could be a participant in the overall war effort to such a degree as to lose his previous noncombatant immunity. Likewise, it became harder to distinguish targets that were clearly military from targets, such as factories or railroad facilities, that were of sufficient military importance to justify their direct intentional attack. It is important to note that this issue arose before the great increase in the range, areas of impact, and destructive effects of modern weaponry, conventional and nuclear. What we may term *countervalue warfare* was carried out in the American Civil War not because it was dictated by the weapons systems but because the civilian population and war-related industries and activities were considered to be critical and legitimate targets to be attacked.

In World War I this kind of attack was carried out primarily by the belligerents with their maritime blockades. Above all, these blockades caused the apparent demise of the principle of noncombatant immunity in the positive international law of war. Other factors in this demise were developments that revealed potentials not fully realized until World War II (for example, aerial bombardment of population centers and unrestricted submarine warfare). In World War II aerial bombardment of population centers was preeminent as a source of attacks on traditional noncombatants and nonmilitary targets. By this time the concept of total mobilization had advanced so far that a plausible argument could be made that vast segments of belligerent populations and complexes of industry and housing had become so integral to the war effort as to lose their noncombatant immunity.

ALVA MYRDAL

The Game of Disarmament

"You cannot simultaneously prevent and prepare for war," wrote Albert Einstein. This sentiment can be carried further, to the more positive assertion: You can prevent war by getting rid of the weapons with which war is carried out. But not everyone would agree. Indeed, no one—not even the most ardent advocate of disarmament—claims that doing away with weapons will solve the problem of war. So long as the underlying causes persist, and so long as people have the capacity and inclination to resort to violence—especially organized violence—under certain circumstances, war will continue to haunt us.

Nonetheless, the connection between weaponry and war, although complex, is well established and legitimate. The dream of disarmament is thus an ancient one, intimately connected with the yearning for peace itself: "And they shall beat their swords into plowshares, and their spears into pruning hooks; nation shall not lift up sword against nation, neither shall they learn war any more" (Micah 4:3–4). The actual history of disarmament, however, is not especially encouraging. All too often, disarmament proposals have been self-serving, in which one side urges elimination of those weapons in which the other has an advantage, or which are obsolete, or both sides make proposals simply for their publicity value, confident that they will be rejected.

Although general and complete disarmament has thus far eluded our grasp, there have been a number of modest successes, including prohibitions on specific weapons (dum-dum bullets, biological agents, antiballistic missiles), as well as mutual agreements to forego arms races in particular places (e.g., Antarctica, the sea-bed). These and other accomplishments fall within the category of disarmament's "poor sister," arms control.

From *The Game of Disarmament* by Alva Myrdal. 1976. New York: Pantheon.

Arms control is controversial; within the peace studies community, it is often seen as potentially pernicious if it shifts attention from the ultimate goal of disarmament, while also seeming to legitimize various arms races and even sometimes accelerating them in areas not explicitly prohibited. There is also a long and sorry history of using arms control negotiations as a smokescreen to build yet more weapons, under the guise that one must be able to "negotiate from strength."

However, peace specialists acknowledge four potential benefits of well-constructed arms control agreements, even if they serve largely as stop-gap measures: (1) reduce the chances of war breaking out (if each side worries less that its opponent is accumulating weapons that makes it likely to initiate an attack); (2) reduce the destructiveness of war if it does break out (for instance, by eliminating weapons of mass destruction or those conventional weapons that are especially brutal); (3) reduce the economic costs of preparing for war (by permitting the redirection of society's resources away from certain weapons); and (4) develop cooperation and confidence-building, which can lead to yet further agreements (assuming that the agreed measures are in fact lived up to).

Most of all, it is important to recognize that disarmament is a *process*, not an *event*, more a way of progressing than a finished masterpiece to be unveiled to the admiring world with a grand "voila!" Like perfect grace, total disarmament may never be achieved, but that doesn't diminish its worth as a goal or, rather, as a route toward possible salvation. Famed Swedish disarmament advocate and Nobel Peace Prize winner Alva Myrdal long deplored the manipulativeness and dishonesty of many so-called disarmament efforts, especially those involving the United States and the former Soviet Union. She makes a specific case for non-nuclear as well as nuclear disarmament; the former is excerpted here. Nuclear weapons are addressed in the next selection.

Disarmament Efforts Before World War II

The questions of how to preserve peace and promote disarmament were burning issues after World War I. It was called the Great War or the World War and consensus reigned that it should not, and would not, be repeated. The world should be made to "return to normalcy."

There were two aspects of the disarmament issue. The first, motivated by sheer revulsion against war itself, led to attempts to proscribe the *use of cruel weapons*. The horrifying experience of the use of gas and the hundreds of thousands of victims killed, maimed, or blinded emphasized the need. Such work tied in with the traditions from the turn-of-the-century Hague Conferences which had established rules of international law for the conduct of warfare. In this first area, the work was crowned with considerable success in the form of the Geneva Protocol of 1925, which prohib-

ited the use not only of gas warfare but of chemical and biological weapons in general.

The second approach was aimed at *reduction of armaments* by mutually agreed limitations on possession and production. The reaction against the arms race that had preceded the War and, according to popular view, had been a cause of the War was one of the main constituent factors when the Versailles Peace Treaty was made and the League of Nations created in 1920. The Covenant of the League demanded that armaments be reduced to "the lowest point consistent with national safety." There was a strong political commitment to the League's work on the issues of disarmament, especially after 1926 when a Preparatory Disarmament Commission was established wherein both the United States and the Soviet Union (at the time nonmembers) participated, as did Germany (a new League member).

There were times when negotiations were on the verge of major breakthroughs, as often has been emphasized by Philip Noel-Baker, a prominent participant. These potentialities were not realized, however. Governments were too preoccupied with what they considered to be their own security interests. They could not free themselves from questions of prestige, and they underestimated the greater security that could have been gained by mutual agreement. Then when Hitler came to power the disarmament negotiations had to be abandoned as being unrealistic. The world was drifting towards a new world war.

We ought nevertheless to learn a lesson from the sincerity and the boldness with which the disarmament tasks were tackled in that period. The situation was, of course, more manageable at the time of the League of Nations since the organization consisted largely of advanced European countries with similar problems. Technologies were then far less diversified. Wars traditionally had been fought on the surface of the earth and on the seas and only recently had the submarine environment and the air been opened up to military pursuit. Rules for the conduct of wars, from Grotius to the Hague Conferences, had traditionally been based on comparatively manageable environments.

After World War I efforts were made to restrict armaments by matching, item for item, the number of troops, guns, tanks, warships, etc. in order to agree on a low ceiling or to eliminate arms altogether. There were early successes in a limited way and for a limited time such as the Washington Naval Treaty of 1922, which restricted the tonnage and gunpower of the navies of the major powers. Although it soon became obvious that the intent of the Treaty was forfeited by the *qualitative* improvement of cruisers and destroyers, the tradition of setting *quantitative* norms, or ratios, persisted and persists to this day.

Nonetheless, the progress of the League of Nations in settling disarmament issues was, all matters considered, remarkable. The leading statesmen of the era set high stakes on farreaching proposals. Strong support came also from powerful civic-interest bodies like the trade unions and the cooperative movement. Their views were presented at the Preparatory Commission. For more than five years this body labored ambitiously on plans to be negotiated at the World Conference for the Reduction and Limitation of Armaments, which finally met in February 1932. As a matter of fact,

it was at the first appearance of Soviet delegates at a meeting of the Preparatory Commission that Russia's Foreign Minister Litvinov introduced a plan for "general and complete disarmament," a term revived after World War II— a high aspiration which fifty years later seems to lie farther and farther away.

Strikingly ambitious proposals about specific arms reductions were made, beginning in the Preparatory Commission. Lord Cecil of Britain submitted a proposal on naval disarmament, suggesting that all countries should forgo three types of fighting vessels (which the Versailles Treaty explicitly had forbidden Germany to possess): surface vessels over 10,000 tons' displacement, all submarines, and aircraft carriers. The underlying principle was that weapons with primarily offensive functions should be outlawed. In relation to the interesting new weapons category of airplanes, this criterion meant that all military air forces be forbidden, including naval ones. In today's reality the principle would apply to almost all major weapons systems with high mobility, as being principally offensive in character, whether intended for preemptive defense of home territories or more farflung undertakings. . . .

United Nations and Disarmament

The statesmen who had lived through the cataclysm of World War II, reflecting the feelings of the peoples in all countries, declared their determination that wars should be prevented by collective efforts. The United Nations was created in order "to save succeeding generations from the scourge of war." Peace was its primary purpose. The responsibility for enforcing peace was laid upon the Security Council, while the General Assembly was to have the right to consider questions of peace and security and to make recommendations to the members and to the Security Council on all matters within the scope of the Charter.

In the spirit of optimism and mutual confidence that reigned when the Charter was drafted, the question of disarmament was not brought forward as a major task or one of immediate urgency. The Charter did not prescribe that the Member nations should reduce their armaments or even that they should not increase them. Restraints were only placed on the defeated nations, but this was done through settlements by the victors outside of the United Nations. . . .

Almost immediately after the end of World War II the cold war broke out between the two superpowers, within a few years leading to the establishment of the system of military alliances . . .

In Chapters VI and VII of the UN Charter the Security Council's main functions had been laid down to be "pacific settlements of disputes" and taking "action with respect to threats to the peace, breaches of the peace, and acts of aggression." These functions of the Security Council have become largely immobilized by the veto and, more fundamentally, by the deep-rooted disagreements between the superpowers. But rather hidden in Chapter V, otherwise dealing with the rules for the constitution of and the decision-making in the Council, there is an Article 26, prescribing:

> In order to promote the establishment and maintenance of international peace and security with the least diversion for armaments of the world's human and economic resources, the Security Council shall be responsible for formulating, with the assistance of the Military Staff Committee referred to in Article 47, plans to be submitted to the Members of the United Nations for the establishment of a system for the regulation of armaments.

This task of regulating armaments has never in a systematic way been performed or even approached by the Council. . . .

Reversing the Conventional Arms Race

Little thought has been given to measures that might block and perhaps reverse the race for building up the conventional armories. . . . Measures to cope realistically with this problem must perforce be enmeshed in the complicated web of development, production, and sales of arms, where individual threads can hardly be kept separate. A first step is to lay bare the somber facts. Active measures for introducing restraint must then be sought, either by the indirect method of reducing military expenditures across the board or by the direct way of prohibiting certain lines of production and of trade in conventional weapons. Because of the

interdependent nature of the problem, the steps I propose will necessarily follow a somewhat zig-zag course.

DISCLOSURE OF MILITARY EXPENDITURES

The first requirement for an international taking stock of where the world is heading is to lay all the facts on the table. An annual yearbook on armaments and arms trade was published by the League of Nations until 1938. At that time the publication of national military budgets was recommended, a standardized accounting system was beginning to be developed, and a number of states did, in fact, submit their military budgets to the League Secretariat in roughly standardized form.

There is no reason why these traditions could not be taken up again. The most practical why to obtain a registration of military expenditures would be to request through a majority of the General Assembly that the Secretary General appoint an expert group to spell out the procedures for gathering the required information from the Member countries for its central compilation by an agency of the United Nations. . . . An International Verification Agency could undertake such a duty among its other fact-finding chores.

Emphatically, the military budgets should become part of international public knowledge. There are difficult problems in making figures for military expenditures comparable, particularly because some are often hidden in other parts of a national budget. But these do not pose insurmountable technical problems. A deeper difficulty comes from the imperfect methods of estimating the sacrifice of gains that might have been won through alternative use of resources.

The problem of abolishing the secrecy of military expenditures has a long history. It has usually been connected with the further issue of recommendations for freezing or reducing military budgets. As far back as 1899 at a Hague Conference the Russian Czar proposed ceilings for military expenditures with the aim of capping an arms race. During the time of the League of Nations the Preparatory Disarmament Commission again wrestled with the problem of standardizing military budgets as a step towards agreeing on their reduction. . . .

Making public the military expenditures and monitoring them . . . would also draw attention to ill-advised outlays not in proportion to actual needs in many countries. In this way, it would to some extent serve disarmament purposes.

But, of course, the purpose of more openness about military expenditures has always been and should today be to make possible international agreements to reduce these very expenditures. The simplest form would be a straight reduction of a percentage of the military budget, but only the availability of standardized and fairly specialized national accounts for military expenditures, according to procurement categories, would open up the way for critical comparisons and disarmament advocacy. Points will then be won for abolition or reduction of spending for specified weapons or other war preparations, including R&D expenditures.

DISCLOSURE OF PRODUCTION
AND TRADE IN ARMS

There are many arguments against any restriction of aid and trade in arms which must be met head on. A prohibition against transfer of arms from outside states, presumed to be neutral, to any state taking part in warfare is already laid down in the Hague Convention of 1907. Like many other stipulations of international law, this one has often been broken, without drawing much criticism from either legal scholars or concerned citizens. Neither have such violations, common as they are, been discussed within the United Nations.

. . . Many problems are now more complicated than in the time of the League; exceptions must be made for sharing of weapons within formal military alliances. Other problems are: if the prohibition to import and export arms should be clearly stipulated to cover all undeclared wars, which have become a modern fashion; if it should cover those situations where countries are more or less imperceptibly drifting towards wars; and if it should cover civil wars.

With the development in the Middle East uppermost in mind, it might be reasonable to question whether arms-exporting countries should not be urged to agree to balance their arms deliveries and do so at lower levels. . . .

There is a need to scrutinize the rules various countries unilaterally have laid down for the transfer of weapons to war-prone countries. Most countries seem to have no hard and fast regulations but let government policies be decided from case to case. Another method, utilized in Sweden, is to legislate as a general principle the rule of no arms sales abroad, granting exceptions only on application in special cases, thus greatly facilitating strict restraint. Such a rule is easier to administer and have accepted, both at home and abroad, than the practice of allowing the transfer of weapons to flourish unregulated. An expert group should see whether a uniform international rule could be recommended for arms transference. Full disclosure of the arms trade and all military aid should be given, the aim to be a continual registration by a United Nations agency of all arms transfers in any category.

Proposals in the United Nations for divulgence of the arms trade . . . have met with resistance, mostly from underdeveloped countries who strongly argue that accounting for trade in arms without accounting for production of arms is discriminatory. Some of them would resent revealing how much of their foreign exchange reserve pays for armaments. Countries which have little or no domestic production themselves often fear that any control over arms transfers would be directly discriminatory against them. The mere fact that developed countries produce most of their weapons at home and have a surplus to sell for profit or to give away is felt as discrimination by the underdeveloped countries. . . .

RESTRAINING PRODUCTION
AND TRADE IN ARMS

Registration of military budgets in some standardized form and publication of statistics on production and transfer of weapons is only a first step towards agreement on controls. In addition to the need to reach agreed limitations of the whole arms budget, it would be possible to seek out certain items on which to forbid production and transfer. Obvious candidates for such limited disarmament measures are mass-destruction weapons, such as the biological and chemical ones, which are already under a ban against use and near to being banned on production.

Highest priority for international prohibition must be given to the huge number of conventional weapons which are cruel and inhumane: high-velocity weapons, fragmentation bombs, napalm, etc. They are now in ample stocks in many military establishments and have been massively used in wars, although that is contrary to international law. Their eradication from national armories and the prohibition of their production should be thought of as part of the reestablishment of the rules of international law. The benign neglect with which military violations of these rules have been treated must cease. To forbid the transfer of cruel weapons from one country to another would be a suitable entering wedge for total prohibition of these devices.

Particularly important would be the forbidding of, or at the very least restraint of the production and transfer of, arms that are typically offensive in character, while leaving purely defensive capacities less restrained. . . .

Admittedly, the classification must have been easier to make in the days of less sophisticated weapons and less tolerance of total warfare. But the issue must be brought to life again. . . . Once more I see the need for an expert group working under the aegis of the United Nations and drawing on experiences

from many countries. It would, for instance, lead us much farther in understanding what weapons are truly needed for defense if the analysis took as a point of departure a neutral and independent country like Switzerland. The superpowers are so engaged in dreaming up nuclear deterrence and war-fighting capabilities that conventional defense has been overshadowed.

While these approaches are addressed to partial disarmament in regard to specific conventional weapons, a wider and more general approach is essential to bring to a halt the competition for ever more sophisticated weaponry. As with nuclear weaponry, the same request for stalling the qualitative arms race must be made and stressed. To some extent such a desirable development may be pursued through limitation of military budgets. The constant modernization of weapons is so tremendously expensive that sheer cost considerations should support this request in all countries.

JONATHAN SCHELL

The Gift of Time

Nuclear weapons represent the greatest of all violent threats to life on earth. With the end of the Cold War, a problem that had seemed as intractable as it was immense now offers exciting possibilities for genuine progress, including perhaps that ancient dream: disarmament. Even in the strait jacket of the nuclear arms race, treaties were negotiated that banned above ground nuclear tests and restricted competition in antiballistic missiles, and restrained nuclear proliferation, as well. In 1996, a Comprehensive Test Ban Treaty was signed; its future was marred however, by Indian, then Pakistani, nuclear testing in 1998.

Not surprisingly, nuclear competition in south Asia raised the specter of nuclear proliferation generally, a danger that is especially worrisome because, unlike the United States and the former Soviet Union, India and Pakistan share a common border and have already engaged in several wars. (This problem also applies to other potential proliferators, such as Brazil and Argentina, Israel and the Arab states, and so forth.) Ironically, small nuclear arsenals may also be *less* secure than large ones. Small nuclear arsenals may tempt an opponent to try a "pre-emptive strike," whereas if a country possessed a large supply of nuclear weapons, it could maintain a secure "second strike capabil-

From "The Gift of Time" by Jonathan Schell, *The Nation*, Feb. 2/9. 1998. Reprinted by permission of *The Nation*.

ity," being able to absorb an initial attack and still retaliate. The result, at least in theory, would be "deterrence," or at least, a degree of "crisis stability." It is also possible, of course, that nuclear arsenals will make hostile countries more cautious, and thus less likely to initiate or—if hostilities begin—to escalate wars. On the other hand, the greatest crisis stability would seem to derive from nuclear disarmament, which offers the added benefit of allowing desperately poor countries to invest in their people instead of their weapons.

Just as the end of the Cold War effectively cut through the Gordian knot of the U.S.–Soviet arms race, the present time seems right for making dramatic progress in completely undoing our current reliance on nuclear weapons. After all, the build-up and retention of nuclear weapons by the United States and the Soviet Union was largely rationalized by each side mimicking the behavior of the other. Jonathan Schell helped energize the antinuclear movement of the 1980s with his eloquent description of the consequences of nuclear war, *The Fate of the Earth*. In his book, *The Gift of Time*, Schell argues for a more activist antinuclear policy, now that the Cold War is over. Schell's distinction between "vertical" and "horizontal" nuclear disarmament is especially important and provocative.

What we might call the first nuclear era, which lasted from 1945 until 1991, has come to an end, and a second nuclear era has begun. Its basic shape remains to be decided. Some 35,000 nuclear weapons remain in the world. Whether these are merely a monstrous leftover from a frightful era that has ended, and will soon follow it into history, or whether, on the contrary, they are the seeds of a new, more virulent nuclear era, in which nuclear weapons are held more widely and rooted more deeply, is not a matter for prediction; it is a matter for choice.

By choosing to call for the elimination of nuclear weapons, the new abolitionists have revived a vision that had all but disappeared since the beginning of the nuclear age, when the United States placed the Baruch plan, which called for eliminating nuclear weapons, before the United Nations. The proposal was vetoed by the Soviet Union, and the United States, the sole possessor of nuclear arms at the time, proceeded with a nuclear buildup, which it justified as a desperate, temporary measure to counter a threat that Soviet conventional forces were thought to pose to a ruined Europe. In Western minds, the two evils were soon equated: Nuclear weapons, it was admitted, were a horrifying expedient, but so, many said, was the threat they kept at bay—world domination by a totalitarian power. . . .

In the 1950s, a reassuring gloss was placed on the nuclear peril by the rise in the West of the theory of deterrence, which taught that safety from nuclear weapons could be found only in the threat to use those same weapons—that relief from terror could be found only in terror itself. Official acceptance of this doctrine, in which nuclear arsenals appeared to provide their own justification, gave the nuclear buildup a legitimacy and a self-propelling momentum that at first it had lacked. The horrifying expedient came to be seen as a lasting necessity, even a positive good. The belief that great benefit could be extracted from nuclear arms perfectly complemented the belief that their abolition was impossible. If you could not eliminate nuclear weapons, it was comforting to discover that you would not want to anyway. Abolition was doubly ruled out. Nuclear terror, once regarded as intolerable, came to be seen as the new foundation of the world's safety.

The conviction that abolition was impossible played a pivotal role in moral as well as political thinking about the nuclear question. Nuclear weapons are distinguished above all by their unparalleled destructive power. Their singularity, from a moral point of view, lies in the fact that the use of just a few would carry the user beyond every historical benchmark of indiscriminate mass slaughter. Is it necessary, fifty-three years after Hiroshima, to rehearse the basic facts? Suffice it to recall the old rule of thumb that one bomb can destroy one city. A large nuclear weapon today may possess a thousand times the explosive power of the bomb that destroyed Hiroshima—far more than enough to annihilate any city on earth. A single Trident II submarine has the capacity to deliver nearly 200 warheads, which could lay waste any nation, giving the further rough rule of thumb: one boat, one nation. The use of a mere dozen nuclear weapons against, say, the dozen largest cities of the United States, Russia or China, causing tens of millions of deaths, would be a human catastrophe without parallel. The use of a few hundred nuclear weapons, not to speak of a thousand, would raise these already incomprehensible losses by orders of magnitude, leaving the imagination in the dust. Because so few weapons can kill so many people, even far-reaching disarmament proposals would leave us implicated in plans for unprecedented slaughter of innocent people. The sole measure that can free us from this burden is abolition. But abolition, during the forty or so years of the cold war, was ruled out.

The moral crisis created by the invention of nuclear weapons, then, lay in the fact that politically realistic people have felt themselves virtually barred during the cold war from being able to champion the only measure that would return governments and their peoples to the realm of minimal moral sense. . . .

Today, the terms of the nuclear predicament have been altered fundamentally. The barrier of impossibility has fallen. The Soviet Union has unexpectedly—almost magically— cleared itself out of the way. Gone is the murderous, implacable hostility between global rivals, which just a few years ago seemed destined to last forever; gone the totalitarian empire; and gone the obstacles to inspection that have been considered the main brake on nuclear disarmament. The elimination of nuclear weapons has always been much to be desired. What distinguishes our moment is that, for the first time since the invention of the weapons, it is entirely reasonable to believe that the goal actually can be reached. The opportunity for action that has now opened up is, above all else, an opportunity to heal our fractured selves. It is an opportunity to end the forced cohabitation with horror, the shotgun marriage with final absurdity—to snap out of the trance of the cold war, annul the suicide

pact dictated by the doctrine of deterrence and take the step that alone can free us from nuclear danger and corruption, namely, the abolition of nuclear weapons. Abolition is the great threshold. It is the logical and necessary destination because only abolition gets us out of the zone of mass slaughter, both as perpetrators and as victims.

Since the beginning of the nuclear age, it has been a commonplace to say that humanity's technical achievement has outstripped its political achievement. Now the situation is reversed. The world's political achievements have raced ahead of its technical achievements. In the political realm, peace reigns, but in the technical realm hostility—indeed, threats of "mutual assured destruction"—remain the order of the day. Today, we require a technical event as great as the political event that was the end of the cold war. To use a homely metaphor, the West in the wake of the Soviet collapse is like a person who has won $50 million in the lottery and then declares, "Wonderful—now I can redecorate my living room!" Why not buy a whole new house? History has handed us a political windfall. Why do we refuse to spend it? Political assets, unlike financial ones, are not apt to increase over time. If not made use of, they can, in an instant of crisis or war, evaporate.

The questions that need to be addressed are moral, political and strategic. The moral question for the United States is whether, during the cold war, we so accustomed ourselves to threatening nuclear annihilation that it became second nature to us. Why shouldn't America's leaders, by agreeing together with Russia's leaders to abolish nuclear weapons, rescue our people from the threat of annihilation by a Russian nuclear attack when the only price to be paid is giving up the threat, itself morally intolerable, of annihilating our new friends the Russian people? Was the cold war not, as we first hoped, the apogee of the era of nuclear weapons, to be succeeded by an era of disarmament and peace, but instead a period of initiation, in which not only Americans and Russians but Chinese, Indians, Pakistanis, Israelis, Koreans, Iraqis, Iranians and others were unlearning their horror of nuclear destruction—were learning to think the unthinkable? Was the cold war a sort of Trojan horse whereby nuclear weapons were being smuggled into the moral and political life of the world? Have we, in a silent but deep moral revolution in which the United States has played the leading role, come to regard threats of mass destruction as normal—as the proper and ordinary procedure of any self-respecting nation, whether or not it faces an extraordinary danger from without? Can we still remember that to destroy hundreds of millions of human beings is an atrocity beyond all history? Or have we, so to speak, forgotten this before we had ever quite learned it? And have we, accordingly, adopted the strange vocation—so deeply at odds with the principles on which our nation was founded—of salesman of terror to the world?

The chief political question is whether nuclear proliferation can be stopped and reversed while the current nuclear powers declare by their actions as well as their words that they believe that nuclear bombs are indispensable instruments of power. Or should proliferation perhaps be reluctantly accepted, or even enthusiastically embraced? The development that sets the stage for proliferation is, of course, the spread of nuclear technology. Although politically speaking it may in a sense be 1945 again, technically speaking it is much later than that. While the world was understandably transfixed by the mortal rivalry between the two superpowers, dissemination of the knowledge underlying the bomb and the technical wherewithal for building it was proceeding. During the cold war, the "secret" of the bomb was held by a few governments. Now it is published in magazines. Back then, the nuclear club was exclusive. Now just about anyone can join. Then, the necessary scientific knowledge was centralized in a few places. Now it is ubiquitous, protean, osmotic—fully up- and down-loadable, just like any other information in the information age.

The principal strategic question is whether the doctrine of deterrence, having been framed during the cold war, will now be discredited as logically absurd and morally bankrupt or, on the contrary, recommended to nations all over the world as the soundest and most sensible solution to the nuclear dilemma. The question then will not be whether a particular quarreling pair of nations or blocs (the United States and the Soviet Union during the cold war) is better off with nuclear arsenals but whether any such pair (India and Pakistan, Greece and Turkey,

Iraq and Israel, or Iran and Iraq will do as examples) is better off. If, as many analysts say, deterrence was successful solution to the dangers of the cold war, then why should it not be adopted by all nations prone to conflict? Why resist proliferation? Wouldn't it be better to step it up—to proceed knowingly and deliberately to an increasingly nuclearized world? This is the direction in which events now appear to be drifting, and a few theorists are honest and unflinching enough to champion the goal. For example, John Mearsheimer of the University of Chicago has called nuclear weapons a "powerful force for peace" and advocates "well-managed proliferation." He hopes that Germany will acquire nuclear weapons and advises the world to "let proliferation occur in Eastern Europe." In statements like his, we can see the elements of a new conventional wisdom, in which nuclear weapons become entrenched in the plans and policies not just of a few great powers but of the world at large. . . .

In the face of these questions, the citizens who oppose nuclear arms are as sorely in need of fresh thinking as the governments that possess them. The starting point of this thinking must be recognition that even as the main obstacles to abolition have been removed the main goad to getting there—the immediate danger of a full-scale nuclear holocaust—has been greatly reduced. The fact is that the public at large, enjoying a reprieve from immediate, universal terror bestowed by the end of the cold war, is not paying much attention to the nuclear question. It's also true that the public is actively worried—and with good reason—that a terrorist group or government will use one or more nuclear weapons somewhere in the world. But the feeling of relief dominates. During the cold war, abolition, though perhaps highly desired, was found impossible. Now it appears possible but is not so urgently desired. The combination of comparatively low nuclear danger and high opportunity to solve the nuclear dilemma is new. During the cold war, opposition to nuclear arms was driven by immediate, overwhelming fear—fear that ran headlong into the wall of political impossibility. Today, in sharp contrast, fear has been radically reduced. Our primary inspiration for attending to the nuclear question, accordingly, should not be fear but fear's opposites, hope and faith—hope that, in the transformed and brightened political scene, the goal of abolition is achievable, and faith that we possess the nerve, stamina and wisdom to reach it. At the very least, all who, at one terror-stricken moment or another of the cold war, picked up a sign or shouted a slogan or organized to protest nuclear danger should now stir themselves again to seize the present opportunity actually to rid the world of the weapons. Protest is not something undertaken for its own sake; it is supposed to inspire constructive action. And the time for action has come. . . .

The task is of course immense. But history has given us the gift of time—a limited time, perhaps, but enough to proceed, without haste, to scout the obstacles in our path, to weigh carefully and thoroughly the course to be followed, and then to create the structures that will carry us to the goal and keep us there. If we use the gift properly and rid the species for good of nuclear danger, we will secure the greatest of time's gifts, assurance of a human future. Of course, some will say the goal is a utopian dream of human perfection. We needn't worry. There will be more than enough sins left for everyone to commit after we have taken nuclear bombs away from ourselves. Others will say the obstacles in the way of success are too great. We can answer, as George Washington once did, "Let us raise a standard to which the wise and the honest can repair. The event is in the hand of God."

If it seems paradoxical to call for the greatest exertions at a time of relaxed urgency, we should remind ourselves that the opportunity is greater for the same reason that the danger is less: the end of the cold war. That people can be inspired to act as much by the appeal of reaching a great goal in a time of peace as by immediate and overwhelming terror in a time of conflict is admittedly an unproven proposition. Terror, unquestionably, is a powerful spur to action. If we wait for terror to revive, however, what price will we pay? Will it be New York City? Teheran? Berlin? Beijing? And are we sure that after such a catastrophe we would act wisely? Our reasons for acting are bound to shape the character of our action. Measures taken abruptly, after the abrupt end of fifty years of nuclear peace, possibly in an atmosphere of global suspicion, bewilderment, panic and calls for revenge, seem unlikely to be as sensible as measures adopted now, after thorough and careful discussion and preparation. The nuclear crises of the cold war called

for the swift, sharp shock of protest. On June 12, 1982, a million people, dismayed by the acceleration of the arms race, gathered in New York City to call for a freeze on nuclear arms. In the years that followed, their wishes were more than granted: Nuclear arsenals were not merely frozen, they were reduced. The million never gathered again. In our new circumstances, what is needed is not just a moment of protest but the steady engagement of citizens and their representatives over many years of constructive purpose. Can a movement based on hope, confidence in the concerted powers of human beings and faith in the human future be as great as one based on terror? It must, in fact, be greater. In the words of Jody Williams, on the day her campaign to ban landmines became a treaty signed by 121 nations, "Together we are a superpower. It's a new definition of superpower. It's not one of us; it's all of us." The abolition of nuclear arms—to cite a chapter of American history—would be to the end of the cold war what the Constitutional Convention was to the War of Independence. The end of the cold war was a liberation. Abolition is the act of foundation toward which that liberation points as its natural consequence and completion.

To succeed in the task would, by securing human survival through human resolve and action, go far toward restoring our faith, so badly shaken in this century, in our capacity to make use of the amazing products of our hands and minds for our benefit rather than our destruction. It would bring undying honor to those who carried it to fulfillment and to their generation. It would have the character not of a desperate expedient resorted to under pressure of terror but of a tremendous free act, following upon calm public deliberation in every nation—among all humankind. In a way, it would be the foundation of humankind. . . .

In the years since the end of the cold war, a striking number of the men (there were almost no women among them) who had responsibility for nuclear policy in the United States, Russia and Europe have undergone changes of heart about nuclear weapons. They now support a position unthinkable for most of them even a decade or so ago—the global elimination of nuclear weapons—and many have come to question the cold war strategies they once devised. . . . Both the post-cold war political situation and the dilemmas it poses are radically new, and so, in many cases, are the positions taken. Some of the abolitionists have been on the political right, some on the political left and some in the center. Some favor antinuclear defenses in a nuclear-free world, some oppose them. Some believe that all the functions now served by nuclear weapons in U.S. military planning could be better served by high-technology conventional arms; others think these weapons are not as effective as advertised or wouldn't want them used even if they were that effective. Some wish to retain a right to nuclear armament if a nation violates an abolition agreement; others are dismayed by the idea. Some want to embrace the goal of abolition all at once; others prefer to proceed step by step. . . .

Two other groups, broadly speaking, have begun to call for nuclear abolition. One consists of the traditional antinuclear and antiwar groups, working at the grassroots level. The other consists of politicians and diplomats from nonnuclear-weapon states. For both groups, which have cooperated extensively, the United Nations has been a center of activity. The spark that ignited the fledgling movement was struck in April 1995, at the Nuclear Weapons Non-Proliferation Treaty review conference, where a gathering of representatives of nongovernmental organizations founded a group called Abolition 2000, which issued an appeal for abolition. The appeal went out over the Internet, and in the next few days, 300 groups around the world joined; today the number is nearly 900. Most of the founding and joining groups were veterans of the antinuclear cause. Among them were the International Network of Engineers and Scientists Against Proliferation, which is based in Europe; the International Physicians for Prevention of Nuclear War; the Lawyers' Committee on Nuclear Policy; and the American Friends Service Committee. . . . A decision by the World Court sharply restricting the legal use of nuclear weapons has aided the activist groups. The decision, taken in response to a request from the World Health Organization and the U.N. General Assembly, found that "the threat and use of nuclear weapons would generally be contrary to the rules of international law applicable in armed conflict, and particularly the principles and rules of humanitarian law"—except, possibly, in "an extreme circumstance of self-defense, in which the very survival of the state would be at stake." . . .

In the United States, official voices have persisted, for the most part, in the message of the cold war: nuclear deterrence works; only nuclear weapons can protect us from nuclear weapons; full nuclear disarmament is dangerous; nuclear arsenals are necessary indefinitely. . . .

The nuclear dilemma is in its essence a global human dilemma; but in several ways the role of the United States in nuclear matters has been outsized. . . .

First, there is the simple fact that our arsenals are such a large part of the problem—a little under 50 percent of it, if we reckon in numbers of strategic warheads.

Second, Americans have, for fifty-three years, had both occasion and cause to think deeply about the nuclear question. Hiroshima and Nagasaki lie uneasy on the American conscience. It seems safe to say that, whether we have thought soundly or not, no other people has thought as much about the bomb. (There is also a sense in which no people has strained harder not to think about it.) America needed a bridge between the humane ideals it professed and the reality of unlimited slaughter it was now threatening. The doctrine of nuclear deterrence, which teaches that nuclear armament is not only justified but inescapable, provided such a bridge. Now, we should ask, do we need that bridge any longer? It would be fitting if the United States, which led the nuclear powers every step of the way up the slope of the nuclear precipice, were to help lead the world back down again.

Third, the United States has a particular interest in abolition, owing to its prominence as a potential target of nuclear destruction. Can we fail to see that, with nuclear technology spreading rapidly and probably unstoppably around the world, the destruction we once visited on others may, sooner or later, visit our shores? . . .

Fourth, as a practical matter, the United States seems destined to play a disproportionately large role in the world's decisions regarding nuclear weapons. If the United States were, after a process of national deliberation, to decide in favor of a world without nuclear weapons, there is good reason to assume that the other nuclear powers would follow suit. At the very least, it is scarcely conceivable that nuclear weapons can be abolished without the energetic and willing participation of this country.

The 180 nations that have, under the terms of the Non-Proliferation Treaty, renounced nuclear weapons manage very well without fission bombs, fusion bombs, nuclear-powered submarines or multiple independently targetable re-entry vehicles, and give no thought to nuclear deterrence, mutual assured destruction, flexible response or any of the rest of it. If we say that we seek a nuclear-weapon-free world, the goal seems ambitious, perhaps utopian. But if we say that our goal is a nuclear-free United States, Russia, China, France, England, India, Pakistan and Israel, the problem suddenly looks more manageable.

Fifth and finally, in the nuclear age, as long as the United States believed itself menaced by great, malevolent powers bent on its defeat or destruction, a degree of separation could be maintained between the country's underlying principles and the dread means we were employing, temporarily, in their name. From the moment of the founding of the Manhattan Project, such enemies—first Hitler's Germany, then Imperial Japan, then the Soviet Union—were in the field. Now the United States is left with the dread means but without any extraordinary threat. In these circumstances, if we keep nuclear weapons, they will become as much a part of what we are and stand for as the Constitution. . . .

Recently, however, voices have been raised suggesting that abolition is possible. In 1997, the Henry L. Stimson Center, a nonprofit public policy research institution, published a report advocating the elimination of nuclear weapons at the end of a four-stage process. The report was surprising not only because of its conclusions but because it had been signed by, among others, former Defense Secretary Robert McNamara; Gen. Charles Horner, commander of the allied air forces in the Gulf War; and Paul Nitze, President Reagan's chief arms control negotiator. It was the first U.S. proposal for abolition since the Baruch plan to enjoy widespread support among established Washington figures. Although the report placed elimination in a quite distant future, it embraced the goal without qualification. "Regardless of the amount of time required," it stated in its closing words, "it is virtually certain that the world will never be rid of nuclear risks without a serious political commitment to the objective of progressively eliminating weapons of mass destruction from all countries. The time to start is now."

In August 1996, the Canberra Commission on the Elimination of Nuclear Weapons, a group established by the Australian government to consider abolition, presented its report. It, too, was notable for the distinction of its signatories, which included Gen. George Lee Butler, a former commander of the U.S. Strategic Air Command; Field Marshal Lord Michael Carver, former Chief of the British Defense Staff; Michel Rocard, a former Prime Minister of France; and Joseph Rotblat, the winner of the 1995 Nobel Peace Prize for his work as president of the Pugwash Conference on Science and World Affairs. The tone of the Canberra report was more urgent and impassioned, and its prescriptions for action more detailed. Asserting that "the proposition that nuclear weapons can be retained in perpetuity and never used—accidentally or by decision— defies credibility," it declared that "the only complete defence is the elimination of nuclear weapons [and] assurance that they will never be produced again." The report backed up this conclusion with closely reasoned advocacy of ways to achieve a nuclear-weapon-free world and rebuttal of the principal arguments opposing this goal. The commission also specified some immediate steps. They were: taking nuclear forces off alert, removing warheads from delivery vehicles, ending deployment of tactical nuclear weapons, ending nuclear testing, pursuing reductions in U.S. and Russian arsenals and the global adoption of a no-nuclear-first-use policy.

Voices from surprising quarters in favor of abolition were heard for a third time in 1996, when a statement in favor of abolition was made by sixty-three active and retired military men from seventeen countries. Among them were Adm. Andrew Goodpaster, former Supreme Allied Commander of Europe; General Butler; and Gen. Aleksandr Lebed, the former National Security Adviser to President Yeltsin. . . .

During the cold war, the number of nuclear weapons in U.S. and Soviet arsenals first grew exponentially and then, after reaching their high-water mark of some 60,000 to 80,000 warheads in the mid-eighties, began to drop. The success of nuclear arms control negotiations was measured, above all, in numbers of weapons. Nuclear disarmament of this kind may be called numerical, or vertical, disarmament. Abolition, obviously, occurs when the number falls to zero. However, abolition so conceived in a world of nuclear deterrence gave rise to a doctrinal crisis, for if deterrence theoretically placed a ceiling above which more nuclear weapons were useless, it also placed a floor beneath which it would be dangerous to reduce them. If safety depended on possessing nuclear forces, then reducing them too far—not to speak of abolishing them—was bound to seem perilous. In fact, as long as deterrence doctrine guides military policy, abolition is impossible.

In the doctrinal crisis lies one of the reasons for the immunity that nuclear arsenals have shown to otherwise powerful winds of political change. It also helps explain why there are, among dovish arms controllers, so many proposals for "minimum deterrence" or "deep cuts," in which numerical reductions are allowed to proceed very far but then—at the last minute, so to speak—are pulled up short, leaving perhaps a thousand, or a few hundred, or maybe even as few as a couple of dozen nuclear weapons to serve in the deterrent role. For to go to zero would be to dissolve deterrence and thus dissolve security. It is this fear of excessive reductions that also sets the stage for the most alarmist statements regarding breakout, in which a nation shorn of its retaliatory nuclear force is portrayed as helpless in the face of just a few nuclear weapons. In the land of the disarmed, according to deterrence theorists, the possessor of one nuclear bomb is king.

If deterrence cannot countenance abolition, then some other strategic or political framework for disarmament seems to be needed. But what is that new framework to be? The current debate can be seen as a many-sided search for an answer to this question. Wilsonian collective security—or even world federalism—is one possible candidate. But . . . that venerable, noble, quintessentially American idea is in eclipse at present.

It is into the space between deterrence and full-fledged Wilsonianism that a younger generation of analysts has stepped to offer a new approach to nuclear disarmament that we might call the horizontal path. Although they do not constitute a self-conscious school, their thinking, taken as a whole, contains many of the elements of a new conceptual framework. If vertical disarmament involves lowering the number of weapons in nuclear arsenals, hori-zontal disarmament involves progressively standing down, dispersing, disassembling or partially dismantling arsenals. Establishing ceilings on nuclear arsenals, abolishing certain classes of weapons and drawing down the number of weapons are steps along the vertical path. "De-alerting" weapons, "de-mating" warheads from delivery vehicles, storing warheads at a distance from delivery vehicles, removing parts from warheads or delivery vehicles (or adding parts that spoil their performance) or adulterating weapons-grade fissile materials are steps along the horizontal path. Vertical disarmament makes a catastrophe, should it ever occur, smaller. Horizontal disarmament makes a catastrophe of any size less likely to occur. The verticalist looks at the size of arsenals. The horizontalist looks at their operation.

Vertical disarmament has reached its destination when the last nuclear weapon has been destroyed. The final destination of horizontal disarmament is harder to define. Absolute zero along the horizontal path would, technically speaking, consist of the disassembly of every last component of every last nuclear warhead and delivery vehicle, leaving in existence only the bare knowledge of how to rebuild nuclear weapons. This knowledge is, in the last analysis, the bedrock of the nuclear age, which neither disarmament nor any other human act can remove. The perdurability of this underlying knowledge is the irreducible basis for the danger of cheating or breakout in a nuclear-weapon-free world. As the possessionists see it, the country that uses this knowledge to violate an abolition agreement stands to gain an insuperable advantage. The violator, they seem to suggest, would put itself in the position of the United States in August 1945, while those obedient to the treaty would be in the position of Japan at that time. To such pessimism, however, the horizontal disarmer offers an answer: Because that knowledge must remain in the world, it is possessed just as much by those who obey the agreement as by those who violate it. In obeying the agreement, they do not render themselves helpless before their enemies. Both cheater and victim remain in the nuclear age. Those who have remained faithful to the treaty retain the capacity, if all else fails, to reconstitute their own nuclear arsenals. The violator's advantage, therefore, would be at best temporary.

In actuality, it would not be feasible to

disassemble all the devices that could be used as parts of nuclear weapons or delivery vehicles. Many of them are deeply embedded in civilian life or in arsenals of conventional weaponry. If abolition were defined in a treaty in terms of precise levels of disassembly, a great many levels, ranging from de-alerting and de-mating to prohibitions on virtually all nuclear technology, including nuclear power plants, would be imaginable. Yet while each step along the horizontal path would further attenuate the danger of nuclear holocaust, there would never come a point at which, through technical measures alone, nuclear danger finally disappears. Like the possessionist, the horizontal abolitionist knows that nuclear danger has descended upon the world forever and draws conclusions from that fact.

Vertical and horizontal disarmament are not mutually exclusive. They are, to a certain degree, two angles of vision on the same process. Every weapon that has been "reduced" has also been "disassembled" to one degree or another. (For example, all arms-control agreements so far have pertained solely to delivery vehicles. No warheads have yet been destroyed; they have only been recycled or stored. This does not make these agreements fraudulent. It only means that the "reductions" they secure are of a more horizontal nature than common parlance might suggest.) Likewise, when a nuclear weapon has been (horizontally) dismantled to a certain point, it would not be wrong to say that it has been (vertically) "eliminated." Nevertheless, the vertical and the horizontal approaches to nuclear disarmament are substantively different. It's quite possible, for example, to imagine disarmament agreements that leave a large, horizontally disarmed arsenal (many warheads, all kept under inspection in locations distant from any delivery vehicles), just as it is possible to imagine ones that leave a small, fully constituted arsenal (few warheads, all on full alert). . . .

At issue, broadly speaking, is the role to be played by nuclear terror. Must we rely on it—in one form or another—for our safety? Must its use be immediate and overwhelming or can it somehow be attenuated, or rolled back? In a world that has acquired the fateful know-how, can nuclear terror be eliminated from military and political calculation?

The distinction between technical zero and political zero, though apparently arcane, leads into both the moral and the practical center of these vexing issues. My conversations made clear that defining technical zero is not easy. But difficulty is not impossibility. There is clearly a difference, as Morton Halperin has suggested, between scattered nuclear "materials" and nuclear "weapons." Perhaps the line between the two is crossed, as he also suggests, when the plutonium "pits" are removed from war-heads. But whether we choose this point or another point, farther along the horizontal path of disarmament, it is unquestionably possible, through technical means, to turn something that is a nuclear weapon into a collection of materials that plainly is not. It therefore would be perfectly accurate to say that when every nuclear weapon has been dismantled to a certain extent, abolition has occurred. And this word, it seems to me, remains fitting whether or not a nation retains the intention to reconstitute nuclear weapons in the event that another nation builds them.

The definition of political zero requires an entirely different set of calculations, having to do with human will, not with things. It would, for instance, theoretically be possible to reduce one's society technically to the Stone Age while still not ruling out the intention of building nuclear weapons and using them one day. It would also be possible to possess nuclear arsenals while having no intention of using them. Britain and the United States are, in their nuclear relations, at political zero, even though each has a nuclear arsenal with which it could attack the other. The defining feature of political zero, which can exist independently of any existing nuclear materials, is a complete disavowal by political authorities of the intention to use nuclear weapons, in any circumstances whatsoever. Britain and the United States feel no need to go to a mutual technical zero because their confidence in their political zero is so strong.

Political will, admittedly, is a less tangible thing than nuclear technology, but, it, too, can be given institutional expression. A no-first-use policy, for instance, is a declaration of intention that would have both technical and legal consequences. The technical consequences would be a shift in the composition of military forces to provide defense without using nuclear weapons first. The legal consequences would be adherence to a treaty agreeing on no-first-use. However, the great—the transforming—step along the path to political zero would certainly be the renunciation of the retaliatory strike—no second use—for only this step would render renunciation of nuclear weapons complete. The consequences would of course be profound. In the first place, the path then would be clear to criminalizing possession and use of nuclear weapons as a crime against humanity. (This, of course, would not be possible if nations reserved the right to reconstitute nuclear weapons. Then only first use, or first possession, would be a crime.) In addition, a far deeper reconfiguration of military forces as well as international alliances would be required. In the third place, the "social verification"—the universal whistle-blowing—of nuclear disarmament could be established both in international and national law. . . .

Let us turn the familiar image of nuclear escalation upside down, and picture the path to nuclear safety as a de-escalatory ladder, leading, at its end, to the prohibition of nuclear weapons. If we picture that this ladder is suspended from the high and dangerous precipice on which we now sit, we would like to know, before we start climbing down, that it reaches all the way to the ground. According to current deterrence theory, many of the lower rungs are missing. According to the advocates of virtual arsenals, all the rungs are present. The ladder proceeds step by descendable step to safety. The way to abolition—and beyond abolition to prohibition—lies open.

If that destination were reached, would the infernal paradoxes of nuclear deterrence then at last be dissolved once and for all? They would. No "side," in that world, would threaten "the other side" with nuclear weapons, whether credibly or incredibly, thinkably or unthinkably. No citizen would be drawn into the barbarism of threatening to kill millions of innocent people. All political efforts would truly bend toward preventing such acts, which would unambiguously be named as crimes. However, this answer requires a footnote. Although nuclear threats would be gone, nuclear danger would remain—far, far in the background of our affairs, perhaps, but present nevertheless. Moreover, everyone would know this. If the world returned to anarchy, nuclear weapons could reappear. This is the truly ineradicable political consequence of the fact that nuclear weapons cannot be disinvented. There is, in the last analysis, no turning back to a pre-nuclear age. In that sense, you could even say that a kind of nuclear deterrence would persist. The fear of returning to a nuclear-armed world would always stand guard over the treaty by which the world had eliminated such weapons. The difference from the present would be that rather than one nation deterring another, all would jointly deter all from starting back down the path toward the nuclear abyss. If, in a last gasp of the paradoxical language of deterrence, we wished to assign a "use" to nuclear danger in that world, we would say that the purpose of nuclear danger is to prevent ourselves from ever again possessing—not to speak of using—nuclear weapons. This would be deterrence that truly works. . . .

On August 9, 1945, the day the atomic bomb was dropped on Nagasaki, Yosuke Yamahata, a photographer serving in the Japanese Army, was dispatched to the destroyed city. The hundred or so pictures he took the next day constitute the fullest photographic record of nuclear destruction in existence.

. . . Yamahata's pictures afford a glimpse of the end of the world. Yet in our day, when the challenge is not just to apprehend the nuclear peril but to seize a God-given opportunity to dispel it once and for all, we seem to need, in addition, some other picture to counterpoise against ruined Nagasaki—one showing not what we would lose through our failure but what we would gain by our success. What might that picture be, though? How do you show the opposite of the end of the world? Should it be Nagasaki, intact and alive, before the bomb was dropped . . . Should it be a child, or a mother and child, or perhaps the Earth itself? None seems adequate, for how can we give a definite form to that which can assume infinite forms, namely the lives of all human beings, now and in the future? Imagination, faced with either the end of the world or its continuation, must remain incomplete. Only action can satisfy. Once, the arrival in the world of new generations took care of itself. Now, they can come into existence only if, through an act of faith and collective will, we insure their right to exist. Performing that act is the greatest of the responsibilities of the generations now alive. The gift of time is the gift of life, forever, if we know how to receive it.

Finding the Future: The Role of Economic Conversion in Shaping the Twenty-First Century

During the Cold War, it was routinely acknowledged that about 85 to 90% of the U.S. military budget was driven by competition with communism generally, and with the Soviet Union in particular. Now that the Soviet Union and the Cold War are both defunct, and only remnant Communist regimes are still in power (in Cuba, Vietnam, and North Korea), the U.S. military budget has declined, but only by about 10%. Clearly, any "peace dividend" has been elusive, which is troublesome for many reasons. For one thing, a militarized economy distorts and ultimately weakens any society. "Every gun that is made," said President Dwight D. Eisenhower in his 1961 Farewell Address, "every warship launched, every rocket fired signifies, in the final sense, a theft from those who hunger and are not fed, those who are cold and are not clothed."

These costs are devastating enough to warrant "economic conversion" as part of any peace-oriented future. But additionally, a war-oriented economy is probably more likely to be war-prone, so that the prevention of war may well require a re-orientation of priorities away from the military and toward the domestic economy. This point has been made by many serious thinkers, including economist Joseph Schumpeter, who wrote that "the orientation toward war is mainly fostered by the domestic interests of ruling classes, but also by the influence of all those who tend to gain individually from a war policy, whether economically or socially."[7] Following World War I, concern focused increasingly on the role of the armaments industry, the so-called "merchants of death," in fostering wars.

Interestingly, however, it was President Eisenhower once again—no starry-eyed idealist or soft-headed pacifist—who gave voice to the most influential, critical (and regrettably accurate) description of this problem, when he warned in his Farewell Address that,

> We have been compelled to create a permanent armaments industry of vast proportions.... The total influence—economic, political, even spiritual—is felt in every city, every statehouse, every office of the federal government. ... In the councils of government, we must guard against the acquisition of unwarranted influence ... by the military-industrial complex.

This alliance of military and industrial sectors that Eisenhower so decried has now become a military-industrial-labor-science-governmental complex, and it has shown itself to be firmly entrenched indeed. But, we presume, not entrenched permanently. The stage may now be set for "economic conversion," whose long-term advantages would go beyond the immediately economic, to embrace the prospect of a society, economy, and a politics oriented toward meeting human needs.

From "Finding the Future: The Role of Economic Conversion in Shaping the Twenty-First Century" by Lloyd J. Dumas. In L. J. Dumas, ed., *The Socio-Economics of Conversion from War to Peace*. 1995. Armonk, NY: M. E. Sharp. Reprinted by permission of M. E. Sharp.

---

[7]Joseph Schumpeter. 1955. *Imperialism and Social Classes*. New York: Meridian.

During the long Cold War, the military budget was the largest single category of federal expenditure on goods and services. For nearly half a century, with the armed might of a rival military superpower as a foil, the budget supported a large military establishment, serviced by an unparalleled system of laboratories and industrial facilities. The military budget is an expenditure, not an investment. As such, it had a particular though vaguely defined goal, to provide for the nation's security. Now the Cold War is over, the Soviet Union is no more, and the United States is the only global military superpower.

Although much has been made of the threats of international terrorism and Third World conflict by those who seek to maintain as large a military as possible, these threats, such as they are, were no less serious before the demise of the Soviet Union. The "Soviet threat" was indisputably the main driver and rationale for those huge Cold War budgets, and it no longer exists. Thus, apart from the issue of whether there was ever any justification for the huge military budgets that characterized the Cold War, it is inconceivable that the continuation of military spending at anywhere near that level is justifiable today. Furthermore, many large and expensive military systems, from the MX missile to the B1 (and B2) bomber to the Trident submarine, have absolutely no relevance to dealing with Third World conflict or international terrorism.

Arguments for an even-handed approach to budget reduction, balanced between military spending and domestic programs, are simplistic and make no sense. They are appealing because they have the appearance of fairness. But fairness is not the issue. Fairness may be an appropriate criterion for judging what levels of support make sense for programs of income transfer that benefit one or another segment of the population, but it is wholly inappropriate in the case of mission-oriented programs such as education, roadbuilding, or the military. Within the bounds of affordability, levels of support for the military should be based on what is needed to achieve the mission of securing the nation against real and significant external military threats. According to such a criterion, disproportionately large cuts in the military budget are entirely sensible and justifiable. That is not a matter of ideology, it is a matter of common sense.

This situation does not call for 5 or 10 percent cuts in military spending. A military budget no larger than half, and probably more like a quarter to a third of the Cold War average, properly spent, will give us a military force strong enough to provide as much security as military forces are capable of providing in the present and foreseeable future. In any case, by some estimates more than half the United States' Cold War military budget was designed to defend other nations with standards of living comparable to our own, against a threat that no longer exists. Why then, even with all the pressures to cut the federal budget deficit, are we so reluctant to recognize the enormity of excess in present military expenditures and to do what so obviously needs doing?

This is a classic case of a set of vested interests resisting every attempt to move decisively into the future. These interests have become so intertwined with the existing political and socioeconomic structure that it is extremely difficult to disentangle them. Like a tumor that has attached itself to the body's vital organs, it cannot be safely removed by simply chopping it away. It must be detached with the care and precision of a skilled surgeon's knife. . . .

Economic conversion is just such a careful structural approach. Conversion reaches into the economy and redirects human and capital resources from military to civilian-oriented activity. It involves the retraining and reorientation of work forces and the restructuring of organizations and facilities that have been serving the military sector so that they can *efficiently* produce civilian goods and services. It is a way of reassuring the individuals, companies, and communities whose income, profits, and economic base are currently locked into the military system that the realization of the dream of peacefully ending the Cold War need not be the beginning of an economic nightmare for them. It is a way of removing obstacles to change, of helping them let go.

But it can be much more than that. Economic conversion can play a critical role in directing key economic resources to the kinds of investment that are so important to rebuilding the competitiveness of U.S. industry and generating real economic growth that can help put an end to our trade and budget deficits. To fully understand why conversion is at the fulcrum of this important change of direction, it is first necessary to understand why the military budgets of the Cold War were so peculiarly damaging to our economic well-being.

Military Spending and Economic Decay

The predominant view among economists is that money value is the arbiter of economic value. As a reflection of this, the most commonly used measure of the total economic output of a society, the gross national product (GNP) (or its close relative, the gross domestic product—GDP), includes only goods and services for which money has been paid. That goods and services produced without money exchange (for example, within the household) can be useful is not denied. But they are clearly not considered part of the "economy," and are therefore not counted as part of economic output. . . .

It is more productive to define the economy as that part of the society whose central function is to provide material well-being. It generates and distributes both the goods and services that directly satisfy material needs (i.e., consumer goods, such as televisions and furniture) and the means required to supply them (i.e., producer goods, such as metal-cutting machines and industrial furnaces). This definition of the economy means that money value is no longer the same as economic value. The proper criterion of economic value becomes the extent to which a good or service contributes to material well-being. A bookcase made at home is just as much a part of economic output as a comparable bookcase bought from a furniture store. Whether or not it has money value, any activity that results in such a good or service contributes to the economy's goal of improving material well-being. Therefore, it makes sense to call that activity economically "contributive."

On the other hand, not all goods and services with money value add to the material standard of living. Some goods and services are created to satisfy other human wants and needs. Churches are not constructed and bibles printed to provide material well-being, but to help fulfill the need for spiritual guidance; courthouses and law books are not aimed at increasing the material wealth of society, but at providing political order and control; battle tanks and missiles do not themselves add to the material standard of living, they are produced to enhance physical security. Though these goods may carry a very hefty money price, and may be very useful for the purposes they serve, they do not directly contribute to the central purpose of the economy and so do not have any *economic* value. It is logical, then, to classify activities that result in goods or services that do not have economic value as economically "noncontributive."

Although noncontributive activities are without *economic value*, to the extent that they use productive resources they do have *economic cost*, in terms of opportunities foregone. In other words, the economic cost of a noncontributive activity is measured by the economic value that could have been created by using the same labor, machinery, and equipment to produce goods and services that have economic value.

Economically productive resources that are used for noncontributive activity can be said to be "diverted" to other than economic purposes. An economy in which significant amounts of critical economic resources have been persistently diverted to noncontributive activities will tend to experience a long-term decline in its productive competence—that is, in its ability to produce efficiently. And declining productive competence will lead to a deteriorating standard of living in the long run.

There is no question that the production of military goods and services is noncontributive activity. Whatever else may be said for such products, they do not add to the present standard of living as consumer goods do, or to the economy's capacity to produce standard-of-living goods and services in the future, as producer goods do. Military-oriented activity may be only one of many forms of noncontributive activity, but it is one of the largest and most important in the world today. And the voracious appetite of modern military sectors for both capital and engineers and scientists creates a particularly damaging kind of resource diversion. Why is the diversion of technologists and capital so damaging?

The majority of the population earns the largest part of its money income in the form of wages and salaries. Ongoing increases in wages and salaries that outrun inflation are thus key to producing sustained, broad-based improvement in the standard of living. But, since wages and salaries are the largest part of cost for most producers, increases in labor costs will squeeze profits, creating strong cost-push pressure for price increases. . . .

The ability to offset cost-push pressures depends crucially on the rise of productivity. Although many things affect the rate of productivity increase, more than anything else, rising productivity depends on improving the techniques of production and the quantity and quality of capital available to workers. Improvements in the techniques of production come primarily from research and development (R&D) aimed at discovering and applying new civilian-oriented technology. Regardless of the amount of money spent, without a great enough quantity and quality of engineers and scientists available to perform the work, such R&D will not be successful. Money does not create technological progress, engineers and scientists do. However, if enough capital is not available, it may be difficult to provide the required research facilities, or to widely deploy the results of successful R&D to the factory floor throughout industry.

A persistent, large-scale diversion of engineers and scientists and/or capital to economically noncontributive military activity will unavoidably reduce their availability to contributive civilian activity. The stream of civilian-oriented, productivity-enhancing technological innovation will slow down, causing the rate of productivity growth to drop. Reduced productivity growth will, in turn, undermine the ability of domestic producers to offset the rising cost of labor, or for that matter, of any other input to production and supply. . . .

How large has the diversion of technological and capital resources been in the service of the arms race? For decades now, about 30 percent of the nation's engineers and scientists (full-time equivalent) have been engaged in military R&D. Because pay has been higher and access to state-of-the-art facilities and equipment better in that arena, the military has tended to attract a disproportionate number of the "best and the brightest" technologists. Thus, although the quantitative diversion of engineers and scientists is large enough, adjusted for quality, the "brain drain" is even larger. Concerning capital diversion, as of 1990 the total book value of physical capital directly owned by the Department of Defense (DoD) (including plant equipment, structures, weapons, and related equipment and supplies) was

more than 80 percent of the total book value of capital equipment and structures in all U.S. manufacturing facilities combined!

The standard of living in the United States has been declining since the mid-1970s. The failure of American industrial competitiveness has been highlighted by the replacement of more than three-quarters of a century of continuous trade surpluses (1894–1970) by decades of trade deficits. Hundreds of thousands of high-paying manufacturing jobs have been lost, while job creation has focused on "MacJobs"—low-paying, no-future jobs in the downscale part of the service sector. And all this alongside a national orgy of borrowing that quadrupled the national debt and transformed the United States from the world's largest net creditor internationally to the world's largest net debtor. Had the huge amount of capital borrowed just since 1980 been used for contributive investment and combined with the talents of otherwise diverted engineers and scientists, the United States would have undergone an industrial renaissance. Instead, such resources were lavished on largely noncontributive activity, and all we have to show for all that debt is protracted economic decline.

One clear implication of this analysis is that not all parts of the military budget have equal economic meaning. Roughly half the military budget has traditionally been operations and maintenance expense, including the salaries and benefits of those in the armed services. Although these outlays involve a great deal of money, they have relatively little economic impact. *The main economic action lies in procurement and R&D expenditures, because those are the outlays that draw engineers and scientists, industrial capital, and other productive economic resources into the military sector.* Compared with cutbacks in military procurement and R&D, troop reductions and base closings thus do very little to release the economic resources critical to industrial renewal. Yet the military spending cuts to date have been concentrated mainly on operations and maintenance.

Conversion and Reconversion

Economic conversion is key to economic renewal for two related reasons. First, it provides a means for efficiently reconnecting labor and capital resources released from the noncontributive military sector to contributive work in the civilian economy. It is, after all, not what diverted resources are doing (noncontributive activity), but what they are *not* doing (contributive activity) that causes economic decay. *Shrinking the military sector will do nothing to repair the economic damage of the arms race unless the released resources are reconnected to contributive civilian activity.* In economic terms, nothing will have been accomplished if those people and facilities are released from the military sector and become unemployed. Second, conversion can help reduce the natural resistance of entrenched vested interests to this restructuring by reassuring them that in fact reconnection, rather than unemployment, lies at the end of the road.

At the end of the World War II, the United States faced a great challenge. A large fraction of the nation's output had to be moved from military to civilian production. With a combination of private sector and federal, state, and local government planning, the challenge was met with flying colors. Some 30 percent of U.S. output was transferred in one year without the unemployment rate ever rising above 3 percent. This experience made it clear that it is possible to redirect enormous amounts of productive resources from military to civilian activity without intolerable economic disruption. But it is an experience that must be interpreted with care.

First of all, rationing during the war combined with high incomes to create considerable pent-up demand for all manner of consumer products. When rationing ended with the war, there was a ready-made, unsatisfied market for a wide variety of goods to which war producers could turn. There was little foreign competition to challenge American producers, since every major industrial nation except the United States had been severely damaged by the war. Even more important, the companies that supplied the military during the war were basically civilian companies that shifted to military production for a few years from their normal business of making civilian products. All of their workers, including managers, engineers, and scientists, knew how to operate in a civilian commercial market environment. That is what they had spent most of their working lives doing. Though modifications had been made during the war, most production facilities and equipment had originally been designed and configured for efficient civilian production. For these firms and their work forces, this was a "reconversion"—that is, they were going back to business as usual.

The situation today is quite different. There is no deep well of unsatisfied pent-up demand, and there is fierce foreign competition. Decades, rather than a few years, of high military expenditures have drained the U.S. economy and put many domestic producers far behind their overseas rivals. It is no coincidence that the two most successful industrial economies in competition with the United States have been the two industrialized nations prevented by the World War II terms of surrender from building massive military forces—Germany and Japan.

Today there are generations of managers, engineers, scientists, and production and maintenance workers whose employment experience includes little or nothing but military-oriented work. Many present-day military-industrial firms have never operated in civilian commercial markets. Even those that are large-scale manufacturers of both military and civilian products (e.g., Boeing and Rockwell International) typically have operationally insulated military and civilian divisions functioning as separate, wholly owned subsidiaries reporting to the same overall top management.

Furthermore, during World War II, both the means of production and the technologies used in designing and manufacturing military goods were still fairly similar to those in the civilian economy. Over the past half century, the physical plant, machinery, and technologies involved in military and civilian manufacturing have sharply diverged. The technologies embodied in the designs of the products themselves are even more different. For the major military producers, moving into civilian commercial markets is most assuredly not returning to "business as usual." It is movement into new and unexplored territory. It is conversion, not reconversion.

That makes the process more difficult. But with some care and advanced planning, there is little question that it can be successful.

The Nature of the Conversion Problem

The United States' military sector does not operate by market principles. It is the closest thing to centrally planned socialism in the United States. The nature, quantity, and price of output are not determined by impersonal market forces. They are set by the interaction of the Pentagon's central planners and the managers of military industry. The vast majority of Department of Defense business is negotiated rather than awarded through a serious and enforced competitive bidding process. In practice, virtually all major military contracts operate as if they were "cost-plus"—with producers reimbursed for whatever they have spent, "plus" a guaranteed profit. Under such a contract, the manufacturer bears virtually no risk and can increase revenues without hurting profits by high-cost, inefficient operation. In a competitive commercial marketplace, this kind of inefficient operation would cause serious, if not fatal, problems for the company. In the sheltered and subsidized world of the centrally planned military sector, it is a recipe for growth and success. . . .

Policies for Successful Conversion

Given a thorough understanding of the endpoints of conversion—the very different operating environments of the military and of the civilian sectors—policies can be designed to carry workers and facilities successfully through this difficult transition. For technical reasons, some things must be done regardless of the particular shape the conversion process takes. It is abundantly clear, for example, that any sensible conversion process must take seriously the need both to retrain and to reorient managers, engineers, and scientists. But other things are greatly affected by whether conversion is internal or external to the firm.

"Internal" conversion involves the transition of work force, facilities, and equipment within a formerly military-oriented firm that is shifting to servicing a civilian market. "External" conversion involves the transition of workers, facilities, and equipment that are released by a military-oriented firm and so must find reemployment elsewhere. Internal conversion has much to recommend it. It minimizes disruption of the lives of workers and their families, since it aims at keeping as much of the work force intact as is economically sensible. It minimizes disruption of the surrounding community as well by maintaining

the tax base and the geographic patterns of living, spending, and commuting. And working within the familiar context of an existing firm and workplace means that less on-the-job adjustment is required on the part of the affected work force. On the other hand, some external conversion is unavoidable. . . .

Both public and private sectors have key roles to play in converting the economy. There are things they should do, and just as important, there are things they should not do. It is very helpful to have the coordination and assistance that the federal government can provide, but if the conversion process is not highly decentralized, it has very little chance of working well. The search for productive and profitable civilian activities to replace the previous military mission, and the plans for the reshaping of capital and labor they imply, must be tailored to the details of each particular facility and workplace. This is one case where a one-size-fits-all approach virtually guarantees that nothing will fit anyone. It is a mistake for the federal government to try to blueprint facility and work-force conversion. There is no good substitute for a high degree of decentralization in the detailed planning and plan implementation process. Even close oversight of microlevel conversion by the federal government is a poor idea. It is unlikely to improve the effectiveness of conversion plans and highly likely to be inefficient and expensive. Although this is more obviously true of internal conversion, it is important for external conversion as well. . . .

It may also be time to resurrect, in updated form, one of the most successful federal investment programs in the nation's history, the World War II vintage GI Bill of Rights. Under the provisions of the GI Bill, millions of individuals who had served in the armed forces received training and educational benefits to help them improve their earning capacity and employment opportunities. According to former Senator Ralph Yarborough, who chaired a committee that evaluated the performance of the program, the GI Bill was an investment with an enormous rate of return. The extra federal taxes collected out of the higher incomes earned because of the training amounted to some thirty times the program's cost to the taxpayer. And this does not even begin to consider the plethora of other benefits to the economy and society that attend a better-trained and better-educated work force and citizenry. A new GI Bill for all workers in the military sector would make a great deal of sense in facilitating conversion today. I see no reason why this approach could not eventually be broadened to cover all displaced workers. However, it is important to recognize that workers undergoing conversion (particularly engineers, scientists, and managers) do have special problems. Even more important, *the successful conversion of these workers, especially of engineers and scientists, holds the key to the kind of industrial renewal that can and will brighten the economic prospects of the entire labor force....*

Conversion and the Twenty-First Century

Times of transition are always difficult. They call on us to break old familiar patterns that have come to feel comfortable. Effort is required where habit and routine once carried us through. It takes some courage to face up to the need for change, even when it is clear that the patterns of the past are no longer tenable. It takes some creativity and determina-tion to recast our lives in ways that are not just different, but better.

We are living in an era of profound change. That can be frightening, but it can also be liberating. Where the structures of the past have crumbled, there is the opportunity to create new and better structures for the future. And it is easier to build bridges when walls come down.

In the last decades of the twentieth century, structures have crumbled and walls have come down all over the world. That we are passing through a time of profound change is undeniable. What we do—or fail to do—now will change the shape of the century to come. The enormous, worldwide preemption of productive resources for military purposes over the past fifty years says a great deal about the world we have created and the priorities we have established. If we have courage, foresight, and determination, we can break with the deadly, fear-driven legacy of this tortured century. We can find a more productive, life-enhancing way to use our talents and capabilities. Conversion, properly understood and implemented, can help us work our way through the myriad of details needed to build a practical path to a world that is both more prosperous and more humane.

DAVID P. BARASH

International Law

For some people, international law is one of the great hopes of humanity, offering the prospect of subjecting the often chaotic interactions of countries to the same reason and order that—at least in theory—governs the interactions of individuals. For others, international law is laughably inadequate, primarily because it has no clear-cut enforcement mechanism. On the other hand, in the aftermath of genocidal cruelty in Bosnia and Rwanda, many of the perpetrators were declared international outlaws, and at least some have been brought before the International Court of Justice. This is a pattern that may become increasingly common in the future.

International law may be held to an unfairly strict standard. Breaches of international law, for example, are sometimes thought to show the absurdity of international law itself, perhaps because such offenses (genocide, torture, etc.) are often so egregious.

From *Introduction to Peace Studies* by David P. Barash. 1991. Belmont, Calif: Wadsworth.

But by contrast, violations of national or local law are virtually never taken as reasons to disavow legal systems. Presumably, this is because nearly everyone recognizes the need for law, even if existing laws are not perfect or perfectly complied with. The "law of nations" is and will be what we make it. Depending on our choice, international law offers the prospect of restraining, or possibly ending, war, and promoting a more lawful world, which may also be more predictable, just, and peaceful.

The international community should support a system of laws to regularize international relations and maintain the peace in the same manner that law governs national order.
—*Pope John Paul II*

Schemes for ending war—for creating negative peace and, ultimately, positive peace as well—often founder at the level of states. By zealously guarding their sovereignty, states undermine, or at best diminish, the authority and effectiveness of international organizations such as the United Nations. Even when these organizations operate in a manner that recognizes the primacy of state sovereignty, an unavoidable tension arises between a state-centered world system and one organized around different fundamental values. By providing a unit around which dangerous and misleading notions such as peace through strength can congeal, nationalism and state-centeredness legitimize the use of violence in settling disputes. By emphasizing the similarities and often suggesting some kind of superiority on the part of each group of people, and cutting them off from others, the current political divisions of our planet make prospects for disarmament seem terribly difficult, perhaps impossible. By rewarding those who behave violently—so long as such violence, or the threat of violence, is successful—our current world system works strongly against peaceful ethical or religious resolutions of conflict. And by fractionating the people of the world, our current political organization makes it very difficult to deal effectively with problems that cross traditional borders and that require global solutions. . . .

In short, many people are becoming increasingly aware that our current state-centric system is part of the problem, and that we must move beyond the nation-state to find the solution. . . . All governments operate by laws, the rules of behavior that specify what is per-

missible and, more commonly, what is not. Even in our current system of separate states, a legal framework undergirds the relationship of states to one another. It is known as international law. . . .

The Sources of International Law

We are all familiar with domestic law, with its prohibitions against violent crimes such as murder, robbery, and assault, as well as with the way it regulates the nonviolent conduct of daily living, from the flow of traffic to the affairs of business and the standards of acceptable conduct in private and public life. Less familiar, by contrast, is international law, the acknowledged principles that guide the interactions between states, and that set limits upon what is and what is not permissible. People live within societies, not between them, so we have done far more to encourage *intra*national law than *inter*national law. And yet, international law does exist; in fact, the current body of international law is very large. Just as most daily life among individuals within a society is peaceful, most interactions among states on the world scene is also peaceful, in accord with expectations, and thus, in a sense, "legal."

Unlike domestic law, which in the United States is codified in constitutions and amendments, as well as in the specific laws passed by federal, state, and municipal law-making bodies, the body of international law is relatively chaotic, spread over history and generated in many different ways. There are four major sources of international law: (1) classical writings that have become widely accepted, (2) custom, (3) treaties, and (4) the rulings of international courts.

CLASSICAL WRITINGS

In the sixteenth century, the Spanish legal scholar Francisco de Victoria developed the thesis that war must be morally justifiable, and could not simply be fought over differences of religion or for the glory of a ruler. He also maintained that soldiers were not obliged to fight in unjust wars, even if so commanded by their king. But the best-known and most influential example of classical international law is found in the work of the Dutch legal scholar Hugo Grotius. In his treatise *On the Law of War and Peace* (1625), Grotius maintained that there was a fundamental "natural law," which transcended that of nations, and which emanated from the fact that people were ultimately members of the same community. Grotius argued strongly for the sovereignty of individual states, within their own realms. From this, he concluded that states must avoid interference in the internal affairs of other states. Grotius pointed to the agreements that states have made among themselves, and that have proved to be durable: peace treaties, decisions as to the allocation of fishing and navigation rights, commonly accepted boundaries, and so on. The Grotian tradition thus derives the legitimacy of international law from the legitimacy of states themselves. But it goes further in seeking to derive principles whereby the behavior of one state toward another can be regulated, arguing that "natural right" must govern the interactions among states, and that this supercedes the authority of the states themselves. As Grotius saw it (and subsequent international law has affirmed), international "society" exists, which requires certain norms of conduct among states, including rules governing what is acceptable during war itself. For Grotius, war was not a breakdown in the law of nations, but rather a special condition to which law still applied. . . .

The term *international law* first appeared in 1783, with the publication of Jeremy Bentham's *Principles of International Law.* Accordingly, it is worth emphasizing that, whatever its shortcomings, nearly all our progress in international law has taken place in just a few hundred years; in fact, things have really gathered steam in the last fifty years. We might therefore be on the threshold of dramatic new developments.

CUSTOM

Custom is one of the most important and least appreciated sources of international law. For example, consider the "rules of diplomatic protocol," whereby diplomats from one country are considered immune to arrest or detention in another. Clearly, these "rules" are in the interest of all countries, since, if the representatives of opposing states could legally be harrassed, communication between states could quickly cease, to the disadvantage of all sides. Diplomats occasionally are expelled from a host country, usually for "activities incompatible with their diplomatic status" (that is, for spying), in which case some of the other side's diplomats typically are expelled in retaliation. But normally—that is, customarily, and thus by international law—diplomats are allowed substantial leeway, including the ability to communicate freely and secretly with their home government, as well as guarantees of their safety. (The strength of this presumption is shown by the outrage when it is violated, as when U.S. diplomats were held hostage in Iran in 1979–1980.) . . .

TREATIES

International treaties are analogous to contracts among individuals. And of course, there have been many treaties, covering not only the termination of wars, but also agreements about boundaries, fishing and navigation rights, and mutually agreed restrictions as to permissible actions during war. Treaties are not always honored, but in the vast majority of cases, they have been. Backing away from treaty obligations results in a substantial loss of face, and once branded a treaty-breaker, a state may not be able to establish useful, reliable relationships with other states. Through treaties as well as customary practice, international law provides "rules of the road" by which international interaction, beneficial to each side, can be conducted. As a result, states have a strong interest in abiding by them.

COURTS

Finally, international law—just like domestic law—requires courts to hear disputed cases and render decisions. The first example of an international court was the Central American Court of Justice, established by treaty in 1908 by five Central American republics. . . .

Best known and most important, however, is the International Court of Justice (formerly the Permanent Court of International Justice, during its tenure under the League of Nations), located at The Hague, Netherlands, and administered by the UN. Also known as the World Court, this institution consists of a rotating membership of world jurists. It issues decisions about international law that are generally considered authoritative, although typically unenforceable. The verdict on international courts is thus mixed. On the one hand, states are gradually becoming accustomed to letting go of enough sovereignty to settle disputes in court instead of in combat. On the other, adherence to the dictates of the World Court is entirely "consensual"—it is up to the consent of those involved—whereas adherence to domestic law is obligatory. Imagine a community in which accused lawbreakers could only be brought to trial if they agreed that the laws applied to them; further, imagine that they could then decide whether or not to abide by the ruling of the courts!

Enforcement of International Law

The major problem with international law, therefore, aside from its diffuseness, is enforcement. Because enforcement provisions are generally lacking, some people contend that international "law" is not, strictly speaking, law at all, but rather, a set of acknowledged customs, or norms of behavior. The importance of norms alone should not be underestimated; in fact, most human behavior is conducted according to widely shared norms, not law itself. Nonetheless, domestic law is the last resort (short of violence, which domestic law typically prohibits), and law is effective at least in part because if worst comes to worst, and a lawbreaker is apprehended and found guilty of violating the law, he or she can be held accountable, suffering fines, prison terms, and the like. In the case of domestic law, individuals acknowledge (whether overtly or not) that they are subordinate to the state and its machinery of enforcement: the police, court bailiffs, the national guard, and so on. When it comes to relations among states, by contrast, the "individuals" insist on their sovereignty; they most emphatically do not recognize that any authority supercedes their own. If individual people behaved this way, domestic law could not effectively regulate their behavior. The major problem with international law, therefore, is that individual states insist on a kind of latitude that they would never allow their own citizens.

Let us briefly consider the role of sanctions (punishments for noncompliance) in law more generally. There are three primary incentives for obeying any law, domestic or international: self-interest, duty, and coercion. For example, most individuals stop at red lights not because they fear getting a traffic ticket, but rather because they know that otherwise, they are more likely to have an accident. Rules may therefore be followed out of purely utilitarian concerns, in this case, interest in one's own personal safety. Laws provide a way of regulating human conduct, for the benefit of all: You can proceed with reasonable safety through an intersection when your light is green, because you know that opposing traffic has a red light, and you have some confidence that other drivers will respect this law, just as you do.

In addition, individuals may follow the law because they feel themselves duty-bound to contribute toward an orderly society that functions with respect for authority. As members of society, who benefit from it, individuals assume a responsibility toward it. That is, some are influenced by normative considerations, or a kind of Kantian categorical imperative to do what is right and good for its own sake. And finally, some people are induced to be law-abiding by fear that "violators may be prosecuted" and forced to succumb to the state's authority if they are found guilty. Although the role of such coercive factors cannot be denied, coercion is not the only reason why most people obey the law. And similarly, the absence of such coercion does not invalidate international law, or render it toothless.

States have numerous incentives, both positive and negative, for abiding by their legal obligations to other states. If a state defects from its legal obligations, adversaries may well retaliate, one's friends and allies are liable to disapprove, and world opinion is likely to be strongly negative, leading to ostracism and possible economic, political, and cultural sanctions. Moreover, governments themselves have a strong stake in their own legitimacy, and—even in totalitarian states—adherence to law is fundamental to such legitimacy. . . .

The Conflict with State Sovereignty

It simply isn't true that all is anarchy in the international arena, any more than it is true that all is peaceful in the domestic sphere: More than one quarter of all wars, for example, are civil wars. States generally obey the law—out of a combined sense of duty and self-interest—even though coercive sanctions, as understood in domestic law, are absent. States engage in nonviolent commerce—exchange of tourists, diplomats, ideas, trade—according to certain regulations, and usually with goodwill and amity. Moreover, states usually do not enter into treaties unless they intend to abide by them, and they only acquiesce with customary norms of behavior when they anticipate that over the long run, they will benefit by doing so. At the same time, however, they typically cling to various aspects of sovereignty. Most treaties—notably those involving nuclear weapons—include a provision permitting signatories to withdraw within a set period of time, typically three or six months, if their "supreme national interests" are jeopardized. And who makes this decision? The state itself.

We have defined states as those political entities that are granted a monopoly of legitimate violence within their borders. When they engage in what they claim is lawful violence outside their borders, states typically maintain that (1) they are acting in self-defence (the U.S.S.R. in World War II, Israel in the Six Day War), (2) they are fulfilling treaty obligations (France and Britain in World War II), (3) they are intervening on the side of legitimate authority (the United States in Vietnam, the U.S.S.R. in Afghanistan), (4) the situation is anarchic and lacks a legitimate authority (the UN in the Congo), or (5) the conflict is within the realm of international obligations (the UN in Korea). In short, state sovereignty continues to reign, although a semblance of international law is generally invoked as well. States have been especially hesitant, however, to circumscribe their day-to-day authority. It is significant that whereas the Hague Conferences produced a few halting restrictions on the waging of war, they were unable to establish any significant binding rules for peace.

States are also selective when it comes to accepting the jurisdiction of the International Court of Justice, a process known as "adjudication." Adjudication is similar to arbitration in that the decision of the third party is binding. The only difference is that in adjudication, the decision is based on international law, rather than made by an arbitrator. The Soviet Union, for example, has historically refused to submit disputes to this body, although ... the United States has been no better, despite the fact that in 1946, it formally agreed to submit all of its international disputes to the International Court of Justice. At that time, the U.S. Senate attached an amendment, known as the Connally Reservation, stipulating that the Court would not have authority over any disputes that "are essentially within the domestic jurisdiction of the United States of America as determined by the United States of America." With this loophole, the United States is free to "determine" that any dispute is essentially within its domestic jurisdiction, thereby avoiding international adjudication whenever it wishes. . . .

Law is an important part of modern human life; some would even say that it is crucial to civilization. Despite concerns about enforcement—and anxiety when, as in the case of international law, enforcement powers are lacking—law is in many ways the antithesis of rule by brute force. Might does not make right; law does (or better yet, it reflects what is right). As a result, most good, decent people are presumed to be "law-abiding," and in fact, rule by law is almost inevitably seen as preferable to rule by force. We should also be aware, however, that law can be an instrument of oppression. Laws are made by those in power, and as such, they serve to perpetuate that power, and to prevent change. Thus, laws—international as well as domestic—serve best in a conservative environment. Third World and revolutionary states often point out that international laws were established by Western powers in support of their domination. The clearest example might well be the Treaty of Tordesillas (1494), following Columbus's "discovery" of the New World, whereby the pope "legally" divided that world into Spanish and Portuguese domains ... without any regard for the people already living there. . . .

International law must be flexible, if only because of the march of technology. For several centuries, for example, ever since a Dutch ruling in 1737, "territorial waters" have been considered to extend three miles from shore; this distance was based on the effective range of shore-based cannons. Now, new guidelines are being sought, with controversy fueled by disagreement among states, especially between the exploiters and the exploited. The former, particularly the developed industrialized states with relatively little shoreline (such as Britain and Japan) argue for narrow territorial waters, while those with extensive coastal waters (like Brazil and Burma), which seek to protect their fishing industry from foreign fleets, argue for a 200-mile limit.

These issues were partly resolved by the Law of the Sea Treaty, completed after decades of wrangling. This treaty also arranged for mechanisms of dispute resolution, waste disposal, and navigation procedures, but under the Reagan administration, the United States refused to sign, maintaining that the treaty's call for an intergovernmental body to supervise mining on the deep-sea bed constituted "international socialism." This also highlights once again the susceptibility of international law to asserted claims of state sovereignty, as well as the growing pressure of north/south cleavages.

Hidden Strengths of International Law

GOVERNMENTAL RESPECT FOR LAW

Yet, governments do not routinely flout the law, not even their own domestic statutes, over which they have complete control. In most democratic countries, governments accede to legal decisions, even those that go against them. Citizens of the United States, for example, often take for granted the fact that in many cases, they can, if they wish, bring legal action against their own government. And if the courts—which are themselves organs of the government—rule against the government, citizens can receive compensation or other redress for their grievances, even though governments, not the courts, have the strong-arm potential of enforcing their will. This emphasizes the primacy of law over force. For example, following a strike during the Korean War—an action that supposedly threatened U.S. war production at a critical time—President Truman sought to nationalize the U.S. steel industry. The Supreme Court, however, overruled this action, whereupon the government obeyed the law, albeit reluctantly. Because democratic governments have a long-range interest in settling disputes amicably, that supercedes any short-term interest in winning a given dispute, they tend to abide by legal rulings, even those that they dislike.

In international affairs, as we have seen, major powers are less likely to abide by international laws ... unless the opponents are so balanced that the potential costs of losing a case are less than those of further wrangling, and possibly war....

International law often appears weaker than it really is, however. This is because violations, when they occur, are often sensational and dramatic, whereas compliance is taken for granted. When domestic law is broken by individuals, only rarely are we moved to question the appropriateness of the law itself, and never to doubt the existence of such law. But a different standard seems to be applied to international law. When states violate international law, they may or may not be condemned by public opinion, but almost invariably, the law itself is called into question, and the purported weakness of international law is once again lamented. Just as we are not told about the vast majority of people who obey domestic law every day, we do not see news stories proclaiming that "Paraguay today complied with its treaty obligations regarding its border with Bolivia, and therefore, no invasion took place."

Virtually the entire civilized world was shocked, by contrast, when Chancellor Theobald von Bethmann-Hollweg justified the German invasion of Belgium in the early days of World War I by describing the international guarantee of Belgian neutrality as a "mere scrap of paper" that could readily be torn up. On the one hand, this announcement—and even more so, the brutal invasion itself—showed the truth of the chancellor's assertion: Belgian neutrality was in fact "only" an international agreement, lacking any guarantee and incapable, by itself, of keeping the invading German divisions out. On the other hand, the level of international outrage showed that international law, even when it lacks explicit means of enforcement, has undeniable effects on public perception. (In addition, we should note that the immediate reason for Britain entering the war against Germany was the German violation of Belgian neutrality; so, in a sense, international treaty law was ultimately enforced in this case. Had Germany respected the law, it might have won the war.)

THE LAW OF WAR

War—the violent resolution of conflict—can be seen as the antithesis of law, whose goal after all is the ordering of relations without recourse to violence. Cicero first wrote that *inter arma silent legis* ("in war the law is silent"). This is taken to mean that the justifiability of any given war is outside the purview of international law, since states are sovereign authorities unto themselves, and free to make war or not, as they choose. Under this view, since there is no higher authority than a state, no one can claim that a state is making war unlawfully. . . .

Nonetheless, a body of law is widely thought to apply to states under conditions of war. War itself can even be defined as "the legal condition which equally permits two or more hostile groups to carry on a conflict by armed force." Therefore—at least according to some experts—war represents a highly formalized interval during which violence may legitimately be practiced between two opposing groups. Enough agreement exists within the community of nations that belligerents and neutrals alike recognize the existence of certain accepted standards: "Although war manifests the weakness of the community of nations, it also manifests the existence of that community."

The Nuremberg Principles

States that are party to international treaties may find themselves subject, even against their will, to the legal restraints of these treaties. The losers in World War II, for example, were tried—and many were convicted— for having waged aggressive war in defiance of their obligations under the Kellogg-Briand Treaty. These trials, conducted in the German city of Nuremberg, were unique in developing the legal doctrine that individuals are personally liable to criminal prosecution for crimes against international law. This includes illegal resort to war as well as violations of accepted restraints as to appropriate conduct during war, notably the treatment of prisoners and the waging of genocide. Thus, the chief Allied prosecutor at Nuremberg wrote that

> war consists largely of acts that would be criminal if performed in time of peace— killing, wounding, kidnapping, destroying or carrying off other people's property. Such conduct is not regarded as criminal if it takes place in the course of war, because the state of war lays a blanket of immunity over the warriors. . . . But the area of immunity is not unlimited and its boundaries are marked by the laws of war.

It should also be pointed out, however, that critics objected to these proceedings, claiming that the Nuremberg Trials were simply examples of "victors' justice," and not concerned with genuine international law. Nevertheless, the so-called Nuremberg Principles have served as a benchmark in efforts to introduce humane and reasoned limits to acceptable wartime behavior. Thus, the international military tribunal that convened in Nuremberg specified a series of international crimes. Article 6 of the Nuremberg Charter identified the following:

1. Crimes against the peace, namely planning, preparation, initiation or waging of a war of aggression, or a war in violation of international treaties . . .
2. Crimes against humanity, namely murder, extermination, enslavement, deportation, and other inhumane acts committed against any civilian population . . .
3. War crimes, namely, violations of the laws or customs of war. Such violations shall include, but not be limited to, murder, ill-treatment or deportation to slave labor or for any other purpose of civilian population of or in occupied territory, murder or ill-treatment of prisoners of war or persons on the seas, killing of hostages, plunder of public or private property, wanton destruction of cities, towns or villages, or devastation not justified by military necessity.

Article 7 specified that "the official position of defendants, whether as Heads of State or responsible officials of Government departments, shall not be considered as freeing them from their responsibility or mitigating their punishment." And according to Article 8, "the fact that the defendant acted pursuant to orders of this Government or of a superior shall not free him from responsibility."

Whereas the German defendants at Nuremberg were tried for crimes they had committed in violation of international law, a series of lesser-known trials were also conducted in Tokyo, of Japanese officials accused in large part of crimes of *omission*—that is, illegal failure to act.

   . . . Several decades later, when U.S. army lieutenant William Calley was tried and found guilty for his role in the My Lai massacre during the Vietnam War, it marked the first time a state had accused one of its own soldiers of war crimes. Calley's highest-ranking commanding officers were not tried, however, . . . So again, whereas international laws exist, and have been enforced, such enforcement has been highly selective.

The treaties that were violated by the Nuremberg defendants, originating from the Geneva and Hague Conventions, specified limitations on such actions as naval or aerial bombardment. But they also made allowances for "military necessity," which can be stretched to permit nearly any act in wartime, however outrageous. Similarly, even the toothless Kellogg-Briand Treaty was interpreted by many as permitting "wars of self-defense," as does the current UN Charter: Article 51 grants states the "inherent right of individual or collective self-defense." Self-defense would clearly justify Poland's short-lived response in seeking to resist the German invasion in 1939, but what about France's response, namely, declaring war on Germany (France was treaty-bound to help defend Poland)? And what about the Israeli invasion of Egypt in 1967, in which Israel clearly struck first, but in which it was argued that Egyptian behavior constituted a real provocation as well as an imminent threat that justified a "preemptive" attack by Israel? Similarly, the "Brezhnev Doctrine," by which the U.S.S.R.

justified its invasion of Czechoslovakia, was described as laudable pan-socialist self-defense against Western-inspired counterrevolutionaries. And the "Reagan Doctrine," under which the United States assisted right-wing revolutionaries in Marxist states such as Angola or Afghanistan, has been described by its supporters as providing aid to people seeking to defend themselves. Apologists for wars of self-defense and self-determination have thus far always been able to find loopholes in international treaties large enough to drive an army through. . . .

A Final Note on International Law

International law has many imperfections. It appears to have exerted some useful restraints in some cases, while being woefully inadequate in others. The major powers give it less credence than do the lesser states, in part because the former have recourse to their military strength, whereas the latter must depend on the rule of law to offer them the possibility of a "level playing field" in contests with larger, stronger opponents. Some authorities recommend only a modest role for international law in the future, avoiding "the Charybdis of subservience to state ambitions and the Scylla of excessive pretensions of restraint," and recognizing that "it is the interest of international law itself to put states' consciences neither to sleep nor to torture." Another view holds that international law is a beginning, something on which to build a world without boundaries, or at least, one in which the sanctity of state sovereignty is greatly curtailed in the interest of human survival as well as quality of life.

The Evolution of United Nations Peacekeeping

Conflict situations can be resolved in two basic ways: "associative" or "disassociative." The latter relies on military strength and political separation, based on the notion that "good fences make good neighbors." Associative solutions, by contrast, involve tearing down walls and joining together. As we have seen, prominent among the causes of war is the existence of feisty, sovereign states that are, by definition, disassociative relative to each other. Associative solutions include heightened reliance on international law, shared ethical norms, and the joining together of otherwise independent countries to form international organizations. As with the other "solutions" considered in this chapter, international organizations are not perfect or foolproof. Although their record is imperfect, there is much to applaud in the activities of various international organizations, especially the United Nations, which offers a way of ameliorating—although not eliminating—the often troublesome role of states.

When considering the U.N., it is important to recognize what it is *not:* It is not a world government, since its members retain their sovereignty. Also, it has not proven effective in preventing conflicts among the major powers, since these powers were granted vetoes over any U.N. led enforcement activities. However, the U.N. has been effective occasionally in peacekeeping and in monitoring compliance with cease-fires and other negotiated settlements and, often, in mediating disputes that might otherwise have turned violent. The U.N. also provides a valuable forum for debates. Its various "functional" agencies (such as the Food and Agriculture Organization, the World Health Organization, UNESCO, UNICEF, etc.) contribute to the alleviatation of much human misery, and creatively help undermine reliance on states as the sole units of political/economic/social recourse.

Thus, the benefits of the United Nations go beyond simply contributing to "negative peace." The U.N. may also represent a partial step in the progression from individualism through tribalism, to nationalism, and then globalism. This is a transition that may well be essential if we are ever to give peace a realistic chance. As might be expected, the United Nations is regularly criticized, especially by right-wing militarists and ardent nationalists . . . which in itself suggests that it may have a major role to play in preventing war! The following selection is by a former U.N. Under-Secretary-General for Peacekeeping Operations.

The title, 'The evolution of peacekeeping', was chosen about a year ago. At the time, it seemed to make sense; with the phasing out of the Cold War, the United Nations had been given new opportunities to help control and resolve conflicts. As a result, new tasks and new methods had evolved from what had previously been a fairly homogeneous activity. The biological metaphor seemed an accurate way of describing what was going on.

From "The Evolution of United Nations Peacekeeping" by Marrack Goulding, *International Affairs* 69:451–64. 1993. Reprinted by permission of *International Affairs*, London.

However, the word evolution implies a comparatively leisurely process in which, by trial and error, organisms develop more efficient ways of responding to a changing environment. A year later, the metaphor seems less apt. 1992 saw an almost five-fold increase in United Nations peacekeeping activity; we had some 11,000 military and police personnel deployed at the beginning of the year; by its end the total was over 52,000. Today 'the forced development of peacekeeping' might be a better title.

I propose first to analyse what peacekeeping had become by the time the Cold War ended; then to classify the different types (I would have referred to 'species' if the evolution metaphor was still appropriate) of peacekeeping operations which are currently deployed or being planned; then to discuss the current trend from peacekeeping to peace-enforcement and the implications it has for the United Nations' ability to develop into an effective system of collective security; and finally to draw some brief conclusions about the heavy responsibilities which bear upon the Secretary-General and the Security Council.

What Is Peacekeeping?

Peacekeeping is a technique which has been developed, mainly by the United Nations, to help control and resolve armed conflicts. There is no agreed definition of it nor even agreement on when the first peacekeeping operation was set up. . . .

The official view in the United Nations is that the United Nations Truce Supervision Organization (UNTSO) was the first United Nations peacekeeping operation. It consisted of unarmed military observers who were sent to Palestine in June 1948 to supervise a truce negotiated by Count Bernadotte in the first war between Israel and its Arab neighbours. It stayed on when, a month later, the Security Council, acting under Chapter VII of the Charter, 'ordered' a ceasefire. A similar group was deployed a few months later in Kashmir. A major step forward was taken when the first armed United Nations force—the United Nations Emergency Force (UNEF)—was deployed in Egypt following the Anglo-French-Israeli attack on that country in October 1956. . . .

The golden age—dare I say the *first* golden age?—of United Nations peacekeeping was from 1956 to 1974, though there was a hiatus for six years after the disaster that befell UNEF in 1967. Those 18 years gave birth to 10 of the 13 peacekeeping operations established before the revival of demand for peacekeeping in the late 1980s. On the whole they succeeded well in helping to control regional conflicts, especially in the Near East, at a time when the Cold War made it difficult for the Security Council to take effective action to resolve them.

The Congo operation (1960–64) deserves special mention. It is often described as a failure, but in fact it succeeded in its objectives, albeit at a very high cost, including the life of Dag Hammarskjöld and a major constitutional-cum-financial crisis at the United Nations. It is interesting in the contemporary context for three reasons. First, it was deployed in a country where the institutions of state were collapsing—the first case of what the Foreign Secretary recently called 'painting a country blue'. Second, it was the first peacekeeping operation to include very substantial civilian elements. Third, it was initially deployed as a peacekeeping operation; but when it became clear that the peacekeeping mode would not enable it to achieve its objectives, the Security Council authorized it to use force on a considerable scale to end the secession of Katanga—the first, and until Somalia the only, case of a transition from peacekeeping to peace-enforcement.

The Near East war of October 1973 gave rise to two other remarkable achievements: the interposition of the second United Nations Emergency Force between the Egyptian and Israeli armies in an exceedingly dangerous and complicated military situation; and, eight months later, the deployment of a United Nations force (UNDOF) to control an agreed buffer zone between Israeli and Syrian forces on the Golan Heights in Syria. That force is still there—unpublicized because it does its job so well.

After those two successes, the line went almost dead until in 1988 the new readiness of the United States and the Soviet Union to work together revived opportunities for resolving regional conflicts and created a renewed demand for peacekeeping.

During the intervening 14 years, only one new operation was set up—UNIFIL in southern Lebanon. UNIFIL also is interesting in the contemporary context. It is an operation about whose viability the then Secretary-General and his senior advisers had doubts. It was nevertheless pushed through the Security Council by the United States for pressing, if passing, political reasons: President Carter was launching the negotiations which were to lead to the Camp David Accords and did not want that process derailed by the Israeli invasion of Lebanon which had just taken place.

UNIFIL has not been able to carry out its mandate because it has never enjoyed the necessary cooperation from all the parties concerned. But its presence has brought succour to the people of southern Lebanon and its withdrawal would certainly lead to an intensification of hostilities. It has thus become a quasi-permanent fixture. It illustrates how much easier it is to get into a peacekeeping operation than to get out of it—and the need therefore for the Security Council to satisfy itself that conditions exist for successful peacekeeping before taking the decision to set up a new operation.

The 13 operations established during the Cold War (of which five remain in existence) fostered the gradual evolution of a body of principles, procedures and practices for peacekeeping. Few of them were formally enacted by the legislative organs of the United Nations. But they came to constitute a corpus of case law or customary practice which was by and large accepted by all concerned, though until the mid-1980s Moscow continued from time to time to grumble about peacekeeping's lack of legitimacy because it was not explicitly provided for in the Charter.

The established principles of peacekeeping can be summarized under five headings.

First, peacekeeping operations were *United Nations* operations. Their United Nationsness derived from various factors: they were established by one of the legislative organs of the United Nations (unlike the enforcement operations in Korea or (subsequently) Kuwait and Somalia where the Security Council's role has been only to authorize certain member states to undertake military action for a specific purpose); they were under the command and control of the Secretary-General, who acted with authority delegated

to him by the Security Council and reported regularly to the Council; and their costs were met collectively by the member states as 'expenses of the Organization' under Article 17 of the Charter—a principle which was established with much difficulty during the 1960s. It was this United Nationsness which had made United Nations peacekeeping operations acceptable to member states who would not otherwise have accepted foreign troops on their territory. Suspicions that peacekeepers were acting as instruments of their governments' policy, rather than of the collective will of the international community, could be fatal for the credibility of an operation. It had been learnt the hard way that it could also—literally—be fatal for the peacekeepers themselves.

Second, it had become established over time that peacekeeping operations could be set up only with the *consent of the parties to the conflict* in question. It had also been learnt that they could succeed only with the continuing consent and cooperation of those parties. This had turned out to be both a strength and a weakness.

It was a strength in that, for the parties, it made peacekeeping less threatening and more acceptable. For the troop-contributing countries, it reduced to a very low level the risk of combat casualties. It was supposed also, in theory, to improve the chances of success; the parties would have agreed in advance to what the peacekeepers were going to do.

In practice, the consent principle had sometimes turned out to be more of a weakness than a strength. Consent once given could later be withdrawn. President Nasser's withdrawal of Egypt's consent to the presence of UNEF I on Egyptian territory in May 1967 had been the classic example. It tragically illustrated the perennial truth that if one of the parties takes the decision to go to war there is very little that peacekeepers can do to prevent war. . . .

Third, it had been established that the peacekeepers must be *impartial between the parties*. They were not there to advance the interests of one party against those of the other. It was not like Korea where the United States and its allies had been authorized by the Security Council to use force against North Korea for the benefit of South Korea. This principle of impartiality arose from the fact that peacekeeping operations were interim arrangements set up, as UNEF had been, without prejudice to the claims and positions of the parties.

Of course, the peacekeepers had to criticize, use pressure, mobilize international support, even in certain circumstances take more forceful action when a party violated agreed arrangements. But, beyond that, they could not take sides. Otherwise they themselves would violate the terms on which the operation had been accepted by the parties. This requirement for absolute impartiality sometimes obliged peacekeepers to maintain normal relations with a party whose behaviour was being censured by most of the international community and thus exposed them to the charge of condoning that behaviour.

The fourth principle related to the *troops required for United Nations peacekeeping* operations. It was recognized that it would not be practicable for the United Nations to maintain a standing army. National armies and police forces could be the only source for the uniformed personnel the United Nations required. The Charter provided for member states to enter into binding agreements with the Security Council under which they would commit themselves to provide it with troops. There had been no agreement between the major powers on the conclusion of such agreements for peacekeeping operations—or indeed for peace enforcement. Successive Secretaries-General had perforce, therefore, to rely on member states to provide the necessary personnel and equipment on a voluntary basis. Member states had responded readily to the call.

The fifth principle concerned the *use of force*. More than half the organization's peacekeeping operations before 1988 had consisted only of unarmed military observers. But when operations were armed, it had become an established principle that they should use force only to the minimum extent necessary and that normally fire should be opened only in self-defence.

However, since 1973 self-defence had been deemed to include situations in which peacekeepers were being prevented by armed persons from fulfilling their mandate. This was a wide definition of 'self-defence'. In practice commanders in the field had only very rarely taken advantage of the authority to open fire

on, for instance, soldiers at a roadblock who were denying passage to a United Nations convoy. This reluctance was based on sound calculations related to impartiality, to their reliance on the continued cooperation of the parties and to the fact that their force's level of armament was based on the assumption that the parties would comply with their commitments. The peacekeepers could perhaps win the firefight at that first roadblock. But, in lands of the vendetta, might they not find themselves out-gunned in the third or fourth encounter?

On the basis of these principles established during the first four decades of United Nations peacekeeping, a definition of peacekeeping could perhaps read as follows:

> Field operations established by the United Nations, with the consent of the parties concerned, to help control and resolve conflicts between them, under United Nations command and control, at the expense collectively of the member states, and with military and other personnel and equipment provided voluntarily by them, acting impartially between the parties and using force to the minimum extent necessary.

Six Types of Peacekeeping Operation

The revival of peacekeeping since 1988 has officially seen the establishment of 13 new operations so far. My personal count is 16. One of the 13, the United Nations Protection Force (UNPROFOR) in the former Yugoslavia, the largest operation yet fielded, is in fact a conglomerate of three separate operations. I would also add the electoral mission in Haiti in 1990. . . .

During these hectic five years of forced development, the Secretary-General and his staff have applied the established principles, procedures and practices of peacekeeping. On the whole they have stood the test well and have been able to accommodate a much wider range of activities than—with one or two exceptions—peacekeepers had undertaken during the Cold War years. . . .

Since 1988 this emphasis on the military has changed and peacekeeping operations frequently now contain substantial civilian elements. This is mainly because the United

Nations is more often involved in internal conflicts than in inter-state ones. As it had already learned in the Congo, these are messy affairs in which success is hard to achieve and more than military skills are required. Helping to end a civil war is likely to involve a third party in a whole range of civilian activities which are less often required in the interstate context. Such settlements almost always, for instance, include some electoral act which needs to be impartially monitored. In some cases reform or replacement of state institutions can also be a part of the settlement. Even in interstate conflicts, experience has shown that there is a greater role for civilian peacekeepers than had been apparent in earlier years.

Before 1988, peacekeeping had been regarded, not entirely accurately, as a rather homogeneous activity. It is now possible to identify at least six different types of peacekeeping. . . .

Type One is the *preventive deployment* of United Nations troops before a conflict has actually begun, at the request of one of the parties and on its territory only. The troops' function is partly early warning but mainly to increase the political price that would be paid by the potential aggressor. This idea, which came originally from Mikhail Gorbachev, was adopted by the present Secretary-General in his report *An agenda for peace*. It is currently being applied for the first time in Macedonia.

Type Two is *traditional peacekeeping*. The function is to support peacemaking efforts by helping to create conditions in which political negotiation can proceed. It involves monitoring ceasefires, controlling buffer zones, and so on. These are supposed to be interim arrangements but they can last for a very long time if the peacemaking efforts are slow to succeed: UNTSO has been deployed in the Near East for almost 45 years and UNFICYP in Cyprus for 29 years. Slow progress in peacemaking does not necessarily create a case for ending the peacekeeping; a long-standing peacekeeping operation may sometimes be the least bad option available to the international community if renewed war is to be avoided.

There are three sub-types: unarmed military observer groups as currently in the Near East, Kashmir and Western Sahara; armed infantry-based forces which are deployed in cases where the task is to control territory, as in Cyprus, Syria, southern Lebanon (in theory only, alas) and Croatia; and operations, armed or unarmed, which are established as an adjunct of, or sequel to, a peace enforcement operation, as on the Iraq-Kuwait border. . . .

Type Three consists of operations set up to support *implementation of a comprehensive settlement* which has already been agreed by the parties. This has been the area of most rapid growth since 1988, largely because the end of the Cold War and the new effectiveness of the Security Council have made it possible to negotiate partial or comprehensive settlements of several regional conflicts. In the case of comprehensive settlements, the peacekeepers have had to undertake a wide range of functions old and new. These can include: monitoring ceasefires, the cantonment and demobilization of troops, the destruction of weapons and the formation and training of new armed forces; monitoring existing police forces and forming new ones; supervizing, or even in Cambodia controlling, existing administrations; verifying respect for human rights; observing, supervizing or even conducting elections; undertaking information campaigns to explain the settlement, the opportunities it offers the people concerned and the role of the United Nations.

The paradigm is the very successful operation in Namibia in 1989–90. The United Nations is currently conducting similar operations in El Salvador, Angola, Cambodia, and Mozambique. It will do so in Western Sahara also, if conditions can be agreed for holding the planned referendum. . . .

Type Four (a new one) consists of operations *to protect the delivery of humanitarian relief supplies* in conditions of continuing warfare. This has been tried in recent months in Somalia and in Bosnia and Herzegovina. In Somalia it failed. This was not, as is often alleged, because of inadequate rules of engagement. It was mainly because of the absence of recognized political authorities with whom the United Nations could reliably conclude agreements for the deployment and activities of the peacekeepers, and because the unrecognized pretenders to power who controlled different parts of Somalia were not willing or, in some cases, able to provide the cooperation needed for the United Nations to succeed. . . .

In Bosnia and Herzegovina United Nations peacekeepers have had more success than is generally acknowledged in protecting humanitarian operations. But there too local warlords have denied them access to many areas of need and have continuously harassed and obstructed their efforts. Their rules of engagement permit them to use force against such obstruction but for reasons already explained their commanders have judged that 'fighting the aid through' is not a practicable proposition.

A feature common to Somalia and Bosnia is the difficulty of making peacekeeping work *vis-à-vis* armed groups outside the control of recognized political authorities with whom the United Nations can conclude the necessary political and practical agreements. This problem will grow as the organization becomes involved more frequently in internal conflicts. It is one of the impulses pushing it strongly in the direction of a greater readiness to use force.

Type Five is arguably not peacekeeping at all because it is likely to involve enforcement. It will also involve peacemaking (that is the fashioning of a political settlement) and what the Secretary-General has called post-conflict peacebuilding. This is *the deployment of a United Nations force in a country where the institutions of state have largely collapsed,* anarchy and lawlessness abound, the breakup of the country may be imminent and some external agency is needed to put it together again. It is Foreign Secretary Hurd's scenario of 'painting a country blue'. It requires an integrated programme including humanitarian relief, a ceasefire, demobilization of troops, a political process of national reconciliation, the rebuilding of political and administrative structures, economic rehabilitation and so on. As already mentioned the United Nations undertook this task successfully in the Congo in the 1960s. The new United Nations force in Somalia will have the same task and, like its predecessor in the Congo, is likely to have to use force to achieve it.

Type Six is, again, not really peacekeeping but I include it because it is currently under active discussion in the Bosnian context and because it illustrates the extent to which, in the public and the political mind at any rate, peacekeeping's evolution is taking it across the threshold into peace-enforcement. It can be called *ceasefire*

enforcement and is essentially a forceful variant of the traditional peacekeeping which I have classified as Type Two. A United Nations force would be deployed, after an agreement had been reached between the parties, with the authority and armament to use force against any party which violated the ceasefire or other agreed military arrangements. The mandate would be analogous to peacekeeping in that the parties would agree to the initial deployment of the force and the force would act impartially in enforcing the agreed arrangements. But it would differ from peacekeeping in that the force could open fire in situations other than self-defence, for example to silence guns that persisted in violating the ceasefire. . . .

From Peacekeeping to Peace-Enforcement: Desirable, Practicable?

During the last five years the established principles, procedures and practices of peacekeeping have, as I have said, stood up remarkably well to an unprecedented increase in the demand for United Nations peacekeeping services. . . .

The increase in activity has highlighted some shortcomings in existing arrangements. By common consent, the departments concerned at United Nations Headquarters in New York need to be strengthened if they are to have the planning and command and control capability to support operations on the scale currently deployed. Financial and logistic procedures need to be streamlined. There needs to be a working capital fund for peacekeeping and a reserve stock of basic peacekeeping equipment to enable the Secretary-General to respond more quickly when the Security Council decides to establish new peacekeeping operations. Present arrangements by which a few member states commit themselves to have troops on stand-by to serve with the United Nations at specified terms of notice need to be refined and extended to many more countries. The United Nations needs to do more to help member states train their personnel for peacekeeping service and perhaps to undertake more training itself.

Much work is in hand in New York on all these issues, in spite of the crushing pressure of the day to day management of existing operations. I believe that the wind stands fair for peacekeeping to continue as an effective United Nations instrument for the control and resolution of conflicts.

However, in recent months governments and public opinion in many countries have increasingly questioned whether peacekeeping is enough. Its reliance on the consent and cooperation of the parties has, it is said, shown it to be incapable of taking the forceful action required in situations like those in Bosnia and Somalia. Perhaps that is partly due to the fact that the Security Council may sometimes have deployed peacekeeping operations in situations where it was not entirely clear that conditions actually existed for successful peacekeeping. . . .

Creating this kind of grey area between peacekeeping and peace-enforcement can give rise to considerable dangers. In political, legal and military terms, and in terms of the survival of one's own troops, there is, on the one hand, all the difference in the world between being deployed with the consent and cooperation of the parties to help them carry out an agreement they have reached and, on the other hand, being deployed without their consent and with powers to use force to compel them to accept the decisions of the Security Council.

To take that view, however, is not to say that the United Nations should not use force. On the contrary, if the organization is to evolve into an effective system of collective security, it must, as was recognized in the Charter, have an enforcement capability. In that context, the greater readiness of the international community to contemplate enforcement action by the United Nations is to be welcomed and could represent a decisive moment in the development of the organization. It nevertheless gives rise to a number of questions which need to be urgently addressed.

1. By what criteria does the Security Council decide to use force, which in effect means going to war, against countries or groups which fail to comply with its decisions? There may be sound reasons why it is right to use force against Iraq and the Bosnian Serbs, but not against other member states which continue to occupy their neighbours' territory contrary to the Security Council's wishes, or against other movements which fail to heed the Council's decisions. But if the Security

Council is to escape the charge of double standards it—and especially its Western members—need to be more careful in defining those reasons and getting them accepted. The same question of criteria arises in relation to forceful intervention for humanitarian purposes. Why Bosnia, Kurdish Iraq and Somalia, but not Angola, or Liberia or southern Sudan where equally atrocious situations exist?

2. How can the Security Council ensure that its use of force will succeed? The credibility of the organization already suffers when a peacekeeping operation fails. During the Reagan era the inability of UNIFIL, through no fault of its own, to implement its mandate was used remorselessly in Washington to discredit the United Nations. Think how much greater the damage will be if resort to force by the Security Council does not succeed or if it gets bogged down in an interminable conflict like Britain's in Northern Ireland or India's in Kashmir (which seem more appropriate analogies than the often quoted Vietnam).

The answer to that question must lie, first, in very careful military appreciation of the task to be performed and, second, in deployment of sufficient forces to ensure its accomplishment. Equally, it is necessary to define a credible and practicable end-game, so that the United Nations force can be withdrawn without leaving behind chaos, tyranny or some other result which causes continued suffering or otherwise discredits the United Nations. . . .

3. Is the international community ready to pay for peace-enforcement? This is a vastly more expensive action than peacekeeping. During Desert Storm, on the basis of press estimates of its cost, we calculated that one day's expenditure on that operation would have been more than enough to finance United Nations peacekeeping for the whole of 1991. There is also the question of whether the costs of peace-enforcement operations should, as in the case of Kuwait, be borne by the governments contributing the troops, with financial support from their friends and allies, or whether they should be borne collectively by the member states as a whole. The latter principle was, with great travail, established for peacekeeping during the 1960s. If peace-enforcement is to strengthen the credibility of the United Nations as a world system of collective security, it is desirable that it too should be financed collectively.

4. Will enough member states be willing to contribute to peace-enforcement operations with the increased risk of casualties which they entail? And how many of those who are willing will have the armament and training necessary to engage in combat operations in unfamiliar terrain? Member states so far have been admirably willing to contribute military and police personnel to the organization's peacekeeping operations, in which almost 40 per cent of them are currently represented. If the credibility and effectiveness of the United Nations are to be strengthened, it is desirable that peace-enforcement operations, like peacekeeping, should include a wide enough spread of member states to reflect the composition of the organization as a whole.

5. How should command and control of peacekeeping operations be organized in the future? As already mentioned, peacekeeping operations take place under the command and control of the Secretary-General, who is responsible to the Security Council. Existing structures in New York have found it increasingly difficult to plan, command and control the greatly increased peacekeeping activities of recent years. When the Security Council authorized the despatch of additional troops to protect the delivery of humanitarian supplies in Bosnia and Herzegovina, it was decided to take 'off the shelf' elements of a NATO headquarters to establish the new command in Bosnia. This has not been an entirely happy experiment. . . .

It is to be assumed that the Security Council will continue to move in the direction of more forceful action, especially in response to civil wars involving intolerable human suffering. There is therefore likely to be continuing debate about whether this is better done by national forces and coalitions authorized by the Security Council or by forces under the command of the Secretary-General, and about how such operations should be financed. The outcome of this debate will have major implications for the future evolution of the United Nations as a system of collective security.

Conclusion

The future development or evolution of peacekeeping—and peace-enforcement—lies in the hands of two of the principal organs of the United Nations: the Security Council and the Secretary-General. They carry a heavy responsibility.

During the first four decades of the United Nations' existence, peacekeeping evolved in a less than benign environment. The Cold War blighted the organization's ability to perform many of the tasks envisaged for it in the Charter; and the Soviet Union maintained considerable reservations about the legitimacy of peacekeeping. On some occasions, notably in 1956 and 1973, the establishment and efficient functioning of a peacekeeping operation clearly served Soviet national interests and objections were not raised. But there was always hesitation about the Secretary-General's political role and opposition to his acquiring a military staff, let alone any stock of military equipment.

During those years Ralph Bunche and then Brian Urquhart, together with the Secretaries-General whom they served with such distinction, nurtured the evolution of peacekeeping and, with resourcefulness, and even stealth sometimes, established its credibility as a United Nations technique for conflict control and resolution. . . .

On the one hand, the Secretary-General has to try to ensure that peacekeepers are not deployed in conditions where failure is likely; on the other hand, he has to avoid appearing so cautious as to create doubts about the real usefulness of the United Nations or provide a pretext for member states to return to the bad old ways of unilateral military action.

This is not a responsibility which the Secretary-General should be asked to bear alone. The power of decision in these matters rests with the Security Council. It is important that the members of the Council should, if necessary, stand up to the clamour of domestic or regional pressures and take care to satisfy themselves in advance that conditions do really exist for a proposed peacekeeping operation to succeed.

Those conditions are well known, but they bear repeating. The mandate or task must be clear, practicable and accepted by the parties; the parties must pledge themselves to cooperate with the peacekeepers and their pledges must be credible; and the member states of the United Nations must be ready to provide the human and material resources needed to do the job. On any particular day, unfortunately, only a minority of the actual or potential conflicts in the world fulfil those con- ditions. It is often frustratingly necessary to wait until a conflict is ripe for the United Nations peacekeeping treatment. But when the conditions are fulfilled, there is almost no limit to what peacekeeping can achieve.

IMMANUEL KANT

Perpetual Peace

Next: world government. It is tempting to be disdainful of this, the classic case of pie-in-the-sky idealism, so far removed from reality as to seem mere "globaloney." And yet, maybe the idea of world government isn't so foolish or unrealistic after all.

For one thing, the current system of international states has only been in existence since 1648, when the Treaty of Westphalia ended the Thirty Years War in Europe. Current political boundaries are themselves temporary (consider the breakup of the Soviet Union, the unification of Germany, and so forth), not God-given. Moreover, the system of war-making is intimately connected to the existence of nation-states, which have fractured the human community along ideological, social, and geopolitical lines, and which are therefore at least part of the problem—maybe the largest part. The solution may accordingly require structures of coordination and a recognition of unity that demands nothing less than a global revolution, albeit a nonviolent one. In short, it may well be necessary to rethink and rebuild the world. Whereas self-styled "realists" may scoff, it is worth considering whether they are in fact realistic in assuming that the current world system can—or should—go on indefinitely.

Prior to 1648, in a "pre-Westphalian" world, primary loyalties were local, to one's family, tribe, feudal lord, or city. We currently live in a "Westphalian" world of states and nation-states, in which these structures may have become as obsolete as their feudal antecedents. Our mounting problems—notably pollution, poverty, resource deple- tion, and the destructive effects of war—supersede the old, traditional political bound- aries, making it imperative that we think as planetary citizens. The world, in short, has become functionally integrated, even while it remains politically fragmented.

At one level, the appeal of world government is eminently practical: superior author- ities ought to be able to force quarreling subordinates to refrain from violence, to respect larger, common interests and to solve their disputes in some other way. When two indi- viduals disagree about something, they are expected to settle the dispute in a law-abid- ing manner, not by contests of force. Similarly, individual households are not "sover- eign," nor, for example, one Oregon or California within the United States, or Ontario or Alberta within Canada. The hope, then, is that just as Supreme Courts and federal authority prevent states or provinces from going to war against each other, an overrid- ing world government could do the same in regulating disputes among countries. (An

From *Perpetual Peace* by Immanuel Kant. 1795. Translated by Mary Campbell Smith, 1917. London: Allen and Unwin.

interesting precedent can be cited from the history of the United States itself. Under the Articles of Confederation, independent states had been virtually sovereign, had their own military forces, had numerous and occasionally violent disputes, and had even had their own currency. With the adoption of the federal Constitution, the United States became a kind of "world government" in miniature, a political amalgamation that has been quite successful.)

There are, to be sure, widespread fears that any world government would necessarily be dangerous, perhaps dictatorial, even if it were feasible. But it is also debatable whether world government needs to be "all or nothing." Thus, systems are conceivable whereby countries retain their ethnic, economic, and historical identities, while foregoing certain circumscribed powers, notably the authority to wage war (and possibly, to pollute across borders, etc.). Although "the devil is in the details," many detailed plans for potential world governments have already been proposed, involving among other things, elaboration of the U.N. into a world peacekeeping authority, while still permitting national autonomy in nonmilitary arenas (for example, Clark and Sohn, 1966).

In his book, *Perpetual Peace*, Immanuel Kant, renowned German philosopher of the Enlightenment, presaged much of the current work by "One Worlders" and "World Federalists," arguing strongly for world government. Rather than simply proposing yet another kind of international parliament, Kant also made the first major effort to focus specifically on the dangers of armaments. Consistent with his Enlightenment orientation, he argued that, in spite of the evil of which human beings are capable, the continuing cultural progress of humanity will enable people to use reason to act increasingly on behalf of moral perfection. Although his work was published in 1795 and is necessarily somewhat dated today, it remains cogent in many respects, especially in his identification of the state as the prime war-causing culprit, and in his placing blame for this on the "lawlessness" of how, as a last resort, states interact with one another.

"No state having an independent existence—whether it be great or small—shall be acquired by another through inheritance, exchange, purchase or donation."

For a *state is not a property (patrimonium),* as may be the ground on which its people are settled. *It is a society of human beings over whom no one but itself has the right to rule and to dispose.* Like the trunk of a tree, it has its own roots, and to graft it on to another state is to do away with its existence as a moral person, and to make of it a thing. Hence it is in contradiction to the idea of the original contract without which no right over a people is thinkable. . . .

"Standing armies (*miles perpetuus*) shall be abolished in course of time."

For they are always threatening other states with war by appearing to be in constant readiness to fight. They incite the various states to outrival one another in the number of their soldiers, and to this number no limit can be set. Now, since owing to the sums devoted to this purpose, peace at last becomes even more oppressive than a short war, these standing armies are themselves the cause of wars of aggression, undertaken in order to get rid of this burden. To which we must add that the practice of hiring men to kill or to be killed seems to imply a use of them as mere machines and instruments in the hand of another (namely, the state) which cannot easily be reconciled with the right of humanity in our own person. . . .

"No state shall violently interfere with the constitution and administration of another."

For what can justify it in so doing? The scandal which is here presented to the subjects of another state? The erring state can much more serve as a warning by exemplifying the great evils which a nation draws down on itself through its own lawlessness. Moreover, the bad example which one free person gives another, (as *scandalum acceptum*) does no injury to the latter. In this connection, it is true, we cannot count the case of a state which has become split up through internal corruption into two parts, each of them representing by itself an individual state which lays claim to the whole. Here the yielding of assistance to one faction could not be reckoned as interference on the part of a foreign state with the constitution of another, for here anarchy prevails. So long, however, as the inner strife has not yet reached this stage the interference of other powers would be a violation of the rights of an independent nation which is only struggling with internal disease. It would therefore itself cause a scandal, and make the autonomy of all states insecure. . . .

A state of peace among men who live side by side is not the natural state, which is rather to be described as a state of war: that is to say, although there is not perhaps always actual open hostility, yet there is a constant threatening that an outbreak may occur. Thus the state of peace must be *established*. For the mere cessation of hostilities is no guarantee of continued peaceful relations, and unless this guarantee is given by every individual to his neighbour—which can only be done in a state of society regulated by law—one man is at liberty to challenge another and treat him as an enemy. . . .

"The civil constitution of each state shall be republican."

The only constitution which has its origin in the idea of the original contract, upon which the lawful legislation of every nation must be based, is the republican. It is a constitution, in the first place, founded in accordance with the principle of the freedom of the members of society as human beings: secondly, in accordance with the principle of the dependence of all, as subjects, on a common legislation: and, thirdly, in accordance with the law of the equality of the members as citizens. It is then, looking at the question of right, the only constitution whose fundamental principles lie at the basis of every form of civil constitution.

And the only question for us now is, whether it is also the one constitution which can lead to perpetual peace.

Now the republican constitution apart from the soundness of its origin, since it arose from the pure source of the concept of right, has also the prospect of attaining the desired result, namely, perpetual peace. And the reason is this. If, as must be so under this constitution, the consent of the subjects is required to determine whether there shall be war or not, nothing is more natural than that they should weigh the matter well, before undertaking such a bad business. For in decreeing war, they would of necessity be resolving to bring down the miseries of war upon their country. This implies: they must fight themselves; they must hand over the costs of the war out of their own property; they must do their poor best to make good the devastation which it leaves behind; and finally, as a crowning ill, they have to accept a burden of debt which will embitter even peace itself, and which they can never pay off on account of the new wars which are always impending. On the other hand, in a government where the subject is not a citizen holding a vote, (i.e., in a constitution which is not republican), the plunging into war is the least serious thing in the world. For the ruler is not a citizen, but the owner of the state, and does not lose a whit by the war, while he goes on enjoying the delights of his table or sport, or of his pleasure palaces and gala days. He can therefore decide on war for the most trifling reasons, as if it were a kind of pleasure party. . . .

"The law of nations shall be founded on a federation of free states."

Nations, as states, may be judged like individuals who, living in the natural state of society—that is to say, uncontrolled by external law—injure one another through their very proximity. Every state, for the sake of its own security, may—and ought to—demand that its neighbour should submit itself to conditions, similar to those of the civil society where the right of every individual is guaranteed. This would give rise to a federation of nations which, however, would not have to be a State of nations. That would involve a contradiction. For the term "state" implies the relation of one who rules to those who obey—that is to say, of lawgiver to the subject people: and many nations in one state would constitute only one nation, which contradicts our hypothesis, since here we have to consider the right of one nation against another, in so far as they are so many separate states and are not to be fused into one. . . .

The depravity of human nature shows itself without disguise in the unrestrained relations of nations to each other, while in the law-governed civil state much of this is hidden by the check of government. This being so, it is astonishing that the word "right" has not yet been entirely banished from the politics of war as pedantic, and that no state has yet ventured to publicly advocate this point of view. For Hugo Grotius, Puffendorf, Vattel and others—Job's comforters, all of them—are always quoted in good faith to justify an attack, although their codes, whether couched in philosophical or diplomatic terms, have not—nor can have—the slightest legal force, because states, as such, are under no common external authority; and there is no instance of a state having ever been moved by argument to desist from its purpose, even when this was backed up by the testimony of such great men. This homage which every state renders—in words at least—to the idea of right, proves that, although it may be slumbering, there is, notwithstanding, to be found in man a still higher natural moral capacity by the aid of which he will in time gain the mastery over the evil principle in his nature, the existence of which he is unable to deny. And he hopes the same of others; for otherwise the word "right" would never be uttered by states who wish to wage war, unless to deride it like the Gallic Prince who declared:—"The privilege which nature gives the strong is that the weak must obey them."

. . . A treaty of peace makes, it may be, an end to the war of the moment, but not to the conditions of war which at any time may afford a new pretext for opening hostilities; and this we cannot exactly condemn as unjust, because under these conditions everyone is his own judge. Notwithstanding, not quite the same rule applies to states according to the law of nations as holds good of individuals in a lawless condition according to the law of nature, namely, "that they ought to advance out of this condition." This is so, because, as states, they have already within themselves a legal constitution, and have therefore advanced beyond the stage at which others, in accordance with their ideas of right, can force them to come under a wider legal constitution. Meanwhile, however, reason, from her throne of the supreme law-giving moral power, absolutely condemns war as a morally lawful proceeding. . . .

For states, in their relation to one another, there can be, according to reason, no other way of advancing from that lawless condition which unceasing war implies, than by giving up their savage lawless freedom, just as individual men have done, and yielding to the coercion of public laws. Thus they can form a State of nations (*civitas gentium*), one, too, which will be ever increasing and would finally embrace all the peoples of the earth. States, however, in accordance with their understanding of the law of nations, by no means desire this, and therefore reject *in hypothesi* what is correct *in thesi*. Hence, instead of the positive idea of a world-republic, if all is not to be lost, only the negative substitute for it, a federation averting war, maintaining its ground and ever extending over the world may stop the current of this tendency to war and shrinking from the control of law. But even then there will be a constant danger that this propensity may break out.

Third Definitive Article of Perpetual Peace

> "The rights of men, as citizens of the world, shall be limited to the conditions of universal hospitality."

We are speaking here, as in the previous articles, not of philanthropy, but of right; and in this sphere hospitality signifies the claim of a stranger entering foreign territory to be treated by its owner without hostility. The latter may send him away again, if this can be done without causing his death; but, so long as he conducts himself peaceably, he must not be treated as an enemy. It is not a right to be treated as a guest to which the stranger can lay claim—a special friendly compact on his behalf would be required to make him for a given time an actual inmate—but he has a right of visitation. This right to present themselves to society belongs to all mankind in virtue of our common right of possession on the surface of the earth on which, as it is a globe, we cannot be infinitely scattered, and must in the end reconcile ourselves to existence side by side: at the same time, originally no one individual had more right than another to live in any one particular spot. . . .

The intercourse, more or less close, which has been everywhere steadily increasing between the nations of the earth, has now extended so enormously that a violation of right in one part of the world is felt all over it. Hence the idea of a cosmopolitan right is no fantastical, high-flown notion of right, but a complement of the unwritten code of law— constitutional as well as international law— necessary for the public rights of mankind in general and thus for the realisation of perpetual peace. For only by endeavouring to fulfil the conditions laid down by this cosmopolitan law can we flatter ourselves that we are gradually approaching that ideal.

. . . The idea of international law presupposes the separate existence of a number of neighbouring and independent states; and, although such a condition of things is in itself already a state of war, (if a federative union of these nations does not prevent the outbreak of hostilities) yet, according to the Idea of reason, this is better than that all the states should be merged into one under a power which has gained the ascendency over its neighbours and gradually become a universal monarchy. For the wider the sphere of their jurisdiction, the more laws lose in force; and soulless despotism, when it has choked the seeds of good, at last sinks into anarchy. Nevertheless it is the desire of every state, or of its ruler, to attain to a permanent condition of peace in this very way; that is to say, by subjecting the whole world as far as possible to its sway. But nature wills it otherwise. She employs two means to separate nations, and prevent them from inter-

mixing: namely, the differences of language and of religion. These differences bring with them a tendency to mutual hatred, and furnish pretexts for waging war. But, none the less, with the growth of culture and the gradual advance of men to greater unanimity of principle, they lead to concord in a state of peace which, unlike the despotism we have spoken of, (the churchyard of freedom) does not arise from the weakening of all forces, but is brought into being and secured through the equilibrium of these forces in their most active rivalry.

As nature wisely separates nations which the will of each state, sanctioned even by the principles of international law, would gladly unite under its own sway by stratagem or force; in the same way, on the other hand, she unites nations whom the principle of a cosmopolitan right would not have secured against violence and war. And this union she brings about through an appeal to their mutual interests. The commercial spirit cannot co-exist with war, and sooner or later it takes possession of every nation. For, of all the forces which lie at the command of a state, the power of money is probably the most reliable. Hence states find themselves compelled—not, it is true, exactly from motives of morality—to further the noble end of peace and to avert war, by means of mediation, wherever it threatens to break out, just as if they had made a permanent league for this purpose. For great alliances with a view to war can, from the nature of things, only very rarely occur, and still more seldom succeed.

In this way nature guarantees the coming of perpetual peace, through the natural course of human propensities: not indeed with sufficient certainty to enable us to prophesy the future of this ideal theoretically, but yet clearly enough for practical purposes. And thus this guarantee of nature makes it a duty that we should labour for this end, an end which is no mere chimera.

STUDY QUESTIONS

1. Identify and discuss some ways of preventing war that were *not* touched upon in this chapter.

2. Choose one or more of the selections in this chapter and disagree with it, pointing out, for example, how it is unrealistic, or undesirable, or might be counterproductive.

3. Consider a current source of conflict and describe how "principled negotiation" might help both sides reach an acceptable agreement.

4. Now that the Cold War is over, is arms control still important? If yes, in what sphere would you like to see it concentrated? If no, why not?

5. Look into the current status of international organizations *other* than the United Nations. Which of these seem especially promising? Do any seem liable to be especially troublesome? Why?

6. Are there any weaknesses in international law other than the problem of enforcement? Describe them.

7. What are some reasons for thinking that the current system of sovereign states is inappropriate for meeting the problems of the twenty-first century? Are there any reasons to think that this system is weakening? If so, what dangers might this pose?

8. Look into schemes for world government that have been proposed since Kant. Are they necessarily as unrealistic as some critics suggest?

9. Describe ways in which Osgood's strategy of GRIT might be applied to a current situation of conflict.

10. What similarities exist between attempts to achieve negative peace on the international level and on the personal level?

Suggestions for Further Reading

Benton, Barbara, ed. 1996. *Soldiers for Peace: Fifty Years of United Nations Peacekeeping*. New York: Facts On File.

Best, Geoffrey F. A. 1994. *War and Law Since 1945*. New York: Oxford University Press.

Bischak, Gregory A. ed. 1991. *Towards a Peace Economy in the United States: Essays on Military Industry, Disarmament and Economic Conversion*. London: Macmillan.

Brauer, Jurgen and Manas Chatterji, eds. 1993. *Economic Issues of Disarmament: Contributions from Peace Economics and Peace Science*. New York: New York University Press.

Burns, Richard Dean, ed. 1993. *Encyclopedia of Arms Control and Disarmament*. New York: Charles Scribner's Sons.

Cassidy, Kevin J. and Gregory A. Bischak. 1993. *Real Security: Converting the Defense Economy and Building Peace*. Albany: State University of New York Press.

Clark, Grenville and Louis Sohn. 1966. *World Peace Through World Law: Two Alternative Plans*. Cambridge, Mass: Harvard University Press.

Durch, William J. ed. 1996. *UN Peacekeeping, American Politics, and the Uncivil Wars of the 1990s*. New York: St. Martin's Press.

Falk, Richard, Friedrich Kratochwil, and Saul H. Mendlovitz. eds. 1985. *International Law: A Contemporary Perspective*. Boulder, Colo: Westview Press.

Findlay, Trevor. ed. 1996. *Challenges for the New Peacekeepers*. New York: Oxford University Press.

Goldman, Ralph Morris and Willard M. Hardman. 1997. *Building Trust: An Introduction to Peacekeeping and Arms Control*. Brookfield, VT: Ashgate.

Isard, Walter and Charles H. Anderton. eds. 1992. *Economics of Arms Reduction and the Peace Process: Contributions from Peace Economics and Peace Science*. New York: Elsevier.

von Lipsey, Roderick K. ed. 1997. *Breaking the Cycle: A Framework for Conflict Intervention*. New York: St. Martin's Press.

3

~~~

Building "Positive Peace"

It is important to be against war. But it is not enough. We also need to be in favor of something—something positive and affirming: namely, peace. Peace studies is unique not only because it is multidisciplinary and forthrightly proclaims its adherence to "values," but also because it identifies positive visions of peace as being greater than the absence of war.

The "positive peace" toward which peace studies strives may be, if anything, even more challenging than the prevention of war. It is a variation on what has been called the "dog–car problem." Imagine a dog that has spent years barking and running after cars. Then, one day, it catches one. What does it *do* with it? What would devotees of peace *do* with the world if they had the opportunity?

This is not a useless exercise, as before any future can be established, it must first be imagined. And moreover, unlike our hypothetical car-chasing dog, the establishment of positive peace is not an all-or-nothing phenomenon. The movement toward positive peace is likely to be halting and fragmentary, with substantial success along certain dimensions, likely failures along others. On balance, the project is formidable, nothing less than a fundamental effort to rethink the relationship of human beings to each other and to their shared planet. If war and its causes are difficult to define—and this is assuredly the case—positive peace is even more elusive. (It can even be dangerous, since disagreements over what constitutes a desirable "peace" can lead to war.)

Earlier, we briefly considered "Just War" doctrine. The conditions for a "just peace" are no less strenuous or important. The relevant issues include—but are not limited to— aspirations for human rights, economic fairness and opportunity, democratization, and environmental well-being and sustainability. Nonetheless, there is no agreement as to what, specifically, is desired, or how much emphasis to place on each goal.

The pursuit of positive peace nonetheless leads to certain agreed principles, one of which is a minimization of violence, not only the overt violence of war, but also what has been called "structural violence," a condition that is typically built into many social and cultural institutions. A slave-holding society may be at "peace" in that it is not literally at war, but it is also rife with structural violence. Structural violence has the effect of denying people important rights such as economic opportunity, social and political equality, a sense of fulfillment and self-worth, and access to a healthy natural environment. When people starve to death, or even go hungry, a kind of violence is taking place. Similarly, when human beings suffer from diseases that are preventable, when

129

they are denied a decent education, housing, an opportunity to play, to grow, to work, to raise a family, to express themselves freely, to organize peacefully, or to participate in their own governance, a kind of violence is occurring, even if bullets or clubs are not being used. Society visits violence on human rights and dignity when it forcibly stunts the optimum development of each human being, whether because of race, religion, sex, sexual preference, age, ideology, and so on. In short, structural violence is another way of identifying oppression, and positive peace would be a situation in which structural violence and oppression are minimized.

In addition, social injustice is important not only in its contribution to structural violence, but also as a major contributor to war, often in unexpected ways. For many citizens of the United States and Europe, as well as privileged people worldwide, current lifestyles are fundamentally acceptable. Hence, peace for them has come to mean the continuation of things as they are, with the additional hope that overt violence will be prevented. For others—perhaps the majority on our planet—change of one sort or another is desired. And for a small minority, peace is something to fight for! A Central American peasant was quoted in *The New York Times* as saying "I am for peace, but not peace with hunger."

There is a long tradition suggesting that injustice is a primary cause of war. The French philosopher Denis Diderot, for example, was convinced that a world of justice and plenty would mean a world free of tyranny and war. Hence, in his 18th-century treatise, the *Encyclopedia*, Diderot sought to establish peace by disseminating all the world's technical information, from bee-keeping to iron forging. And, of course, similar efforts continue today, although few advocates of economic and social development claim that the problem of violence can be solved simply by spreading knowledge or even by keeping everyone's belly full.

The troubling relationship of human beings to their natural environment must also be reworked, perhaps in fundamental ways. A world at peace must be one in which environmental, human rights, and economic issues all cohere to foster maximum well-being; ecological harmony cannot realistically be separated from questions of human rights or economic justice (or, for that matter, from the issues of democratization and demilitarization).

In relation to the environment, political or economic ideology do not appear to be significant. Environmental degradation is, to be sure, intimately connected to poverty: wealthy states often export their most odious environmental abuses, and impoverished states are often forced by their poverty to accept the situation. Moreover, within any given state, wealthy people are able to purchase certain amenities, while the poor find themselves living in degraded, and downright dangerous surroundings. But in general, left-leaning governments have not shown themselves to be more environmentally sensitive than their right-leaning counterparts. In avowedly socialist or communist societies, for example, "production goals" typically replaced the capitalist pursuit of "profit" as the "bottom line" to which environmental values were all too frequently sacrificed.

A very important shift in human consciousness—intimately related to the agenda of peace studies—is the realization that "national security" must be defined in ways that go far beyond military strength, and that as our planet becomes increasingly interconnected politically, economically, and socially, and also as our global environment is increasingly endangered, the health, well-being, and security of every individual becomes inseparable from the health, well-being, and security of the earth itself.

The Land Ethic

An ecological perspective demands that we recognize the reality of connectedness, which, as the poet Francis Thompson put it, "all things . . . near and far, hiddenly to each other, connected are, that thou canst not stir a flower without the troubling of a star." This is true not only for biology, but also for social, political, and economic systems. Thus, not only do wars ruin the environment, but environmental destruction—and its threat—can lead to wars. Millions of refugees regularly flee environmental disasters such as drought, floods, famine, and disease. These refugees, who constitute a humanitarian disaster in themselves, can also raise international tensions.

The destruction of rain forests, for example, is not only a deeply troubling environmental issue with worldwide implications, but it arises from particular economic systems (notably a free-market free-for-all), with no small dose of racism (devaluing the rights of indigenous peoples). The poverty resulting from deforestation and displacement leads to land degradation and the growing problem of desertification as hungry, desperate people clear and cultivate regions that should be left untouched. This in turn leads to yet more poverty and social unrest. Intensive farming of highly erodable land permanently destroys soil; large-scale intrusions into wildlife habitat (which contribute to species extinction) are in large part responses to land hunger in rural, developing countries, where a small minority of wealthy people own most of the arable land, thereby pushing others to environmentally abusive behavior. Worldwide, the burning of fossil fuels produces greenhouse gases; resulting global climate warming may increase food insecurity by reducing agricultural productivity. All of these factors—plus many others—are intertwined in complex ways with the exponential growth of the human population.

There is an enormous and growing literature on specific solutions to environmental problems, such as mass transportation; improved energy efficiency and co-generation; "soft" energy paths such as solar, wind and tidal power; organic agriculture; enhanced recycling; eating "lower on the food chain"; and an enlightened population policy that encourages family planning, especially by empowering women.

The word "ecology" derives from the Greek *oikos*, meaning house. It refers to the interrelations between living things and their environment, with the latter including other living things (plants, animals, microorganisms) as well as inanimate objects and processes such as climate, rock, water, and air. Despite dreams of space travel and the colonization of other planets, the fact remains that human beings have only one home, and good planets are hard to find.

In the final analysis, a world at peace must be one in which all living things experience themselves as being "at home." In recent times, some of the crucial relationships among the world's species, and between those species and their environments, have become increasingly tenuous, which in turn has begun to threaten the quality of life,

---

and even its continuation. At risk is nothing less than the integrity of various life-support systems: the air we breathe, the water we drink, the food we eat, as well as the diverse fabric of life that provides emotional and spiritual sustenance.

The following selection—written by one of the great figures in ecology, and the founder of "wildlife management"—attempts to look broadly at the problem, and to suggest the beginning of a solution: notably, a code of environmental ethics.

When god-like Odysseus returned from the wars in Troy, he hanged all on one rope a dozen slave-girls of his household whom he suspected of misbehavior during his absence.

This hanging involved no question of propriety. The girls were property. The disposal of property was then, as now, a matter of expedience, not of right and wrong.

Concepts of right and wrong were not lacking from Odysseus' Greece: witness the fidelity of his wife through the long years before at last his black-prowed galleys clove the wine-dark seas for home. The ethical structure of that day covered wives, but had not yet been extended to human chattels. During the three thousand years which have since elapsed, ethical criteria have been extended to many fields of conduct, with corresponding shrinkages in those judged by expediency only.

The Ethical Sequence

This extension of ethics, so far studied only by philosophers, is actually a process in ecological evolution. Its sequences may be described in ecological as well as in philosophical terms. An ethic, ecologically, is a limitation on freedom of action in the struggle for existence. An ethic, philosophically, is a differentiation of social from antisocial conduct. These are two definitions of one thing. The thing has its origin in the tendency of interdependent individuals or groups to evolve modes of co-operation. The ecologist calls these symbioses. Politics and economics are advanced symbioses in which the original free-for-all competition has been replaced, in part, by co-operative mechanisms with an ethical content.

The complexity of co-operative mechanisms has increased with population density, and with the efficiency of tools. It was simpler, for example, to define the anti-social uses of sticks and stones in the days of the mastodons than of bullets and billboards in the age of motors.

The first ethics dealt with the relation between individuals; the Mosaic Decalogue is an example. Later accretions dealt with the relation between the individual and society. The Golden Rule tries to integrate the individual to society; democracy to integrate social organization to the individual.

There is as yet no ethic dealing with man's relation to land and to the animals and plants which grow upon it. Land, like Odysseus' slave-girls, is still property. The land-relation is still strictly economic, entailing privileges but not obligations.

The extension of ethics to this third element in human environment is, if I read the evidence correctly, an evolutionary possibility and an ecological necessity. It is the third step in a sequence. The first two have already been taken. Individual thinkers since the days of Ezekiel and Isaiah have asserted that the despoliation of land is not only inexpedient but wrong. Society, however, has not yet affirmed their belief. I regard the present conservation movement as the embryo of such an affirmation.

An ethic may be regarded as a mode of guidance for meeting ecological situations so new or intricate, or involving such deferred reactions, that the path of social expediency is not discernible to the average individual. Animal instincts are modes of guidance for the individual in meeting such situations. Ethics are possibly a kind of community instinct in-the-making.

The Community Concept

All ethics so far evolved rest upon a single premise: that the individual is a member of a community of interdependent parts. His instincts prompt him to compete for his place in that community, but his ethics prompt him also to co-operate (perhaps in order that there may be a place to compete for).

The land ethic simply enlarges the boundaries of the community to include soils, waters, plants, and animals, or collectively: the land.

This sounds simple: do we not already sing our love for and obligation to the land of the free and the home of the brave? Yes, but just what and whom do we love? Certainly not the soil, which we are sending helter-skelter downriver. Certainly not the waters, which we assume have no function except to turn turbines, float barges, and carry off sewage. Certainly not the plants, of which we exterminate whole communities without batting an eye. Certainly not the animals, of which we have already extirpated many of the largest and most beautiful species. A land ethic of course cannot prevent the alteration, management, and use of these "resources," but it does affirm their right to continued existence, and, at least in spots, their continued existence in a natural state.

In short, a land ethic changes the role of *Homo sapiens* from conqueror of the land-community to plain member and citizen of it. It implies respect for his fellow-members, and also respect for the community as such.

In human history, we have learned (I hope) that the conqueror role is eventually self-defeating. Why? Because it is implicit in such a role that the conqueror knows, *ex cathedra*, just what makes the community clock tick, and just what and who is valuable, and what and who is worthless, in community life. It always turns out that he knows neither, and this is why his conquests eventually defeat themselves.

In the biotic community, a parallel situation exists. Abraham knew exactly what the land was for: it was to drip milk and honey into Abraham's mouth. At the present moment, the assurance with which we regard this assumption is inverse to the degree of our education.

The ordinary citizen today assumes that science knows what makes the community clock tick; the scientist is equally sure that he does not. He knows that the biotic mechanism is so complex that its workings may never be fully understood. . . .

The Ecological Conscience

Conservation is a state of harmony between men and land. Despite nearly a century of propaganda, conservation still proceeds at a snail's pace; progress still consists largely of letterhead pieties and convention oratory. On the back forty we still slip two steps backward for each forward stride.

The usual answer to this dilemma is "more conservation education." No one will debate this, but is it certain that only the *volume* of education needs stepping up? Is something lacking in the *content* as well?

It is difficult to give a fair summary of its content in brief form, but, as I understand it, the content is substantially this: obey the law, vote right, join some organizations, and practice what conservation is profitable on your own land; the government will do the rest.

Is not this formula too easy to accomplish anything worth-while? It defines no right or wrong, assigns no obligation, calls for no sacrifice, implies no change in the current philosophy of values. In respect of land-use, it urges only enlightened self-interest. Just how far will such education take us?

No important change in ethics was ever accomplished without an internal change in our intellectual emphasis, loyalties, affections, and convictions. The proof that conservation has not yet touched these foundations of conduct lies in the fact that philosophy and religion have not yet heard of it. In our attempt to make conservation easy, we have made it trivial.

Substitutes for a Land Ethic

When the logic of history hungers for bread and we hand out a stone, we are at pains to explain how much the stone resembles bread. I now describe some of the stones which serve in lieu of a land ethic.

One basic weakness in a conservation system based wholly on economic motives is that most members of the land community have no economic value. Wildflowers and songbirds are examples. Of the 22,000 higher plants and animals native to Wisconsin, it is doubtful whether more than 5 per cent can be sold, fed, eaten, or otherwise put to economic use. Yet these creatures are members of the biotic community, and if (as I believe) its stability depends on its integrity, they are entitled to continuance.

When one of these non-economic categories is threatened, and if we happen to love it, we invent subterfuges to give it economic importance. At the beginning of the century songbirds were supposed to be disappearing.

Ornithologists jumped to the rescue with some distinctly shaky evidence to the effect that insects would eat us up if birds failed to control them. The evidence had to be economic in order to be valid.

It is painful to read these circumlocutions today. We have no land ethic yet, but we have at least drawn nearer the point of admitting that birds should continue as a matter of biotic right, regardless of the presence or absence of economic advantage to us.

A parallel situation exists in respect of predatory mammals, raptorial birds, and fish-eating birds. Time was when biologists somewhat overworked the evidence that these creatures preserve the health of game by killing weaklings, or that they control rodents for the farmer, or that they prey only on "worthless" species. Here again, the evidence had to be economic in order to be valid. It is only in recent years that we hear the more honest argument that predators are members of the community, and that no special interest has the right to exterminate them for the sake of a benefit, real or fancied, to itself. . . .

Lack of economic value is sometimes a character not only of species or groups, but of entire biotic communities: marshes, bogs, dunes, and "deserts" are examples. Our formula in such cases is to relegate their conservation to government as refuges, monuments, or parks. The difficulty is that these communities are usually interspersed with more valuable private lands; the government cannot possibly own or control such scattered parcels. The net effect is that we have relegated some of them to ultimate extinction over large areas. . . .

Industrial landowners and users, especially lumbermen and stockmen, are inclined to wail long and loudly about the extension of government ownership and regulation to land, but (with notable exceptions) they show little disposition to develop the only visible alternative: the voluntary practice of conservation on their own lands.

When the private landowner is asked to perform some unprofitable act for the good of the community, he today assents only with outstretched palm. If the act costs him cash this is fair and proper, but when it costs only forethought, open-mindedness, or time, the issue is at least debatable. The overwhelming growth of land-use subsidies in recent years must be ascribed, in large part, to the government's own agencies for conservation education: the land bureaus, the agricultural colleges, and the extension services. As far as I can detect, no ethical obligation toward land is taught in these institutions.

To sum up: a system of conservation based solely on economic self-interest is hopelessly lopsided. It tends to ignore, and thus eventually to eliminate, many elements in the land community that lack commercial value, but that are (as far as we know) essential to its healthy functioning. It assumes, falsely, I think, that the economic parts of the biotic clock will function without the uneconomic parts. It tends to relegate to government many functions eventually too large, too complex, or too widely dispersed to be performed by government.

An ethical obligation on the part of the private owner is the only visible remedy for these situations.

The Land Pyramid

An ethic to supplement and guide the economic relation to land presupposes the existence of some mental image of land as a biotic mechanism. We can be ethical only in relation to something we can see, feel, understand, love, or otherwise have faith in.

The image commonly employed in conservation education is "the balance of nature." For reasons too lengthy to detail here, this figure of speech fails to describe accurately what little we know about the land mechanism. A much truer image is the one employed in ecology: the biotic pyramid. I shall first sketch the pyramid as a symbol of land, and later develop some of its implications in terms of land-use.

Plants absorb energy from the sun. This energy flows through a circuit called the biota, which may be represented by a pyramid consisting of layers. The bottom layer is the soil. A plant layer rests on the soil, an insect layer on the plants, a bird and rodent layer on the insects, and so on up through various animal groups to the apex layer, which consists of the larger carnivores.

The species of a layer are alike not in where they came from, or in what they look like, but rather in what they eat. Each successive layer depends on those below it for food and often for other services, and each in turn furnishes food and services to those above.

Proceeding upward, each successive layer decreases in numerical abundance. Thus, for every carnivore there are hundreds of his prey, thousands of their prey, millions of insects, uncountable plants. The pyramidal form of the system reflects this numerical progression from apex to base. Man shares an intermediate layer with the bears, raccoons, and squirrels which eat both meat and vegetables.

The lines of dependency for food and other services are called food chains. Thus soil-oak-deer-Indian is a chain that has now been largely converted to soil-corn-cow-farmer. Each species, including ourselves, is a link in many chains. The deer eats a hundred plants other than oak, and the cow a hundred plants other than corn. Both, then, are links in a hundred chains. The pyramid is a tangle of chains so complex as to seem disorderly, yet the stability of the system proves it to be a highly organized structure. Its functioning depends on the co-operation and competition of its diverse parts.

In the beginning, the pyramid of life was low and squat; the food chains short and simple. Evolution has added layer after layer, link after link. Man is one of thousands of accretions to the height and complexity of the pyramid. Science has given us many doubts, but it has given us at least one certainty: the trend of evolution is to elaborate and diversify the biota.

Land, then, is not merely soil; it is a fountain of energy flowing through a circuit of soils, plants, and animals. Food chains are the living channels which conduct energy upward; death and decay return it to the soil. The circuit is not closed; some energy is dissipated in decay, some is added by absorption from the air, some is stored in soils, peats, and long-lived forests; but it is a sustained circuit, like a slowly augmented revolving fund of life. There is always a net loss by downhill wash, but this is normally small and offset by the decay of rocks. It is deposited in the ocean and, in the course of geological time, raised to form new lands and new pyramids.

The velocity and character of the upward flow of energy depend on the complex structure of the plant and animal community, much as the upward flow of sap in a tree depends on its complex cellular organization. Without this complexity, normal circulation would presumably not occur. Structure means the char-acteristic numbers, as well as the characteristic kinds and functions, of the component species. This interdependence between the complex structure of the land and its smooth functioning as an energy unit is one of its basic attributes.

When a change occurs in one part of the circuit, many other parts must adjust themselves to it. Change does not necessarily obstruct or divert the flow of energy; evolution is a long series of self-induced changes, the net result of which has been to elaborate the flow mechanism and to lengthen the circuit. Evolutionary changes, however, are usually slow and local. Man's invention of tools has enabled him to make changes of unprecedented violence, rapidity, and scope.

One change is in the composition of floras and faunas. The larger predators are lopped off the apex of the pyramid; food chains, for the first time in history, become shorter rather than longer. Domesticated species from other lands are substituted for wild ones, and wild ones are moved to new habitats. In this world-wide pooling of faunas and floras, some species get out of bounds as pests and diseases, others are extinguished. Such effects are seldom intended or foreseen; they represent unpredicted and often untraceable readjustments in the structure. Agricultural science is largely a race between the emergence of new pests and the emergence of new techniques for their control.

Another change touches the flow of energy through plants and animals and its return to the soil. Fertility is the ability of soil to receive, store, and release energy. Agriculture, by overdrafts on the soil, or by too radical a substitution of domestic for native species in the superstructure, may derange the channels of flow or deplete storage. Soils depleted of their storage, or of the organic matter which anchors it, wash away faster than they form. This is erosion.

Waters, like soil, are part of the energy circuit. Industry, by polluting waters or obstructing them with dams, may exclude the plants and animals necessary to keep energy in circulation.

Transportation brings about another basic change: the plants or animals grown in one region are now consumed and returned to the soil in another. Transportation taps the energy stored in rocks, and in the air, and uses it elsewhere; thus we fertilize the garden with nitrogen gleaned by the guano birds from the fishes of seas on the other side of the Equator. Thus the formerly localized and self-contained circuits are pooled on a world-wide scale.

The process of altering the pyramid for human occupation releases stored energy, and this often gives rise, during the pioneering period, to a deceptive exuberance of plant and animal life, both wild and tame. These releases of biotic capital tend to becloud or postpone the penalties of violence.

This thumbnail sketch of land as an energy circuit conveys three basic ideas:

1. That land is not merely soil.
2. That the native plants and animals kept the energy circuit open; others may or may not.
3. That man-made changes are of a different order than evolutionary changes, and have effects more comprehensive than is intended or foreseen.

These ideas, collectively, raise two basic issues: Can the land adjust itself to the new order? Can the desired alterations be accomplished with less violence? . . .

The combined evidence of history and ecology seems to support one general deduction: the less violent the man-made changes, the greater the probability of successful readjustment in the pyramid. Violence, in turn, varies with human population density; a dense population requires a more violent conversion. In this respect, North America has a better chance for permanence than Europe, if she can contrive to limit her density.

This deduction runs counter to our current philosophy, which assumes that because a small increase in density enriched human life, that an indefinite increase will enrich it indefinitely. Ecology knows of no density relationship that holds for indefinitely wide limits. All gains from density are subject to a law of diminishing returns.

Whatever may be the equation for men and land, it is improbable that we as yet know all its terms. Recent discoveries in mineral and vitamin nutrition reveal unsuspected dependencies in the up-circuit: incredibly minute quantities of certain substances determine the value of soils to plants, of plants to animals.

What of the down-circuit? What of the vanishing species, the preservation of which we now regard as an esthetic luxury? They helped build the soil; in what unsuspected ways may they be essential to its maintenance? [It has been proposed] . . . that we use prairie flowers to reflocculate the wasting soils of the dust bowl; who knows for what purpose cranes and condors, otters and grizzlies may some day be used?

Land Health and the A-B Cleavage

A land ethic, then, reflects the existence of an ecological conscience, and this in turn reflects a conviction of individual responsibility for the health of the land. Health is the capacity of the land for self-renewal. Conservation is our effort to understand and preserve this capacity.

Conservationists are notorious for their dissensions. Superficially these seem to add up to mere confusion, but a more careful scrutiny reveals a single plane of cleavage common to many specialized fields. In each field one group (A) regards the land as soil, and its function as commodity-production; another group (B) regards the land as a biota, and its function as something broader. How much broader is admittedly in a state of doubt and confusion.

In my own field, forestry, group A is quite content to grow trees like cabbages, with cellulose as the basic forest commodity. It feels no inhibition against violence; its ideology is agronomic. Group B, on the other hand, sees forestry as fundamentally different from agronomy because it employs natural species, and manages a natural environment rather than creating an artificial one. Group B prefers natural reproduction on principle. It worries on biotic as well as economic grounds about the loss of species like chestnut, and the threatened loss of the white pines. It worries about a whole series of secondary forest functions: wildlife, recreation, watersheds, wilderness areas. To my mind, Group B feels the stirrings of an ecological conscience.

In the wildlife field, a parallel cleavage exists. For Group A the basic commodities are sport and meat; the yardsticks of production are ciphers of take in pheasants and trout. Artificial propagation is acceptable as a permanent as well as a temporary recourse—if its unit costs permit. Group B, on the other hand, worries about a whole series of biotic side-issues. What is the cost in predators of producing a game crop? Should we have further recourse to exotics? How can management restore the shrinking species, like prairie grouse, already hopeless as shootable game? How can management restore the threatened rarities, like trumpeter swan and whooping crane? Can management principles be extended to wildflowers? Here again it is clear to me that we have the same A-B cleavage as in forestry. . . .

The ecological fundamentals of agriculture are just as poorly known to the public as in other fields of land-use. For example, few educated people realize that the marvelous advances in technique made during recent decades are improvements in the pump, rather than the well. Acre for acre, they have barely sufficed to offset the sinking level of fertility.

In all of these cleavages, we see repeated the same basic paradoxes: man the conqueror *versus* man the biotic citizen; science the sharpener of his sword *versus* science the searchlight on his universe; land the slave and servant *versus* land the collective organism. Robinson's injunction to Tristram may well be applied, at this juncture, to *Homo sapiens* as a species in geological time:

> Whether you will or not
> You are a King, Tristram, for you are one
> Of the time-tested few that leave the
> world,
> When they are gone, not the same place it
> was.
> Mark what you leave.

The Outlook

It is inconceivable to me that an ethical relation to land can exist without love, respect, and admiration for land, and a high regard for its value. By value, I of course mean something far broader than mere economic value; I mean value in the philosophical sense.

Perhaps the most serious obstacle impeding the evolution of a land ethic is the fact that our educational and economic system is headed away from, rather than toward, an intense consciousness of land. Your true modern is separated from the land by many middlemen, and by innumerable physical gadgets.

He has no vital relation to it; to him it is the space between cities on which crops grow. Turn him loose for a day on the land, and if the spot does not happen to be a golf links or a "scenic" area, he is bored stiff. If crops could be raised by hydroponics instead of farming, it would suit him very well. Synthetic substitutes for wood, leather, wool, and other natural land products suit him better than the originals. In short, land is something he has "outgrown."

Almost equally serious as an obstacle to a land ethic is the attitude of the farmer for whom the land is still an adversary, or a taskmaster that keeps him in slavery. Theoretically, the mechanization of farming ought to cut the farmer's chains, but whether it really does is debatable.

One of the requisites for an ecological comprehension of land is an understanding of ecology, and this is by no means co-extensive with "education"; in fact, much higher education seems deliberately to avoid ecological concepts. An understanding of ecology does not necessarily originate in courses bearing ecological labels; it is quite as likely to be labeled geography, botany, agronomy, history, or economics. This is as it should be, but whatever the label, ecological training is scarce.

The case for a land ethic would appear hopeless but for the minority which is in obvious revolt against these "modern" trends.

The "key-log" which must be moved to release the evolutionary process for an ethic is simply this: quit thinking about decent land-use as solely an economic problem. Examine each question in terms of what is ethically and esthetically right, as well as what is economically expedient. A thing is right when it tends to preserve the integrity, stability, and beauty of the biotic community. It is wrong when it tends otherwise.

It of course goes without saying that economic feasibility limits the tether of what can or cannot be done for land. It always has and it always will. The fallacy the economic determinists have tied around our collective neck, and which we now need to cast off, is the belief that economics determines *all* land-use. This is simply not true. An innumerable host of actions and attitudes, comprising perhaps the bulk of all land relations, is determined by the land-user's tastes and predilections, rather than by his purse. The bulk of all land relations hinges on investments of time, forethought, skill, and faith rather than on investments of cash. As a land-user thinketh, so is he.

I have purposely presented the land ethic as a product of social evolution because nothing so important as an ethic is ever "written." Only the most superficial student of history supposes that Moses "wrote" the Decalogue; it evolved in the minds of a thinking community, and Moses wrote a tentative summary of it for a "seminar." I say tentative because evolution never stops.

The evolution of a land ethic is an intellectual as well as emotional process. Conservation is paved with good intentions which prove to be futile, or even dangerous, because they are devoid of critical understanding either of the land, or of economic land-use. I think it is a truism that as the ethical frontier advances from the individual to the community, its intellectual content increases.

The mechanism of operation is the same for any ethic: social approbation for right actions: social disapproval for wrong actions.

By and large, our present problem is one of attitudes and implements. We are remodeling the Alhambra with a steam-shovel, and we are proud of our yardage. We shall hardly relinquish the shovel, which after all has many good points, but we are in need of gentler and more objective criteria for its successful use.

P. FREIRE

The Pedagogy of the Oppressed

Peace implies a state of satisfaction. But it is very difficult to be satisfied when denied basics such as food, clothing, shelter, education, medical care, and hope. Not surprisingly, therefore, there is little peace in a world characterized by painful differences between the rich and poor, between the haves and the have-nots. Poverty and social oppression may not lead directly to war, but they certainly are not conducive to peace. Indeed, a substantial motivation for military expenditures may well be concern on the part of the "haves" with preventing any fundamental reorganization in the worldwide distribution of power and wealth.

And yet, fundamental changes have begun. With the end of the Cold War, the primary division among the world's inhabitants has shifted from an East-West to a North-South axis. The search for peace must therefore include a search for economic and social betterment.

Measured by life expectancy, calories consumed, years of education, per capita gross domestic product, and so forth, there are extraordinary disparities in wealth, both within and between countries. Especially in so-called Third World countries, grinding poverty is persistent, degrading, miserable, life-shortening, life-threatening and life-denying. Although "development" has long been the preferred solution for poverty among Western elites, others have criticized such approaches as mere masks for continued oppression. Thus, "dependencia" theory—based on the Spanish word for "dependency"—suggests that indigenous peoples and resources are simply being exploited by the wealthier, industrialized states of the North, and that poor people and poor countries are not so much underdeveloped as overexploited, such that poverty results not from neglect but from altogether too much attention! Dependencia theorists point out, for example, that Indonesia, Brazil, and Sudan are rich; only their people are poor.

Poverty is fundamental to the appeal long exerted by communism. Once again, however, our focus is less on specific, ideological proposals than on understanding some of the background issues. One of the most stimulating (and radical) approaches to the issue of poverty is found in the work of revolutionary Brazilian educator and social theorist Paulo Freire, who has long been concerned with those who are oppressed. Freire explores how to break down the wall between the oppressed and their oppressors, between between theory and practice, between teacher and those taught—to achieve true "dialogue," with the goal of moving toward a more egalitarian society.

While the problem of humanization has always, from an axiological point of view, been humankind's central problem, it now takes on the character of an inescapable concern.[1] Concern for humanization leads at once to the recognition of dehumanization, not only as an ontological possibility but as an historical reality. And as an individual perceives the extent of dehumanization, he or she may ask if humanization is a viable possibility. Within history, in concrete, objective contexts, both humanization and dehumanization are possibilities for a person as an uncompleted being conscious of their incompletion.

But while both humanization and dehumanization are real alternatives, only the first is the people's vocation. This vocation is constantly negated, yet it is affirmed by that very negation. It is thwarted by injustice, exploitation, oppression, and the violence of the oppressors; it is affirmed by the yearning of the oppressed for freedom and justice, and by their struggle to recover their lost humanity.

Dehumanization, which marks not only those whose humanity has been stolen, but also (though in a different way) those who have stolen it, is a *distortion* of the vocation of becoming more fully human. This distortion occurs within history; but it is not an historical vocation. Indeed, to admit of dehumanization as an historical vocation would lead either to cynicism or total despair. The struggle for humanization, for the emancipation of labor, for the overcoming of alienation, for the affirmation of men and women as persons would be meaningless. This struggle is possible only because dehumanization, although a concrete historical fact, is *not* a given destiny but the result of an unjust order that engenders violence in the oppressors, which in turn dehumanizes the oppressed.

Because it is a distortion of being more fully human, sooner or later being less human leads the oppressed to struggle against those who made them so. In order for this struggle to have meaning, the oppressed must not, in seeking to regain their humanity (which is a way to create it), become in turn oppressors of the oppressors, but rather restorers of the humanity of both.

This, then, is the great humanistic and historical task of the oppressed: to liberate themselves and their oppressors as well. The oppressors, who oppress, exploit, and rape by virtue of their power, cannot find in this power the strength to liberate either the oppressed or themselves. Only power that springs from the weakness of the oppressed will be sufficiently strong to free both. Any attempt to "soften" the power of the oppressor in deference to the

---

[1] The current movements of rebellion, especially those of youth, while they necessarily reflect the peculiarities of their respective settings, manifest in their essence this preoccupation with people as beings in the world and with the world—preoccupation with *what* and *how* they are "being." As they place consumer civilization in judgment, denounce bureaucracies of all types, demand the transformation of the universities (changing the rigid nature of the teacher-student relationship and placing that relationship within the context of reality), propose the transformation of reality itself so that universities can be renewed, attack old orders and established institutions in the attempt to affirm human beings as the Subjects of decision, all these movements reflect the style of our age, which is more anthropological than anthropocentric.

weakness of the oppressed almost always manifests itself in the form of false generosity; indeed, the attempt never goes beyond this. In order to have the continued opportunity to express their "generosity," the oppressors must perpetuate injustice as well. An unjust social order is the permanent fount of this "generosity," which is nourished by death, despair, and poverty. That is why the dispensers of false generosity become desperate at the slightest threat to its source.

True generosity consists precisely in fighting to destroy the causes which nourish false charity. False charity constrains the fearful and subdued, the "rejects of life," to extend their trembling hands. True generosity lies in striving so that these hands—whether of individuals or entire peoples—need be extended less and less in supplication, so that more and more they become human hands which work and, working, transform the world.

This lesson and this apprenticeship must come, however, from the oppressed themselves and from those who are truly in solidarity with them. As individuals or as peoples, by fighting for the restoration of their humanity they will be attempting the restoration of true generosity. Who is better prepared than the oppressed to understand the terrible significance of an oppressive society? Who suffers the effects of oppression more than the oppressed? Who can better understand the necessity of liberation? They will not gain this liberation by chance but through the praxis of their quest for it, through their recognition of the necessity to fight for it. And this fight, because of the purpose given it by the oppressed, will actually constitute an act of love opposing the lovelessness which lies at the heart of the oppressors' violence, lovelessness even when clothed in false generosity.

But almost always, during the initial stage of the struggle, the oppressed, instead of striving for liberation, tend themselves to become oppressors, or "sub-oppressors." The very structure of their thought has been conditioned by the contradictions of the concrete, existential situation by which they were shaped. Their ideal is to be men; but for them, to be men is to be oppressors. This is their model of humanity. This phenomenon derives from the fact that the oppressed, at a certain moment of their existential experience, adopt an attitude of "adhesion" to the oppressor. Under these circumstances they cannot "consider" him sufficiently clearly to objectivize him—to discover him "outside" themselves. This does not necessarily mean that the oppressed are unaware that they are downtrodden. But their perception of themselves as oppressed is impaired by their submersion in the reality of oppression. At this level, their perception of themselves as opposites of the oppressor does not yet signify engagement in a struggle to overcome the contradiction;[2] the one pole aspires not to liberation, but to identification with its opposite pole.

In this situation the oppressed do not see the "new man" as the person to be born from the resolution of this contradiction, as oppression gives way to liberation. For them, the new man and woman themselves become oppressors. Their vision of the new man or woman is individualistic; because of their identification with the oppressor, they have no consciousness of themselves as persons or as members of an oppressed class. It is not to become free that they want agrarian reform, but in order to acquire land and thus become landowners—or, more precisely, bosses over other workers. It is a rare peasant who, once "promoted" to overseer, does not become more of a tyrant towards his former comrades than the owner himself. This is because the context of the peasant's situation, that is, oppression, remains unchanged. In this example, the overseer, in order to make sure of his job, must be as tough as the owner—and more so. Thus is illustrated our previous assertion that during the initial stage of their struggle the oppressed find in the oppressor their model of "manhood."

Even revolution, which transforms a concrete situation of oppression by establishing the process of liberation, must confront this phenomenon. Many of the oppressed who directly or indirectly participate in revolution intend—conditioned by the myths of the old order—to make it their private revolution. The shadow of their former oppressor is still cast over them.

The "fear of freedom" which afflicts the oppressed,[3] a fear which may equally well lead

---

[2]As used throughout this book, the term "contradiction" denotes the dialectical conflict between opposing social forces.—Translator's note.

---

[3]This fear of freedom is also to be found in the oppressors, though, obviously, in a different form. The oppressed are afraid to embrace freedom; the oppressors are afraid of losing the "freedom" to oppress.

them to desire the role of oppressor or bind them to the role of oppressed, should be examined. One of the basic elements of the relationship between oppressor and oppressed is *prescription*. Every prescription represents the imposition of one individual's choice upon another, transforming the consciousness of the person prescribed to into one that conforms with the prescriber's consciousness. Thus, the behavior of the oppressed is a prescribed behavior, following as it does the guidelines of the oppressor.

The oppressed, having internalized the image of the oppressor and adopted his guidelines, are fearful of freedom. Freedom would require them to eject this image and replace it with autonomy and responsibility. Freedom is acquired by conquest, not by gift. It must be pursued constantly and responsibly. Freedom is not an ideal located outside of man; nor is it an idea which becomes myth. It is rather the indispensable condition for the quest for human completion.

To surmount the situation of oppression, people must first critically recognize its causes, so that through transforming action they can create a new situation, one which makes possible the pursuit of a fuller humanity. But the struggle to be more fully human has already begun in the authentic struggle to transform the situation. Although the situation of oppression is a dehumanized and dehumanizing totality affecting both the oppressors and those whom they oppress, it is the latter who must, from their stifled humanity, wage for both the struggle for a fuller humanity; the oppressor, who is himself dehumanized because he dehumanizes others, is unable to lead this struggle.

However, the oppressed, who have adapted to the structure of domination in which they are immersed, and have become resigned to it, are inhibited from waging the struggle for freedom so long as they feel incapable of running the risks it requires. Moreover, their struggle for freedom threatens not only the oppressor, but also their own oppressed comrades who are fearful of still greater repression. When they discover within themselves the yearning to be free, they perceive that this yearning can be transformed into reality only when the same yearning is aroused in their comrades. But while dominated by the fear of freedom they refuse to appeal to others, or to listen to the appeals of others, or even to the appeals of their own con-

science. They prefer gregariousness to authentic comradeship; they prefer the security of conformity with their state of unfreedom to the creative communion produced by freedom and even the very pursuit of freedom.

The oppressed suffer from the duality which has established itself in their innermost being. They discover that without freedom they cannot exist authentically. Yet, although they desire authentic existence, they fear it. They are at one and the same time themselves and the oppressor whose consciousness they have internalized. The conflict lies in the choice between being wholly themselves or being divided; between ejecting the oppressor within or not ejecting them; between human solidarity or alienation; between following prescriptions or having choices; between being spectators or actors; between acting or having the illusion of acting through the action of the oppressors; between speaking out or being silent, castrated in their power to create and re-create, in their power to transform the world. This is the tragic dilemma of the oppressed which their education must take into account. . . .

The central problem is this: How can the oppressed, as divided, unauthentic beings, participate in developing the pedagogy of their liberation? Only as they discover themselves to be "hosts" of the oppressor can they contribute to the midwifery of their liberating pedagogy. As long as they live in the duality in which *to be* is *to be like,* and *to be like* is *to be like the oppressor,* this contribution is impossible. The pedagogy of the oppressed is an instrument for their critical discovery that both they and their oppressors are manifestations of dehumanization. . . .

Any situation in which "A" objectively exploits "B" or hinders his or her pursuit of self-affirmation as a responsible person is one of oppression. Such a situation in itself constitutes violence, even when sweetened by false generosity, because it interferes with the individual's ontological and historical vocation to be more fully human. With the establishment of a relationship of oppression, violence has *already* begun. Never in history has violence been initiated by the oppressed. How could they be the initiators, if they themselves are the result of violence? How could they be the sponsors of something whose objective inauguration called forth their existence as oppressed? There would be no oppressed had there been no prior situation of violence to establish their subjugation.

Violence is initiated by those who oppress, who exploit, who fail to recognize others as persons—not by those who are oppressed, exploited, and unrecognized. It is not the unloved who initiate disaffection, but those who cannot love because they love only themselves. It is not the helpless, subject to terror, who initiate terror, but the violent, who with their power create the concrete situation which begets the "rejects of life." It is not the tyrannized who initiate despotism, but the tyrants. It is not the despised who initiate hatred, but those who despise. It is not those whose humanity is denied them who negate humankind, but those who denied that humanity (thus negating their own as well). Force is used not by those who have become weak under the preponderance of the strong, but by the strong who have emasculated them.

For the oppressors, however, it is always the oppressed (whom they obviously never call "the oppressed" but—depending on whether they are fellow countrymen or not—"those people" or "the blind and envious masses" or "savages" or "natives" or "subversives") who are disaffected, who are "violent," "barbaric," "wicked," or "ferocious" when they react to the violence of the oppressors.

Yet it is—paradoxical though it may seem—precisely in the response of the oppressed to the violence of their oppressors that a gesture of love may be found. Consciously or unconsciously, the act of rebellion by the oppressed (an act which is always, or nearly always, as violent as the initial violence of the oppressors) can initiate love. Whereas the violence of the oppressors prevents the oppressed from being fully human, the response of the latter to this violence is grounded in the desire to pursue the right to be human. As the oppressors dehumanize others and violate their rights, they themselves also become dehumanized. As the oppressed, fighting to be human, take away the oppressors' power to dominate and suppress, they restore to the oppressors the humanity they had lost in the exercise of oppression.

It is only the oppressed who, by freeing themselves, can free their oppressors. The latter, as an oppressive class, can free neither others nor themselves. It is therefore essential that the oppressed wage the struggle to resolve the contradiction in which they are caught; and the contradiction will be resolved by the appearance of the new man: neither oppressor nor oppressed, but man in the process of liberation. If the goal of the oppressed is to become fully human, they will not achieve their goal by merely reversing the terms of the contradiction, by simply changing poles.

. . . An act is oppressive only when it prevents people from being more fully human. Accordingly, these necessary restraints do not *in themselves* signify that yesterday's oppressed have become today's oppressors. Acts which prevent the restoration of the oppressive regime cannot be compared with those which create and maintain it, cannot be compared with those by which a few men and women deny the majority their right to be human.

However, the moment the new regime hardens into a dominating "bureaucracy" the humanist dimension of the struggle is lost and it is no longer possible to speak of liberation. Hence our insistence that the authentic solution of the oppressor-oppressed contradiction does not lie in a mere reversal of position, in moving from one pole to the other. Nor does it lie in the replacement of the former oppressors with new ones who continue to subjugate the oppressed—all in the name of their liberation. . . .

A careful analysis of the teacher-student relationship at any level, inside or outside the school, reveals its fundamentally *narrative* character. This relationship involves a narrating Subject (the teacher) and patient, listening objects (the students). The contents, whether values or empirical dimensions of reality, tend in the process of being narrated to become lifeless and petrified. Education is suffering from narration sickness.

The teacher talks about reality as if it were motionless, static, compartmentalized, and predictable. Or else he expounds on a topic completely alien to the existential experience of the students. His task is to "fill" the students with the contents of his narration—contents which are detached from reality, disconnected from the totality that engendered them and could give them significance. Words are emptied of their concreteness and become a hollow, alienated, and alienating verbosity.

The outstanding characteristic of this narrative education, then, is the sonority of words, not their transforming power. "Four times four is sixteen; the capital of Pará is Belém." The student records, memorizes, and repeats these phrases without perceiving what four times four really means, or realizing the true significance of "capital" in the affirmation "the capital of Pará is Belém," that is, what Belém means for Pará and what Pará means for Brazil.

Narration (with the teacher as narrator) leads the students to memorize mechanically the narrated content. Worse yet, it turns them into "containers," into "receptacles" to be "filled" by the teacher. The more completely she fills the receptacles, the better a teacher she is. The more meekly the receptacles permit themselves to be filled, the better students they are.

Education thus becomes an act of depositing, in which the students are the depositories and the teacher is the depositor. Instead of communicating, the teacher issues communiqués and makes deposits which the students patiently receive, memorize, and repeat. This is the "banking" concept of education, in which the scope of action allowed to the students extends only as far as receiving, filing, and storing the deposits. They do, it is true, have the opportunity to become collectors or cataloguers of the things they store. But in the last analysis, it is the people themselves who are filed away through the lack of creativity, transformation, and knowledge in this (at best) misguided system. For apart from inquiry, apart from the praxis, individuals cannot be truly human. Knowledge emerges only through invention and re-invention, through the restless, impatient, continuing, hopeful inquiry human beings pursue in the world, with the world, and with each other.

In the banking concept of education, knowledge is a gift bestowed by those who consider themselves knowledgeable upon those whom they consider to know nothing. Projecting an absolute ignorance onto others, a characteristic of the ideology of oppression, negates education and knowledge as processes of inquiry. The teacher presents himself to his students as their necessary opposite; by considering their ignorance absolute, he justifies his own existence. The students, alienated like the slave in the Hegelian dialectic, accept their ignorance as justifying the teacher's existence—but, unlike the slave, they never discover that they educate the teacher.

The *raison d'être* of libertarian education,

on the other hand, lies in its drive towards reconciliation. Education must begin with the solution of the teacher-student contradiction, by reconciling the poles of the contradiction so that both are simultaneously teachers *and* students. . . .

Dialogue cannot exist, . . . in the absence of a profound love for the world and for people. The naming of the world, which is an act of creation and re-creation, is not possible if it is not infused with love. Love is at the same time the foundation of dialogue and dialogue itself. It is thus necessarily the task of responsible Subjects and cannot exist in a relation of domination. Domination reveals the pathology of love: sadism in the dominator and masochism in the dominated. Because love is an act of courage, not of fear, love is commitment to others. No matter where the oppressed are found, the act of love is commitment to their cause—the cause of liberation. And this commitment, because it is loving, is dialogical. As an act of bravery, love cannot be sentimental; as an act of freedom, it must not serve as a pretext for manipulation. It must generate other acts of freedom; otherwise, it is not love. Only by abolishing the situation of oppression is it possible to restore the love which that situation made impossible. If I do not love the world—if I do not love life—if I do not love people—I cannot enter into dialogue.

On the other hand, dialogue cannot exist without humility. The naming of the world, through which people constantly re-create that world, cannot be an act of arrogance. Dialogue, as the encounter of those addressed to the common task of learning and acting, is broken if the parties (or one of them) lack humility. How can I dialogue if I always project ignorance onto others and never perceive my own? How can I dialogue if I regard myself as a case apart from others—mere "its" in whom I cannot recognize other "I"s? How can I dialogue if I consider myself a member of the in-group of "pure" men, the owners of truth and knowledge, for whom all non-members are "these people" or "the great unwashed"? How can I dialogue if I start from the premise that naming the world is the task of an elite and that the presence of the people in history is a sign of deterioration, thus to be avoided? How can I dialogue if I am closed to—and even offended by—the contribution of others? How can I dialogue if I am afraid of being displaced, the mere possibility causing me torment and weakness? Self-sufficiency is incompatible with dialogue. Men and women who lack humility (or have lost it) cannot come to the people, cannot be their partners in naming the world. Someone who cannot acknowledge himself to be as mortal as everyone else still has a long way to go before he can reach the point of encounter. At the point of encounter there are neither utter ignoramuses nor perfect sages; there are only people who are attempting, together, to learn more than they now know.

Dialogue further requires an intense faith in humankind, faith in their power to make and remake, to create and re-create, faith in their vocation to be more fully human (which is not the privilege of an elite, but the birthright of all). Faith in people is an *a priori* requirement for dialogue; the "dialogical man" believes in others even before he meets them face to face. His faith, however, is not naïve. The "dialogical man" is critical and knows that although it is within the power of humans to create and transform, in a concrete situation of alienation individuals may be impaired in the use of that power. Far from destroying his faith in the people, however, this possibility strikes him as a challenge to which he must respond. He is convinced that the power to create and transform, even when thwarted in concrete situations, tends to be reborn. And that rebirth can occur—not gratuitously, but in and through the struggle for liberation—in the supersedence of slave labor by emancipated labor which gives zest to life. Without this faith in people, dialogue is a farce which inevitably degenerates into paternalistic manipulation.

Founding itself upon love, humility, and faith, dialogue becomes a horizontal relationship of which mutual trust between the dialoguers is the logical consequence. It would be a contradiction in terms if dialogue—loving, humble, and full of faith—did not produce this climate of mutual trust, which leads the dialoguers into ever closer partnership in the naming of the world. Conversely, such trust is obviously absent in the anti-dialogics of the banking method of education. Whereas faith in humankind is an *a priori* requirement for dialogue, trust is established by dialogue. Should it founder, it will be seen that the preconditions were lacking. False love, false humility, and feeble faith in others cannot create trust. Trust is contingent on the evidence which one party provides the others of his true, concrete intentions; it cannot exist if that party's words do not coincide with their actions. To say one thing and do another—to take one's own word lightly—cannot inspire trust. To glorify democracy and to silence the people is a farce; to discourse on humanism and to negate people is a lie.

Nor yet can dialogue exist without hope. Hope is rooted in men's incompletion, from which they move out in constant search—a search which can be carried out only in communion with others. Hopelessness is a form of silence, of denying the world and fleeing from it. The dehumanization resulting from an unjust order is not a cause for despair but for hope, leading to the incessant pursuit of the humanity denied by injustice. Hope, however, does not consist in crossing one's arms and waiting. As long as I fight, I am moved by hope; and if I fight with hope, then I can wait.

MARTIN LUTHER KING, JR.

Letter from a Birmingham Jail

Martin Luther King, Jr., was especially concerned with racial prejudice and the absence of civil rights for African Americans in the United States. (As time went on, he expanded this focus to include the problems of poverty and the war in Vietnam.) His "Letter from

From *Why We Can't Wait* by Martin Luther King, Jr. Copyright 1963, 1991. New York: Harper & Row. Reprinted by arrangement with the Heirs to the Estate of Martin Luther King, Jr., c/o Writers House, Inc.

a Birmingham Jail," one of the signal documents of the U.S. civil rights movement, was originally written on the margins of a local newspaper which had published a statement by a number of Georgia ministers denouncing the civil rights campaign in which Rev. King, and many others, had been engaged. This selection could also have been placed in the next chapter, on nonviolence. As a passionate and influential call for social justice, it seems equally appropriate to any consideration of positive peace.

... I am in Birmingham because injustice is here. Just as the prophets of the eighth century B.C. left their villages and carried their "thus saith the Lord" far beyond the boundaries of their home towns, and just as the Apostle Paul left his village of Tarsus and carried the gospel of Jesus Christ to the far corners of the Greco-Roman world, so am I compelled to carry the gospel of freedom beyond my own home town. Like Paul, I must constantly respond to the Macedonian call for aid.

Moreover, I am cognizant of the interrelatedness of all communities and states. I cannot sit idly by in Atlanta and not be concerned about what happens in Birmingham. Injustice anywhere is a threat to justice everywhere. We are caught in an inescapable network of mutuality, tied in a single garment of destiny. Whatever affects one directly, affects all indirectly. Never again can we afford to live with the narrow, provincial "outside agitator" idea. Anyone who lives inside the United States can never be considered an outsider anywhere within its bounds.

... You may well ask: "Why direct action? Why sit-ins, marches and so forth? Isn't negotiation a better path?" You are quite right in calling for negotiation. Indeed, this is the very purpose of direct action. Nonviolent direct action seeks to create such a crisis and foster such a tension that a community which has constantly refused to negotiate is forced to confront the issue. It seeks so to dramatize the issue that it can no longer be ignored. My citing the creation of tension as part of the work of the nonviolent-resister may sound rather shocking. But I must confess that I am not afraid of the word "tension." I have earnestly opposed violent tension, but there is a type of constructive, nonviolent tension which is necessary for growth. Just as Socrates felt that it was necessary to create a tension in the mind so that individuals could rise from the bondage of myths and half-truths to the unfettered realm of creative analysis and objective ap-

praisal, so must we see the need for nonviolent gadflies to create the kind of tension in society that will help men rise from the dark depths of prejudice and racism to the majestic heights of understanding and brotherhood. ...

Lamentably, it is an historical fact that privileged groups seldom give up their privileges voluntarily. Individuals may see the moral light and voluntarily give up their unjust posture; but, as Reinhold Niebuhr has reminded us, groups tend to be more immoral than individuals.

We know through painful experience that freedom is never voluntarily given by the oppressor; it must be demanded by the oppressed. Frankly, I have yet to engage in a direct-action campaign that was "well timed" in the view of those who have not suffered unduly from the disease of segregation. For years now I have heard the word "Wait!" It rings in the ear of every Negro with piercing familiarity. This "Wait" has almost always meant "Never." We must come to see, with one of our distinguished jurists, that "justice too long delayed is justice denied."

We have waited for more than 340 years for our constitutional and God-given rights. The nations of Asia and Africa are moving with jetlike speed toward gaining political independence, but we still creep at horse-and-buggy pace toward gaining a cup of coffee at a lunch counter. Perhaps it is easy for those who have never felt the stinging darts of segregation to say, "Wait." But when you have seen vicious mobs lynch your mothers and fathers at will and drown your sisters and brothers at whim; when you have seen hate-filled policemen curse, kick and even kill your black brothers and sisters; when you see the vast majority of your twenty million Negro brothers smothering in an airtight cage of poverty in the midst of an affluent society; when you suddenly find your tongue twisted and your speech stammering as you seek to explain to your six-year-old daughter why she can't go to the public amusement park that has just been advertised on television, and see tears welling up in her eyes when she is told that Funtown is closed to colored children, and see ominous clouds of inferiority beginning to form in her little mental sky, and see her beginning to distort her personality by developing an unconscious bitterness toward white people; when you have to concoct an answer for a five-year-old son who is asking: "Daddy, why do white people treat colored people so mean?"; when you take a cross-country drive and find it necessary to sleep night after night in the uncomfortable corners of your automobile because no motel will accept you; when you are humiliated day in and day out by nagging signs reading "white" and "colored"; when your first name becomes "nigger," your middle name becomes "boy" (however old you are) and your last name becomes "John," and your wife and mother are never given the respected title "Mrs."; when you are harried by day and haunted by night by the fact that you are a Negro, living constantly at tiptoe stance, never quite knowing what to expect next, and are plagued with inner fears and outer resentments; when you are forever fighting a degenerating sense of "nobodiness"— then you will understand why we find it difficult to wait. There comes a time when the cup of endurance runs over, and men are no longer willing to be plunged into the abyss of despair. I hope, sirs, you can understand our legitimate and unavoidable impatience.

You express a great deal of anxiety over our willingness to break laws. This is certainly a legitimate concern. Since we so diligently urge people to obey the Supreme Court's decision of 1954 outlawing segregation in the public schools, at first glance it may seem rather paradoxical for us consciously to break laws. One may well ask: "How can you advocate breaking some laws and obeying others?" The answer lies in the fact that there are two types of laws: just and unjust. I would be the first to advocate obeying just laws. One has not only a legal but a moral responsibility to obey just laws. Conversely, one has a moral responsibility to disobey unjust laws. I would agree with St. Augustine that "an unjust law is no law at all."

Now, what is the difference between the two? How does one determine whether a law is just or unjust? A just law is a man-made code

that squares with the moral law or the law of God. An unjust law is a code that is out of harmony with the moral law. To put it in the terms of St. Thomas Aquinas: An unjust law is a human law that is not rooted in eternal law and natural law. Any law that uplifts human personality is just. Any law that degrades human personality is unjust. All segregation statutes are unjust because segregation distorts the soul and damages the personality. It gives the segregator a false sense of superiority and the segregated a false sense of inferiority. Segregation, to use the terminology of the Jewish philosopher Martin Buber, substitutes an "I–it" relationship for an "I–thou" relationship and ends up relegating persons to the status of things. Hence segregation is not only politically, economically and sociologically unsound, it is morally wrong and sinful. Paul Tillich has said that sin is separation. Is not segregation an existential expression of man's tragic separation, his awful estrangement, his terrible sinfulness? Thus it is that I can urge men to obey the 1954 decision of the Supreme Court, for it is morally right; and I can urge them to disobey segregation ordinances, for they are morally wrong.

Let us consider a more concrete example of just and unjust laws. An unjust law is a code that a numerical or power majority group compels a minority group to obey but does not make binding on itself. This is *difference* made legal. By the same token, a just law is a code that a majority compels a minority to follow and that it is willing to follow itself. This is *sameness* made legal.

Let me give another explanation. A law is unjust if it is inflicted on a minority that, as a result of being denied the right to vote, had no part in enacting or devising the law. Who can say that the legislature of Alabama which set up that state's segregation laws was democratically elected? Throughout Alabama all sorts of devious methods are used to prevent Negroes from becoming registered voters, and there are some counties in which, even though Negroes constitute a majority of the population, not a single Negro is registered. Can any law enacted under such circumstances be considered democratically structured? . . .

We should never forget that everything Adolf Hitler did in Germany was "legal" and everything the Hungarian freedom fighters did in Hungary was "illegal." It was "illegal" to aid and comfort a Jew in Hitler's Germany.

Even so, I am sure that, had I lived in Germany at the time, I would have aided and comforted my Jewish brothers. If today I lived in a Communist country where certain principles dear to the Christian faith are suppressed, I would openly advocate disobeying that country's antireligious laws. . . .

I had hoped that the white moderate would understand that law and order exist for the purpose of establishing justice and that when they fail in this purpose they become the dangerously structured dams that block the flow of social progress. I had hoped that the white moderate would understand that the present tension in the South is a necessary phase of the transition from an obnoxious negative peace, in which the Negro passively accepted his unjust plight, to a substantive and positive peace, in which all men will respect the dignity and worth of human personality. Actually, we who engage in nonviolent direct action are not the creators of tension. We merely bring to the surface the hidden tension that is already alive. We bring it out in the open, where it can be seen and dealt with. Like a boil that can never be cured so long as it is covered up but must be opened with all its ugliness to the natural medicines of air and light, injustice must be exposed, with all the tension its exposure creates, to the light of human conscience and the air of national opinion before it can be cured.

. . . Human progress never rolls in on wheels of inevitability; it comes through the tireless efforts of men willing to be co-workers with God, and without this hard work, time itself becomes an ally of the forces of social stagnation. We must use time creatively, in the knowledge that the time is always ripe to do right. Now is the time to make real the promise of democracy and transform our pending national elegy into a creative psalm of brotherhood. Now is the time to lift our national policy from the quicksand of racial injustice to the solid rock of human dignity. . . .

Oppressed people cannot remain oppressed forever. The yearning for freedom eventually manifests itself, and that is what has happened to the American Negro. Something within has reminded him of his birthright of freedom, and something without has reminded him that it can be gained. Consciously or unconsciously, he has been caught up by the *Zeitgeist*, and with his black brothers of Africa and his brown and yellow brothers of Asia, South America and the Caribbean, the United States Negro is moving with a sense of great urgency toward the promised land of racial justice. If one recognizes this vital urge that has engulfed the Negro community, one should readily understand why public demonstrations are taking place. The Negro has many pent-up resentments and latent frustrations, and he must release them. So let him march; let him make prayer pilgrimages to the city hall; let him go on freedom rides—and try to understand why he must do so. If his repressed emotions are not released in nonviolent ways, they will seek expression through violence; this is not a threat but a fact of history. So I have not said to my people: "Get rid of your discontent." Rather, I have tried to say that this normal and healthy discontent can be channeled into the creative outlet of nonviolent direct action. And now this approach is being termed extremist.

But though I was initially disappointed at being categorized as an extremist, as I continued to think about the matter I gradually gained a measure of satisfaction from the label. Was not Jesus an extremist for love: "Love your enemies, bless them that curse you, do good to them that hate you, and pray for them which despitefully use you, and persecute you." Was not Amos an extremist for justice: "Let justice roll down like waters and righteousness like an ever-flowing stream." Was not Paul an extremist for the Christian gospel: "I bear in my body the marks of the Lord Jesus." Was not Martin Luther an extremist: "Here I stand; I cannot do otherwise, so help me God." And John Bunyan: "I will stay in jail to the end of my days before I make a butchery of my conscience." And Abraham Lincoln: "This nation cannot survive half slave and half free." And Thomas Jefferson: "We hold these truths to be self-evident, that all men are created equal . . ." So the question is not whether we will be extremists, but what kind of extremists we will be. Will we be extremists for hate or for love? Will we be extremists for the preservation of injustice or for the extension of justice? In that dramatic scene on Calvary's hill three men were crucified. We must never forget that all three were crucified for the same crime—the crime of extremism. Two were extremists for immorality, and thus fell below their environment. The other, Jesus Christ, was an extremist for love, truth and goodness, and thereby rose above his environment. Perhaps the South, the nation and the world are in dire need of creative extremists.

I had hoped that the white moderate would see this need. Perhaps I was too optimistic; perhaps I expected too much. I suppose I should have realized that few members of the oppressor race can understand the deep groans and passionate yearnings of the oppressed race, and still fewer have the vision to see that injustice must be rooted out by strong, persistent and determined action. I am thankful, however, that some of our white brothers in the South have grasped the meaning of this social revolution and committed themselves to it.

. . . I hope the church as a whole will meet the challenge of this decisive hour. But even if the church does not come to the aid of justice, I have no despair about the future. I have no fear about the outcome of our struggle in Birmingham, even if our motives are at present misunderstood. We will reach the goal of freedom in Birmingham and all over the nation, because the goal of America is freedom. Abused and scorned though we may be, our destiny is tied up with America's destiny. Before the pilgrims landed at Plymouth, we were here. Before the pen of Jefferson etched the majestic words of the Declaration of Independence across the pages of history, we were here. For more than two centuries our forebears labored in this country without wages; they made cotton king; they built the homes of their masters while suffering gross injustice and shameful humiliation—and yet out of a bottomless vitality they continued to thrive and develop. If the inexpressible cruelties of slavery could not stop us, the opposition we now face will surely fail. We will win our freedom because the sacred heritage of our nation and the eternal will of God are embodied in our echoing demands.

. . . One day the South will recognize its real heroes. They will be the James Merediths, with the noble sense of purpose that enables them to face jeering and hostile mobs, and with the agonizing loneliness that characterizes the life of the pioneer. They will be old, oppressed, battered Negro women, symbolized in a seventy-two-year-old woman in Montgomery, Alabama, who rose up with a sense of dignity and with her people decided not to ride segregated buses, and who responded with ungrammatical profundity to one who inquired about her weariness: "My feets is tired, but my soul is at rest." They will be the young high school and college students, the young ministers of the gospel and a host of their elders, courageously and nonviolently sitting in at lunch counters and willingly going to jail for conscience' sake. One day the South will know that when these disinherited children of God sat down at lunch counters, they were in reality standing up for what is best in the American dream and for the most sacred values in our Judaeo-Christian heritage, thereby bringing our nation back to those great wells of democracy which were dug deep by the founding fathers in their formulation of the Constitution and the Declaration of Independence.

Never before have I written so long a letter. I'm afraid it is much too long to take your precious time. I can assure you that it would have been much shorter if I had been writing from a comfortable desk, but what else can one do when he is alone in a narrow jail cell, other than write long letters, think long thoughts and pray long prayers?

If I have said anything in this letter that overstates the truth and indicates an unreasonable impatience, I beg you to forgive me. If I have said anything that understates the truth and indicates my having a patience that allows me to settle for anything less than brotherhood, I beg God to forgive me.

I hope this letter finds you strong in the faith. I also hope that circumstances will soon make it possible for me to meet each of you, not as an integrationist or a civil-rights leader but as a fellow clergyman and a Christian brother. Let us all hope that the dark clouds of racial prejudice will soon pass away and the deep fog of misunderstanding will be lifted from our fear-drenched communities, and in some not too distant tomorrow the radiant stars of love and brotherhood will shine over our great nation with all their scintillating beauty.

Yours for the cause of
Peace and Brotherhood,
Martin Luther King, Jr.

DAVID P. BARASH

Human Rights

Like Mark Twain's celebrated remark about the weather, it sometimes appears that everyone talks about human rights, but no one does anything about it. The truth, fortunately, is otherwise. To some extent, moreover, talking about human rights *is* doing something about it, since in many cases a focused attention to human rights, combined with the power of the international community's approval or disapproval, can be surprisingly effective.

The situation, however, is rather grim: nearly half the world's people are denied democratic freedoms and participation; more than half of Asia and black Africa do not have access to safe water; jails are filled with political prisoners, many of them held without trial and victimized by torture; child labor is widespread; women are often deprived of the economic, social, and political rights that men take for granted; many workers are not only non-unionized, but prohibited even from forming unions; the right of conscientious objection to military service is not recognized in most countries; censorship is widespread; many millions of people are illiterate, chronically sick, without adequate shelter, and just plain hungry; the basic rights of homosexuals, indigenous people, the elderly, and the deviant are routinely trampled. And yet, concern with human rights has been growing, and real progress is being made, with more anticipated.

A Brief History of Human Rights

It is tempting to claim that human rights are as old as the human species, but in truth, this is not so. Even if human rights themselves are God-given, inalienable, and fundamental, the conception of human rights as such—and respect for them—is relatively new. Individuals may possess rights and privileges, but these have traditionally been considered the province of society, to be bestowed or revoked by the larger unit (band, tribe, village, city, state) at will. In virtually all societies, for virtually all of human history, ultimate value derived from the social order, not the individual. Hence, an individual human being could not claim entitlement to very much, if anything, simply because he or she existed as a human being. . . .

It was not until the Enlightenment, particularly in Europe, that the concept of universal human rights for all people first gained prominence. It had existed before, but prima-

rily as a smattering of isolated thought rather than a consistent, widespread trend.

According to this new perspective, a body of human rights exists that are intrinsic and not provable; they stem ultimately from the natural order of things, not from the laws of society or from human logic. Hence, this approach derives human rights from what is called "natural law," with its implication that such rights are established by an authority even higher than that of governments. Heraclitus (about 500 B.C.) wrote that "all human laws are nourished by one, which is divine. For it governs as far as it will, and is sufficient for all, and more than enough." And Aristotle, in his *Ethics*, advanced the notion that "of political justice, part is natural, part legal—natural, that which everywhere has the same force and does not exist by people's thinking this or that." When the natural law viewpoint reappeared during the Enlightenment, it was used especially to counter claims that kings ruled

From *Introduction to Peace Studies* by David P. Barash. 1991. Belmont, Calif: Wadsworth.

with absolute authority and by divine right. Finally, by the seventeenth and eighteenth centuries, the concept crystalized that people possess inherent rights, and that it is society's job to *recognize* these preexisting rights, not to create them.

The idea of human rights as currently understood . . . is largely a Western tradition, deriving especially from the work of John Locke and John Stuart Mill. Locke maintained that the fundamental human right was the right to property, the primary one being the right to the secure ownership of one's own body; civil and political rights flowed, in his view, from this. And Mill strove to identify a set of rights not covered by the state. Thus, there is some truth to the criticism that Western human rights advocates may occasionally be guilty of moral arrogance, seeking to export their own rather culture-bound ideas, especially their emphasis on civil/political freedom.

It should also be emphasized that Western political thought is not limited to individualism and human rights; rather, it coexists with respect for—and often, virtual worship of—the state. According to influential theorists such as Hegel and Herder, rights are enlarged and created for individuals only through the actions of the state. And for orthodox Marxists, value derives only from the social order; in Marxist analysis, individual rights do not exist unless they are explicitly granted by society. Although communist societies are supposedly designed to maximize the benefits of every person, the "rights" of each individual come to naught if they run counter to the greater good of society as a whole. Individuals can expect to receive benefits from a community only insofar as they participate in it, and further its goals. And as we shall see, even today—with ever-increasing agreement on the meaning and desirability of human rights— there continues to be substantial disagreement as to priorities.

HUMAN RIGHTS IN THE TWENTIETH CENTURY

Internationally, there was very little concern with human rights until quite recently, after World War II. Despite the Enlightenment, despite capitalism's emphasis on individual property rights, and despite democracy's emphasis on individual political rights, as a practical matter, state sovereignty has long superceded human rights. When the worldwide state system was established in the mid-seventeenth century, governments agreed— ostensibly in the interest of world peace—not to concern themselves very much with how other governments treated their own citizens. Within its own boundaries, each state was supreme and could do as it wished.

Gradually, however, human rights law developed, initially out of concern for protecting persons during armed conflict. The Geneva Convention of 1864, for example, sought to establish standards for treatment of wounded soldiers and of prisoners. (It is ironic that war—the most inhumane of situations— should have led to the first organized recognition of shared humanitarian values.) The International Committee of the Red Cross is a notable nongovernmental organization long concerned with international human rights; it was organized by a group of Swiss citizens, involved in the 1864 Geneva Conference. . . .

Following World War I, there was widespread recognition that one cause of that conflict had been the denial of national rights within large empires such as Austria's. Hence, human rights received explicit attention from the League of Nations, which emphasized that the rights of minorities must be respected by larger federal governments. Labor rights—the right to organize and to decent working conditions and wages, and restrictions on child labor—were the focus of the International Labor Organization, which later functioned within the United Nations. Opposition to slavery catalyzed numerous early human rights organizations, such as the Anti-Slavery League. (Most Americans do not realize that in many countries, slavery was only abolished during the 1950s; some claim that it is still being practiced today, in Mauritania and Pakistan.)

Organized, worldwide concern for human rights did not really coalesce until after World War II, perhaps in part as a reaction to the devastating denials of rights that occurred in association with that conflict. In the aftermath of the Nazi Holocaust most especially, the world's conscience was finally activated— partly out of regret for those who had suffered, and partly, too, out of enlightened self-interest. Martin Niemoeller put it memorably:

> First they came for the Jews and I did not speak out—because I was not a Jew. Then

they came for the communists and I did not speak out—because I was not a communist. Then they came for the trade unionists and I did not speak out—because I was not a trade unionist. Then they came for me—and there was no one left to speak out for me.[4]

In recent decades, the world's people have begun to speak out for themselves and for human rights of every sort. Before we review some of the legal protections, conventions, and treaties that have resulted, let us consider the question of what is meant by human rights, and how they have come to be asserted.

The Political Philosophy of Human Rights

Human rights implies a new way of viewing the relationship of governments and their peoples, whereby governance is intended to enhance the dignity of human beings, not exploit them. With this in mind, let us examine three major political philosophies of human rights, each of which is divisible into two branches.

LIBERALISM

In traditional liberal thought, human rights exist not only because of their contribution to human dignity, but also because human beings, themselves, naturally possess such rights. "The object of any obligation," wrote the philosopher Simone Weil,

> in the realm of human affairs, is always the human being as such. There exists an obligation towards every human being for the sole reason that he or she is a human being, ...

In Jefferson's phrase, people have certain "inalienable rights" that may not be denied. The liberal view of human rights thus corresponds to the "natural law" perspective. One of the great classical liberals, John Locke, argued that civil law, to be valid, must be tested against this "natural law," which is the ultimate arbiter of justice. And when the

framers of the Declaration of Independence complained of a "long train of abuses and usurpations" on the part of King George III, it was precisely natural law that they believed was being abused and usurped.

Another liberal theory of human rights derives from "utilitarianism," especially the works of John Stuart Mill and Jeremy Bentham. The idea here is that society should value whatever is utilitarian, or useful, in maximizing human happiness and freedom. The best-known motto of utilitarianism is "the greatest good for the greatest number," although individual freedom and equality are recognized as well, so as to prevent tyranny by the majority. Social betterment is to be achieved through equality and maximum personal liberty. . . .

CONSERVATISM

Traditional conservatism is rarely articulated today with respect to human rights, because it is in large part a philosophy of unequal rights and privileges, and as such, difficult to defend in an avowedly egalitarian age. But the unspoken tenets of conservatism are nonetheless influential in actual practice. Classical conservatism can be said to have originated with Plato, who argued in *The Republic* that all people are not equal, and that the best form of government is therefore not democracy, but rule by a philosopher–king. This belief in unequal rights underpins many right-wing governments, from the "classical conservatism" of the military juntas that ruled Brazil and Greece, as well as the various U.S.-sponsored Central American governments (Guatemala, Honduras, Panama), to the neo-fascist dictatorships that arose in Chile and Paraguay, where rights were reserved only for the most powerful.

GROUP-ORIENTED PHILOSOPHIES

Finally, there is a third branch of human rights philosophy, which, for want of a better term, might be called "group-oriented." It can be subdivided into two branches, Marxist and nationalist. For Karl Marx, individuals were not independent actors; rather, they were controlled by economic forces, pawns in a relentless class struggle. In the Marxist view, the liberal emphasis on individual rights is therefore misplaced, a bourgeois luxury, form without substance. Instead, rights are conferred by society, and they should belong exclusively to

---

[4]In fact, Pastor Niemoeller himself became a victim of the Nazis.

the proletariat (the working class). Such an approach leads automatically to an embrace of socioeconomic rights and material equality, with a downplaying of civil/political rights. Thus, in Marxist societies, freedom of speech and opinion are permitted insofar as they do not conflict with the stated goals of group advancement and welfare. The state, and not the working class, typically becomes paramount. . . .

The second version of group-oriented human rights has a leftist flavor, but is not, strictly speaking, Marxist. It originates instead in the experience of national liberation movements, and places special emphasis on the right to national self-determination and economic development, from which all other rights are then derived. Believers in the human right to national self-determination downplay the individual as well as the social class, although they remain committed to equal rights. Emphasis instead is on the rights of a national grouping. This approach lay behind the "Universal Declaration of the Rights of Peoples," which grew out of a meeting of highly regarded, nongovernmental Third World spokespersons in 1976. The first three articles in this thirty-article document read as follows:

1. Every people has the right to existence.
2. Every people has the right to the respect of its national and cultural identity.
3. Every people has the right to retain peaceful possession of its territory and to return to it if it is expelled.

. . . The emphasis on "people's rights" clearly distinguishes this approach from the Western focus on "individual rights."

Nationalist group-oriented regimes are found in many Third World states, such as Algeria and Zimbabwe, which are often leftist, but rarely communist. Tanzanian president Julius Nyerere was one of the most articulate spokespersons for the nationalist group-oriented point of view:

> For what do we mean when we talk of freedom? First, there is national freedom; that is, the ability of the citizens of Tanzania to determine their own future, and to govern themselves without interference from non-Tanzanians. Second, there is freedom from hunger, disease, and poverty. And third,

there is personal freedom for the individual; that is, his right to live in dignity and equality with all others, his right to freedom of speech.

The difference between this viewpoint and the others (classical and egalitarian liberal, classical and neo-fascist conservative, Marxist group-oriented) is more one of emphasis than of absolutes. But the "rights" associated with individual competition—so dear to the liberal conception of human rights—are devalued. "The important thing for us," explains Nyerere, "is the extent to which we succeed in preventing the exploitation of one man by another, and in spreading the concept of working together cooperatively for the common good instead of competitively for individual private gain." . . .

On balance, capitalist democracies give insufficient attention to socioeconomic rights, while socialist governments take inadequate account of civil/political ones. Recent evidence suggests that economic development is more rapid under capitalism: but relatively little benefit from such development actually reaches the poorest citizens. . . .

Those who are wealthy and privileged characteristically favor maximum freedom (especially, freedom of economic competition) and a minimal role for government, which, at least in the United States, often leads in turn to opposition to the "welfare state" or resistance to affirmative action plans. Those lacking in wealth and power are typically more in need of laws and specified rights, to be assured by society. Hence, Western governments tend to describe socioeconomic rights as not really "human rights" at all, but rather, goals or aspirations for society.

As we shall see, human rights can be characterized in many ways, although a global consensus has been developing that incorporates not only the traditional American concern with political liberty, but also the Second and Third World concern with socioeconomic rights, as well as additional values that are difficult to pigeonhole. Many other rights are also asserted—states' rights, consumer rights—but to suggest that something is a "human right" is to claim something particularly fundamental and weighty, and should not be done lightly. . . .

Citizens of the United States need to recognize the importance that large numbers of people, especially in the Second and Third Worlds, attribute to socioeconomic rights. In the words of Leopold Senghor, former president of Senegal, "human rights begin with breakfast." Without such an awareness, relatively well-off Westerners too quickly sneer at the poor "rights" records of other countries, oblivious to their own shortcomings in the eyes of others. In addition, once we recognize the validity of socioeconomic rights, then governments such as Libya under Qaddafi or Cuba under Castro—which to many in the West are failures in the civil/political sphere because of their lack of representative government, widespread censorship, and torture and abuse of political prisoners—can be recognized as effective, even admirable, in other domains, such as public health or literacy. (This is not to claim that success in some dimensions of human rights cancels outrages in another; rather, it helps permit a more balanced perception of systems that might otherwise seem unidimensionally evil, and whose high level of domestic acceptance would otherwise be difficult for Americans to understand.) Thus, in an effort to identify basic human rights, Richard Falk has proposed the following:

1. *Basic human needs:* the rights of individuals and groups to food, housing, health, and education; the duty of governments to satisfy these rights . . .
2. *Basic decencies:* the rights of individuals and groups to be protected against genocide, torture, arbitrary arrest, detention, and execution, or their threat; . . .
3. *Participatory rights:* the rights of individuals and groups to participate in the processes that control their lives, including choice of political leadership, of job, of place of residence, or cultural activity and orientation; . . .
4. *Security rights:* the rights of individuals and groups (including those of unborn generations) to be reasonably secure about their prospects of minimal physical well-being and survival; the duty of governments and peoples to uphold this right by working to achieve sustainable forms of national and ecological security. . . .

THE RIGHTS OF CATEGORIES OF PEOPLE

We have thus far focused on the various rights themselves (civil, political, social, economic, and so on), rather than on the categories of people in whom such rights are supposed to inhere. But these categories are in many cases so important that, by themselves, they constitute major areas of concern. Women's rights is one example. Women comprise more than 50 percent of the world's population, and yet they are without doubt an oppressed group. For centuries, women have suffered from patriarchal social structures that devalue their personhood and deny many of their basic human rights. This includes a diverse array of abuses, such as footbinding in precommunist China, the forced seclusion and isolation of women in certain modern-day Hindu and Moslem societies, sexual mutilation as currently practiced on millions of young women in several African societies, polygamy, restricted or nonexistent choice as to marriage, and—even in ostensibly "liberated" societies such as those of the United States and Great Britain—greatly restricted economic and professional opportunities along with underrepresentation in political life.

Other groups also deserve attention. There are about 200 million indigenous people worldwide, representing national majorities in such states as Guatemala and Bolivia, and small minorities in such states as Brazil, Australia, and the United States. Regardless of their numbers, indigenous people are generally in dire straits, sometimes—as in Guatemala or Brazil—being subjected to out-right genocide. In other cases, they are severely maltreated, and/or they enjoy dramatically fewer opportunities and privileges than their nonnative counterparts. Australian aborigines are the most imprisoned people on Earth, with an incarceration rate sixteen times that of the Caucasian population; the life expectancy of Mayan Indians in Guatemala is eleven years shorter than that of the nonindigenous population; the average per capita income of native Americans is one half that of the rest of the U.S. population; large dams have devastated the homelands of indigenous peoples in Canada, Brazil, Norway, the Philippines, and India, depriving them of an arguably crucial human right: to live in their ancestral homelands. And this is but a partial list.

Other groups can also be identified as having particular human rights claims and vulnerabilities: the mentally ill, children, the homeless, racial minorities, the handicapped, convicts, unskilled workers, migrant laborers, refugees, political dissidents, the elderly, and so on. Ideally, human rights such as civil freedoms, economic opportunity, protection from mass destruction, and the right to a safe and clean environment will be equally shared by all people. In practice, these rights must often be defended most vigilantly for those groups that have thus far been the most victimized. . . .

It seems unavoidable that various rights will conflict. In a famous opinion, U.S. Supreme Court justice Oliver Wendell Holmes concluded that the right to free speech did not extend to yelling "Fire" in a crowded theater. The "right" to a drug-free environment may conflict with the "rights" to privacy, just as the "right" of Third World people to healthy babies has already been found to conflict with the "right" of the Nestlé company to market substandard infant formula. In Islamic states, women's "rights" are often subordinated to the "rights" of people to practice the religion of their choice. A woman's "right" to control her own body, including an abortion if she desires, runs contrary to a fetus's "right" to life; the "right" of religious freedom can conflict with a child's "right" to necessary medical care, as when fundamentalist parents refuse life-saving treatment for their child; the public's "right" to safe air travel appears to have triumphed over individual "rights" not to be searched without a warrant; and the list goes on. . . .

However they are sliced, many human rights are essentially claims against the authority of governments. As such, they are freedoms *from*—guarantees that governments will refrain from behaving badly toward their own people. These can be distinguished from freedoms *to*—the asserted obligations of society to help its members to achieve a better life. This distinction somewhat parallels the one between negative and positive peace—between those rights asserted *against* governments (no war, no intrusions into personal freedom) and those expected *of* them (establish positive peace, provide for basic human needs). In most cases, the first category (negative rights) seems easier for governments to achieve; certain states may simply lack the resources to make substantial improvements in socioeconomic conditions, but they all can stop torturing, murdering, and otherwise oppressing their people. . . .

UN-RELATED AGREEMENTS

In assessing the legal status of human rights, the UN Charter represents a useful starting point. Its major reference to human rights appears in Article 55:

> With a view to the creation of conditions of stability and well-being which are necessary for peaceful and friendly relations among nations based on respect for the principle of equal rights and self-determination of peoples, the United Nations shall promote: a. higher standards of living, full employment, and conditions of economic and social progress and development; b. solutions of international economic, social, health, and related problems, and international cultural and educational cooperation; and c. universal respect for, and observance of, human rights and fundamental freedoms for all without distinction as to race, sex, language, or religion.

But if the UN Charter serves as a constitution, it lacks a bill of rights, specifying which human rights are to be "respected" and "observed." This was accomplished largely by the UN-sponsored Universal Declaration of Human Rights (UDHR), passed unanimously in 1948. Thus, after the UN Charter endorsed human rights, the Universal Declaration went ahead and enumerated them. The United States was a major contributor to the UDHR; much of its impetus came from Eleanor Roosevelt, widow of the late U.S. president. The UDHR consists of thirty articles, of which the first twenty-one are primarily civil/political, prohibiting torture and arbitrary arrest, and guaranteeing freedom of assembly, religion, speech, emigration, and even the right to vote by secret ballot. The remaining articles are concerned with socioeconomic and cultural rights, including the right to work, to an "adequate" standard of living, to an education, and to some form of social security, and even specifying the right to vacations with pay.

The Universal Declaration is not technically binding in the sense of an international treaty; it is a recommendation only, and makes no provisions for enforcement. Nonetheless, it has had substantial impact on thinking worldwide. The UDHR is widely respected, and has legitimated concern with human rights; it has even been incorporated into many national constitutions. To some degree, it has become part of customary international law; accordingly, many judicial scholars argue that it has the literal force of law, although it is often violated. (It should be noted that customary law is more universal and more durable than treaty law.) . . .

People dispute precisely what obligations member states undertake when, in the UN Charter, they agree to "promote universal respect for and observance" of human rights. Nonetheless, an underlying consensus has emerged. The accepted phrase is that governments have no business engaging in a "consistent pattern of gross violations of human rights." Thus, isolated incidents are unlikely to generate worldwide outrage. By contrast, "gross violations"—that is, serious, recurring acts—merit condemnation and, ultimately, such actions as censure, economic boycott, and possibly even military intervention. Abuses of this sort could include widespread torture, mass arrests and imprisonment without trial, genocide, and vicious policies of racial segregation and debasement. . . .

THE PROBLEM OF ENFORCEMENT

Faced with the awesome, sovereign power of states, the international human rights regime can seem woefully inadequate, based as it is on mere legalisms or exhortations, and devoid of enforcement mechanisms. But legal systems always have difficulty controlling powerful actors—labor unions in Britain, for example, or large corporations in the United States. And ultimately, most of them rely on voluntary compliance. Some states have in fact complied voluntarily with international human rights norms, largely to achieve international legitimacy as well as to avoid ostracism.

Frustration with the rights-denying policies of states occasionally spills over into efforts to transcend the authority of states. Although lacking in legal authority, individuals of high moral and international standing have on occasion gathered together to fill what they see as a vacuum in the protection of human rights. So-called people's tribunals have periodically convened to draw attention to various human rights abuses. Most notable of these was the Russell Tribunal, which roundly criticized U.S. policy during the Vietnam War. The League for the Rights of Peoples, established in Rome in 1976, has held numerous sessions, evaluating

repression under Marcos in the Philippines, offering a retrospective on Turkish genocide against Armenians from 1915 to 1916, and criticizing Brazil's behavior toward its indigenous Amazonian population, Indonesia's strong-arm tactics in East Timor, U.S. intervention in Central America, and Soviet intervention in Afghanistan, as well as questioning the legitimacy of nuclear weapons. Such actions are of uncertain effectiveness, but they do attract a degree of public attention, while also serving to undercut the presumption that only state-centered approaches are relevant in dealing with violations of human rights. . . .

An approach that emphasizes human rights represents a fundamentally new way of thinking about human dignity and world politics, reflecting as it does the determination that states must meet certain standards, both in their own domestic affairs and in their international relations. Even today, after several decades of vigorous prohuman rights advocacy, states typically act with primary regard to their power and perceived national interests, rather than according to the ideals of human rights. There is, as a result, the constant danger that concern for human rights will be sacrificed on the altar of state sovereignty, expediency, and realpolitik.

Human rights advocacy involves a different perspective from which to view the human condition and the goals of society and politics—as citizens of a larger community than individual states or nation-states. As opposed to the relatively narrow focus of states, concern with superordinate human rights requires that political barriers be transcended, in the search for human dignity on the widest possible scale. . . .

Human Rights and Peace

Human rights and peace are inextricably connected, in several ways. First, the denial of human rights is itself a denial of peace. A world in which there is no armed conflict, but in which fundamental human rights are thwarted, could not in any meaningful sense be considered peaceful. Speaking at the United Nations, Pope John Paul II explicitly linked human rights and war:

> The Universal Declaration of Human Rights has struck a real blow against the

many deep roots of war since the spirit of war in its basic primordial meaning springs up . . . where the inalienable rights of men are violated. This is a new and deeply relevant vision of the cause of peace. One that goes deeper and is more radical.

The pope's perspective applies to socioeconomic rights no less than civil/political ones. As one Scandinavian peace researcher has noted, "Whether a child dies in infancy due to poverty and consequent malnutrition and lack of hygiene, or if it grows up and at a later stage is executed as a political opponent, the society in which this happens must be considered hostile to human rights." And, we might add, to peace as well.

Second, there appears to be a connection between the way a state treats its own population and its inclinations toward other states. As Franklin Roosevelt put it, "We in this nation still believe that it [self-determination] should be predicated on certain freedoms which we think are essential everywhere. We know that we ourselves will never be wholly safe at home unless other governments recognize such freedoms." . . .

Third, a denial of human rights can provoke breaches of the peace, if other states become involved. Humanitarian intervention of this sort may be legal; certainly, there is ample precedent in the classical writings of international law. . . .

On the other hand, claims of humanitarian intervention have often been used as an excuse for aggression (of which the Spanish-American War may well be an example). Hitler claimed that dismemberment of Czechoslovakia and, later, the invasion of Poland were warranted to stop the persecution of both countries' German-speaking minorities. Vietnam invaded Cambodia ostensibly to oust the genocidal Khmer Rouge regime, and the United States explained its invasion of Grenada at least partly as a response to human rights violations on that Caribbean island. . . . (No comparable justifications were ever used by the United States to overthrow rightist regimes, including the Somoza dictatorship, which was far more abusive of human rights, or the government of El Salvador. . . .)

Finally, one of the widely recognized human rights—specified in the first articles of both 1966 human rights conventions—is that of national self-determination. Abuses of this right often lead directly to war, especially civil war . . . which makes this issue a difficult one. The pursuit of human rights may in fact lead more to violence than to peace, since human rights often are won by struggle and confrontation. Furthermore, it is not obvious whether all claims for national self-determination are worthy of success: Should there be independent states for . . . Basques, Welsh, Scots, Quebecois, and native Americans? For its part, the UN Security Council has determined that, at least in certain cases, such as anticolonial struggles, a continuing denial of human rights constitutes a formal threat to international peace (this was applied to Zimbabwe, Namibia, and South Africa).

In summary, the connection between human rights and peace is complex and multifaceted. It is useful to claim that human rights contribute to peace, but the most fundamental connection may well be that such claims encourage adherence to human rights, for their own sake, regardless of whether this actually promotes peace as narrowly defined.

The Future

What of the future? Several things can be said with confidence. The first is that the question of human rights will continue to demand attention on the international agenda. . . .

A second safe conclusion is that the question of human rights will continue to be controversial, with different conceptions competing with one another, while the very notion of human rights competes with the basic inclination of states to engage in amoral, realpolitik maneuverings. The dilemma may be profound. Consider these realpolitik questions, for example, from the perspective of a government leader. What should a state do when confronted with this choice: It desires a particular strategic relationship with another state, but that other state engages in human rights abuses? Which should be sacrificed, national strategy or a commitment to human rights? . . .

Perhaps, on the other hand, the "natural law" school is correct, and support of human rights is simply the right thing to do, period, regardless of its practical consequences. . . .

There is yet another possibility, a way

station between the amorality of realpolitik and the absolutism of morality for its own sake. Some argue that power (or at least, security) can readily be reconciled with human rights. . . . Former Secretary of State Cyrus Vance echoed this sentiment when he observed: "We pursue our human rights objectives, not only because they are right, but because we have a stake in the stability that comes when people can express their hopes and find their futures freely. Our ideals and our interests coincide."

PROMOTING HUMAN RIGHTS

It is difficult to imagine exactly what a U.S. foreign policy would be if it was organized primarily around the promotion of human rights worldwide. However, the following specific actions, which have already been taken at different times in support of human rights, suggest the benefits to be gained from a continuation, to say nothing of an expansion, of such policies:

- *Subtle diplomacy.* Quiet, persistent pressure raised with offending governments has the advantage that the government in question need not worry about losing face if and when abuses are corrected. A disadvantage, beyond the high chance of being ignored, is that a government may claim that it is employing subtle diplomacy while it is actually doing nothing.

- *Public statements.* This involves drawing world attention to specific abuses and to governments that violate human rights. It may involve publicly dissociating one's own government from the unacceptable behavior of another. Human rights compliance can be promoted by publicizing violations through the publication of reports conducted by respected, impartial investigative commissions; especially in a world climate committed to human rights, most governments seek to avoid the embarrassment that comes with being branded a violator of these rights.

- *Symbolic acts.* Sending support to dissidents, either by words, by contact with opposition figures, or by otherwise indicating disapproval of abuses, is a way of

emphasizing to both the offending government and its people that human rights violations are noticed and rejected.

- *Cultural penalties.* By isolating offenders at international cultural events, including athletic contests and other exchanges, such governments are made to feel like pariahs. Although it is easy to scoff at such minimal "penalties," pride and the universal desire to be accepted enhance the impact of such actions.

- *Economic penalties.* Applying trade embargoes, renouncing investment in the offending country, refusing development loans and other forms of foreign aid—these actions can hurt the economy of offending countries, thereby putting pressure (often on the more wealthy and influential citizens) to modify policies and/or oust the government. . . .

- *Immigration.* Human rights activists, dissidents, and those being deprived of their human rights can be permitted to enter the United States. In the recent past, the "right" of immigration has been applied quite selectively, facilitating immigration by people fleeing leftist countries whose human rights policies the United States wishes to criticize, while making it very difficult for refugees from rightist countries that are allied to the United States, and whose human rights policies it is inclined to ignore or whitewash.

- *Legal approaches.* International law can be applied more vigorously, by indicting violators of human rights overseas, just as people involved in the international drug trade have occasionally been indicted and, when possible, extradited for trial.

- *Multilateral approaches.* The United States can commit itself to the various human rights organizations now active worldwide, especially the United Nations Commission on Human Rights. . . .

- *Destabilization and belligerency.* The United States has actively sought to destabilize the governments of certain countries—for example, Nicaragua—at least in part, we are told, for their human rights abuses. This remains an option, although of questionable legality or morality, unless the abuses are sufficiently flagrant, and unless the policy is applied even-handedly to all regimes, regardless of ideology. Certainly, the human rights abuses of Nazi Germany and imperial Japan were influential in the U.S. decision to make war upon them, although these abuses actually became more serious after war was declared. The Tanzanian invasion of Uganda, which ultimately toppled the government of Idi Amin, won widespread support because that regime's human rights record was particularly atrocious. . . .

We conclude our discussion of human rights with an account by Jerome Shestack, a long-time human rights activist. Shestack recognizes the extraordinarily difficult and seemingly hopeless task of securing human rights worldwide, in the face of human cruelty,

frailty, misunderstandings, and the power of states. He conjures up the Greek myth of Sisyphus, who was condemned to spend eternity pushing a boulder up a hill, only to have it roll back again just as he reached the top. Sisyphus' task is absurd, and yet—echoing the existential philosopher Albert Camus—Shestack points out that

> Sisyphus may turn out to be a more enduring hero than Hercules. For if, as Camus taught, life itself is absurd, Sisyphus represents the only triumph possible over that absurdity. In his constancy to reach that summit, even with failure preordained, Sisyphus demonstrated that the human spirit is indomitable and that dedication to a higher goal is in itself man's reason for living. . . . The realities of the world may foredoom a great part of the struggle and make most of the effort seem abysmal. Yet, the very struggle itself takes on symbolic meaning, enhancing human dignity. And when all is said and done, there is no other humane course to pursue.

OXFAM

An Agenda for Change

Poverty persists as an underlying cause, as well as an effect, of structural violence. It also lurks behind much of the world's overt violence and is, in any event, a constant rebuke to any conception of human dignity and positive peace. Although the world as a whole is, in a sense, wealthy, great disparities exist and, in some places, these disparities have been increasing. Many factors contribute to this, including (but not limited to) population pressure, environmental degradation, governmental corruption, traditions of helplessness and hopelessness, exploitation by local socio-economic systems as well as by foreign countries and multinational corporations. In the struggle against world poverty and economic injustice—as with many efforts towards positive peace—so-called "NGOs" have been especially prominent. Because of their independence from state authority and narrowly defined state interests, these Non-Governmental Organizations have often been on the cutting edge of practical action as well as theoretical concept development. In the

From *The Oxfam Poverty Report* by Kevin Watkins, ed. 1995. Reprinted by permission of Oxfam, U.K. (Oxfam GB is a development and relief agency working to put an end to poverty world-wide. Oxfam GB is a member of Oxfam International.)

arena of world poverty, a prominent and effective organization is the British-based Oxfam, source of the following selection. It is worth noting that some of Oxfam's recommendations—such as a ban on antipersonnel land mines—have been instituted, although the United States, along with certain other countries, has refused to sign.

People are not developed, they develop themselves.

—Julius Nyerere

Working for an alternative approach to development has to be seen as a process ... It implies continuous changes, as well as uniting people from across the entire social spectrum in a common purpose. There are many obstacles to be overcome, one of the main ones being to deal with the present situation, while simultaneously working to build an alternative to it.

—Eduardo Klien, Oxfam Deputy Regional Representative, Central America

Though the challenges are great and the situation is complex, we have hope that we can change conditions and build a better tomorrow.

—Declaration from Southern Women's Organisations presented at Women Linking for Change Conference, Thailand, 1994

The Challenge of Poverty

There can be no greater indictment of our world than the fact that one in four of its inhabitants is consigned to poverty. This represents a denial of rights and a wastage of human potential on a massive scale. If the present pattern of development is allowed to continue unchallenged, the future is a frightening prospect, of a world of deep divisions, of societies segregated between the 'haves' and the 'have-nots'; between those with skills and opportunities, jobs and wealth, and those with none; between those who 'count' in economic, social, and political terms, and those who do not. This is a prescription for deepening instability.

The only enduring solution is to tackle poverty and injustice, so that all people have a stake in society. For without a cohesive spirit of social justice no society can achieve security and stability for its members. This requires not only the state, but individual citizens, as part of an active civil society, to take responsibility for ensuring that all can enjoy their full rights.

Creating a world order which realises the ambitions of the UN Charter and the goal of ending poverty will require a transformation in attitudes, policies, and institutions. It will necessitate a renewed sense of vision on the part of political leaders, and a willingness to sacrifice short-term political expediency in the interest of achieving long-term human development gains. It will mean creating equal opportunities, and sharing wealth in a more equitable manner, both nationally and internationally. It will also require a transformation of the post-war institutions of global governance, which have become increasingly irrelevant to the challenges of today.

Oxfam's vision of transformation is rooted in the energy and creativity of people who are looking for alternatives and shaping a new agenda. It is based on a conviction that people have the power to effect change—whether they are part of a women's group in Mali organising to obtain credit, indigenous people in Brazil struggling to secure their land rights, Windward Islands banana producers trying to keep open their lifeline to the European market, or citizens in developed countries, who can exercise consumer power in the supermarket by buying fairly-traded goods, or lobby their governments to write off debt as part of a wider poverty-reduction strategy.

Community-based groups of peasant producers, shanty-town dwellers, women's groups, indigenous and ethnic minority groups, trade unions, and NGOs are all working to achieve change, whether in the household, or the community, at district, regional, national, and international levels. On the basis of its work with such groups, Oxfam is convinced that real change must come from the bottom up. Far from being powerless victims of poverty, poor women and men show extraordinary resilience in challenging inequitable power structures. Their success in bringing about positive change will depend on the creation of effective democracies and strong civil societies, which enable people to have a voice, to campaign, and to assert their rights. At the same time, a new sense of responsibility for the rights of others is needed, together with an emphasis on building new alliances to achieve change. . . .

The five critical elements of that enabling environment are:

- democratic participation
- enhanced opportunity
- increased equity
- peace and security
- a sustainable future.

Oxfam's Agenda for Change

PARTICIPATION

. . . There is no one form of democracy appropriate to all people and transferable between countries; but transparent and accountable government, and respect for the rule of law and for civil and political rights, are crucial ingredients of democracy and participation. Some governments claim that the dictates of economic growth demand the suspension of such rights until a higher level of development has been attained. But while several countries, notably China, have achieved high rates of growth while maintaining oppressive political structures, it does not follow that autocracy is necessary for development. More importantly, civil and political rights are inalienable rights which all people are entitled to enjoy, irrespective of the stage of economic development in the country in which they live. . . .

Institutional development To provide a framework for democratic participation, it is essential to strengthen institutions at all levels, from village associations to an independent judiciary capable of implementing the rule of law.

Equality of opportunity Genuine participation also requires equality of opportunity. It is time for governments to take effective steps to implement all the principles agreed at the Vienna Human Rights Conference—particu-

larly that the human rights of women and of girl children are an inalienable, integral and indivisible part of universal human rights—and eliminate all forms of discrimination, against women and other disadvantaged groups. . . .

A stronger institutional framework to safeguard rights The UN remains the one global institution able—by virtue of its Charter and universal membership—to play a decisive role in poverty reduction. Charged with finding solutions to international social and economic problems, and promoting and protecting human rights and fundamental freedoms, the UN will be able to carry out its role only if the steady erosion of its power and authority is reversed. . . .

- The ECOSOC (Economic and Social Council) should have a strengthened role for monitoring the impact of global macro-economic policies on social development and basic rights. . . .

- ECOSOC should adopt a system of periodic national reports which would streamline existing reporting requirements on governments and move towards a more balanced and integrated approach to civil, political, economic, social, and cultural rights, and implementation of the Earth Summit agreements. In order to ensure that such reports do not become token exercises, citizens' groups and NGOs should be encouraged to present additional relevant information to ECOSOC.

- Governments should support the long overdue creation of a complaints mechanism, open to individuals and groups, to investigate alleged denials of basic rights under the International Covenant on Economic, Social and Cultural Rights.

Accountability of the international financial institutions There is increasing acceptance that IFIs as part of the UN family have obligations both to promote social and economic rights (which they themselves acknowledge) and to further the social development goals identified by the United Nations. The World Bank and IMF wield enormous influence over social and economic policy in developing countries, yet for too long they have operated outside the UN's human rights framework. . . .

Citizens' movements and campaign groups
The problems of poverty and denial of rights can seem insurmountable. Yet taking campaigning action to get poverty issues on the agenda and generate public pressure for change, as the Brazilian Campaign against Hunger, Misery and for Life has successfully done, or developing a co-ordinated approach to advocacy between groups in the South and North, can be both motivating and effective in changing attitudes and policies.

- Northern and international NGOs should concentrate more on building the advocacy capacity of community-based organisations and Southern NGOs working for change at national and international levels.

- To be effective in attempting to relieve poverty, NGOs should develop advocacy, research, networking, and policy dialogue with governments, multilateral agencies, and the corporate sector, as an integral part of fulfilling their mandates.

OPPORTUNITY

The eradication of poverty demands that poor men and women have control over the productive assets and resources on which their livelihoods depend. But to be capable of making use of opportunities, they also need enough to eat, clean water to drink and wash in, health-care, education, shelter, political freedom, and protection from violence.

Health-care, primary education, and other forms of welfare provision, are basic human rights, which governments should be protecting. Moreover, there is compelling evidence to show that investment in health, education, and basic-needs provision, apart from the immediate benefits, also makes good economic sense. Yet deep expenditure cuts and withdrawal of the state from social-service provision, together with the introduction of user fees, have disadvantaged the poorest people. Women are particularly adversely affected by cuts in health-care provision because of their higher exposure to health risks. Young girls are the first to be withdrawn from education in the face of economic stress.

Community groups are organising themselves to improve basic services. They range from community-based organisations in Zambia building their own health posts and schools, and lobbying government to staff them, to women in shanty towns in Peru organising soup-kitchens for destitute urban migrants. Such efforts need the support of governments and financial institutions, who should protect expenditure in areas of concern to the poor.

Provision of health-care and education

- Governments should redirect resources so that at least 20 per cent of government expenditure is allocated to providing services of maximum benefit to the poor, including primary health-care and education, clean water, and sanitation.

- Official aid donors, as part of a '20:20 compact' with recipient governments, should improve the poverty-focus of their aid so that a minimum of 20 per cent is directed towards these social priorities . . .

- To ensure that the poorest people can benefit from service provision, governments should immediately withdraw user fees for primary health and basic education services. . . .

National poverty-eradication plans Governments should prioritise the development of poverty-eradication plans, making time-bound commitments to eradicate absolute poverty, as agreed at the World Summit for Social Development. . . .

Resources for enhanced opportunity There are a range of ways in which new resources could be found to create opportunity and an enabling environment for poor people. These include:

- *Increased aid:* Official aid donors should establish a timetable for reaching the UN target of 0.7 per cent of GNP for their aid budgets.

- *Progressive taxation:* Governments should introduce progressive and equitable taxation systems, with a focus on taxing income and assets. . . .

- *Reduced military spending:* Significant reductions in expenditure on the military and on parastatals could translate into increased public investment in socially useful and productive activities.

- *Debt reduction:* An international conference on debt should be convened by the UN Secretary-General and charged with developing a concrete strategy for reducing the debt-servicing burdens of severely-indebted low-income countries (SILICs) to levels compatible with social and economic recovery by:

  - writing-off between 80 per cent and 100 per cent of the entire stock of official debt owed to governments represented in the Paris Club; . . .

- All debt-relief measures would be linked to concrete commitments by governments to increase provision in social priority areas through debt-for-development contracts negotiated with citizens' groups and the relevant UN agencies.

- *International taxation:* . . . A case can be made for putting aid on a more secure footing, through the introduction of a progressive income-tax on OECD countries. Tax-based transfers would undoubtedly meet with political objections, particularly in countries where governments are committed to lowering taxation. However, . . . international aid should be seen as a financial entitlement, and as part of a compact between citizens in the industrial and developing worlds, as it is in the interests of industrial countries to enhance human welfare in the South. Moreover, in practice aid is already a tax-based transfer. Establishing a formal system would merely ensure that the burden was shared more equitably, and would make the provision of aid more secure. An international tax on currency speculation could serve the dual purpose of providing resources for development and deterring a form of financial activity which is deeply destabilising for all countries.

EQUITY

Inequity in the distribution of wealth and productive assets is a formidable obstacle to reducing poverty and creating social cohesion. So, too, is the battery of disadvantages faced by women. A nation cannot genuinely claim to be 'developing' where half of its population is marginalised and suffers discrimination.

Nor can it expect economic growth to bring improvement in human welfare where vast numbers of people lack rights to the use of land and other productive resources. Patterns of development which exclude poor men and women are not merely socially unjust and politically unsustainable, but also inefficient. One of the central lessons from South-East Asia is that redistributive measures, including land reform, and moves towards more equitable wealth distribution (and investment in primary health and education), can lead to dynamic economic growth. . . .

Community organisations are working at grassroots level to address inequality. Women's organisations across the developing world are working to remove the deep-rooted structures of gender discrimination. In Bangladesh, for example, Saptagram is tackling the violation of women's land rights and enabling women to obtain credit. In Brazil, landless peasants and Indian communities are trying to secure their land rights; and in Chile, women employed in sweatshops are organising to improve their working conditions. Small producers in co-operatives and producer groups across the world are trying to improve their position in the market, and consumers in the North are choosing to buy fairly-traded coffee, tea, and other commodities to help to secure the rights of small producers. To strengthen their efforts, action is needed in the following areas:

Gender equity A major priority must be the elimination of all forms of discrimination against women, particularly in relation to land, credit, and control over productive resources. . . .

Agrarian reform Reform of the rural sector is needed to create more equitable patterns of land ownership and make more efficient use of resources, including measures to:

- redistribute land in favour of poor men and women . . .

- protect the rights of share-croppers and agricultural labourers;

- safeguard customary land rights and access to common property resources (including forests, fish stocks and waterways);

- enhance the land and inheritance rights of women.

Management of markets If poor women and men are not to be disadvantaged in local and national markets, these must be managed in the interests of equity by:

- providing targeted investment in credit, extension services, and economic infrastructure for poor women and men;
- providing market information to help poor producers participate in markets on more equitable terms;
- regulating markets to prevent local, national, and independent monopolies working against the social interest;
- enforcing reasonable and non-discriminatory employment practices in compliance with minimum standards set by the ILO, particularly in the areas of living wages, and safety and security of employment. . . .

Refocusing the role of the IMF The IMF's role should be re-assessed, to ensure that it plays a part in poverty eradication. . . .

Recasting the existing world trade order There is an urgent need for reform of the international trading system, so that trade becomes an engine of equitable economic growth. The major priorities are:

- international co-operation to stabilise commodity markets at remunerative levels;
- the withdrawal of all discriminatory trade barriers . . . targeted at developing countries;
- the introduction into the WTO of a social clause, based on ILO standards, establishing minimum conditions for participation in the multilateral trading system;
- new international trade rules to reconcile the potential conflicts at national and international levels between free trade and sustainable resource management . . .

PEACE AND SECURITY

There is no greater challenge facing the international community than that of creating the conditions for peace and security. Without genuine development and poverty reduction, there can be no lasting peace. But without peace, efforts to eradicate poverty will fail. Poverty, widening social divisions, environmental stresses, and the long-standing suppression of the rights of different social, ethnic, and cultural groups are fuelling conflict, violence, and crime. Civilians, particularly poor women and children, are bearing the brunt of that violence, as rape victims, amputees, and refugees who have suffered the loss of their family and community networks, and their livelihoods.

At the same time, in countries as diverse as El Salvador, Cambodia, Lebanon, and Mozambique, people are facing new challenges as they seek to rebuild their societies after decades of war.

Communities across the world are grappling with these problems. In Southern Sudan, pastoral communities have adapted their survival strategies to cope with the reality of 'permanent emergencies'; in Bosnia, groups are providing counselling and support for women rape victims; and in El Salvador, community organisations built up during the civil war are now involved in struggles for land, health-care, education, and a fairer return for producers. Ultimately, the only lasting solutions will be found within societies and through action at different levels to create the conditions for peace and security through greater equity, opportunity, and participation. However, far more can also be done at an international level.

Currently, the international community is floundering in attempts to find an appropriate response to conflict, having gone from counter-productive intervention in Somalia to inaction in the face of genocide in Rwanda. Much more effort is needed to identify an appropriate role for external actors in conflict, whether the UN, regional bodies, official donors, or NGOs. Below, we list some critical elements of a more appropriate international response.

Conflict prevention More resources should be invested in helping to strengthen local and regional conflict-mediation and conflict-prevention initiatives.

The UN Security Council should respond promptly to early warnings of impending conflict and put much greater emphasis on preventive diplomacy and speedy deployment of human-rights monitors. . . .

Improved UN response to conflicts When conflicts break out, the UN must be able to respond quickly and effectively. This requires:

- member states to establish 'fast track' stand-by arrangements (to provide the UN with the necessary troops, civilian police and logistical support), and the creation of a properly financed and adequately staffed permanent UN rapid-deployment force, deployable by the UNSC;
- financial and logistical support from member states to strengthen regional capacity for conflict prevention and peacekeeping duties;
- all UN interventions to have clear political and humanitarian objectives; troops to be under streamlined UN command structures and strictly observe human rights;
- a thorough and public evaluation of the work of all the UN humanitarian agencies and of the effectiveness of the co-ordinating role of the Department of Humanitarian Affairs, if necessary, exploring options for radical reform;
- the provision by member governments of adequate finance for UN operations (including humanitarian relief, conflict-prevention, peace-keeping, peace-making, and post-conflict reconstruction).

Post-conflict reconstruction Greater priority should be given to supporting post-war reconstruction efforts in a manner which addresses the underlying causes of conflict and creates the conditions for permanent peace.

Reduction in arms sales In order to establish an enforceable code of conduct on international arms transfers, a high-level expert committee needs to be created, reporting to the UN Secretary-General, to administer the UN Arms Register, with wide-ranging powers to investigate arms exports, and subsidies to the weapons industry, and to develop transparent systems of accountability.

The UN Register of Conventional Arms should be extended to cover all small weapons and used to levy a one per cent tax on arms exports that would be channelled into financing UN conflict-prevention initiatives.

A ban on anti-personnel mines A comprehensive and worldwide ban on the manufacture, stockpiling, export, and use of anti-personnel mines should be introduced.

Action to tackle human rights abuse Consideration should be given to creating a permanent International Tribunal for genocide, war crimes, and other serious violations of human rights.

A SUSTAINABLE FUTURE

There can be no sustainable future without peace and prosperity. Poverty is a major destroyer of the environment, since it forces local communities into unsustainable survival strategies. Poor people, and particularly women, who have to walk increasingly long distances to collect water and fuelwood, are all too aware that it is they themselves who bear the brunt of local environmental degradation. A range of community groups are taking action across the developing and developed world to try to conserve resources and protect the environment, such as Beja groups in Sudan taking action to cope with a rapidly changing and risk-prone environment, and the Zabaleen community in the slums of Cairo, who survive by collecting and recycling the city's waste. Their action is paralleled by that of local environmental action groups in the North, who are involved in recycling waste, and regenerating run-down inner city areas.

Citizens' action in industrialised countries is particularly important, because it is there that the bulk of the damage is being done to the global environment, through high levels of energy consumption and wasteful life-styles, which are emulated by the elite in developing countries. By the same token, the industrialised world has no right to demand environmental sustainability in the South until it sets its own house in order—and until it provides the financial resources needed to realise the objectives agreed at the Earth Summit.

It is therefore essential that countries in the North assume their full share of the cost of protecting the global environment, and that governments take tangible steps to reduce the depth of their ecological footprint on that environment by:

- following the Dutch example of assessing the scale and impact of their 'ecological footprint' in key sectors, including energy and agriculture, and committing themselves to setting specific, time-tabled targets to reduce the negative impact of their footprints . . .

- introducing measures to meet more stringent targets on energy use, including a carbon/energy tax, tougher energy efficiency standards, programmes of insulation, investment in renewable energy sources, redesigning the taxation system to tax over-exploitation of resources, rather than employment and investment;

- committing themselves to reduce CO_2 emissions by 30 per cent from 1990 levels by 2005;

- introducing environmental policies that use market mechanisms, including environmental taxes, import and export controls, and recourse to the 'polluter pays' principle, so that environmental costs are more accurately reflected in market prices.

Local environmental action Action by local environmental groups and individual citizens in the North is needed to conserve energy, improve the local environment and make more sustainable use of resources through recycling.

Ultimately, action by citizens and social movements in both South and North, coming together to put pressure on governments to act, provides the best hope of securing rights and ending poverty.

STUDY QUESTIONS

1. Develop the connections between overpopulation, poverty, and environmental destruction.

2. In some ways, "human rights" is like Mom and apple pie: everyone is in favor. But, in fact, the question of human rights can be enormously controversial. Explain.

3. Martin Luther King, Jr. wrote that "Injustice anywhere is an affront to justice everywhere." The merits of this statement are—or should be—obvious. But is there any sense in which this idea could be troublesome?

4. Comment on the notion that human rights are a Western concept, which should not be applied to other societies. Take female circumcision as an example.

5. Look into the question of whether ecological stability and sustainability conflict with economic growth and development.

6. It is often said that one cannot make omelets without breaking eggs. Propose some guidelines as to how many eggs, and of what sort, might legitimately be "broken" in order to establish positive peace.

7. Positive peace is as much a matter of national security as is negative peace. Agree or disagree, trying to be specific and "hard-headed" in your response.

8. Compare and contrast differences in wealth within a country with differences in wealth between countries; is the solution to such differences simply a matter of "development?"

9. When peace becomes a positive goal (as opposed to war prevention), then people feel inclined to fight for it; hence, it is better to aim "lower." Agree or disagree, using historical examples and/or plausible future scenarios.

10. Describe some successes in achieving positive peace. What can we learn from them? Do the same for some failures.

SUGGESTIONS FOR FURTHER READING

Allenby, Braden R. and Deanna J. Richards, eds. 1994. The Greening of Industrial Ecosystems. Washington, DC: National Academy Press.

Andreopoulos, George J. and Richard Pierre Claude. eds. 1997. *Human Rights Education for the Twenty-first Century*. Philadelphia: University of Pennsylvania Press.

Andrzejewski, Julie. ed. 1993. *Oppression and Social Justice: Critical Frameworks*. New York: Routledge.

Brown, Lester Russell, Christopher Flavin, and Sandra Postel. 1991. *Saving the Planet: How to Shape an Environmentally Sustainable Global Economy*. New York: W.W. Norton.

Buergenthal, Thomas. 1995. *International Human Rights in a Nutshell*. St. Paul, Minn: West Pub. Co.

Bullard, Robert D. ed. 1993. *Confronting Environmental Racism: Voices from the Grassroots*. Boston: South End Press.

Conca, Ken, Michael Alberty and Geoffrey D Dabelko. eds. 1995. *Green Planet Blues: Environmental Politics from Stockholm to Rio*. Boulder: Westview Press.

Felice, William. 1996. *Taking Suffering Seriously: The Importance of Collective Human Rights*. Albany: State University of New York Press.

Gurinder S. Shahi, et al. 1997. *International Perspectives on Environment, Development, and Health: Toward a Sustainable World*. New York: Springer.

Harrison, Paul. 1992. *The Third Revolution: Environment, Population, and a Sustainable World*. New York: St. Martin's Press.

Howard, Rhoda E. 1995. *Human Rights and the Search for Community*. Boulder, Colo: Westview Press.

Kothari, Rajni. 1995. *Poverty: Human Consciousness and the Amnesia of Development*. Atlantic Highlands, NJ: Zed Books.

Lal, Deepak and H. Myint. 1996. *The Political Economy of Poverty, Equity and Growth: A Comparative Study*. New York: Oxford University Press.

Renner, Michael. 1996. *Fighting for Survival: Environmental Decline, Social Conflict, and the New Age of Insecurity*. New York: W.W. Norton.

Schuler, Margaret A. ed. 1995. *From Basic Needs to Basic Rights: Women's Claim to Human Rights*. Washington, DC: Women, Law and Development International.

Shields, David L. ed. 1995. *The Color of Hunger: Race and Hunger in National and International Perspective*. Lanham, MD: Rowman & Littlefield.

Suzuki, Y., K. Ueta, and S. Mori. eds. 1996. *Global Environmental Security: From Protection to Prevention*. New York: Springer.

Turpin, Jennifer and Lois Ann Lorentzen. eds. 1996. *The Gendered New World Order: Militarism, Development, and the Environment*. New York: Routledge.

4

~~~

Nonviolence

Much of the human world is structured by violence—the international political and military system perhaps most of all. Hence, a commitment to nonviolence is necessarily radical. Nonviolence is not limited to tactics for overcoming any one oppressive system—whether colonial domination, denial of civil rights, and so forth—but rather it seeks to overthrow all relationships based on violence, oppression, and the unfair domination of some by others. Thus, nonviolence is directly relevant not only to the prevention of war, but also to the establishment of social justice, environmental protection, and the securing of human rights. Nonviolence seeks to change the terms whereby individuals and groups interact: not only with each other, but even with the planet Earth.

It can be argued, for example, that the destructive patterns whereby people and states interact violently with one another are also reflected in the destructive style that characterizes so much of the interaction of people with their environment: the burning of rain forests, the clear-cutting of temperate woodlands, the gouging of the earth during strip-mining, the pollution of water and air, the extinction of plant and animal species. All these can be seen as deriving from a lack of what Gandhi called *ahimsa*, best translated into English, perhaps, as "nonviolent love." This is not love of the sloppy, sentimental kind, but is closer to the Christian concept of *agape*, a transcending love of connection and mutual commitment. It is also similar to Albert Schweitzer's concept of "reverence for life."

The poet Walt Whitman had this love in mind when he wrote:

Were you looking to be held together by lawyers?
Or by an agreement on paper? Or by arms?
Nay, nor the world, nor any living thing, will so cohere.
Only those who love each other shall become indivisible.

It must be emphasized that nonviolence has emerged as a definite, defiant, hard-headed strategy of social transformation. The very word "nonviolence" is thus unfortunate, since it evokes images of passivity, especially in its regrettable counterpart, "passive resistance." This is akin to translating *light* as "nondarkness," or defining *good* as merely the absence of evil. Mohandas Gandhi, the greatest twentieth-century apostle of nonviolence, coined the word *satyagraha*, which can be translated literally from the Sanskrit as "soul-force" or "soul-truth." It incorporates such positive traits as courage, direct-ness, friendly civility, absolute honesty, respect for other living creatures, and willing-ness to suffer in pursuit of deeply felt goals.

Traditionally, when conflicts are resolved by violence, they simply involve the tri-umph of one protagonist over the other. Such a "resolution" may occur via threat, per-suasion, or compulsion by naked force, but, in any event, the presumption is that one side wins and the other loses: what mathematicians call a "zero sum game." (In most competitive sports, for example, for every winner there is a loser, so the sum total of wins and losses equals zero.) By contrast, devotees of nonviolence seek to resolve the conflict at its source, rather than to defeat or annihilate the opponent. The goal is to per-suade the adversary that all parties have more to gain by acting in harmony and love than by persevering in discord and violence: that is, that the parties are not really adver-saries at all!

As we shall see, there have been numerous spokespeople for nonviolence and for creative nonviolent resistance. It was Gandhi, however, who most closely wedded the-ory to practice, employing nonviolence as a coherent approach to peace. For nonviolent activists in the Gandhian mold, violence itself is the enemy, and, thus, there is no room for violence in the arsenal of those who would effect creative, peaceful change. If the goal is a genuine social revolution, then the more violence, the less revolution: "The practice of violence, like all action, changes the world," wrote social philosopher Han-nah Arendt. "But the most probable change is to a more violent world."[1]

For practitioners of nonviolence, therefore, it is crucially important to recognize the interdependence of means and ends: a goal of peace can only be achieved by the use of nonviolence. For example, by using violent methods, revolutions (even the most well-meaning ones) and even antiwar movements can build up reservoirs of resentment and hatred, thereby laying the foundations for additional injustice and yet more violence. Political activists of the far left and far right are generally prone to make compromises with violence, convinced that their vision of the world-as-it-should-be justifies virtually any means of attaining it. Lenin announced, for example, that "to achieve our ends, we will unite even with the Devil."

Similarly, ideologues of the far right did not hesitate to make common cause with oppressive dictatorships—such as Somoza in Nicaragua, Marcos in the Philippines, Chun doo Hwan in South Korea, Pinochet in Chile, Duvalier in Haiti, the Shah in Iran, Suharto in Indonesia, Botha in South Africa—in the interest of a presumed greater good, the defeat or containment of international communism.

Cicero, in *The Letters to His Friends*, asks, "What can be done against force, without force?" Students of nonviolence would answer, "Plenty." They would, in fact, question whether anything effective, lasting, or ultimately worthwhile can be done against force, *with* force. The Rev. Martin Luther King, Jr., nonviolent leader of the civil rights move-ment in the United States—and a visionary who, like Gandhi, was also intensely prac-tical and result-oriented—wrote that "returning violence for violence multiplies vio-lence, adding deeper darkness to a night already devoid of stars. Darkness cannot drive out darkness; only light can do that. Hate cannot drive out hate; only love can do that."

---

[1]Hannah Arendt. 1969. *On Violence*. New York: Harcourt, Brace and World.

This does not mean that the practitioner of nonviolence is forbidden anger, even hate; rather, these feelings must be redirected creatively against various *systems* of evil rather than individuals.

What, then, does nonviolence look like in practice? It takes many forms: marches, boycotts, picketing, leafleting, strikes, civil disobedience, the peaceful occupation of various government facilities, vigils and fasts, mass imprisonment, tax resistance, and a willingness to be abused by the authorities and yet to respond nonviolently, with courage and determination, even politeness. Thus, the nonviolent struggle is if anything more intense and difficult than its violent counterpart. It is not an alternative to fighting, but rather, a different (nonviolent and loving) way of doing so.

When a victim responds to violence with yet more violence, he or she is reacting in predictable, perhaps even instinctive ways. Violent responses validate the original attacker, even, in a way, vindicating the original violence as far as the attacker is concerned: since the opponent is so violent, then presumably he or she "deserved it." Thus, there is a widespread expectation of countervailing power analogous in the social sphere to Newton's First Law, which states that for every action there is an equal and opposite reaction. Accustomed to counter-violence—and even, perhaps, hoping for it—the violent person who encounters a nonviolent opponent who is courageous and respectful, even loving, becomes a "victim" of a kind of moral judo, in which the attacker's own energy is redirected, knocking him or her off balance.

It is said of some people and some nations that "they only understand force," and, therefore, they cannot be moved by anything other than force or the threat of force. The truth, however, may be precisely the opposite: Those who understand and expect force can generally deal with it effectively. By contrast, the British authorities in India, like supporters of segregation laws in the U.S. South, were consistently off balance and flustered by the creative nonviolent tactics employed against their regime.

Historically, violent governmental over-reaction has often worked to the ultimate detriment of the perpetrators, transforming victims into martyrs, who became symbols of their regime's callous wrong-headedness. In 1819, for example, a nonviolent crowd in Manchester, England was attacked by soldiers while listening to speeches calling for the repeal of the Corn Laws; this so-called Peterloo Massacre became a rallying cry for radicals who eventually succeeded in their demands. The slaughter of participants in the Paris Commune of 1871 led to greater solidarity among the French working class. In 1905, a large gathering of nonviolent Russian peasants in St. Petersburg, led by Father Gapon, attempted to submit a petition to Czar Nicholas, whose troops responded by slaughtering hundreds of unarmed people. This led to a general strike, which ushered in some limited democratic reforms but, more importantly, also signaled the beginning of the end for czarist tyranny. When the Russian Revolution finally took place, thirteen years later, it was in many ways the culmination of mounting popular revulsion at the czar's wanton violence toward his own people.

The arrest and beating of U.S. civil rights protesters during the 1950s and early 1960s, along with the murder of civil rights workers and innocent bystanders (including children), was instrumental in bringing about desegregation and the passing of the subsequent Civil Rights and Voting Rights Acts. The "police riot" at the 1968 Democratic Party Convention in Chicago led to widespread condemnation of the political system, just as the killing of four unarmed students at Kent State University in 1970 galvanized sentiment against the Vietnam War. The 1988 Israeli policy of beating Palestinian protesters who sought an end to Israeli occupation of the West Bank led to solidification of Palestinian sentiment, and subjected the Israeli government to greater pressure for a negotiated agreement. In 1989, when nonviolent protesters—mostly students—occupied Tiananmen Square and demanded political reforms, the Chinese government responded with tanks and the slaughter of hundreds, perhaps thousands of protesters. Although the Chinese government has thus far survived this episode, it seems clear that when nonviolent protesters are abused, the world's conscience is aroused, and significant changes are often set in motion.

Nonviolent protest has accomplished much more than the creation of martyrs. In 1986, for example, the corrupt dictatorship of Ferdinand Marcos in the Philippines was toppled, largely due to "people power," the persistent nonviolence of Filipino civilians. Strongly supported by the Catholic church, crowds of unarmed Filipinos at one point interposed themselves between a small number of dissident troops and those ostensibly loyal to Marcos, who had been ordered to suppress their opponents. When it became evident that his own military would not fire on the nonviolent, unarmed populace, it was clear that the end of the Marcos regime had come. Similar campaigns caused the ouster of the long-lasting Duvalier regime in Haiti, and produced the first ever democratic government in South Korea. And the prodemocracy movement in Eastern Europe succeeded in throwing off communist domination with essentially nonviolent techniques (except in Romania). It is also notable that in many countries, this "velvet revolution"—so named because of the virtual absence of bloodshed—was hastened by instances in which the repressive government reacted violently to nonviolent protesters . . . which in turn served to delegitimate the government itself.

This is but a small and highly selective sampling. It is noteworthy that examples of "successful" violence are far better known—although not necessarily more numerous or important—than their successful nonviolent counterparts. The argument can in fact be made that violent outcomes are, by definition, failures, and that nonviolence represents the best in our politics and in human potential.

Civil Disobedience

Henry David Thoreau was not, strictly speaking, an advocate of nonviolence. However, he was deeply troubled by government misbehavior, notably the institution of slavery and the Mexican-American War, which he saw as a blatant act of imperialist aggression by the United States. Thoreau protested by famously refusing to pay taxes, and was imprisoned as a result. He was influential in developing the concept of civil disobedience, and had a powerful effect on the thinking of Leo Tolstoy and Mohandas Gandhi, among many others. Thoreau, in turn—like Gandhi after him—had been influenced by the Bhagavad Gita, the great Hindu epic that emphasized the importance of renouncing personal possessiveness and striving in pursuit of greater aims.

Advocates of civil disobedience have long been considered unpatriotic, not only because they recommend a less bellicose stand toward proclaimed national "enemies," but because their efforts are in some ways subversive of accepted national values. When, in the 1960s, Black Power advocate H. Rap Brown pointed out that violence was "as American as cherry pie," he spoke a part of the truth. So did theologian and peace activist Thomas Merton, when he warned that the sources of violence can be found

> not in esoteric groups but in the very culture itself, its mass media, its extreme individualism and competitiveness, its inflated myths of virility and toughness, and its overwhelming preoccupation [with means of destruction].[2]

Thoreau's call for civil disobedience and for the priority of conscience, combined with the image of him living in relative isolation by the shores of Walden Pond, challenge us to consider the position of the peace activist as principled outsider. Thus, pacifism and tax resistance, for example, are warily tolerated in the United States so long as they are performed by small and uninfluential groups. But as Thomas Merton pointed out,

> There is also an implication that any minority stand against war on grounds of conscience is *ipso facto* a kind of deviant and morally eccentric position, to be tolerated only because there are always a few religious half-wits around in any case, and one has to humor them in order to preserve the nation's reputation for respecting individual liberty.[3]

The following selection is from Thoreau's essay "Civil Disobedience."

From *Civil Disobedience: Theory and Practice* by Henry David Thoreau.

---

[2]Thomas Merton. 1980. *The Non-Violent Alternative.* New York Farrar, Straus & Giroux.

---

[3]Merton, *Non-Violent*

I heartily accept the motto—"That government is best which governs least"; and I should like to see it acted up to more rapidly and systematically. Carried out, it finally amounts to this, which also I believe—"That government is best which governs not at all"; and when men are prepared for it, that will be the kind of government which they will have. Government is at best but an expedient; but most governments are usually, and all governments are sometimes, inexpedient. The objections which have been brought against a standing army, and they are many and weighty, and deserve to prevail, may also at last be brought against a standing government. The standing army is only an arm of the standing government. The government itself, which is only the mode which the people have chosen to execute their will, is equally liable to be abused and perverted before the people can act through it. Witness the present Mexican war, the work of comparatively a few individuals using the standing government as their tool; for, in the outset, the people would not have consented to this measure.

This American government—what is it but a tradition, though a recent one, endeavoring to transmit itself unimpaired to posterity, but each instant losing some of its integrity? It has not the vitality and force of a single living man; for a single man can bend it to his will. It is a sort of wooden gun to the people themselves. But it is not the less necessary for this; for the people must have some complicated machinery or other, and hear its din, to satisfy that idea of government which they have. Governments show thus how successfully men can be imposed on, even impose on themselves, for their own advantage. It is excellent, we must all allow. Yet this government never of itself furthered any enterprise, but by the alacrity with which it got out of its way. *It* does not keep the country free. *It* does not settle the West. *It* does not educate. The character inherent in the American people has done all that has been accomplished; and it would have done somewhat more, if the government had not sometimes got in its way. For government is an expedient by which men would fain succeed in letting one another alone; and, as has been said, when it is most expedient, the governed are most let alone by it. . . .

But, to speak practically and as a citizen, unlike those who call themselves no-govern-ment men, I ask for, not at once no government, but *at once* a better government. Let every man make known what kind of government would command his respect, and that will be one step toward obtaining it.

. . . I think that we should be men first, and subjects afterward. It is not desirable to cultivate a respect for the law, so much as for the right. The only obligation which I have a right to assume, is to do at any time what I think right. It is truly enough said, that a corporation has no conscience; but a corporation of conscientious men is a corporation *with* a conscience. Law never made men a whit more just; and, by means of their respect for it, even the well-disposed are daily made the agents of injustice. A common and natural result of an undue respect for law is, that you may see a file of soldiers, colonel, captain, corporal, privates, powder-monkeys, and all, marching in admirable order over hill and dale to the wars, against their wills, ay, against their common sense and consciences, which makes it very steep marching indeed, and produces a palpitation of the heart. They have no doubt that it is a damnable business in which they are concerned; they are all peaceably inclined. Now, what are they? Men at all? or small movable forts and magazines, at the service of some unscrupulous man in power? . . .

The mass of men serve the state thus, not as men mainly, but as machines, with their bodies. They are the standing army, and the militia, jailers, constables, posse comitatus, & c. In most cases there is no free exercise whatever of the judgment or of the moral sense; but they put themselves on a level with wood and earth and stones; and wooden men can perhaps be manufactured that will serve the purpose as well. Such command no more respect than men of straw or a lump of dirt. They have the same sort of worth only as horses and dogs. Yet such as these even are commonly esteemed good citizens. Others—as most legislators, politicians, lawyers, ministers, and officeholders—serve the state chiefly with their heads; and, as they rarely make any moral distinctions, they are as likely to serve the Devil, without *intending* it, as God. A very few, as heroes, patriots, martyrs, reformers in the great sense, and *men*, serve the state with the consciences also, and so necessarily resist it for the most part; and they are commonly treated as enemies by it. . . .

How does it become a man to behave toward this American government to-day? I answer, that he cannot without disgrace be associated with it. I cannot for an instant recognize the political organization as *my* government which is the *slave's* government also.

All men recognize the right of revolution; that is, the right to refuse allegiance to, and to resist, the government, when its tyranny or its inefficiency are great and unendurable. But almost all say that such is not the case now. But such was the case, they think, in the Revolution of '75. If one were to tell me that this was a bad government because it taxed certain foreign commodities brought to its ports, it is most probable that I should not make an ado about it, for I can do without them. All machines have their friction; and possibly this does enough good to counterbalance the evil. At any rate, it is a great evil to make a stir about it. But when the friction comes to have its machine, and oppression and robbery are organized, I say, let us not have such a machine any longer. In other words, when a sixth of the population of a nation which has undertaken to be the refuge of liberty are slaves, and a whole country is unjustly overrun and conquered by a foreign army, and subjected to military law, I think that it is not too soon for honest men to rebel and revolutionize. What makes this duty the more urgent is the fact, that the country so overrun is not our own, but ours is the invading army.

. . . I quarrel not with far-off foes, but with those who, near at home, co-operate with, and do the bidding of, those far away, and without whom the latter would be harmless. We are accustomed to say, that the mass of men are unprepared; but improvement is slow, because the few are not materially wiser or better than the many. It is not so important that many should be as good as you, as that there be some absolute goodness somewhere; for that will leaven the whole lump. There are thousands who are *in opinion* opposed to slavery and to the war, who yet in effect do nothing to put an end to them; who, esteeming themselves children of Washington and Franklin, sit down with their hands in their pockets, and say that they know not what to do, and do nothing; who even postpone the question of freedom to the question of free-trade, and quietly read the prices-current along with the latest advices from Mexico, after dinner, and, it may be, fall asleep over them both. What is the price-current of an honest man and patriot to-day? They hesitate, and they regret, and sometimes they petition; but they do nothing in earnest and with effect. They will wait, well disposed, for others to remedy the evil, that they may no longer have it to regret. . . .

It is not a man's duty, as a matter of course, to devote himself to the eradication of any, even the most enormous wrong; he may still properly have other concerns to engage him; but it is his duty, at least, to wash his hands of it, and, if he gives it no thought longer, not to give it practically his support. If I devote myself to other pursuits and contemplations, I must first see, at least, that I do not pursue them sitting upon another man's shoulders. I must get off him first, that he may pursue his contemplations too. See what gross inconsistency is tolerated. I have heard some of my townsmen say, "I should like to have them order me out to help put down an insurrection of the slaves, or to march to Mexico—see if I would go"; and yet these very men have each, directly by their allegiance, and so indirectly, at least, by their money, furnished a substitute. . . .

How can a man be satisfied to entertain an opinion merely, and enjoy *it*? Is there any enjoyment in it, if his opinion is that he is aggrieved? If you are cheated out of a single dollar by your neighbor, you do not rest satisfied with knowing that you are cheated, or with saying that you are cheated, or even with petitioning him to pay you your due; but you take effectual steps at once to obtain the full amount, and see that you are never cheated again. Action from principle, the perception and the performance of right, changes things and relations; it is essentially revolutionary, and does not consist wholly with anything which was. It not only divides states and churches, it divides families; ay, it divides the *individual*, separating the diabolical in him from the divine.

Unjust laws exist: shall we be content to obey them, or shall we endeavor to amend them, and obey them until we have succeeded, or shall we transgress them at once? Men generally, under such a government as this, think that they ought to wait until they have persuaded the majority to alter them. They think that, if they should resist, the remedy would be worse than the evil. But it is the fault of the government itself that the remedy *is* worse than the evil. *It* makes it worse. Why is it not more apt to anticipate and provide for reform? Why does it not cherish its wise minority? Why does it cry and resist before it is hurt? Why does it not encourage its citizens to be on the alert to point out its faults, and *do* better than it would have them? Why does it always crucify Christ, and excommunicate Copernicus and Luther, and pronounce Washington and Franklin rebels? . . .

If the injustice is part of the necessary friction of the machine of government, let it go, let it go: perchance it will wear smooth—certainly the machine will wear out. If the injustice has a spring, or a pulley, or a rope, or a crank, exclusively for itself, then perhaps you may consider whether the remedy will not be worse than the evil; but if it is of such a nature that it requires you to be the agent of injustice to another, then, I say, break the law. Let your life be a counter friction to stop the machine. What I have to do is to see, at any rate, that I do not lend myself to the wrong which I condemn. . . .

I do not hesitate to say, that those who call themselves Abolitionists should at once effectually withdraw their support, both in person and property, from the government of Massachusetts, and not wait till they constitute a majority of one, before they suffer the right to prevail through them. I think that it is enough if they have God on their side, without waiting for that other one. Moreover, any man more right than his neighbors constitutes a majority of one already.

. . . I know this well, that if one thousand, if one hundred, if ten men whom I could name—if ten *honest* men only—ay, if *one* HONEST man, in this State of Massachusetts, *ceasing to hold slaves*, were actually to withdraw from this copartnership, and be locked up in the county jail therefore, it would be the abolition of slavery in America. For it matters not how small the beginning may seem to be: what is once well done is done forever. . . .

Under a government which imprisons any unjustly, the true place for a just man is also a prison. The proper place to-day, the only place which Massachusetts has provided for her freer and less desponding spirits, is in her prisons, to be put out and locked out of the State by her own act, as they have already put themselves out by their principles. It is there that the fugitive slave, and the Mexican prisoner on parole, and the Indian come to plead the wrongs of his race, should find them; on that separate, but more free and honorable ground, where the State places those who are not *with* her, but *against* her—the only house in a slave State in which a free man can abide with honor. If any think that their influence would be lost there, and their voices no longer afflict the ear of the State, that they would not be as an enemy within its walls, they do not know by how much truth is stronger than error, nor how much more eloquently and effectively he can combat injustice who has experienced a little in his own person. Cast your whole vote, not a strip of paper merely, but your whole influence. A minority is powerless while it conforms to the majority; it is not even a minority then; but it is irresistible when it clogs by its whole weight. If the alternative is to keep all just men in prison, or give up war and slavery, the State will not hesitate which to choose. If a thousand men were not to pay their tax-bills this year, that would not be a violent and bloody measure, as it would be to pay them, and enable the State to commit violence and shed innocent blood. This is, in fact, the definition of a peaceable revolution, if any such is possible. If the tax-gatherer, or any other public officer, asks me, as one has done, "But what shall I do?" my answer is, "If you really wish to do anything, resign your office." When the subject has refused allegiance, and the officer has resigned his office, then the revolution is accomplished. But even suppose blood should flow. Is there not a sort of blood shed when the conscience is wounded? Through this wound a man's real manhood and immortality flow out, and he bleeds to an everlasting death. I see this blood flowing now. . . .

I have paid no poll-tax for six years. I was put into a jail once on this account, for one night; and, as I stood considering the walls of solid stone, two or three feet thick, the door of wood and iron, a foot thick, and the iron grating which strained the light, I could not help being struck with the foolishness of that institution which treated me as if I were mere flesh and blood and bones, to be locked up. I wondered that it should have concluded at length that this was the best use it could put me to, and had never thought to avail itself of my services in some way. I saw that, if there was a wall of stone between me and my townsmen, there was a still more difficult one to climb or break through, before they could get to be as free as I was. I did not for a moment feel confined, and the walls seemed a great waste of stone and mortar. I felt as if I alone of all my townsmen had paid my tax. They plainly did not know how to treat me, but behaved like persons who are underbred. In every threat and in every compliment there was a blunder; for they thought that my chief desire was to stand the other side of that stone wall. I could not but smile to see how industriously they locked the door on my meditations, which followed them out again without let or hindrance, and *they* were really all that was dangerous. As they could not reach me, they had resolved to punish my body; just as boys, if they cannot come at some person against whom they have a spite, will abuse his dog. I saw that the State was half-witted, that it was timid as a lone woman with her silver spoons, and that it did not know its friends from its foes, and I lost all my remaining respect for it, and pitied it.

Thus the State never intentionally confronts a man's sense, intellectual or moral, but only his body, his senses. It is not armed with superior wit or honesty, but with superior physical strength. I was not born to be forced. I will breathe after my own fashion. Let us see who is the strongest. What force has a multitude? They can only force me who obey a higher law than I. They force me to become like themselves. I do not hear of *men* being *forced* to live this way or that by masses of men. What sort of life were that to live? When I meet a government which says to me, "Your money or your life," why should I be in haste to give it my money? It may be in a great strait, and not know what to do: I cannot help that. It must help itself; do as I do. It is not worth the while to snivel about it. I am not responsible for the successful working of the machinery of society. I am not the son of the engineer. I perceive that, when an acorn and a chestnut fall side by side, the one does not remain inert to make way for the other, but both obey their own laws, and spring and grow and flourish as best they can, till one, perchance, overshadows and destroys the other. If a plant cannot live according to its nature, it dies; and so a man.

. . . I have never declined paying the highway tax, because I am as desirous of being a good neighbor as I am of being a bad subject; and, as for supporting schools, I am doing my part to educate my fellow-countrymen now. It is for no particular item in the tax-bill that I refuse to pay it. I simply wish to refuse allegiance to the State, to withdraw and stand aloof from it effectually. I do not care to trace the course of my dollar, if I could, till it buys a man or a musket to shoot one with—the dollar is innocent—but I am concerned to trace the effects of my allegiance. In fact, I quietly declare war with the State, after my fashion, though I will still make what use and get what advantage of her I can, as is usual in such cases.

. . . I sometimes say to myself, When many millions of men, without heat, without ill will, without personal feeling of any kind, demand of you a few shillings only, without the possibility, such is their constitution, of retracting or altering their present demand, and without the possibility, on your side, of appeal to any other millions, why expose yourself to this overwhelming brute force? You do not resist cold and hunger, the winds and the waves, thus obstinately; you quietly submit to a thousand similar necessities. You do not put your head into the fire. But just in proportion as I regard this as not wholly a brute force, but partly a human force, and consider that I have relations to those millions as to so many millions of men, and not of mere brute or inanimate things, I see that appeal is possible, first and instantaneously, from them to the Maker of them, and secondly, from them to themselves. But, if I put my head deliberately into the fire, there is no appeal to fire or to the Maker of fire, and I have only myself to blame. . . .

I do not wish to quarrel with any man or nation. I do not wish to split hairs, to make fine distinctions, or set myself up as better than my neighbors. I seek rather, I may say, even an excuse for conforming to the laws of the land. I am but too ready to conform to them. Indeed, I have reason to suspect myself on this head; and each year, as the tax-gatherer comes round, I find myself disposed to review the acts and position of the general and State governments, and the spirit of the people, to discover a pretext for conformity. . . .

The authority of government, even such as I am willing to submit to—for I will cheerfully obey those who know and can do better than I, and in many things even those who neither know nor can do so well—is still an impure one: to be strictly just, it must have the sanction and consent of the governed. It can have no pure right over my person and property but what I concede to it. The progress from an absolute to a limited monarchy, from a limited monarchy to a democracy, is a progress toward a true respect for the individual. Even the Chinese philosopher was wise enough to regard the individual as the basis of the empire. Is a democracy, such as we know it, the last improvement possible in government? Is it not possible to take a step further toward recognizing and organizing the rights of man? There will never be a really free and enlightened State, until the State comes to recognize the individual as a higher and independent power, from which all its own power and authority are derived, and treats him accordingly. I please myself with imagining a State at last which can afford to be just to all men, and to treat the individual with respect as a neighbor; which even would not think it inconsistent with its own repose, if a few were to live aloof from it, not meddling with it, nor embraced by it, who fulfilled all the duties of neighbors and fellow-men. A State which bore this kind of fruit, and suffered it to drop off as fast as it ripened, would prepare the way for a still more perfect and glorious State, which also I have imagined, but not yet anywhere seen.

LEO TOLSTOY

Letter to Ernest Howard Crosby

As a young man, Leo Tolstoy served in the Russian Army during the Crimean War. In his later years, however, Tolstoy increasingly adopted a unique brand of Christianity, embracing personal nonviolence and especially the First Commandment, "Thou Shalt Not Kill," so vigorously that he was widely hailed as the thirteenth apostle. Tolstoy was especially concerned about personal compliance with war, which he denounced as nothing less than murder. As such, his writings stand in marked contrast to the "Christian realist" tradition, which sought to elaborate situations under which recourse to war was acceptable.

Tolstoy maintained a kind of principled anarchism, opposing not only participation in war but the very workings of government, whose institutionalized violence he considered inimical to peace and to religious conscience. In his "Letter on the Peace Conference," Tolstoy wrote,

> Armies can be reduced and abolished only in opposition to the will, but never by the will, of government. Armies will only be diminished and abolished when people cease to trust governments, and themselves seek salvation from the miseries that oppress them, and seek that safety, not by the complicated and delicate combinations of diplomats, but in the simple fulfillment of that law, binding upon every man, inscribed in all religious teachings, and present in every heart, not to do to others what you wish them not to do to you—above all, not to slay your neighbors.
>
> Armies will first diminish, and then disappear, only when public opinion brands with contempt those who, whether from fear, or for advantage, sell their liberty and enter the

From "Letter to Ernest Howard Crosby" by Leo Tolstoy. In *Writings on Civil Disobedience and Nonviolence*, translated by Aylmer Mude. 1987. Philadelphia: New Society Publishers.

ranks of those murderers, called soldiers; and when the men now ignored and even blamed—who, in despite of all the persecution and suffering they have borne—have refused to yield the control of their actions into the hands of others, and become the tools of murder—are recognized by public opinion to be the foremost champions and benefactors of mankind. Only then will armies first diminish and then quite disappear, and a new era in the life of mankind will commence. And that time is near.

Tolstoy was convinced that the common people are as responsible for war as their leaders. This, in turn, contributed to his determination that individuals have the opportunity—indeed, the responsibility—to take things into their own hands and refuse to fight.

In the following selection, the influence of Eastern thought can be seen in Tolstoy's embrace of nonviolence, notably his rejection of ethical egoism and even utilitarianism: "the greatest good for the greatest number."

"What would happen if people were all obliged to obey the law of non-resistance?"

But, in the first place, it is impossible to oblige every one to accept the law of non-resistance. Secondly, if it were possible to do so, such compulsion would in itself be a direct negation of the very principle set up. Oblige all men to refrain from violence? Who then should enforce the decision? Thirdly, and this is the chief point, the question, as put by Christ, is not at all, "Can non-resistance become a general law for humanity?" but, "How much each man act to fulfil his allotted task, to save his soul, and to do the will of God, three things which are really one and the same thing?" . . .

Tradition—the collective wisdom of my greatest forerunners—tells me that I should do unto others as I would that they should do unto me. My reason shows me that only by all men acting thus is the highest happiness for all men attainable. Only when I yield myself to that intuition of love which demands obedience to this law is my own heart happy and at rest. And not only can I then know how to act, but I can and do discern that work, to cooperate in which my activity was designed and is required. I cannot fathom God's whole design, for the sake of which the universe exists and lives; but the divine work which is being accomplished in this world, and in which I participate by living, is comprehensible to me.

This work is the annihilation of discord and strife among men, and among all creatures; and the establishment of the highest unity, concord, and love. It is the fulfilment of the promises of the Hebrew prophets, who foretold a time when all men should be taught by truth, when spears should be turned into reaping-hooks, swords be beaten to plowshares, and the lion lie down with the lamb. So that a man of Christian intelligence not only knows what he has to do, but he also understands the work he is doing. He has to act so as to cooperate toward the establishment of the kingdom of God on earth. For this, a man must obey his intuition of God's will, i.e. he must act lovingly toward others, as he would that others should act toward him. Thus the intuitive demands of man's soul coincide with the external aim of life which he sees before him. . . .

And yet, in spite of such a twofold indication, clear and indubitable to a man of Christian understanding of what is the real aim and meaning of human life, and of what men should do and should not do, we find people (and people calling themselves Christians) who decide that in such and such circumstances men ought to abandon God's law and reason's guidance, and act in opposition to them; because, according to their conception, the effects of actions performed in submission to God's law may be detrimental or inconvenient.

According to the law, contained alike in tradition, in our reason, and in our hearts, man should always do unto others as he would that they should do unto him; he should always cooperate in the development of love and union among created beings. But on the contrary, in the judgment of these people who look ahead, as long as it is premature, in their opinion, to obey this law, man should do violence, imprison or kill people, and thereby evoke anger and venom instead of loving union in the hearts of men. It is as if a bricklayer, set to do a particular task, and knowing that he was cooperating with others to build a house, after receiving clear and precise instructions from the master himself how to build a certain wall, should receive from some fellow bricklayers (who like himself knew neither the plan of the house nor what would fit in with it) orders to cease building his wall, and instead rather to pull down a wall which other workmen had erected.

Astonishing delusion! A being who breathes one day and vanishes the next receives one definite, indubitable law to guide him through the brief term of his life; but instead of obeying that law he prefers to fancy that he knows what is necessary, advantageous, and well-timed for men, for all the world—this world which continually shifts and evolves; and for the sake of some advantage (which each man pictures after his own fancy) he decides that he and other people should temporarily abandon the indubitable law given to one and to all, and should act, not as they would that others should act toward them, bringing love into the world, but instead do violence, imprison, kill, and bring into the world enmity whenever it seems profitable to do so. And he decides to act thus, though he knows that the most horrible cruelties, martyrdoms, and murders—from the inquisitions, and the murders, and horrors of all the revolutions, down to the violences of contemporary anarchists, and their slaughter by the established authorities—have only occurred because people will imagine that they know what is necessary for mankind and for the world. But are there not always, at any given moment, two opposite parties, each of which declares that it is necessary to use force against the other—the "law and order" party against the "anarchist"; the "anarchist" against the "law and order" men; English against Americans, and Americans against English, and English against Germans; and so forth in all possible combinations and rearrangements?

A man enlightened by Christianity sees that he has no reason to abandon the law of God, given to enable him to walk with sure foot through life, in order to follow the chance, inconstant, and often contradictory demands of men. But besides this, if he has lived a Christian life for some time, and has developed in himself a Christian moral sensibility, he literally cannot act as people demand of him. Not this reason only, but his feeling also, makes it impossible. To many people of our society it would be impossible to torture or kill a baby, even if they were told that by so doing they could save hundreds of people. And in the same way a man, when he has developed a Christian sensibility of heart, finds a whole series of actions are become impossible for him. For instance, a Christian who is obliged to take part in judicial proceedings in which a man may be sentenced to death, or who is obliged to take part in evictions, or in debating a proposal leading to war, or to participate in preparations for war (not to mention war itself), is in a position parallel to that of a kindly man called on to torture or to kill a baby. It is not reason alone that forbids him to do what is demanded of him; he feels instinctively that he cannot do it. For certain actions are morally impossible, just as others are physically impossible. As a man cannot lift a mountain, and as a kindly man cannot kill an infant, so a man living the Christian life cannot take part in deeds of violence. Of what value then to him are arguments about the imaginary advantages of doing what is morally impossible for him to do?

But how is a man to act when he sees clearly an evil in following the law of love and its corollary law of non-resistance? How (to use the stock example) is a man to act when he sees a criminal killing or outraging a child, and he can only save the child by killing the criminal? When such a case is put, it is generally assumed that the only possible reply is that one should kill the assailant to save the child. But this answer is given so quickly and decidedly only because we are all so accustomed to the use of violence, not only to save a child, but even to prevent a neighboring government altering its frontier at the expense of ours, or to prevent some one from smuggling lace across that frontier, or even to defend our garden fruit from a passer-by. It is assumed that to save the child the assailant should be killed.

But it is only necessary to consider the question, "On what grounds ought a man, whether he be or be not a Christian, to act so?" in order to come to the conclusion that such action has no reasonable foundation, and only seems to us necessary because up to two thousand years ago such conduct was considered right, and a habit of acting so had been formed. Why should a non-Christian, not acknowledging God, and not regarding the fulfilment of His will as the aim of life, decide to kill the criminal in order to defend the child? By killing the former he kills for certain; whereas he cannot know positively whether the criminal would have killed the child or not. But letting that pass, who shall say whether the child's life was more needed, was better, than the other's life? Surely, if the non-Christian knows not God, and does not see life's meaning to be in the performance of His will, the only rule for his actions must be a reckoning, a conception, of which is more profitable for him and for all men, a continuation of the criminal's life or of the child's. To decide that, he needs to know what would become of the child whom he saves, and what, had he not killed him, would have been the future of the assailant. And as he cannot know this, the non-Christian has no sufficient rational ground for killing a robber to save a child.

If a man be a Christian, and consequently acknowledges God, and sees the meaning of life in fulfilling His will, then, however ferocious the assailant, however innocent and lovely the child, he has even less ground to abandon the God-given law, and to do to the criminal as the criminal wishes to do to the child. He may plead with the assailant, may interpose his own body between the assailant and the victim; but there is one thing he cannot do—he cannot deliberately abandon the law he has received from God, the fulfilment of which alone gives meaning to his life. Very probably bad education, or his animal nature, may cause a man, Christian or non-Christian, to kill an assailant, not to save a child, but even to save himself or to save his purse. But it does not follow that he is right in acting thus, or that he should accustom himself or others to think such conduct right. What it does show is that, notwithstanding a coating of education and of Christianity, the habits of the stone age are yet so strong in man that he still commits actions long since condemned by his reasonable conscience.

I see a criminal killing a child, and I can save the child by killing the assailant—therefore, in certain cases, violence must be used to resist evil. A man's life is in danger, and can be saved only by my telling a lie—therefore, in certain cases, one must lie. A man is starving, and I can only save him by stealing—therefore, in certain cases, one must steal. . . . There is no moral law concerning which one might not devise a case in which it is difficult to decide which is more moral, to disobey the law or to obey it? But all such devices fail to prove that the laws, "Thou shalt not lie, steal, or kill," are invalid.

It is thus with the law of non-resistance. People know it is wrong to use violence, but they are so anxious to continue to live a life secured by "the strong arm of the law," that, instead of devoting their intellects to the elucidation of the evils which have flowed, and are still flowing, from admitting that man has a right to use violence to his fellow-men, they prefer to exert their mental powers in defense of that error. "*Fais ce que dois, advienne que pourra*"—"Do what's right, come what may"—is an expression of profound wisdom. We each can know indubitably what we ought to do, but what results will follow from our actions we none of us either do or can know. Therefore it follows that, besides feeling the call of duty, we are further driven to act as duty bids us by the consideration that we have no other guidance, but are totally ignorant of what will result from our action.

Christian teaching indicates what a man should do to perform the will of Him who sent him into life; and discussion as to what results we anticipate from such or such human actions have nothing to do with Christianity, but are just an example of the error which Christianity eliminates. None of us has ever yet met the imaginary criminal with the imaginary child, but all the horrors which fill the annals of history and of our own times came, and come, from this one thing, namely, that people will believe they really foresee speculative future results of actions.

The case is this. People once lived an animal life, and violated or killed whom they thought well to violate or to kill. They even ate one another, and public opinion approved of it. Thousands of years ago, as far back as the times of Moses, a day came when people had realized that to violate or kill one another is bad. But there were people for whom the reign of force was advantageous, and these did not approve of the change, but assured themselves and others that to do deeds of violence and to kill people is not always bad, but that there are circumstances when it is, necessary and even moral. And violence and slaughter, though not so frequent or so cruel as before, continued, only with this difference, that those who committed or commended such acts excused themselves by pleading that they did it for the benefit of humanity.

It was just this sophistical justification of violence that Christ denounced. When two enemies fight, each may think his own conduct justified by the circumstances. Excuses can be made for every use of violence, and no infallible standard has ever been discovered by which to measure the worth of these excuses. Therefore Christ taught us to disbelieve in any excuse for violence, and (contrary to what had been taught by them of old times) never to use violence. One would have thought that those who have professed Christianity would be indefatigable in exposing deception in this matter; for in such exposure lay one of the chief manifestations of Christianity. What really happened was just the reverse. People who profited by violence, and who did not wish to give up their advantages, took on themselves a monopoly of Christian preaching, and declared that, as cases can be found in which non-resistance causes more harm than the use of violence (the imaginary criminal killing the imaginary child), therefore Christ's doctrine of non-resistance need not always be followed;

and that one may deviate from His teaching to defend one's life or the life of others; or to defend one's country, to save society from lunatics or criminals, and in many other cases.

The decision of the question in what cases Christ's teaching should be set aside was left to the very people who employed violence. So that it ended by Christ's teaching on the subject of not resisting evil by violence being completely annulled. . . . The real question is not whether it will be good or bad for a certain human society that people should follow the law of love and the consequent law of non-resistance. But it is this: Do you, who today live and tomorrow will die, you who are indeed tending deathward every moment, do you wish now, immediately and entirely, to obey the law of Him who sent you into life, and who clearly showed you His will, alike in tradition and in your mind and heart; or do you prefer to resist His will? And as soon as the question is put thus, only one reply is possible: I wish now, this moment, without delay or hesitation, to the very utmost of my strength, neither waiting for one or counting the cost, to do that which alone is clearly demanded by Him who sent me into the world; and on no account, and under no conditions, do I wish to, or can I, act otherwise— for herein lies my only possibility of a rational and unharassed life.

EDNA ST. VINCENT MILLAY

Conscientious Objector

Nonviolent antiwar protest takes many forms. Much has been written by way of specific advice for individuals contemplating tax resistance, draft resistance, organized opposition to various government policies, and so forth. Consistent with the goal of this book, however, which is to focus on general principles and to provide lasting food for thought, we present "Conscientious Objector," a remarkable and timeless poem by Edna St. Vincent Millay.

I shall die, but that is all that I shall do for Death.
I hear him leading his horse out of the stall; I hear the clatter on the barn floor.

He is in haste; he has business in Cuba, business in the Balkans, many calls to make this morning.
But I will not hold the bridle while he cinches the girth.

And he may mount by himself: I will not give him a leg up.

Though he flick my shoulders with his whip, I will not tell him which way the fox ran.

With his hoof on my breast, I will not tell him where the black boy hides in the swamp.

I shall die, but that is all I shall do for Death; I am not on his payroll.

I will not tell him the whereabouts of my friends nor of my enemies either.

Though he promise me much, I will not map him the route to any man's door.

Am I a spy in the land of the living, that I should deliver men to Death?

Brother, the password and the plans of our city are safe with me; never through me

Shall you be overcome.

ALBERT CAMUS

Neither Victims nor Executioners

Personal commitment to nonviolence takes many forms. To complement Millay's statement in poetry, and Tolstoy's Christian-based faith, we present a prose, secular selection, from a renowned essay by French philosopher-novelist-playwright Albert Camus. Ironically, "Neither Victims nor Executioners" first appeared in a magazine titled *Combat*, which was edited by Camus on behalf of the anti-Nazi French Resistance during World War II. Somewhat like Tolstoy—although without the latter's religious motivation—Camus eventually committed himself to nonviolence. He was especially concerned with denying the legitimacy of violence on behalf of political ideology, of any persuasion.

The Century of Fear

The seventeenth century was the century of mathematics, the eighteenth that of the physical sciences, and the nineteenth that of biology. Our twentieth century is the century of fear. I will be told that fear is not a science. But science must be somewhat involved since its latest theoretical advances have brought it to the point of negating itself while its perfected technology threatens the globe itself with destruction. Moreover, although fear itself cannot be considered a science, it is certainly a technique.

The most striking feature of the world we live in is that most of its inhabitants—with the exception of pietists of various kinds—are cut off from the future. Life has no validity unless it can project itself toward the future, can ripen and progress. Living against a wall is a dog's life.

. . . I once said that, after the experiences of the last two years, I could no longer hold to any truth which might oblige me, directly or indirectly, to demand a man's life. Certain friends whom I respected retorted that I was living in Utopia, that there was no political truth which could not one day reduce us to such an extremity, and that we must therefore either run the risk of this extremity or else simply put up with the world as it is.

They argued the point most forcefully. But I think they were able to put such force into it only because they were unable to really

From Albert Camus "Neither Victims nor Executioners," *Combat*, fall, 1946. Translated by Dwight MacDonald, 1947. *Politics*, July-August, 1947.

imagine other people's death. It is a freak of the times. We make love by telephone, we work not on matter but on machines, and we kill and are killed by proxy. We gain in cleanliness, but lose in understanding.

But the argument has another, indirect meaning: it poses the question of Utopia. People like myself want not a world in which murder no longer exists (we are not so crazy as that!) but rather one in which murder is not legitimate. Here indeed we are Utopian—and contradictory. For we do live, it is true, in a world where murder is legitimate, and we ought to change it if we do not like it. But it appears that we cannot change it without risking murder. Murder thus throws us back on murder, and we will continue to live in terror whether we accept the fact with resignation or wish to abolish it by means which merely replace one terror with another.

It seems to me every one should think this over. For what strikes me, in the midst of polemics, threats and outbursts of violence, is the fundamental good will of every one. From Right to Left, every one, with the exception of a few swindlers, believes that his particular truth is the one to make men happy. And yet the combination of all these good intentions has produced the present infernal world, where men are killed, threatened and deported, where war is prepared, where one cannot speak freely without being insulted or betrayed. . . .

Little is to be expected from present-day governments, since these live and act according to a murderous code. Hope remains only in the most difficult task of all: to reconsider everything from the ground up, so as to shape a living society inside a dying society. Men must therefore, as individuals, draw up among themselves, within frontiers and across them, a new social contract which will unite them according to more reasonable principles.

More precisely, the latter's task would be to speak out clearly against the confusions of the Terror and at the same time to define the values by which a peaceful world may live. The first objectives might be the drawing up of an international code of justice whose Article No. 1 would be the abolition of the death penalty, and an exposition of the basic principles of a sociable culture (*"civilisation du dialogue"*). Such an undertaking would answer the needs of an era which has found no philosophical justification for that thirst for frater-

nity which today burns in Western man. There is no idea, naturally, of constructing a new ideology, but rather of discovering a style of life.

Let us suppose that certain individuals resolve that they will consistently oppose to power the force of example; to authority, exhortation; to insult, friendly reasoning; to trickery, simple honor. Let us suppose they refuse all the advantages of present-day society and accept only the duties and obligations which bind them to other men. Let us suppose they devote themselves to orienting education, the press and public opinion toward the principles outlined here. Then I say that such men would be acting not as Utopians but as honest realists. They would be preparing the future and at the same time knocking down a few of the walls which imprison us today. If realism be the art of taking into account both the present and the future, of gaining the most while sacrificing the least, then who can fail to see the positively dazzling realism of such behavior?

Whether these men will arise or not I do not know. It is probable that most of them are even now thinking things over, and that is good. But one thing is sure: their efforts will be effective only to the degree they have the courage to give up, for the present, some of their dreams, so as to grasp the more firmly the essential point on which our very lives depend. Once there, it will perhaps turn out to be necessary, before they are done, to raise their voices. . . .

To save what can be saved so as to open up some kind of future—that is the prime mover, the passion and the sacrifice that is required. It demands only that we reflect and then decide, clearly, whether humanity's lot must be made still more miserable in order to achieve far-off and shadowy ends, whether we should accept a world bristling with arms where brother kills brother; or whether, on the contrary, we should avoid bloodshed and misery as much as possible so that we give a chance for survival to later generations better equipped than we are.

For my part, I am fairly sure that I have made the choice. And, having chosen, I think that I must speak out, that I must state that I will never again be one of those, whoever they be, who compromise with murder, and that I must take the consequences of such a decision. . . .

We are asked to love or to hate such and such a country and such and such a people. But some of us feel too strongly our common humanity to make such a choice. Those who really love the Russian people, in gratitude for what they have never ceased to be—that world leaven which Tolstoy and Gorky speak of—do not wish for them success in power-politics, but rather want to spare them, after the ordeals of the past, a new and even more terrible blood-letting. So, too, with the American people, and with the peoples of unhappy Europe. This is the kind of elementary truth we are liable to forget amidst the furious passions of our time.

Yes, it is fear and silence and the spiritual isolation they cause that must be fought today. And it is sociability ("*le dialogue*") and the universal intercommunication of men that must be defended. Slavery, injustice and lies destroy this intercourse and forbid this sociability; and so we must reject them. But these evils are today the very stuff of History, so that many consider them necessary evils. It is true that we cannot "escape History," since we are in it up to our necks. But one may propose to fight within History to preserve from History that part of man which is not its proper province. That is all I have tried to say here. The "point" of this article may be summed up as follows:

Modern nations are driven by powerful forces along the roads of power and domination. I will not say that these forces should be furthered or that they should be obstructed. They hardly need our help and, for the moment, they laugh at attempts to hinder them. They will, then, continue. But I will ask only this simple question: what if these forces wind up in a dead end, what if that logic of History on which so many now rely turns out to be a will o' the wisp? What if, despite two or three world wars, despite the sacrifice of several generations and a whole system of values, our grand-children—supposing they survive—find themselves no closer to a world society? It may well be that the survivors of such an experience will be too weak to understand their own sufferings. Since these forces are working themselves out and since it is inevitable that they continue to do so, there is no reason why some of us should not take on the job of keeping alive, through the apocalyptic historical vista that stretches before us, a modest thoughtfulness which, without pretending to solve everything, will constantly be prepared to give some human meaning to everyday life. The essential thing is that people should carefully weight the price they must pay.

To conclude: all I ask is that, in the midst of a murderous world, we agree to reflect on murder and to make a choice. After that, we can distinguish those who accept the consequences of being murderers themselves or the accomplices of murderers, and those who refuse to do so with all their force and being. Since this terrible dividing line does actually exist, it will be a gain if it be clearly marked. Over the expanse of five continents throughout the coming years an endless struggle is going to be pursued between violence and friendly persuasion, a struggle in which, granted, the former has a thousand times the chances of success than that of the latter. But I have always held that, if he who bases his hopes on human nature is a fool, he who gives up in the face of circumstances is a coward. And henceforth, the only honorable course will be to stake everything on a formidable gamble: that words are more powerful than munitions.

Ahimsa, or the Way of Nonviolence

Mohandas Gandhi is the pre-eminent figure of nonviolence, at least in the twentieth century, if not future centuries. (The word "Mahatma" is an honorific title in the Hindi language, meaning "great soul.") Gandhi may have been the first person—certainly, he was the most effective and influential—to extend nonviolence from a principle of individual behavior to a concerted strategy grounded in a search for political and social justice.

Gandhi's teachings—as well as his practical example—have been carefully studied by many nonviolent leaders, including the Rev. Martin Luther King, Jr., who patterned his leadership of the civil rights struggle in the United States after Gandhi's decades-long efforts in South Africa and then India. (Gandhian thought and practice has also influenced human rights crusaders in China, Burma, Indonesia, and indeed, around the globe.)

"With the increased velocity of modern changes we do not know what the world will be a hundred years hence," wrote S. Radhakrishnan, Vice President and later President of India, in the Introduction to Gandhi's book of autobiographical reflections, *All Men Are Brothers*.

> We cannot anticipate the future currents of thought and feeling. But years may go their way, yet the great principles of *satya* and *ahimsa*, truth and nonviolence, are there to guide us. They are the silent stars keeping holy vigil above a tired and turbulent world. Like Gandhi we may be firm in our conviction that the sun shines above the drifting clouds.
>
> We live in an age which is aware of its own defeat and moral coarsening, an age in which old certainties are breaking down, the familiar patterns are tilting and cracking. There is increasing intolerance and embitterment.... It is our pride that one of the greatest figures of history lived in our generation, walked with us, spoke to us, taught us the way of civilized living. He who wrongs no one fears no one. He has nothing to hide and so is fearless. He looks everyone in the face. His step is firm, his body upright, and his words are direct and straight. Plato said long ago: "There always are in the world a few inspired men whose acquaintance is beyond price."

Gandhi explained that *ahimsa* "does not mean meek submission to the will of the evil-doer, but it means pitting of one's whole soul against the will of the tyrant. Working under this law of our being, it is possible for a single individual to defy the whole might of an unjust empire ..." In addition to *ahimsa* and *satya* (or *satyagraha*), another Gandhian term is crucially important: *tapasya*, a willingness to undergo suffering oneself, and not to shift it onto another—including the opponent—as a consequence of one's commitment to the truth of nonviolence.

Although *tapasya* may be especially difficult for many people to accept or understand (not to mention, to practice!), it should not be especially foreign, especially if one substitutes "courage" for "willingness to suffer," which has the added benefit of helping dispel the frequent misunderstanding that practitioners of nonviolence are lazy or cowardly, seeking an easy way out of conflict.

From *All Men are Brothers* by Mohandas Gandhi. 1980. New York: Continuum.

The courage and commitment of *satyagrahis* come at a price, as revealed in this eye-witness account of the famous "salt *satyagraha*" of 1930. Gandhi and 2,500 peaceful marchers arrived at a police stockade near the Dharasana Salt Works, in defiance of law and in complete silence, approaching and in turn being battered on the head with steel-shod clubs, while no one even raised an arm in self-protection: "From where I stood I heard the sickening whack of the clubs on unprotected skulls. . . . The survivors, without breaking ranks, silently and doggedly marched on until struck down."[4] In the long run, such techniques have in fact been overwhelmingly successful, in no small part because of their powerful appeal to shared human conscience. (Once, when visiting England, Gandhi was asked his impression of Western civilization, to which he replied "It would be a good idea.")

It may be that—as is frequently pointed out—Gandhian nonviolence would not have succeeded against, say, a nuclear-armed Hitler. Perhaps it requires a degree of underlying humanity and good will on the other side. But it is also true that the British empire had not been especially gentle or humane in its treatment of colonial subjects and, in the end, persistent nonviolent tactics succeeded in liberating a nation of (at that time) more than 400 million people, without firing a shot.

Gandhi himself pointed out that nonviolence is more pervasive in ordinary human life than most of us realize, and far more frequently (and successfully) employed than is violence.

It is hoped that the following selections will help acquaintant the reader with the remarkable, inspired person Gandhi was, and, in the process, reveal the potential for nonviolence as an approach to peace.

Nonviolence is the greatest force at the disposal of mankind. It is mightier than the mightiest weapon of destruction devised by the ingenuity of man. Destruction is not the law of the humans. Man lives freely by his readiness to die, if need be, at the hands of his brother, never by killing him. Every murder or other injury, no matter for what cause, committed or inflicted on another is a crime against humanity.

Harijan, July 20, 1931

The first condition of nonviolence is justice all round in every department of life. Perhaps, it is too much to expect of human nature. I do not, however, think so. No one should dogmatize about the capacity of human nature for degradation or exaltation.

Mahatma, V., April, 1940

Just as one must learn the art of killing in the training for violence, so one must learn the art of dying in the training for nonviolence. Violence does not mean emancipation from fear, but discovering the means of combating the cause of fear. Nonviolence, on the other hand, has no cause for fear. The votary of nonviolence has to cultivate the capacity for sacrifice of the highest type in order to be free from fear. He recks not if he should lose his land, his wealth, his life. He who has not overcome all fear cannot practise *ahiṃsā* to perfection. The votary of *ahiṃsā* has only one fear, that is of God. He who seeks refuge in God ought to have a glimpse of the *Atma* that transcends the body; and the moment one has a glimpse of the imperishable *Atma* one sheds the love of the perishable body. Training in nonviolence is thus diametrically opposed to training in violence. Violence is needed for the protection of things external, nonviolence is needed for the protection of the *Atma*, for the protection of one's honour.

Harijan, September 1, 1940

---

[4]quoted in Erik Erikson. 1969. *Gandhi's Truth*. New York: W.W. Norton.

It is no nonviolence if we merely love those that love us. It is nonviolence only when we love those that hate us. I know how difficult it is to follow this grand law of love. But are not all great and good things difficult to do? Love of the hater is the most difficult of all. But by the grace of God even this most difficult thing becomes easy to accomplish if we want to do it.

Letter of December 31, 1934

I have found that life persists in the midst of destruction and therefore there must be a higher law than that of destruction. . . .

It is not that I am incapable of anger, for instance, but I succeed on almost all occasions to keep my feelings under control. Whatever may be the result, there is always in me conscious struggle for following the law of nonviolence deliberately and ceaselessly. Such a struggle leaves one stronger for it. The more I work at this law, the more I feel the delight in my life, the delight in the scheme of the universe. It gives me a peace and a meaning of the mysteries of nature that I have no power to describe.

Young India, October 1, 1931

If we turn our eyes to the time of which history has any record down to our own time, we shall find that man has been steadily progressing towards *ahiṃsā*. Our remote ancestors were cannibals. Then came a time when they were fed up with cannibalism and they began to live on chase. Next came a stage when man was ashamed of leading the life of a wandering hunter. He therefore took to agriculture and depended principally on mother earth for his food. Thus from being a nomad he settled down to civilized stable life, founded villages and towns, and from member of a family he became member of a community and a nation. All these are signs of progressive *ahiṃsā* and diminishing *hiṃsā*. Had it been otherwise, the human species should have been extinct by now, even as many of the lower species have disappeared.

Prophets and *avatārs* have also taught the lesson of *ahiṃsā* more or less. Not one of them has professed to teach *hiṃsā*. And how should it be otherwise? *Hiṃsā* does not need to be taught. Man as animal is violent, but as Spirit is nonviolent. The moment he awakes to the Spirit within, he cannot remain violent. Either he progresses towards *ahiṃsā* or rushes to his doom. That is why the prophets and *avatārs* have taught the lesson of truth, harmony, brotherhood, justice, etc. all attributes of *ahiṃsā*.

Harijan, August 11, 1940

I have never claimed to present the complete science of nonviolence. It does not lend itself to such treatment. So far as I know, no single physical science does, not even the very exact science of mathematics. I am but a seeker.

Harijan, February 22, 1942

In the application of *Satyāgraha*, I discovered in the earliest stages that pursuit of truth did not admit of violence being inflicted on one's opponent but that he must be weaned from error by patience and sympathy. For, what appears to be truth to the one may appear to be error to another. And patience means self-suffering. So the doctrine came to mean vindication of truth, not by infliction of suffering on the opponent, but on one's self.

Young India, November, 1919

In this age of wonders no one will say that a thing or idea is worthless because it is new. To say it is impossible because it is difficult, is again not in consonance with the spirit of the age. Things undreamt of are daily being seen, the impossible is ever becoming possible. We are constantly being astonished these days at the amazing discoveries in the field of violence. But I maintain that far more undreamt of and seemingly impossible discoveries will be made in the field of nonviolence.

Harijan, August 25, 1940

Nonviolence is a universal principle and its operation is not limited by a hostile environment. Indeed, its efficacy can be tested only when it acts in the midst of and in spite of opposition. Our nonviolence would be a hollow thing and worth nothing, if it depended for its success on the goodwill of the authorities.

Harijan, November 12, 1938

No man could be actively nonviolent and not rise against social injustice no matter where it occurred.

Harijan, April 20, 1940

Passive resistance is a method of securing rights by personal suffering; it is the reverse of resistance by arms. When I refuse to do a thing that is repugnant to my conscience, I use soul-force. For instance, the government of the day has passed a law which is applicable to me. I do not like it. If by using violence I force the government to repeal the law, I am employing what may be termed body-force. If I do not obey the law and accept the penalty for its breach, I use soul-force. It involves sacrifice of self.

Everybody admits that sacrifice of self is infinitely superior to sacrifice of others. Moreover, if this kind of force is used in a cause that is unjust, only the person using it suffers. He does not make others suffer for his mistakes. Men have before now done many things which were subsequently found to have been wrong. No man can claim that he is absolutely in the right or that a particular thing is wrong because he thinks so, but it is wrong for him so long as that is his deliberate judgement. It is therefore meet that he should not do that which he knows to be wrong, and suffer the consequence whatever it may be. This is the key to the use of soul-force.

Indian Home Rule, 1909

You might of course say that there can be no nonviolent rebellion and there has been none known to history. Well, it is my ambition to provide an instance, and it is my dream that my country may win its freedom through nonviolence. And, I would like to repeat to the world times without number, that I will not purchase my country's freedom at the cost of nonviolence. My marriage to nonviolence is such an absolute thing that I would rather commit suicide than be deflected from my position. I have not mentioned truth in this connexion, simply because truth cannot be expressed except by nonviolence.

Young India, November 12, 1931

The conviction has been growing upon me, that things of fundamental importance to the people are not secured by reason alone but have to be purchased with their suffering. Suffering is the law of human beings; war is the law of the jungle. But suffering is infinitely more powerful than the law of the jungle for converting the opponent and opening his ears, which are otherwise shut, to the voice of reason. Nobody has probably drawn up more petitions or espoused more forlorn causes than I and I have come to this fundamental conclusion that if you want something really important to be done you must not merely satisfy the reason, you must move the heart also. The appeal of reason is more to the head but the penetration of the heart comes from suffering. It opens up the inner understanding in man. Suffering is the badge of the human race, not the sword.

Young India, November 4, 1931

Nonviolence is a power which can be wielded equally by all—children, young men and women or grown up people—provided they have a living faith in the God of Love and have therefore equal love for all mankind. When nonviolence is accepted as the law of life it must pervade the whole being and not be applied to isolated acts.

Harijan, September 5, 1936

Perfect nonviolence is impossible so long as we exist physically, for we would want some space at least to occupy. Perfect nonviolence whilst you are inhabiting the body is only a theory like Euclid's point or straight line, but we have to endeavour every moment of our lives.

Harijan, July 21, 1940

Taking life may be a duty. We do destroy as much life as we think necessary for sustaining our body. Thus for food we take life, vegetable and other, and for health we destroy mosquitoes and the like by the use of disinfectants, etc., and we do not think that we are guilty of irreligion in doing so ... for the benefit of the species, we kill carnivorous beasts. ... Even man-slaughter may be necessary in certain cases. Suppose a man runs amuck and goes furiously about, sword in hand, and killing anyone that comes in his way, and no one dares to capture him alive. Anyone who despatches this lunatic will earn the gratitude of the community and be regarded as a benevolent man.

Young India, November 4, 1926

A man cannot practise *ahiṃsā* and be a coward at the same time. The practice of *ahiṃsā* calls forth the greatest courage.

Speeches and Writings of Mahatma Gandhi,
no date given.

Nonviolence is 'not a resignation from all real fighting against wickedness.' On the contrary, the nonviolence of my conception is a more active and real fight against wickedness than retaliation whose very nature is to increase wickedness. I contemplate a mental and therefore a moral opposition to immoralities. I seek entirely to blunt the edge of the tyrant's sword, not by putting up against it a sharper-edged weapon, but by disappointing his expectation that I would be offering physical resistance. The resistance of the soul that I should offer would elude him. It would at first dazzle him and at last compel recognition from him, which recognition would not humiliate but would uplift him. It may be urged that this is an ideal state. And so it is.

Young India, October 8, 1925

I object to violence because when it appears to do good, the good is only temporary; the evil it does is permanent. I do not believe that the killing of even every Englishman can do the slightest good to India. The millions will be just as badly off as they are today, if someone made it possible to kill off every Englishman tomorrow. The responsibility is more ours than that of the English for the present state of things. The English will be powerless to do evil if we will but be good. Hence my incessant emphasis on reform from within.

Young India, May 21, 1925

History teaches one that those who have, no doubt with honest motives, ousted the greedy by using brute force against them, have in their turn become a prey to the disease of the conquered.

Young India, May 6, 1926

It is to me a matter of perennial satisfaction that I retain generally the affection and trust of those whose principles and policies I oppose. The South Africans gave me personally their confidence and extended their

friendship. In spite of my denunciation of British policy and system I enjoy the affection of thousands of Englishmen and women, and in spite of unqualified condemnation of modern materialistic civilization, the circle of European and American friends is ever widening. It is again a triumph of nonviolence.

Young India, March 17, 1927

My experience, daily growing stronger and richer, tells me that there is no peace for individuals or for nations without practising truth and nonviolence to the uttermost extent possible for man. The policy of retaliation has never succeeded.

Young India, December 15, 1927

I have been practising with scientific precision nonviolence and its possibilities for an unbroken period of over fifty years. I have applied it in every walk of life—domestic, institutional, economic and political. I know of no single case in which it has failed. Where it has seemed sometimes to have failed, I have ascribed it to my imperfections. I claim no perfection for myself. But I do claim to be a passionate seeker after Truth, which is but another name for God. In the course of that search the discovery of nonviolence came to me. Its spread is my life mission. I have no interest in living except for the prosecution of that mission.

Harijan, July 6, 1940

I do not want to live at the cost of the life even of a snake. I should let him bite me to death rather than kill him. But it is likely that if God puts me to that cruel test and permits a snake to assault me, I may not have the courage to die, but that the beast in me may assert itself and I may seek to kill the snake in defending this perishable body. I admit that my belief has not become so incarnate in me as to warrant my stating emphatically that I have shed all fear of snakes so as to befriend them as I would like to be able to.

An Autobiography

Ahiṃsā is soul-force and the soul is imperishable, changeless and eternal. The atom bomb is the acme of physical force and, as such, subject to the law of dissipation, decay and death that governs the physical universe. Our scriptures bear witness that when soul-force is fully awakened in us, it becomes irresistible. But the test and condition of full awakening is that it must permeate every pore of our being and emanate with every breath that we breathe.

But no institution can be made nonviolent by compulsion. Nonviolence and truth cannot be written into a constitution. They have to be adopted of one's own free will. They must sit naturally upon us like next-to-skin garments or else they become a contradiction in terms.

Mahatma Gandhi, The Last Phase, II, circa, 1947

My creed of nonviolence is an extremely active force. It has no room for cowardice or even weakness. There is hope for a violent man to be some day nonviolent, but there is none for a coward. I have therefore said more than once in these pages that if we do not know how to defend ourselves, our women and our places of worship by the force of suffering, i.e., nonviolence, we must, if we are men, be at least able to defend all these by fighting.

Young India, June 16, 1927

In life, it is impossible to eschew violence completely. Now the question arises, where is one to draw the line? The line cannot be the same for every one. For, although, essentially the principle is the same, yet everyone applies it in his or her own way. What is one man's food can be another's poison. Meat-eating is a sin for me. Yet, for another person, who has always lived on meat and never seen anything wrong in it, to give it up, simply in order to copy me, will be a sin.

If I wish to be an agriculturist and stay in a jungle, I will have to use the minimum unavoidable violence, in order to protect my fields. I will have to kill monkeys, birds and insects, which eat up my crops. If I do not wish to do so myself, I will have to engage someone to do it for me. There is not much difference between the two. To allow crops to be eaten up by animals, in the name of *ahimsā*, while there is a famine in the land, is certainly a sin. Evil and good are relative terms. What is good under certain conditions can become an evil or a sin, under a different set of conditions. . . .

Mahatma, VII, 1946

The people of a village near Bettia told me that they had run away whilst the police were looting their houses and molesting their womenfolk. When they said that they had run away because I had told them to be nonviolent, I hung my head in shame. I assured them that such was not the meaning of my nonviolence. I expected them to intercept the mightiest power that might be in the act of harming those who were under their protection, and draw without retaliation all harm upon their own heads even to the point of death, but never to run away from the storm centre. It was manly enough to defend one's property, honour, or religion at the point of the sword. It was manlier and nobler to defend them without seeking to injure the wrong-doer. But it was unmanly, unnatural and dishonourable to forsake the post of duty and, in order to save one's skin, to leave property, honour or religion to the mercy of the wrong-doer. I could see my way of delivering *ahimsā* to those who knew how to die, not to those who were afraid of death.

Gandhiji in Indian Villages, published in 1927

My nonviolence does not admit of running away from danger and leaving dear ones unprotected. Between violence and cowardly flight, I can only prefer violence to cowardice. I can no more preach nonviolence to a coward than I can tempt a blind man to enjoy healthy scenes. Nonviolence is the summit of bravery. And in my own experience, I have had no difficulty in demonstrating to men trained in the school of violence the superiority of nonviolence. As a coward, which I was for years, I harboured violence. I began to prize nonviolence only when I began to shed cowardice.

Young India, May 28, 1924

Nonviolence cannot be taught to a person who fears to die and has no power of resistance. A helpless mouse is not nonviolent because he is always eaten by pussy. He would gladly eat the murderess if he could, but he ever tries to flee from her. We do not call him a coward, because he is made by nature to behave no better than he does. But a man who, when faced by danger, behaves like a mouse, is rightly called a coward. He harbours violence and hatred in his heart and would kill his enemy if he could without hurting himself. He is a stranger to nonviolence. All sermonizing on it will be lost on him. Bravery is foreign to his nature. Before he can understand nonviolence he has to be taught to stand his ground and even suffer death, in the attempt to defend himself against the aggressor who bids fair to overwhelm him. To do otherwise would be to confirm his cowardice and take him farther away from nonviolence. Whilst I may not actually help anyone to retaliate, I must not let a coward seek shelter behind nonviolence so-called. Not knowing the stuff of which nonviolence is made, many have honestly believed that running away from danger every time was a virtue compared to offering resistance, especially when it was fraught with danger to one's life. As a teacher of nonviolence I must, so far as it is possible for me, guard against such an unmanly belief.

Harijan, July 20, 1935

I am not a visionary. I claim to be a practical idealist. Religion of nonviolence is not meant merely for the *rishis* and saints. It is meant for the common people as well. Nonviolence is the law of our species as violence is the law of the brute. The spirit lies dormant in the brute, and he knows no law but that of physical might. The dignity of man requires obedience to a higher law, to the strength of the spirit.

I have ventured to place before India the ancient law of self-sacrifice. For *Satyāgraha* and its offshoots, non-co-operation and civil resistance, are nothing but new names for the law of suffering. The *rishis*, who discovered the law of nonviolence in the midst of violence, were greater geniuses than Newton. They were themselves greater warriors than Wellington. Having themselves known the use of arms, they realized their uselessness and taught a weary world that its salvation lay not through violence but through nonviolence.

Nonviolence in its dynamic condition means conscious suffering. It does not mean meek submission to the will of the evil-doer, but it means putting of one's whole soul against the will of the tyrant. Working under this law of our being, it is possible for a single individual to defy the whole might of an unjust empire to save his honour, his religion, his soul, and lay the foundation for that empire's fall or its regeneration.

And so I am not pleading for India to practise nonviolence because it is weak. I want her to practise nonviolence being conscious of her strength and power. No training in arms is required for realization of her strength. We seem to need it, because we seem to think that we are but a lump of flesh. I want to recognize that she has a soul that cannot perish and that can rise triumphant above every physical weakness and defy the physical combination of a whole world. . . . If India takes up the doctrine of the sword, she may gain momentary victory. Then India will cease to be the pride of my heart. I am wedded to India because I owe my all to her. I believe absolutely that she has a mission for the world. She is not to copy Europe blindly. India's acceptance of the doctrine of the sword will be the hour of my trial. I hope I shall not be found wanting. My religion has no geographical limits. If I have a living faith in it, it will transcend my love for India herself. My life is dedicated to the service of India through the religion of nonviolence which I believe to be the root of Hinduism.

Mahatma, II, Young India, August 11, 1920

I must continue to argue till I convert opponents or I own defeat. For my mission is to convert every Indian, even Englishmen and finally the world, to nonviolence for regulating mutual relations whether political, economic, social or religious. If I am accused of being too ambitious, I should plead guilty. If I am told that my dream can never materialize, I would answer 'that is possible,' and go my way. I am a seasoned soldier of nonviolence, and I have evidence enough to sustain my faith. Whether, therefore, I have one comrade or more or none, I must continue my experiment.

Mahatma, V, Harijan, January 13, 1940

It has been suggested by American friends that the atom bomb will bring in *ahiṃsā*, as nothing else can. It will, if it is meant that its destructive power will so disgust the world, that it will turn it away from violence for the time being. And this is very like a man glutting himself with the dainties to the point of nausea, and turning away from them only to return with redoubled zeal after the effect of nausea is well over. Precisely in the same manner will the world return to violence with renewed zeal, after the effect of disgust is worn out.

Often does good come out of evil. But that is God's, not man's plan. Man knows that only evil can come out of evil, as good out of good. . . . The moral to be legitimately drawn from the supreme tragedy of the atom bomb is that it will not be destroyed by counter bombs, even as violence cannot be by counter violence. Mankind has to go out of violence only through nonviolence. Hatred can be overcome only by love. Counter hatred only increases the surface, as well as the depth of hatred. . . .

Mahatma, VII, Harijan, July 1946

GENE SHARP

Civilian Resistance as a National Defense

Could nonviolence be applied, as a practical matter, to the defense strategy of modern governments? One of the most seriously considered applications involves civilian-based defense, or CBD, which embraces a variety of nonviolent techniques intended to make it very difficult, if not impossible, for a conquering state to govern another and to gain any benefit from its "victory." CBD must be distinguished from "civil defense," the much less realistic government plan for protecting citizenry in the event of nuclear war, widely derided as neither civil, nor defense. CBD is also different from so-called Nonprovocative Defense (NPD), which emphasizes "defensive defense" via such armaments as antitank devices, anti-aircraft munitions, and mobile infantry, as opposed to potentially provocative, offensive weaponry such as bombers, tanks, and other "power-projecting" technology. NPD is a potential way of helping countries avoid the "security dilemma," whereby the pursuit of military security by one country induces insecurity on the part of others; nonetheless, it clearly fails the test of true nonviolence.

The major theorist of CBD, Gene Sharp, has identified specific tactics of nonviolent action. Civilian defenders would not violently resist the occupation of their country; moreover, they would willingly expose themselves to the possibility of substantial hardship, suffering, and even death. But traditional military defenders, too, must anticipate great hardship and suffering, and even death, even in a "successful," violent war. Advocates of CBD emphasize that substantial training of committed citizens would be required. But again, traditional military training in the ways of violence also requires time, effort, and sacrifice, as well as commitment. Moreover, most efforts at nonviolent resistance—Hungary in the mid-nineteenth century, Norway in World War II, Eastern Europe in 1989—were spontaneous, unplanned, and largely leaderless. Serious CBD, well rehearsed and supported by material resources, has never been tried. Given its impressive track record as a form of resistance when it was essentially extemporized, the future of CBD might be bright indeed if it were ever actually carried out by a well-trained populace. And the prospect of facing a determined and highly disciplined citizenry, committed to denying the invader virtually all fruits of conquest, might deter

From Gene Sharp. *Civilian Resistance as a National Defense: Non-violent Action Against Aggression.* A. Roberts, ed. 1968, Harrisburg, PA: Stackpole Books.

invasion no less effectively than the amassing of military forces, and at substantially less cost and risk of provocation.

As weapons become ever more destructive, doctrines of national security based on traditional military techniques offer less and less prospect of defense. During the Vietnam War, for example, a U.S. major claimed that the village of Ben Tre "had to be destroyed in order for us to save it." Gene Sharp has pointed out that by contrast, CBD alters this dynamic in a crucial way, since would seek nonviolently to "deny the attackers their objectives and to make society politically indigestible and ungovernable."[5]

It is widely believed that military combat is the only effective means of struggle in a wide variety of situations of acute conflict. However, there is another whole approach to the waging of social and political conflict. Any proposed substitute for war in the defense of freedom must involve wielding power, confronting and engaging an invader's military might, and waging effective combat. The technique of nonviolent action, although relatively ignored and undeveloped, may be able to meet these requirements and provide the basis for a defense policy.

Alternative Approach to the Control of Political Power

Military action is based largely on the idea that the most effective way of defeating an enemy is by inflicting heavy destruction on his armies, military equipment, transport system, factories, and cities. Weapons are designed to kill or destroy with maximum efficiency. Nonviolent action is based on a different approach: to deny the enemy the human assistance and cooperation which are necessary if he is to exercise control over the population. It is thus based on a more fundamental and sophisticated view of political power.

A ruler's power is ultimately dependent on support from the people he would rule. His moral authority, economic resources, transport system, government bureaucracy, army, and police—to name but a few immediate sources of his power—rest finally upon the cooperation and assistance of other people. If there is general conformity, the ruler is powerful.

But people do not always do what their rulers would like them to do. The factory manager recognizes this when he finds his workers leaving their jobs and machines, so that the production line ceases operation, or when he finds the workers persisting in doing something on the job which he has forbidden them to do. In many areas of social and political life comparable situations are commonplace....

Nonviolent Action

The "technique" of "nonviolent action," which is based on this approach to the control of political power and the waging of political struggles, has been the subject of many misconceptions. For the sake of clarity the two terms are defined in this section.

The term *technique* is used here to describe the overall means of conducting an action or struggle. One can therefore speak of the technique of guerrilla warfare, of conventional warfare, and of parliamentary democracy.

The term *nonviolent action* refers to those methods of protest, noncooperation, and intervention in which the actionists, without employing physical violence, refuse to do certain things which they are expected, or required, to do, or do certain things which they are not expected, or are forbidden, to do. In a particular case there can of course be a combination of acts of omission and acts of commission.

Nonviolent action is a generic term; it includes the large class of phenomena variously called "nonviolent resistance," "satyagraha," "passive resistance," "positive action," and "nonviolent direct action." While it is not violent, it *is* action, and not inaction; passivity, submission, and cowardice must be surmounted if it is to be used. It is a means of conducting conflicts and waging struggles and is

[5]Gene Sharp. 1985. *Making Europe Unconquerable: The Potential of Civilian-based Deterrence and Defense.* Cambridge, Mass: Ballinger.

not to be equated with (though it may be accompanied by) purely verbal dissent or solely psychological influence. It is not "pacifism," and in fact has in the vast majority of cases been applied by nonpacifists. The motives for the adoption of nonviolent action may be religious or ethical, or they may be based on considerations of expediency. Nonviolent action is not an escapist approach to the problem of violence, for it can be applied in struggles against opponents relying on violent sanctions. The fact that in a conflict one side is nonviolent does not imply that the other side will also refrain from violence. Certain forms of nonviolent action may be regarded as efforts to persuade by action, while others are more coercive.

Methods of Nonviolent Action

There is a very wide range of methods, or forms, of nonviolent action, and at least 125 have been identified. They fall into three classes—nonviolent protest, noncooperation, and nonviolent intervention.

Generally speaking, the methods of *nonviolent protest* are symbolic in their effect and produce an awareness of the existence of dissent. Under tyrannical regimes, however, where opposition is stifled, their impact can in some circumstances be very great. Methods of nonviolent protest include marches, pilgrimages, picketing, vigils, "haunting" officials, public meetings, issuing and distributing protest literature, renouncing honors, voluntary emigration, and humorous pranks.

The methods of *nonviolent noncooperation*, if sufficient numbers take part, are likely to present the opponent with difficulties in maintaining the normal efficiency and operation of the system, and in extreme cases the system itself may be threatened. Methods of nonviolent noncooperation include various types of strike (such as general strike, sit-down strike, industry strike, go-slow, and work-to-rule), various types of boycott (such as economic boycott, consumers' boycott, traders' boycott, rent refusal, international economic embargo, and social boycott), and various types of political noncooperation (such as boycott of government employment, boycott of elections, revenue refusal, civil disobedience, and mutiny).

The methods of *nonviolent intervention* have some features in common with the first two classes but also challenge the opponent more directly, and, assuming that fearlessness and discipline are maintained, relatively small numbers may have a disproportionately large impact. Methods of nonviolent intervention include sit-ins, fasts, reverse strikes, nonviolent obstruction, nonviolent invasion, and parallel government.

The exact way in which methods from each of the three classes are combined varies considerably from one situation to another. Generally speaking, the risks to the actionists on the one hand, and to the system against which they take action on the other, are least in the case of nonviolent protest and greatest in the case of nonviolent intervention. The methods of noncooperation tend to require the largest numbers but not to demand a large degree of special training from all participants. The methods of nonviolent intervention are generally effective if the participants possess a high degree of internal discipline and are willing to accept severe repression; the tactics must also be selected and carried out with particular care and intelligence. . . .

Nonviolent Action versus Violence

There can be no presumption that an opponent, faced with an opposition relying solely on nonviolent methods, will suddenly renounce his capacity for violence. Instead, nonviolent action can operate against opponents able and willing to use violent sanctions and can counter their violence in such a way that they are thrown politically off balance in a kind of political *jiu-jitsu*.

Instead of confronting the opponent's police and troops with the same type of forces, nonviolent actionists counter these agents of the opponent's power indirectly. Their aim is to demonstrate that repression is incapable of cowing the populace and to deprive the opponent of his existing support, thereby undermining his ability or will to continue with the repression. Far from indicating the failure of nonviolent action, repression often helps to make clear the cruelty of the political system being opposed, and so to alienate support from it. Repression is often a kind of recognition from the opponent that the nonviolent action constitutes a serious threat to his policy or regime, one which he finds it necessary to combat.

Just as in war danger from enemy fire does not always force front line soldiers to panic and flee, so in nonviolent action repression does not necessarily produce submission. True, repression *may* be effective, but it may fail to halt defiance, and in this case the opponent will be in difficulties. Repression against a nonviolent group which persists in face of it and maintains nonviolent discipline may have the following effects: it may alienate the general population from the opponent's regime, making them more likely to join the resistance; it may alienate the opponent's usual supporters and agents, and their initial uneasiness may grow into internal opposition and at times into noncooperation and disobedience; and it may rally general public opinion (domestic or international) to the support of the nonviolent actionists. Though the effectiveness of this last factor varies greatly from one situation to another, it may produce various types of supporting actions. If repression thus produces larger numbers of nonviolent actionists, thereby increasing the defiance, and if it leads to internal dissent among the opponent's supporters, thereby reducing his capacity to deal with the defiance, it will clearly have rebounded against the opponent.

Naturally, with so many variables (including the nature of the contending groups, the issues involved, the context of the struggle, the means of repression, and the methods of nonviolent action used), in no two instances will nonviolent action "work" in exactly the same way. However, it is possible to indicate in very general terms the ways in which it does achieve results. It is, of course, sometimes defeated: no technique of action can guarantee its user short-term victory in every instance of its use. It is important to recognize, however, that failure in nonviolent action may be caused not by an inherent weakness of the technique but by weakness in the movement employing it, or in the strategy and tactics used. . . .

The Indirect Approach
to the Opponent's Power

The technique of nonviolent action, and the policy of civilian defense relying upon it, can be regarded as extreme forms of the "strategy of indirect approach" which Liddell Hart has propounded in the sphere of military strategy. He has argued that a direct strategy—confronting the opponent head-on—consolidates the opponent's strength. "To move along the line of natural expectation consolidates the opponent's balance and thus increases his resisting power." An indirect approach, he argues, is militarily more sound, and generally effective results have followed when the plan of action has had "such indirectness as to ensure the opponent's unreadiness to meet it." "Dislocation" of the enemy is crucial, he insists, to achieve the conditions for victory, and the dislocation must be followed by "exploitation" of the opportunity created by the position of insecurity. It thus becomes important "to nullify opposition by paralyzing the power to oppose" and to make "the enemy do something wrong."

These general, and at first glance abstract, principles of strategy can take a concrete form not only in certain types of military action but also in nonviolent action, and therefore in civilian defense. An invader, or other usurper, is likely to be best equipped to apply, and to combat, military and other violent means of combat and repression. Instead of meeting him directly on that level, nonviolent actionists and civilian defenders rely on a totally different technique of struggle, or "weapons system." The whole conflict takes on a very special character: the combatants fight, but with different weapons. Given an extensive, determined, and skillful application of nonviolent action, the opponent is likely to find that the nonviolent actionists' insistence on fighting with their chosen "weapons system" will cause him very special problems which frustrate the effective utilization of his own forces. As indicated above, the opponent's unilateral use of violent repression may only increase the resistance and win new support for the resisters, and even the opponent's supporters, agents, and soldiers may first begin to doubt the rightness of his policies and finally undertake internal opposition.

The use of nonviolent action may thus reduce or remove the very sources of the opponent's power without ever directly confronting him with the same violent means of action on which he had relied. The course of the struggle may be viewed as an attempt by the nonviolent actionists to increase their various types of strength, not only among their usual supporters but also among third parties and in the opponent's camp, and to reduce by various processes the strength of the opponent. This type of change in the relative power positions will finally determine the outcome of the struggle.

Success in nonviolent struggle depends to a very high degree on the persistence of the nonviolent actionists in fighting with *their own* methods and opposing all pressures—whether caused by emotional hostility to the opponent's brutalities, temptations of temporary gains, or *agents provocateurs* employed by the opponent (of which there have been examples)—to fight with the opponent's own, violent, methods. Violence by, or in support of, their side will sharply counter the operation of the very special mechanisms of change in nonviolent action—even when the violence is on a relatively small scale, such as rioting, injury, violent sabotage involving loss of life, or individual assassinations. The least amount of violence will, in the eyes of many, justify severe repression, and it will sharply reduce the tendency for such repression to bring sympathy and support for the nonviolent actionists, and it may well, for several reasons, reduce the number of resisters. Violence will also sharply reduce sympathy and support in the opponent's own camp.

The use of violence by, or in support of, the resisters, has many effects. Its dangers are indicated by, among other things, an examination of the likely effect on the opponent's soldiers and police, who may have become sympathetic to the resisters and reluctant to continue as opposition agents. It is well known that ordinary soldiers will fight more persistently and effectively if it is a matter of survival, and if they and their comrades are being shot, bombed, wounded, or killed. Soldiers and police acting against a nonviolent opposition and not facing such dangers may at times be inefficient in carrying out repression—for example by slackness in searches for "wanted" resisters, firing over the heads of demonstrators, or not shooting at all. In extreme cases they may openly mutiny. When such inefficiency or mutiny occurs, the opponent's power is severely threatened: this will often be an objective of nonviolent actionists or civilian defenders.

The introduction of violence by their side, however, will sharply reduce their chances of undermining opposition loyalty, as the influences producing sympathy are removed and their opponents' lives become threatened. This is simply an illustration of the point that it is very dangerous to believe that one can increase one's total combat strength by combining violent sabotage, assassinations, or types of guerrilla or conventional warfare with civilian defense, which relies on the very different technique of nonviolent action.

Development of the Technique

Nonviolent action has a long history, but because historians have often been more concerned with other matters much information has undoubtedly been lost. Even today, this field is largely ignored, and there is no good history of the practice and development of the technique. But it clearly began early.

A very significant pre-Gandhian expansion of the technique took place in the nineteenth and early twentieth centuries. The technique received impetus from three groups during this period: first, from trade unionists and other social radicals who sought a means of struggle—largely strikes, general strikes, and boycotts—against what they regarded as an unjust social system, and for an improvement in the condition of working men; second, from nationalists who found the technique useful in resisting a foreign enemy; and third, on the level of ideas and personal example, from individuals who wanted to show how a better society might be created. . . .

Since Gandhi's time, the use of nonviolent action has spread throughout the world at an unprecedented rate. In some cases it was stimulated by Gandhi's thought and practice, but where this was so the technique was often modified in new cultural and political settings; in these cases it has already moved beyond Gandhi.

Quite independently of the campaigns led by Gandhi, important nonviolent struggles emerged under exceedingly difficult circumstances in Nazi-occupied and Communist countries: nonviolent action was used to a significant extent in the Norwegian and Danish resistance in the Second World War, in the East German uprising in 1953, in the Hungarian revolution in 1956, and in the strikes in the Soviet political prisoner camps, especially in 1953. There have been other important developments in Africa, Japan, and elsewhere. There have, of course, been setbacks, and the limited and sporadic use of nonviolent action in South Africa, for example, has been followed by advocacy of violence. However, when seen in historical perspective, there is no doubt that the technique of nonviolent action has developed very rapidly in the twentieth century.

In this same perspective, it is only recently that nonviolent resistance has been seen as a possible substitute for war in deterring or defeating invasion and other threats. It is even more recently that any attempt has been made to work out this policy—now called "civilian defense"—in any detail and that an examination of its merits and problems has been proposed.

It is inconceivable that any country will in the foreseeable future permanently abandon its defensive capacity. Threats—some genuine, some exaggerated—are too real to people; there has been too much aggression and seizure of power by dictators to be forgotten. But while defense and deterrence inevitably rely on sanctions and means of struggle, there is much reason for dissatisfaction with the usual military means. The question therefore arises whether there exists an alternative means of struggle which could be the basis of a new defense policy. Nonviolent action is an alternative means of struggle; in this, it has more in common with military struggle than with conciliation and arbitration. Could there then be a policy of civilian defense which relies on this nonviolent technique? The question must be answered, not in terms of philosophy and dogma, but in the practical examination of concrete strategies through which it might operate, the problems which might be faced, and alternative ways in which these might possibly be solved. All this will depend to a large degree on an understanding of the technique of nonviolent action, its methods, dynamics, mechanisms, and requirements.

Learning from the Past

Generally speaking, very little effort has been made to learn from past cases of nonviolent action with a view to increasing our understanding of the nature of the technique, and gaining knowledge which might be useful in future struggles, or which might contribute to an expansion of the use of nonviolent action instead of violence. Study of past cases could provide the basis for a more informed assessment of the future political potentialities of the technique.

There are far too few detailed documentary accounts of past uses of nonviolent action; such accounts can provide raw material for analyses of particular facets of the technique and help in the formulation of hypotheses which might be tested in other situations. An important step, therefore, in the development of research in this field is the preparation of purely factual accounts of a large number of specific cases of nonviolent action, accompanied if possible with collections of existing interpretations and explanations of the events. . . .

Another subject which deserves careful study is the meaning of, and conditions for, success in nonviolent action. The varying meanings of the terms "success" and "defeat" need to be distinguished, and consideration given to concrete achievements in particular struggles. The matter is much more complex than may at first appear. For example, failure within a short period of time to get an invader to withdraw fully from an occupied country may nevertheless be accompanied by the frustration of several of the invader's objectives, the maintenance of a considerable degree of autonomy within the "conquered" country, and the furtherance of a variety of changes in the invader's own regime and homeland; these changes may themselves later lead either to the desired full withdrawal, or to further relaxation of occupation rule. When various types of "success" and "defeat" have been distinguished, it would be desirable to have a study of the conditions under which they have occurred in the past and seem possible in the future. These conditions would include factors in the social and political situation, the nature of the issues in the conflict, the type of opponent and his repression, the type of group using nonviolent action, the type of nonviolent action used (taking into account quality, extent, strategy, tactics, methods, persistence in face of repression, etc.), and lastly the possible role and influence of "third parties."

The question of the viability and political

practicality of the technique of nonviolent action is one which can be investigated by research and analysis, and it is possible that the efficiency and political potentialities of this technique can be increased by deliberate efforts.

STUDY QUESTIONS

1. What is meant by Gandhi's insistence that *satyagraha* must be done by the strong, rather than the weak?

2. Suggest nonreligious bases for nonviolence as a social practice and as a way of life.

3. Black power advocate H. Rap Brown once wrote that violence was "as American as cherry pie." Agree or disagree.

4. "Let no man pull you so low," wrote Martin Luther King, Jr., "as to make you hate him." Analyze and interpret this observation.

5. "My creed of nonviolence is an extremely active force," wrote Gandhi. "It has no room for cowardice or even weakness. There is hope for a violent man to be some day nonviolent, but there is none for a coward." Why not?

6. According to Victor Hugo (and many others), "No army can withstand the force of an idea whose time has come." Is there any evidence that nonviolence is such an idea? Or is this simply wishful thinking?

7. Analyze "selective nonviolence," that is, using violence in some circumstances, and nonviolence in others.

8. Can you find any examples of nonviolence among animals? If so, can we learn from them?

9. Analyze the oft-cited problem of how nonviolence (Gandhian or other) would fare in the face, of a nuclear-armed Hitler, for example.

10. Compare the nonviolent conceptions of Gandhi, Tolstoy, King and one or more modern leaders.

SUGGESTIONS FOR FURTHER READING

Ackerman, Peter and Christopher Kruegler. 1994. *Strategic Nonviolent Conflict: the Dynamics of People Power in the Twentieth Century.* Westport, Conn: Praeger.

Bose, Anima. 1987. *Dimensions of Peace and Nonviolence: The Gandhian Perspective.* Delhi, India: Gian Pub. House.

Burrowes, Robert J. 1996. *The Strategy of Nonviolent Defense: A Gandhian Approach.* Albany: State University of New York Press.

Cooney, Robert and Helen Michalowski, eds. 1987. *The Power of the People: Active Nonviolence in the United States.* Philadelphia: New Society Publishers.

Hanigan, James P. 1984. *Martin Luther King, Jr. and the Foundations of Nonviolence.* Lanham, MD: University Press of America.

Junor, Beth. 1995. *Greenham Common Women's Peace Camp: A History of Non-violent Resistance, 1984–1995.* London: Working Press.

Lakey, George. 1987. *Powerful Peacemaking: A Strategy for a Living Revolution.* Philadelphia: New Society Publishers.

McAllister, Pam. ed. 1982. *Reweaving the Web of Life: Feminism and Nonviolence.* Philadelphia: New Society Publishers.

McCarthy, Colman. 1994. *All of One Peace: Essays on Nonviolence.* New Brunswick, NJ: Rutgers University Press.

McManus, Philip and Gerald Schlabach. eds. 1991. *Relentless Persistence: Nonviolent Action in Latin America.* Philadelphia: New Society Publishers.

Merton, Thomas. 1980. *The Nonviolent Alternative.* New York: Farrar, Straus & Giroux.

Moses, Greg. 1997. *Revolution of Conscience: Martin Luther King, Jr., and the Philosophy of Nonviolence.* New York: Guilford Press.

Powers, Roger S. and William B. Vogele. eds. 1997. *Protest, Power, and Change: An Encyclopedia of Nonviolent Action from ACT-UP to Women's Suffrage.* New York: Garland Pub.

Rummel, R. J. 1997. *Power Kills: Democracy as a Method of Nonviolence.* New Brunswick, NJ: Transaction Publishers.

Sibley, Mulford Quickert. ed. 1964. *The Quiet Battle: Writings on the Theory and Practice of Non-violent Resistance.* Chicago: Quadrangle.

Sponsel, Leslie E. and Thomas Gregor. eds. 1994. *The Anthropology of Peace and Nonviolence.* Boulder, Colo: L. Rienner.

5

~~~

Religious Inspiration

Religious teachings are primarily concerned with humanity's relationship with God. But the world's religions invariably devote substantial attention, as well, to the way human beings treat each other. They are inevitably drawn to questions of war and peace, the former because the taking of life is one of the most intense and consequential human acts, and the latter because systems of "peace" are fundamental to the basic condition of human life, spiritual no less than material or social.

We turn to religious inspiration with hope and gratitude (it is noteworthy, for example, that nonviolence, both in theory and practice, has largely been motivated by religious teaching). Nonetheless, it must also be acknowledged that when it comes to matters of war and peace, religion has been a double-edged sword. It may be that on balance, religious tradition has been as likely to support militarism as to oppose it. Sometimes, religious authorities have been among the most outspoken cheerleaders for war-making; at other times, even if not vigorously supporting prevailing government policy, they have passively acquiesced in the status quo. Historically, religions have buttressed bloodthirsty and unjust activities either from belief that the appropriate stance is to "render unto Caesar that which is Caesar's," and/or out of self-protective or self-serving motives. The following inscription (loosely translated) is commonly seen even today on houses in certain small villages of Bavaria: "Saint Florian, protect our town, pass by my house, burn others down."

The Old Testament is replete with bloody accounts of the so-called "commanded wars" in which God urged his people to destroy others: "when the Lord your God has given them over to you, and you defeat them, then you must utterly destroy them; you shall make no covenant with them, and show no mercy to them" (Deuteronomy 7:2). Other religious traditions also have displayed a positive attitude toward war. Best known among these is the *jihad*, or holy war, among Moslems, in which fallen warriors are guaranteed entry into heaven. Although Hinduism contributed mightily to Gandhian nonviolence, it also has a vigorous military tradition, reflected in such texts as the Mahabharata, in which the devout are urged to fight, even for a cause with which they might disagree. By contrast, peace has long been central to Buddhism, although war resistance as such has not been especially prominent among Buddhist teachings.

Christianity has a complex relationship to war. Because it is the predominant religious tradition of the United States, it deserves special attention here. Although many of its founding principles emphasize pacifism, turning the other cheek, and loving one's neighbor, the reality is that mainstream Christianity has been one of the great warrior religions of history (along with Islam, Hinduism, and Shintoism, the predominant religious tradition of Japan). There is a fundamental Christian ambiguity toward war, reflected in the attitude toward the cross. On the one hand, it is supposed to be the ultimate symbol of peace and love, something with which to replace violence and sin; on the other hand, it has long been seen as a sword with which to smite the forces of evil.

Christians were the eventual heirs of the dying Roman empire, fighting numerous—and increasingly unsuccessful—wars. The "Holy War" tradition in Christianity is a direct descendant of the commanded wars of the Old Testament. This tradition was especially virulent during the Middle Ages, most dramatically during the Crusades, which were fought in an attempt to drive Moslems from Palestine. "Deus Vult" (God wills it) was the battle cry of the Crusaders. "A new sort of army has appeared," preached Saint Bernard of Clairvaux, in the twelfth century.

> It fights a double war; first, the war of the flesh and blood against enemies; second, the war of the spirit against Satan and vice. . . . The soldier of Christ kills with safety; he dies with more safety still. He serves Christ when he kills. He serves himself when he is killed.

And as recently as 1914, the bishop of London urged his countrymen to

> Kill Germans. Kill them, not for the sake of killing, but to save the world, to kill the good as well as the bad, to kill the young men as well as the old . . . I look upon it as a war for purity, I look upon everyone who dies in it as a martyr.[1]

At the same time, not surprisingly, German soldiers were marching into battle with the assurance "Gott mit uns" (God is with us).

Perhaps the final word on this paradox belongs to Blaise Pascal, brilliant mathematician and devout Catholic: "Men never do evil so completely and cheerfully, as when they do it from religious conviction."

Two other aspects of Christian religious tradition—both nearly as troublesome as Holy Wars from the perspective of peace studies—warrant mention. One is an approach that (like the commanded wars) dates from the Old Testament, and was revived especially during the sixteenth to eighteenth centuries. This view teaches that war is undesirable, but deservedly so: a war is a retribution upon the ungodly and the unrighteous, whose function is to chastise those who have displeased God. War was thus seen as God's vengeance upon the wicked, but also a kind of penance for the war-maker, who is thus reminded of his or her sinfulness and of God's greatness. This view is not currently popular.

Another troublesome aspect of the Christian religious tradition has an equally long history, while also remaining currently influential, especially among the more conservative wing of religious orthodoxy. It applies more directly to efforts at achieving pos-

---

[1]quoted in Roland Bainton. 1960. *Christian Attitudes Toward War and Peace.* Nashville: Abingdon Press.

itive peace than to opposing war. This approach is essentially to support the status quo, to counsel submission on the part of people—especially the poor and those otherwise oppressed—to existing social and economic conditions, while trusting to eternal salvation in the afterlife. Not surprisingly, communist doctrine was especially critical of this aspect of religion, referring to it as the "opiate of the masses." Karl Marx had this to say:

> The social principles of Christianity justified the slavery of antiquity, glorified the serfdom of the Middle Ages, and equally know, when necessary, how to defend the oppression of the proletariat. . . . The social principles of Christianity preach the necessity of a ruling and an oppressed class, and all they have for the latter is the pious wish the former will be charitable. . . . The social principles of Christianity declare all vile acts of the oppressors against the oppressed to be either the just punishment of original sin and other sins or trials that the Lord in his infinite wisdom imposes on those redeemed. . . . So much for the social principles of Christianity.[2]

Fortunately, there is another side to Christianity. Despite the impression one might get from Christian conservatives, God is not a right-wing Republican! The biblical Christ, for example, was almost inevitably aligned with the poor, the despised, and the disenfranchised. Established Christian doctrine is not inevitably on the side of entrenched power and opposed to social betterment. The Rev. Martin Luther King, Jr., developed the concept of social sin (notably segregation, economic oppression, and war-making). "Liberation theology," which originated in Latin America, also proclaims a vigorously *social* gospel, emphasizing the need for modern-day Christians to act on the social sensitivities of Christ. In 1979, for example, the General Conference of Latin-American Bishops issued a statement that includes the following:

> From the heart of Latin America, a cry rises to the heavens. . . . It is the cry of a people who suffer and who demand justice, freedom and respect for the fundamental rights of man. . . . In pain and anxiety, the Church discerns a situation of social sin, of a magnitude all the greater because it occurs in countries which call themselves Catholic and have the capacity to change. . . . We identify, as the most devastating and humiliating scourge, the situation of inhuman poverty in which millions of Latin Americans live, with starvation wages, unemployment and underemployment, malnutrition, infant mortality, lack of adequate housing, health problems, and labor unrest.

In *The City of God,* Augustine wrote that "it is the wrong-doing of the opposing party which compels the wise man to wage just wars," and that "war with the hope of peace everlasting" to follow was preferable to "captivity without any thought of deliverance." To Augustine and those in the tradition of "Christian realism" that followed him, peace often requires violence against evil-doers, and the soldier who goes to war in defense of right, and out of love for his neighbor, does not violate the commandment against killing. Still, if a Christian was expected to go to war, it was with a heavy heart and only after carefully examining his conscience, because the presumption was at all times supposed to be in favor of peace.

---

[2]Karl Marx. 1964. *On Religion.* New York: Shocken.

Samuel Johnson once wrote that the prospect of a hanging in the morning does won-ders to clarify the mind. Similarly, the prospect of war in general and of nuclear anni-hilation in particular have done wonders to stimulate thought on religious obligation in the face of war. When it comes to nuclear war, for example, the many and detailed requirements of Just War doctrine cannot be met. Some religious ethicists have even seriously doubted the legitimacy of nuclear deterrence (aside from actual nuclear war), arguing that if something is immoral to do, it is immoral to threaten, since the immoral-ity resides first in the intent, and only later in the act itself. Thus, the United Methodist Council of Bishops refused to condone deterrence:

> The moral case for nuclear deterrence, even as an interim ethic, has been undermined by unrelent-ing arms escalation. Deterrence no longer serves, if it ever did, as a strategy that facilitates disar-mament.... Deterrence must no longer receive the churches' blessing, even as a temporary war-rant for the maintenance of nuclear weapons.

The American Catholic Bishops spoke to this issue in 1983, issuing a "Pastoral Let-ter on War and Peace," after listening to three years of testimony from a wide range of experts. Although they decided that the possession of and threat to employ nuclear weapons (that is, deterrence) was provisionally acceptable, the Catholic Bishops were unequivocal in rejecting the *use* of nuclear weapons under any circumstances.

There is a powerful and persistent tradition of explicit pacifism and antiwar activism within Christianity, as within most of the world's great religions. Many pacifists agree with G. K. Chesterton's sardonic observation that "the Christian ideal has not been tried and found wanting. It has been found difficult and left untried."

We turn now to religiously inspired teachers—not all of them Christian—who urge us toward this ideal, no matter how difficult it may be.

The Bhagavad Gita: Hindu

The famed Hindu epic the *Mahabharata* contains as perhaps its most important treatise the *Bhagavad Gita,* which describes a great civil war in ancient India. During this war, one of the principal warriors, Arjuna, is reluctant to fight because many of his friends and relatives are on the opposing side. He is ultimately persuaded to fight by the God Krishna, who convinces Arjuna that he must act, not out of hatred or hope for personal gain, but from selfless duty. Although the *Gita* can and has been interpreted as calling for caste loyalty and a warrior spirit, it also inspired Gandhi and others as an allegory for the deemphasis of self in the pursuit of higher goals.

The wise grieve neither for the living nor for the dead. There has never been a time when you and I and the kings gathered here have not existed, nor will there be a time when we will cease to exist. As the same person inhabits the body through childhood, youth, and old age, so too at the time of death he attains another body. The wise are not deluded by these changes.

When the senses contact sense objects, a person experiences cold or heat, pleasure or pain. These experiences are fleeting; they come and go. Bear them patiently, Arjuna. Those who are not affected by these changes, who are the same in pleasure and pain, are truly wise and fit for immortality. Assert your strength and realize this!

The impermanent has no reality; reality lies in the eternal. Those who have seen the boundary between these two have attained the end of all knowledge. Realize that which pervades the universe and is indestructible; no power can affect this unchanging, imperishable reality. The body is mortal, but he who dwells in the body is immortal and immeasurable. Therefore, Arjuna, fight in this battle.

One man believes he is the slayer, another believes he is the slain. Both are ignorant; there is neither slayer nor slain. You were never born; you will never die. You have never

changed; you can never change. Unborn, eternal, immutable, immemorial, you do not die when the body dies. Realizing that which is indestructible, eternal, unborn, and unchanging, how can you slay or cause another to slay?

As a man abandons worn-out clothes and acquires new ones, so when the body is worn out a new one is acquired by the Self, who lives within.

The Self cannot be pierced by weapons or burned by fire; water cannot wet it, nor can the wind dry it. The Self cannot be pierced or burned, made wet or dry. It is everlasting and infinite, standing on the motionless foundations of eternity. The Self is unmanifested, beyond all thought, beyond all change. Knowing this, you should not grieve.

O mighty Arjuna, even if you believe the Self to be subject to birth and death, you should not grieve. Death is inevitable for the living; birth is inevitable for the dead. Since these are unavoidable, you should not sorrow. Every creature is unmanifested at first and then attains manifestation. When its end has come, it once again becomes unmanifested. What is there to lament in this?

The glory of the Self is beheld by a few, and a few describe it: a few listen, but many without understanding. The Self of all beings, living within the body, is eternal and cannot be harmed. Therefore, do not grieve. . . .

They live in wisdom who see themselves in all and all in them, who have renounced every selfish desire and sense craving tormenting the heart.

Neither agitated by grief nor hankering after pleasure, they live free from lust and fear and anger. Established in meditation, they are truly wise. Fettered no more by selfish attachments, they are neither elated by good fortune nor depressed by bad. Such are the seers.

Even as a tortoise draws in its limbs, the wise can draw in their senses at will. Aspirants abstain from sense pleasures, but they still crave for them. These cravings all disappear when they see the highest goal. Even of those who tread the path, the stormy senses can sweep off the mind. They live in wisdom who subdue their senses and keep their minds ever absorbed in me.

When you keep thinking about sense objects, attachment comes. Attachment breeds desire, the lust of possession that burns to anger. Anger clouds the judgment; you can no longer learn from past mistakes. Lost is the power to choose between what is wise and what is unwise, and your life is utter waste. But when you move amidst the world of sense, free from attachment and aversion alike, there comes the peace in which all sorrows end, and you live in the wisdom of the Self.

The disunited mind is far from wise; how can it mediate? How be at peace? When you know no peace, how can you know joy? When you let your mind follow the call of the senses, they carry away your better judgment as storms drive a boat off its charted course on the sea.

Use all your power to free the senses from attachment and aversion alike, and live in the full wisdom of the Self. Such a sage awakes to light in the night of all creatures. That which the world calls day is the night of ignorance to the wise.

As rivers flow into the ocean but cannot make the vast ocean overflow, so flow the streams of the sense-world into the sea of peace that is the sage. But this is not so with the desirer of desires.

They are forever free who renounce all selfish desires and break away from the ego-cage of "I," "me," and "mine" to be united with the Lord. This is the supreme state. Attain to this, and pass from death to immortality.

THICH NHAT HANH: BUDDHIST

Being Peace

Buddhism, with its focus on compassion and the connectedness of all things, would seem to be a "natural" for a peace-loving, antiwar constituency. And so it is. On the other hand, "engaged Buddhism" does not represent a majority approach within the tradition, largely because the Buddha's teaching emphasizes personal enlightenment. However, Buddhism undeniably nurtures a nonviolent and socially responsible practice, as exemplified, for example, by organizations such as the Buddhist Peace Fellowship. Because Buddhist teachings are especially difficult for the uninitiated Western reader, we have chosen the following selection from a modern sage, Zen master Thich

From *Being Peace* by Thich Nhat Hanh. 1987. Reprinted with permission of Parallax Press, Berkeley, Calif.

Nhat Hanh. He is a Vietnamese monk who led the Buddhist delegation to the Paris Peace Talks during the Vietnam War and is a leading interpreter of Buddhist practice in today's world.

Meditation is not to get out of society, to escape from society, but to prepare for a reentry into society. We call this "engaged Buddhism." When we go to a meditation center, we may have the impression that we leave everything behind—family, society, and all the complications involved in them—and come as an individual in order to practice and to search for peace. This is already an illusion, because in Buddhism there is no such thing as an individual.

Just as a piece of paper is the fruit, the combination of many elements that can be called non-paper elements, the individual is made of nonindividual elements. If you are a poet, you will see clearly that there is a cloud floating in this sheet of paper. Without a cloud there will be no water; without water, the trees cannot grow; and without trees, you cannot make paper. So the cloud is in here. The existence of this page is dependent on the existence of a cloud. Paper and cloud are so close. Let us think of other things, like sunshine. Sunshine is very important because the forest cannot grow without sunshine, and we humans cannot grow without sunshine. So the logger needs sunshine in order to cut the tree, and the tree needs sunshine in order to be a tree. Therefore you can see sunshine in this sheet of paper. And if you look more deeply, with the eyes of a bodhisattva, with the eyes of those who are awake, you see not only the cloud and the sunshine in it, but that everything is here: the wheat that became the bread for the logger to eat, the logger's father—everything is in this sheet of paper.

The Avatamsaka Sutra tells us that you cannot point to one thing that does not have a relationship with this sheet of paper. So we say, "A sheet of paper is made of non-paper elements." A cloud is a non-paper element. The forest is a non-paper element. Sunshine is a non-paper element. The paper is made of all the non-paper elements to the extent that if we return the non-paper elements to their sources, the cloud to the sky, the sunshine to the sun, the logger to his father, the paper is empty. Empty of what? Empty of a separate self. It has

been made by all the non-self elements, non-paper elements, and if all these non-paper elements are taken out, it is truly empty, empty of an independent self. Empty, in this sense, means that the paper is full of everything, the entire cosmos. The presence of this tiny sheet of paper proves the presence of the whole cosmos. . . .

In Plum Village in France, we receive many letters from the refugee camps in Singapore, Malaysia, Indonesia, Thailand, and the Philippines, hundreds each week. It is very painful to read them, but we have to do it, we have to be in contact. We try our best to help, but the suffering is enormous, and sometimes we are discouraged. It is said that half the boat people die in the ocean; only half arrive at the shores in Southeast Asia.

There are many young girls, boat people, who are raped by sea pirates. Even though the United Nations and many countries try to help the government of Thailand prevent that kind of piracy, sea pirates continue to inflict much suffering on the refugees. One day we received a letter telling us about a young girl on a small boat who was raped by a Thai pirate. She was only twelve, and she jumped into the ocean and drowned herself.

When you first learn of something like that, you get angry at the pirate. You naturally take the side of the girl. As you look more deeply you will see it differently. If you take the side of the little girl, then it is easy. You only have to take a gun and shoot the pirate. But we cannot do that. In my meditation I saw that if I had been born in the village of the pirate and raised in the same conditions as he was, I am now the pirate. There is a great likelihood that I would become a pirate. I cannot condemn myself so easily. In my meditation, I saw that many babies are born along the Gulf of Siam, hundreds every day, and if we educators, social workers, politicians, and others do not do something about the situation, in twenty-five years a number of them will become sea pirates. That is certain. If you or I were born today in those fishing villages, we might become sea pirates in twenty-five years.

If you take a gun and shoot the pirate, you shoot all of us, because all of us are to some extent responsible for this state of affairs. . . .

There is a Zen story about a man riding a horse which is galloping very quickly. Another man, standing alongside the road, yells at him, "Where are you going?" and the man on the horse yells back, "I don't know. Ask the horse." I think that is our situation. We are riding many horses that we cannot control. The proliferation of armaments, for instance, is a horse. We have tried our best, but we cannot control these horses. Our lives are so busy.

In Buddhism, the most important precept of all is to live in awareness, to know what is going on. To know what is going on, not only here, but there. For instance, when you eat a piece of bread, you may choose to be aware that our farmers, in growing the wheat, use chemical poisons a little too much. Eating the bread, we are somehow co-responsible for the destruction of our ecology. When we eat a piece of meat or drink alcohol, we can produce awareness that 40,000 children die *each day* in the third world from hunger and that in order to produce a piece of meat or a bottle of liquor, we have to use a lot of grain. Eating a bowl of cereal may be more reconciling with the suffering of the world than eating a piece of meat. An authority on economics who lives in France told me that if only the people in Western countries would reduce the eating of meat and the drinking of alcohol by 50%, that would be enough to change the situation of the world. Only 50% less.

Every day we do things, we are things, that have to do with peace. If we are aware of our lifestyle, our way of consuming, of looking at things, we will know how to make peace right in the moment we are alive, the present moment. . . .

During the war in Vietnam we young Buddhists organized ourselves to help victims of the war rebuild villages that had been destroyed by the bombs. Many of us died during service, not only because of the bombs and the bullets, but because of the people who suspected us of being on the other side. We were able to understand the suffering of both sides, the communists and the anti-communists. We tried to be open to both, to understand this side and to understand that side, to be one with them. That is why we did not take a side, even though the whole world took sides. We tried

to tell people our perception of the situation: that we wanted to stop the fighting, but the bombs were so loud. Sometimes we had to burn ourselves alive to get the message across, but even then the world could not hear us. They thought we were supporting a kind of political act. They didn't know that it was a purely human action to be heard, to be understood. We wanted reconciliation, we did not want a victory. Working to help people in a circumstance like that is very dangerous, and many of us got killed. The communists killed us because they suspected that we were working with the Americans, and the anti-communists killed us because they thought that we were with the communists. But we did not want to give up and take one side.

The situation of the world is still like this. . . . Reconciliation is to understand both sides, to go to one side and describe the suffering being endured by the other side, and then to go to the other side and describe the suffering being endured by the first side. Doing only that will be a great help for peace. . . .

I would like to present to you a form of Buddhism that may be accepted here in the West. In the past twenty years we have been experimenting with this form of Buddhism, and it seems that it may be suitable for our modern society. It is called the Tiep Hien Order, the Order of "Interbeing."

The Tiep Hien Order was founded in Vietnam during the war. It derives from the Zen School of Lin Chi, and is the forty-second generation of this school. It is a form of engaged Buddhism, Buddhism in daily life, in society, and not just in a retreat center. *Tiep* and *hien* are Vietnamese words of Chinese origin. I would like to explain the meaning of these words, because understanding them helps in understanding the spirit of this order.

Tiep means "to be in touch." The notion of engaged Buddhism already appears in the word tiep. First of all, to be in touch with oneself. In modern society most of us don't want to be in touch with ourselves; we want to be in touch with other things like religion, sports, politics, a book—we want to forget ourselves. Any time we have leisure, we want to invite something else to enter us, opening ourselves to the television and telling the television to come and colonize us. So first of all, "in touch" means in touch with one-self in order to find out the source of wisdom, understanding, and compassion in each of us. Being in touch with oneself is the meaning of meditation, to be aware of what is going on in your body, in your feelings, in your mind. That is the first meaning of tiep.

Tiep also means to be in touch with Buddhas and bodhisattvas, the enlightened people in whom full understanding and compassion are tangible and effective. Being in touch with one-self means being in touch with this source of wisdom and compassion. You know that children understand that the Buddha is in themselves. One young boy claimed to be a Buddha on the first day of the retreat in Ojai, California. I told him that this is partly true, because sometimes he is Buddha, but sometimes he is not; it depends on his degree of being awake.

The second part of the meaning of tiep is "to continue," to make something more long-lasting. It means that the career of understanding and compassion started by Buddhas and bodhisattvas should be continued. This is possible only if we get in touch with our true self, which is like digging deep into the soil until we reach a hidden source of fresh water, and then the well is filled. When we are in touch with our true mind, the source of understanding and compassion will spring out. This is the basis of everything. Being in touch with our true mind is necessary for the continuation of the career started by the Buddhas and bodhisattvas.

Hien means "the present time." We have to be in the present time, because only the present is real, only in the present moment can we be alive. We do not practice for the sake of the future, to be reborn in a paradise, but to be peace, to be compassion, to be joy right now. Hien also means "to make real, to manifest, realization." Love and understanding are not only concepts and words. They must be real things, realized, in oneself and in society. That is the meaning of the word hien.

It is difficult to find English or French words which convey the same meaning as *Tiep Hien*. There is a term from *The Avatamsaka Sutra*, "interbeing," which conveys the spirit, so we have translated Tiep Hien as interbeing. In the sutra it is a compound term which means "mutual" and "to be." Interbeing is a new word in English, and I hope it will be accepted. We have talked about the many in the one, and the one containing the many. In one sheet of paper, we see everything else, the cloud, the forest, the logger. I am, therefore you are. You are, therefore I am. That is the meaning of the word "interbeing." We interare. . . .

In Buddhism, the mind is the root of everything else. These then are the precepts of the Order of Interbeing:

First: Do not be idolatrous about or bound to any doctrine, theory, or ideology, even Buddhist ones. Buddhist systems of thought are guiding means; they are not absolute truth.

This precept is the roar of the lion. Its spirit is characteristic of Buddhism. It is often said that the Buddha's teaching is only a raft to help you cross the river, a finger pointing to the moon. Don't mistake the finger for the moon. The raft is not the shore. If we cling to the raft, if we cling to the finger, we miss everything. We cannot, in the name of the finger or the raft, kill each other. Human life is more precious than any ideology, any doctrine. . . . Peace can only be achieved when we are not attached to a view, when we are free from fanaticism. . . .

Second: Do not think the knowledge you presently possess is changeless, absolute truth. Avoid being narrow-minded and bound to present views. Learn and practice nonattachment from views in order to be open to receive others' viewpoints. Truth is found in life and not merely in conceptual knowledge. Be ready to learn throughout your entire life and to observe reality in yourself and in the world at all times.

This precept springs from the first one. Remember the young father who refused to open the door to his own son, thinking the boy was already dead. The Buddha said, "If you cling to something as the absolute truth and you are caught in it, when the truth comes in person to knock on your door, you will refuse to let it in." . . .

Third: Do not force others, including children, by any means whatsoever, to adopt your views, whether by authority, threat, money, propaganda, or even education. However, through compassionate dialogue, help others renounce fanaticism and narrowness. . . .

Fourth: Do not avoid contact with suffering or close your eyes before suffering. Do not lose awareness of the existence of suffering in the life of the world. Find ways to be with those who are suffering, including personal contact, visits, images, and sounds. By such means, awaken yourself and others to the reality of suffering in the world.

The first Dharma talk given by the Buddha was on the Four Noble Truths. The first truth is the existence of suffering. This kind of contact and awareness is needed. If we don't encounter pain, ills, we won't look for the causes of pain and ills to find a remedy, a way out of the situation.

America is somehow a closed society. Americans are not very aware of what is going on outside of America. Life here is so busy that even if you watch television and read the newspaper, and the images from outside flash by, there is no real contact. I hope you will find some way to nourish the awareness of the existence of suffering in the world. Of course, inside America there is also suffering, and it is important to stay in touch with that. But much of the suffering in the West is "useless" and can vanish when we see the real suffering of other people. Sometimes we suffer because of some psychological fact. We cannot get out of our self, and so we suffer. If we get in touch with the suffering in the world, and are moved by that suffering, we may come forward to help the people who are suffering, and our own suffering may just vanish.

Fifth: Do not accumulate wealth while millions are hungry. Do not take as the aim of your life fame, profit, wealth, or sensual pleasure. Live simply and share time, energy, and material resources with those who are in need.

The Eight Realizations of Great Beings Sutra says, "The human mind is always searching for possessions, and never feels fulfilled. Bodhisattvas move in the opposite direction and follow the principle of self-sufficiency. They live a simple life in order to practice the Way, and consider the realization of perfect understanding as their only career." . . .

Sixth: Do not maintain anger or hatred. Learn to penetrate and transform them

when they are still seeds in your consciousness. As soon as they arise, turn your attention to your breath in order to see and understand the nature of your anger and hatred and the nature of the persons who have caused your anger and hatred.

We have to be aware of irritation or anger as it arises, and try to understand it. Once we understand, we are better able to forgive and love. Meditation on compassion means meditation on understanding. If we do not understand, we cannot love.

"Learn to look at other beings with the eyes of compassion" is quoted from *The Lotus Sutra.* . . .

. . . The original Chinese is only five words: "compassionate eyes looking living beings." The first time I recited *The Lotus Sutra,* when I came to these five words, I was silenced. I knew that these five words are enough to guide my whole life. . . .

Eleventh: Do not live with a vocation that is harmful to humans and nature. Do not invest in companies that deprive others of their chance to live. Select a vocation that helps realize your ideal of compassion.

This is an extremely hard precept to observe. If you are lucky enough to have a vocation that helps you realize your ideal of compassion, you still have to understand more deeply. If I am a teacher, I am very glad to have this job helping children. I am glad that I am not a butcher who kills cows and pigs. Yet the son and the daughter of the butcher come to my class, and I teach them. They profit from my right livelihood. My son and daughter eat the meat that the butcher prepares. We are linked together. I cannot say that my livelihood is perfectly right. It cannot be. Observing this precept includes finding ways to realize a collective right livelihood.

You may try to follow a vegetarian diet, to lessen the killing of animals, but you cannot completely avoid the killing. When you drink a glass of water, you kill many tiny living beings. Even in your dish of vegetables, there are quite a lot of them, boiled or fried. I am aware that my vegetarian dish is not completely vegetarian, and I think that if my teacher, the Buddha, were here, he could not avoid that either. The problem is whether we are determined to go in the direction of compassion or not. If we are, then can we reduce the suffering to a minimum? If I lose my direction, I have to look for the North Star, and I go to the north. That does not mean I expect to arrive at the North Star. I just want to go in that direction.

> Twelfth: Do not kill. Do not let others kill. Find whatever means possible to protect life and prevent war.

The defense budgets in Western countries are enormous. Studies show that by stopping the arms race, we will have more than enough money to erase poverty, hunger, illiteracy, and many diseases from the world. This precept applies not only to humans, but to all living beings. As we have seen, no one can observe this precept to perfection; however, the essence is to respect and protect life, to do our best to protect life. This means not killing, and also not letting other people kill. It is difficult. Those who try to observe this precept have to be working for peace in order to have peace in themselves. Preventing war is much better than protesting against the war. Protesting the war is too late.

> Thirteenth: Possess nothing that should belong to others. Respect the property of others, but prevent others from profiting from human suffering or the suffering of other species on Earth.

Bringing to our awareness the pain caused by social injustice, the thirteenth precept urges us to work for a more livable society. This precept is linked with the fourth precept (the awareness of suffering), the fifth precept (lifestyle), the eleventh precept (right livelihood), and the twelfth precept (the protection of life). In order to deeply comprehend this precept, we must also meditate on these four precepts.

To develop ways to prevent others from enriching themselves on human suffering and the suffering of other beings is the duty of legislators and politicians. However, each of us can also act in this direction. To some degree, we can be close to oppressed people and help them protect their right to life and defend themselves against oppression and exploitation. Letting people enrich themselves from human suffering or the suffering of other beings is something we cannot do. As a community we must try to prevent this. How to work for justice in our own city is a problem that we have to consider. The bodhisattvas' vows—to help all sentient beings—are immense. Each of us can vow to sit in their rescue boats.

Tao De Ching: Taoist

The teachings of Confucius (circa. 551–479 BCE) are often thought by Westerners to revolve exclusively around respect for tradition and authority, especially elders and ancestors. But Confucius did not hold to these ideas because he valued obedience and social order as such but, rather, because he felt that peace was the ultimate human goal and that it was attainable only through social harmony and equilibrium. Another renowned Chinese philosopher and religious leader, Mo-tzu (468–401 BCE), argued against offensive war under any circumstances, embracing instead an ethic of love as the universal human virtue, one that is within the grasp of everyone: "Those who love others will be loved in return. Do good to others and others will do good to you. . . . What is hard about that?" (Confucius, in his Analects, had written, similarly: "Treat your subordinates as you would like to be treated by your superiors." It is hard not to notice the seeming ubiquity of this "Golden Rule.")

However, the most directly peace-relevant teachings of Chinese religious philisophy derives from Lao Tse (sixth century BCE), founder of Taoism and author of *Tao De Ching*. He emphasized that military force is not the "Tao" (pronounced "Dow") or "way" for human beings to follow. Taoists frequently refer to peaceful images of water or wind, both of them soft and yielding, yet ultimately triumphant over such "hard" substances as rock or iron. The following selections are from the *Tao De Ching*.

Fine weapons are instruments of evil.
They are hated by men.
Therefore those who possess Tao turn away from them.
The good ruler when at home honors the left.
When at war he honors the right.
Weapons are instruments of evil, not the instruments of a good ruler.
When he uses them unavoidably, he regards calm restraint as the best principle.
Even when he is victorious, he does not regard it as praiseworthy.
For to praise victory is to delight in the slaughter of men.

He who delights in the slaughter of men will not succeed in the empire.

In auspicious affairs, the left is honored.
In inauspicious affairs, the right is honored.
The lieutenant general stands on the left.
The senior general stands on the right.
This is to say that the arrangement follows that of funeral ceremonies.
For the slaughter of the multitude, let us weep with sorrow and grief.
For a victory, let us observe the occasion with funeral ceremonies. . . .

Act without action.
Do without ado.
Taste without tasting.
Whether it is big or small, many or few, repay hatred with virtue.
Prepare for the difficult while it is still easy.
Deal with the big while it is still small.
Difficult undertakings have always started with what is easy.

And great undertakings have always started with what is small.
Therefore the sage never strives for the great,
And thereby the great is achieved.
He who makes rash promises surely lacks faith.
He who takes things too easily will surely encounter much difficulty.
For this reason even the sage regards things as difficult.
And therefore he encounters no difficulty. . . .

All the world says that my Tao is great and does not seem to resemble (the ordinary).
It is precisely because it is great that it does not resemble (the ordinary).
If it did resemble, it would have been small for a long time.
I have three treasures. Guard and keep them:
The first is deep love,
The second is frugality,
And the third is not to dare to be ahead of the world.
Because of deep love, one is courageous.
Because of frugality, one is generous.
Because of not daring to be ahead of the world, one becomes the leader of the world.
Now, to be courageous by forsaking deep love,
To be generous by forsaking frugality,
And to be ahead of the world by forsaking following behind—
This is fatal.

For deep love helps one to win in the case of attack,
And to be firm in the case of defense.
When Heaven is to save a person,
Heaven will protect him through deep love. . . .

There is nothing softer and weaker than
water,
    And yet there is nothing better for
attacking hard and strong things.
    For this reason there is no substitute
for it.
    All the world knows that the weak
overcomes the strong and the soft
overcomes the hard.
    But none can practice it.
    Therefore the sage says:
    He who suffers disgrace for his country
Is called the lord of the land.
    He who takes upon himself the country's
misfortunes
    Becomes the king of the empire.
    Straight words seem to be their
opposite. . . .

    To patch up great hatred is surely to
leave some hatred behind.
    How can this be regarded as good?
    Therefore the sage keeps the left-hand
portion (obligation) of a contract
    And does not blame the other party.
    Virtuous people attend to their left-hand
portions,

While those without virtue attend to other
people's mistakes.

    "The Way of Heaven has no favorites.
It is always with the good man." . . .
    Let there be a small country with few
people.
    Let there be ten times and a hundred
times as many utensils
    But let them not be used.
    Let the people value their lives highly
and not migrate far.
    Even if there are ships and carriages,
none will ride in them.
    Even if there are arrows and weapons,
none will display them.
    Let the people again knot cords and
use them (in place of writing).
    Let them relish their food, beautify
their clothing, be content with their
homes, and delight in their customs.
    Though neighboring communities
overlook one another and the crowing
of cocks and barking of dogs can be heard,
    Yet the people there may grow old
and die without ever visiting one
another.

JEWISH

The Old Testament

Peace as such is not prominent in the Old Testament. The God of Abraham, Moses,
and David is in fact rather bellicose, even bloodthirsty, and the ancient Israelites were successful and merciless warriors. Exceptions exist, however, such as the prophets reprinted
here, most of whom nonetheless retain a kind of "peaceful ferocity." Despite the violence
of the Maccabees and the Zealots (early terrorist opponents of Roman rule in Palestine)—
not to mention the military prowess of modern Israel—Jewish practice has strongly
endorsed peacefulness as opposed to the warrior traditions of the Christian and Islamic
societies within which most Jews have lived. Perhaps it is more accurate, however, to say
that Jewish, Christian, and Islamic traditions all have bellicose components and periods
in their history. A key question, then, is whether these warrior activities represent faith-
fulness to or deviation from their underlying religious values.

Hosea 10:12–15

Sow for yourselves righteousness,
reap the fruit of steadfast love;

break up your fallow ground,
for it is the time to seek the Lord,
that he may come and rain
salvation upon you.

You have plowed iniquity,
you have reaped injustice,
you have eaten the fruit of lies.
Because you have trusted in your
chariots
and in the multitude of your warriors,
therefore the tumult of war shall arise
among your people,
and all your fortresses shall be destroyed,
as Shalman destroyed Betharbel on the day
of battle;
mothers were dashed to pieces with their
children.
Thus it shall be done to you, O house of
Israel,
because of your great wickedness.
In the storm the king of Israel
shall be utterly cut off. . . .

Micah 3:9–12

Hear this, you heads of the house of Jacob
and rulers of the house of Israel,
who abhor justice
and pervert all equity,
who build Zion with blood
and Jerusalem with wrong.
Its heads give judgment for a bribe,
its priests teach for hire,
its prophets divine for money;
yet they lean upon the Lord and say,
"Is not the Lord in the midst of us."
Therefore because of you
Zion shall be plowed as a field;
Jerusalem shall become a heap of ruins,
and the mountain of the house a wooded
height. . . .

Micah 4:1–4

It shall come to pass in the latter days
that the mountain of the house of the Lord
shall be established as the highest of the
mountains,
and shall be raised up above the hills;
and peoples shall flow to it,
and many nations shall come, and say:
"Come, let us go up to the mountain
of the Lord,

to the house of the God of Jacob;
that he may teach us his ways
and we may walk in his paths."
For out of Zion shall go forth the law,
and the word of the Lord from
Jerusalem.
He shall judge between many peoples,
and shall decide for strong nations afar
off;
and they shall beat their swords into
plowshares,
and their spears into pruning hooks;
nation shall not lift up sword against
nation,
neither shall they learn war any more;
but they shall sit every man under
his vine and under his fig tree,
and none shall make them afraid;
for the mouth of the Lord of hosts has
spoken.

Amos 5:11–15

Therefore because you trample upon the
poor
and take from him exactions of wheat,
you have built houses of hewn stone,
but have not dwelt in them;
you have planted pleasant vineyards,
but you shall not drink their wine.
For I know how many are your
transgressions,
and how great are your sins—
you who afflict the righteous, who take a
bribe,
and turn aside the needy in the gate.
Therefore he who is prudent will keep
silent in such a time;
for it is an evil time.

Seek good, and not evil, that you may
live;
and so the Lord, the God of hosts, will
be with you,
as you have said.
Hate evil, and love good, and establish
justice in the gate;
it may be that the Lord, the God of hosts,
will be gracious to the remnant of Joseph.

The New Testament: Christian

It is in the doctrine of pacifism that Christianity makes its unique contribution to the religious ethics of war and peace. The First Commandment tells us not to kill, and the Second Commandment, to love our neighbor as ourselves. But the New Testament goes further, enjoining believers to love their *enemy*, and actively to return good for evil. Among modern Christian churches, the historic "peace churches," including the Society of Friends (Quakers), Mennonites, and the Church of the Brethren, are notable for their literal adherence to pacifist doctrines. Mennonite theologian John Howard Yoder speaks for this pacifist tradition, based largely on the New Testament selections in this section.

Christians whose loyalty to the Prince of Peace puts them out of step with today's nationalistic world, because of a willingness to love their nation's friends but not to hate the nation's enemies, are not unrealistic dreamers who think that by their objections all wars will end. The unrealistic dreamers are rather the soldiers who think that they can put an end to wars by preparing for just one more . . . Christians love their enemies not because they think the enemies are wonderful people, nor because they believe that love is sure to conquer those enemies. They do not love their enemies because they fail to respect their native land or its rulers; nor because they are unconcerned for the safety of their neighbors; nor because another political or economic system may be favored . . . [but] because God does, and God commands His followers to do so; that is the only reason, and that is enough.[3]

Luke 4:23–25

And he came to Nazareth, where he had been brought up; and he went to the synagogue, as his custom was, on the sabbath day. And he stood up to read; and there was given to him the book of the prophet Isaiah. He opened the book and found the place where it was written,

> "The Spirit of the Lord is upon me,
> because he has anointed me to preach
> good news to the poor.
> He has sent me to proclaim release to the captives
> and recovering of sight to the blind,
> to set at liberty those who are oppressed,
> to proclaim the acceptable year of the
> Lord." . . .

Matthew 4:23–5:10

And he went about all Galilee, teaching in their synagogues and preaching the gospel of the kingdom and healing every disease and every infirmity among the people. So his fame spread throughout all Syria, and they brought him all the sick, those afflicted with various diseases and pains, demoniacs, epileptics, and paralytics, and he healed them. And great crowds followed him from Galilee and the Decapolis and Jerusalem and Judea and from beyond the Jordan.

Seeing the crowds, he went up on the mountain, and when he sat down his disciples came to him. And he opened his mouth and taught them, saying:

> "Blessed are the poor in spirit, for theirs is the kingdom of heaven.
> "Blessed are those who mourn, for they shall be comforted.

---

[3]John Howard Yoder. 1982. *Living the Disarmed Life: Christ's Strategy for Peace.* in J. Wallis, ed., *Waging Peace.* New York: Harper & Row.

"Blessed are the meek, for they shall inherit the earth.

"Blessed are those who hunger and thirst for righteousness, for they shall be satisfied.

"Blessed are the merciful, for they shall obtain mercy.

"Blessed are the pure in heart, for they shall see God.

"Blessed are the peacemakers, for they shall be called children of God.

"Blessed are those who are persecuted for righteousness' sake, for theirs is the kingdom of heaven."

Matthew 6: 38–48

"You have heard that it was said, 'An eye for an eye and a tooth for a tooth.' But I say to you, Do not resist one who is evil. But if any one strikes you on the right cheek, turn to him the other also; and if any one would sue you and take your coat, let him have your cloak as well; and if any one forces you to go one mile, go with him two miles. Give to him who begs from you, and do not refuse him who would borrow from you.

"You have heard that it was said, 'You shall love your neighbor and hate your enemy.' But I say to you, Love your enemies and pray for those who persecute you, so that you may be sons of your Father who is in heaven; for he makes his sun rise on the evil and on the good, and sends rain on the just and on the unjust. For if you love those who love you, what reward have you? Do not even the tax collectors do the same? And if you salute only your brethren, what more are you doing than others? Do not even the Gentiles do the same? You, therefore, must be perfect, as your heavenly Father is perfect. . . .

Corinthians 13:1–13

If I speak in the tongues of men and of angels, but have not love, I am a noisy gong or a clanging cymbal. And if I have prophetic powers, and understand all mysteries and all knowledge, and if I have all faith, so as to remove mountains, but have not love, I am nothing. If I give away all I have, and if I deliver my body to be burned, but have not love, I gain nothing.

Love is patient and kind; love is not jealous or boastful; it is not arrogant or rude. Love does not insist on its own way; it is not irritable or resentful; it does not rejoice at wrong, but rejoices in the right. Love bears all things, believes all things, hopes all things, endures all things.

Love never ends; as for prophecies, they will pass away; as for tongues, they will cease; as for knowledge, it will pass away. For our knowledge is imperfect and our prophecy is imperfect; but when the perfect comes, the imperfect will pass away. When I was a child, I spoke like a child, I thought like a child, I reasoned like a child; when I became a man, I gave up childish ways. For now we see in a mirror dimly, but then face to face. Now I know in part; then I shall understand fully, even as I have been fully understood. So faith, hope, love abide, these three; but the greatest of these is love.

A. J. MUSTE

Holy Disobedience

Elders—whether parents or teachers, secular or religious—are often concerned with inculcating obedience. And yet, it may well be that more harm has come into the world by virtue of obedience than disobedience! At the same time, there is something self-con-

From *Holy Disobedience* by A. J. Muste, 1952. New York: Harper. (First appeared in 1952 as a Pendle Hill pamphlet.)

tradictory about teaching disobedience! Protestant minister A. J. Muste was especially convinced of the value of personal disobedience when informed by individual conscience. He was one of the foremost advocates of religiously based pacifism in the United States, and the world. Muste's approach is reflected in this selection from his book, aptly titled *Holy Disobedience*.

It is pretty certainly an oversimplification to suggest . . . that the entire totalitarian, mechanized 'system' under which men today live or into which they are increasingly drawn even in countries where a semblance of freedom and spontaneity remains, can be traced to its source in the military conscription which was instituted by the French Revolution in the eighteenth century. But what cannot, it seems to me, be successfully denied is that today totalitarianism, depersonalization, conscription, war, and the conscripting, war-making power-state are inextricably linked together. They constitute a whole, a 'system'. It is a disease, a creeping paralysis, which affects all nations, on both sides of the global conflict. Revolution and counter-revolution, 'peoples' democracies' and 'western democracies', the 'peace-loving' nations on both sides in the war, are cast in this mold of conformity, mechanization and violence. This is the Beast which, in the language of the Apocalypse, is seeking to usurp the place of the Lamb.

We know that 'war will stop at nothing' and we are clear that as pacifists we can have nothing to do with it. But I do not think that it is possible to distinguish between war and conscription, to say that the former is and the latter is not an instrument or mark of the Beast.

Disobedience Becomes Imperative

Non-conformity, Holy Disobedience, becomes a virtue and indeed a necessary and indispensable measure of spiritual self-preservation, in a day when the impulse to conform, to acquiesce, to go along, is the instrument which is used to subject men to totalitarian rule and involve them in permanent war. To create the impression at least of outward unanimity, the impression that there is no 'real' opposition, is something for which all dictators and military leaders strive assiduously. The more it seems that there is no opposition, the less worthwhile it seems to an ever larger number of people to

cherish even the thought of opposition. Surely, in such a situation it is important not to place the pinch of incense before Caesar's image, not to make the gesture of conformity which is involved, let us say, in registering under a military conscription law. When the object is so plainly to create a situation where the individual no longer has a choice except total conformity or else the concentration camp or death; when reliable people tell us seriously that experiments are being conducted with drugs which will paralyze the wills of opponents within a nation or in an enemy country, it is surely neither right nor wise to wait until the 'system' has driven us into a corner where we cannot retain a vestige of self-respect unless we can say No. It does not seem wise or right to wait until this evil catches up with us, but rather to go out to meet it—to *resist*—before it has gone any further.

. . . Why should we hesitate to have ourselves branded on the cheek or on the buttock, with a hot iron, like cattle? The purges of "wrong-thinkers", so dear to the totalitarian regimes, would thus become infinitely easier.

To me it seems that submitting to conscription even for civilian service is permitting oneself thus to be branded by the State. It makes the work of the State in preparing for war and in securing the desired impression of unanimity much easier. It seems, therefore, that pacifists should refuse to be thus branded.

In the introductory chapter to Kay Boyle's volume of short stories about occupied Germany, *The Smoking Mountain*, there is an episode which seems to me to emphasize the need of Resistance and of not waiting until it is indeed too late. She tells about a woman, professor of philology in a Hessian university who said of the German experience with Nazism: 'It was a gradual process.' When the first *Jews Not Wanted* signs went up, 'there was never any protest made about them, and, after a few months, not only we, but even the Jews who lived in that town, walked past without noticing any more that they were there. Does it seem impossible to you that this should have happened to civilized people anywhere?'

The philology professor went on to say that after a while she put up a picture of Hitler in her classroom. After twice refusing to take the oath of allegiance to Hitler, she was persuaded by her students to take it. 'They argued that in taking this oath, which so many anti-Nazis had taken before me, *I was committing myself to nothing, and that I could exert more influence as a professor than as an outcast in the town.'*

She concluded by saying that she now had a picture of a Jew, Spinoza, where Hitler's picture used to hang, and added: 'Perhaps you will think that I did this ten years too late, and perhaps you are right in thinking this. *Perhaps there was something else we could all of us have done, but we never seemed to find a way to do it, either as individuals or as a group, we never seemed to find a way.*' A decision by the pacifist movement in this country to break completely with conscription, to give up the idea that we can 'exert more influence' if we conform in some measure, do not resist to the uttermost—this might awaken our countrymen to a realization of the precipice on the edge of which we stand. It might be the making of our movement. . . .

It is, of course, possible, perhaps even likely, that if we set ourselves apart as those who will have no dealings whatever with conscription, will not place the pinch of incense before Caesar's image, our fellow-citizens will stone us, as Stephen was stoned when he reminded his people that it was they who had 'received the law as it was ordained by angels, and kept it not'. So may we be stoned for reminding our people of a tradition of freedom and peace which was also, in a real sense, 'ordained by angels' and which we no longer keep. But, it will thus become possible for them, as for Paul, even amidst the search for new victims to persecute, suddenly to see again the face of Christ and the vision of a new Jerusalem. . . .

Our generation will not return to a condition under which every man may sit under his own vine and fig tree, with none to make him afraid, unless there are those who are willing to pay the high cost of redemption and deliverance from a regime of regimentation, terror and war.

Finally, it is of crucial importance that we should understand that for the individual to pit himself in Holy Disobedience against the war-making and conscripting State, wherever it or he be located, is not an act of despair or defeatism. Rather, I think we may say that precisely this individual refusal to 'go along' is now the beginning and the core of any realistic and practical movement against war and for a more peaceful and brotherly world. For it becomes daily clearer that political and military leaders pay virtually no attention to protests against current foreign policy and pleas for peace when they know perfectly well that when it comes to a showdown, all but a handful of the millions of protesters will 'go along' with the war to which the policy leads. All but a handful will submit to conscription. Few of the protesters will so much as risk their jobs in the cause of 'peace'. The failure of the policy-makers to change their course does not, save perhaps in very rare instances, mean that they are evil men who want war. They feel, as indeed they so often declare in crucial moments, that the issues are so complicated, the forces arrayed against them so strong, that they 'have no choice' but to add another score of billions to the military budget, and so on and on. Why should they think there is any reality, hope or salvation in 'peace advocates' who when the moment of decision comes also act on the assumption that they 'have no choice' but to conform?

Precisely in a day when the individual appears to be utterly helpless, to 'have no choice', when the aim of the 'system' is to convince him that he is helpless as an individual and that the only way to meet regimentation is by regimentation, there is absolutely no hope save in going back to the beginning. The human being, the child of God, must assert his humanity and his sonship again. He must exercise the choice which he no longer has as something accorded him by society, which he 'naked, weaponless, armourless, without shield or spear, but only with naked hands and open eyes' must create again. He must understand that this naked human being is the one *real* thing in the face of the mechanics and the mechanized institutions of our age. He, by the grace of God, is the seed of all the human life there will be on earth in the future, though he may have to die to make that harvest possible.

A Devout Meditation in Memory of Adolf Eichmann

We conclude this chapter with two selections confronting the issue of nuclear weapons. Although with the end of the Cold War, the risk of all-out nuclear war is lower than at any time in the past several decades, the threat of accidental or terrorist use, or of small-scale nuclear "exchanges" between conflicting countries (e.g., India and Pakistan) may be at an all time high. Moreover, the spiritual—no less than practical—aspects of nuclear weaponry remain as consequential as ever.

Thomas Merton was a Trappist monk, a writer and poet, and a powerful voice of Christian conscience. He stands in a tradition of dedicated Catholic clergy, including Dorothy Day, Philip and Daniel Berrigan, Raymond Hunthausen, and Jim Douglass. His critique of "sanity"—as defined by nuclear strategic planning—is valid for atheists too, although it may be especially relevant from faith-based perspectives. Adolf Eichmann, whose capture and trial provide the setting for the essay reprinted below, was an official directly responsible for the Nazi Holocaust, which killed six million innocent people.

One of the most disturbing facts that came out in the Eichmann trial was that a psychiatrist examined him and pronounced him *perfectly sane*. I do not doubt it at all, and that is precisely why I find it disturbing.

If all the Nazis had been psychotics, as some of their leaders probably were, their appalling cruelty would have been in some sense easier to understand. It is much worse to consider this calm, "well-balanced," unperturbed official conscientiously going about his desk work, his administrative job which happened to be the supervision of mass murder. He was thoughtful, orderly, unimaginative. He had a profound respect for system, for law and order. He was obedient, loyal, a faithful officer of a great state. He served his government very well.

He was not bothered much by guilt. I have not heard that he developed any psychosomatic illnesses. Apparently he slept well. He had a good appetite, or so it seems. True, when he visited Auschwitz, the Camp Commandant, Hoss, in a spirit of sly deviltry, tried to tease the big boss and scare him with some of the sights. Eichmann was disturbed, yes. He was disturbed. Even Himmler had been disturbed, and had gone weak at the knees. Perhaps, in the same way, the general manager of a big steel mill might be disturbed if an accident took place while he happened to be somewhere in the plant. But of course what happened at Auschwitz was not an accident: just the routine unpleasantness of the daily task. One must shoulder the burden of daily monotonous work for the Fatherland. Yes, one must suffer discomfort and even nausea from unpleasant sights and sounds. It all comes under the heading of duty, self-sacrifice, and obedience. Eichmann was devoted to duty, and proud of his job.

The sanity of Eichmann is disturbing. We equate sanity with a sense of justice, with humaneness, with prudence, with the capacity to love and understand other people. We rely on the sane people of the world to preserve it from barbarism, madness, destruction. And now it begins to dawn on us that it is precisely the *sane* ones who are the most dangerous.

It is the sane ones, the well-adapted ones,

who can without qualms and without nausea aim the missiles and press the buttons that will initiate the great festival of destruction that they, *the sane ones*, have prepared. What makes us so sure, after all, that the danger comes from a psychotic getting into a position to fire the first shot in a nuclear war? Psychotics will be suspect. The sane ones will keep them far from the button. No one suspects the sane, and the sane ones will have *perfectly good reasons*, logical, well-adjusted reasons, for firing the shot. They will be obeying sane orders that have come sanely down the chain of command. And because of their sanity they will have no qualms at all. When the missiles take off, then, *it will be no mistake.*

We can no longer assume that because a man is "sane" he is therefore in his "right mind." The whole concept of sanity in a society where spiritual values have lost their meaning is itself meaningless. A man can be "sane" in the limited sense that he is not impeded by his disordered emotions from acting in a cool, orderly manner, according to the needs and dictates of the social situation in which he finds himself. He can be perfectly "adjusted." God knows, perhaps such people can be perfectly adjusted even in hell itself.

And so I ask myself: what is the meaning of a concept of sanity that excludes love, considers it irrelevant, and destroys our capacity to love other human beings, to respond to their needs and their sufferings, to recognize them also as persons, to apprehend their pain as one's own? Evidently this is not necessary for "sanity" at all. It is a religious notion, a spiritual notion, a Christian notion. What business have we to equate "sanity" with "Christianity"? None at all, obviously. The worst error is to imagine that a Christian must try to be "sane" like everybody else, that we *belong* in our kind of *society*. That we must be "realistic" about it. We must develop a *sane* Christianity:

and there have been plenty of sane Christians in the past. Torture is nothing new, is it? We ought to be able to rationalize a little brainwashing, and genocide, and find a place for nuclear war, or at least for napalm bombs, in our moral theology. Certainly some of us are doing our best along those lines already. There are hopes! Even Christians can shake off their sentimental prejudices about charity, and become sane like Eichmann. They can even cling to a certain set of Christian formulas, and fit them into a Totalist Ideology. Let them talk about justice, charity, love, and the rest. These words have not stopped some sane men from acting very sanely and cleverly in the past. . . .

No, Eichmann was sane. The generals and fighters on both sides, in World War II, the ones who carried out the total destruction of entire cities, these were the sane ones. Those who have invented and developed atomic bombs, thermonuclear bombs, missiles; who have planned the strategy of the next war; who have evaluated the various possibilities of using bacterial and chemical agents: these are not the crazy people, they are the *sane* people. The ones who coolly estimate how many millions of victims can be considered expendable in a nuclear war, I presume they do all right with the Rorschach ink blots too. On the other hand, you will probably find that the pacifists and the ban-the-bomb people are, quite seriously, just as we read in *Time,* a little crazy.

I am beginning to realize that "sanity" is no longer a value or an end in itself. The "sanity" of modern man is about as useful to him as the huge bulk and muscles of the dinosaur. If he were a little less sane, a little more doubtful, a little more aware of his absurdities and contradictions, perhaps there might be a possibility of his survival. But if he is sane, too sane . . . perhaps we must say that in a society like ours the worst insanity is to be totally without anxiety, totally "sane."

A Christian's View of the Arms Race

Diplomat and long-time Sovietologist George F. Kennan delivered the following lecture at the Princeton Theological Seminary in 1982, a time when the nuclear arms race was especially heated and frightening.

The public discussion of the problems presented by nuclear weaponry which is now taking place in this country is going to go down in history, I suspect (assuming, of course, that history is to continue at all and does not itself fall victim to the sort of weaponry we are discussing), as the most significant that any democratic society has ever engaged in.

I myself have participated from time to time in this discussion, whenever I thought I might usefully do so; but in doing so, I have normally been speaking only in my capacity as a citizen talking to other citizens; and since not all of those other citizens were Christians, I did not feel that I could appeal directly to Christian values. Instead, I have tried only to invoke those values which, as it seemed to me, had attained the quality of accepted ideals of our society as a whole.

In this article, I would like to address myself to some of these same problems more strictly from the Christian standpoint. I do this with some hesitation, because while I hold myself to be a Christian, in the imperfect way that so many others do, I am certainly no better a one than millions of others; and I can claim no erudition whatsoever in the field of Christian theology. If, therefore, I undertake to look at the problems of nuclear weaponry from a Christian standpoint, I am aware that the standpoint, in this instance, is a primitive one, theologically speaking, and that this places limitations on its value. This is, however, the way that a great many of us have to look at the subject; and if primitive paintings are conceded to have some aesthetic value, perhaps the same sort of indulgence can be granted to a layperson's view of the relationship of nuclear weaponry to his own faith.

There are, I believe, two ways in which one may view the nuclear weapon, so-called. One way is to view it just as one more weapon, like any other weapon, only more destructive. This is the way it is generally viewed, I am afraid, by our military authorities and by many others. I personally do not see it this way. A weapon is something that is supposed to serve some rational end—a hideous end, as a rule, but one related to some serious objective of governmental policy, one supposed to promote the interests of the society which employs it. The nuclear device seems to me not to respond to that description.

But for those who do see it this way I would like to point out that if it is to be considered a weapon like other weapons, then it must be subjected to the same restraints, to the same rules of warfare, which were supposed, by international law and treaty, to apply to other forms of weaponry. One of these was the prescription that weapons should be employed in a manner calculated to bring an absolute minimum of hardship to noncombatants and to the entire infrastructure of civilian life. This principle was of course offended against in the most serious way in World War II; and our nuclear strategists seem to assume that, this being the case, it has now been sanctioned and legitimized by precedent.

But the fact is that it remains on the books as a prescription both of the laws of war and of

From "A Christian's View of the Arms Race" by George F. Kennan, *Theology Today*, July. Copyright © 1982 by George F. Kennan.

international treaties to which we are parties; and none of this is changed by the fact that we ourselves liberally violated it thirty or forty years ago. And even if it were not thus prescribed by law and treaty, it should, as I see it, be prescribed by Christian conscience. For the resort to war is questionable enough from the Christian standpoint even in the best of circumstances; and those who, as believing Christians, take it upon their conscience to give the order for such slaughter (and I am not saying that there are never situations where this seems to be the lesser of the two evils)—those who do this owe it to their religious commitment to assure that the sufferings brought to innocent and helpless people by the military operations are held to the absolute minimum—and this, if necessary, even at the cost of military victory. For victory itself, even at its apparent best, is a questionable concept. I can think of no judgments of statesmanship in modern times where we have made greater mistakes, where the relationship between calculations and results have been more ironic, than those which related to the supposed glories of victory and the supposed horrors of defeat. Victory, as the consequences of recent wars have taught us, is ephemeral; but the killing of even one innocent child is an irremedial fact, the reality of which can never be eradicated.

Now the nuclear weapon offends against this principle as no other weapon has ever done. Other weapons can bring injury to noncombatants by accident or inadvertence or callous indifference; but they don't always have to do it. The nuclear weapon cannot help doing it, and doing it massively, even where the injury is unintended by those who unleash it.

Worse still, of course, and utterly unacceptable from the Christian standpoint as I see it, is the holding of innocent people hostage to the policies of their government, and the readiness, or the threat, to punish them as a means of punishing their government. Yet how many times—how many times just in these recent years—have we seen that possibility reflected in the deliberations of those who speculate and calculate about the possible uses of nuclear weapons? How many times have we had to listen to these terrible euphemisms about how many cities or industrial objects we would "take out" if a government did not do what we wanted it to do, as though what were involved here were only some sort of neat obliteration of an inanimate object, the removal of somebody else's pawn on the chessboard, and not, in all probability, the killing and mutilation of innocent people on a scale previously unknown in modern times (unless it be, if you will, in the Holocaust of recent accursed memory)?

These things that I have been talking about are only those qualities of the nuclear weapon which violate the traditional limitations that were supposed to rest even upon the conduct of conventional warfare. But there is another dimension to this question that carries beyond anything even conceived of in the past; and that is, of course, the possible, if not probable, effect of nuclear warfare on the entire future of civilization—and, in a sense, on its past as well. It has recently been forcefully argued (and not least in Jonathan Schell's powerful book, *The Fate of the Earth*, 1982) that not only would any extensive employment of nuclear weapons put an end to the lives of many millions of people now alive, but it would in all probability inflict such terrible damage to the ecology of the Northern Hemisphere and possibly of the entire globe as simply to destroy the very capacity of our natural environment for sustaining civilized life, and thus to put an end to humanity's past as well as its future.

Only scientists are qualified, of course, to make final judgments on such matters. But we nonscientists are morally bound, surely, to take into account not only the certain and predictable effects of our actions but also the possible and probable ones. Looking at it from this standpoint, I find it impossible not to accept Schell's thesis that in even trifling with the nuclear weapon, as we are now doing, we are placing at risk the entire civilization of which we are a part.

Just think for a moment what this means. If we were to use these devices in warfare, or if they were to be detonated on any considerable scale by accident or misunderstanding, we might be not only putting an end to civilization as we now know it but also destroying the entire product of humanity's past efforts in the development of civilized life, that product of which we are the beneficiaries and without which our own lives would have no meaning: the cities, the art, the learning, the mastery of nature, the philosophy—what you will. And it would be not just the past of civilization that we were destroying; we would, by the same token, be denying to countless generations as yet unborn, denying to them in our unlimited pride and selfishness, the very privilege of leading a life on this earth, the privilege of which we ourselves have taken unquestioning and greedy advantage, as though it were something owed to us, something to be taken for granted, and something to be conceded or denied by us to those who might come after us—conceded or denied, as we, in our sovereign pleasure, might see fit.

How can anyone who recognizes the authority of Christ's teaching and example accept, even as a humble citizen, the slightest share of responsibility for doing this—and not just for doing it, but for even incurring the risk of doing it? This civilization we are talking about is not the property of our generation alone. We are not the proprietors of it; we are only the custodians. It is something infinitely greater and more important than we are. It is the whole; we are only a part. It is not our achievement; it is the achievement of others. We did not create it. We inherited it. It was bestowed upon us; and it was bestowed upon us with the implicit obligation to cherish it, to preserve it, to develop it, to pass it on—let us hope improved, but in any case intact—to the others who were supposed to come after us.

And this obligation, as I see it, is something more than just a secular one. The great spiritual and intellectual achievements of Western civilization: the art (including the immense Christian art), the architecture, the cathedrals, the poetry, the prose literature—these things were largely unthinkable without the faith and the vision that inspired them and the spiritual and intellectual discipline that made possible their completion. Even where they were not the products of a consciously experienced faith, how can they be regarded otherwise than as the workings of the divine spirit—the spirit of beauty and elevation and charity and harmony—the spirit of everything that is the opposite of meanness, ugliness, cynicism, and cruelty?

Must we not assume that the entire human condition out of which all this has arisen—our own nature, the character of the natural world that surrounds us, the mystery of the generational continuity that has shaped us, the entire environmental framework, in other words, in which the human experiment has proceeded—must we not assume that this was the framework in which God meant it to proceed—that this was the house in which it was meant that we should live—that this was the stage on which the human drama, our struggle out of beastliness and savagery into something higher, was meant to be enacted? Who are we, then, the actors, to take upon ourselves the responsibility of destroying this framework, or even risking its destruction?

Included in this civilization we are so ready to place at risk are the contributions of our own parents and grandparents—of people we remember. These were, in many instances, humble contributions, but ones wrung by those people from trouble and sacrifice, and all of them equal, the humble ones and the momentous ones, in the sight of God. These contributions were the products not just of our parents' efforts but of their hopes and their faith. Where is the place for these efforts, these hopes, that faith, in the morbid science of mutual destruction that has so many devotees, official and private, in our country? What becomes, in that mad welter of calculations about who could take out whom, and how many millions might survive, and how we might hope to save our own poor skins by digging holes in the ground, and thus perhaps surviving into a world not worth surviving into—what becomes in all this of the hopes and the works of our own parents? Where is the place, here, for the biblical injunction to "honor thy father and mother"—that father and mother who stand for us not only as living memories but as symbols of all the past out of which they, too, arose, and without which their own lives, too, had no meaning?

I cannot help it. I hope I am not being unjust or uncharitable. But to me, in the light of these considerations, the readiness to use nuclear weapons against other human beings—against people whom we do not know, whom we have never seen, and whose guilt or innocence it is not for us to establish—and, in doing so, to place in jeopardy the natural structure upon which all civilization rests, as though the safety and the perceived interests of our own generation were more important than everything that has ever taken place or could take place in civilization: this is nothing less than a presumption, a blasphemy, an indignity—an indignity of monstrous dimensions—offered to God!

STUDY QUESTIONS

1. Given that most religions have had a checkered history when it comes to war and violence, how is it possible to be confident that any one religious approach to war and peace is valid?

2. Look into historical trends concerning religious pacifism. Is there any reason to think that it is increasing or decreasing?

3. Describe and evaluate some religious writings that are especially relevant to postive peace.

4. Compare Christian "realism" with anti-war "idealism."

5. Can you begin to identify a truly encompassing, ecumenical, and nonsectarian religious peace tradition that is not limited to your own personal up-bringing?

6. The famed military strategist Karl von Clausewitz argued that "to introduce into a philosophy of war a principle of moderation would be an absurdity. War is an act of violence pushed to its utmost bounds." Is there any way that a religious person could agree with this?

7. Do systems of animism, polytheism, paganism, etc. have any wisdom to offer on the question of war, violence, and peace?

8. Consider and compare systems of religious thought with regard to their underlying assumptions about human nature; for example, whether people are "inherently" good or evil.

9. Learn about "theodicy," the effort to make sense of how the suffering of innocent humans can co-exist with an all-powerful and benevolent God. Relate theodicy to the topic of this chapter.

10. To what extent have famous peace-makers (of the past or the present) been inspired by religious teaching? What about war-makers?

SUGGESTIONS FOR FURTHER READING

Alt, Franz. 1985. *Peace is Possible: the Politics of the Sermon on the Mount.* New York: Schocken Books.

Bainton, Roland Herbert. 1960. *Christian Attitudes Toward War and Peace: a Historical Survey and Critical Re-evaluation.* New York: Abingdon Press.

Berryman, Phillip. 1989. *Our Unfinished Business: The U.S. Catholic Bishops' Letters on Peace and the Economy.* New York: Pantheon Books.

Burns, J. Patout. ed. 1996. *War and its Discontents: Pacifism and Quietism in the Abrahamic Traditions.* Washington, DC: Georgetown University Press.

Cecchini, Rose Marie. 1988. *Women's Action for Peace and Justice: Christian, Buddhist and Muslim Women Tell Their Story.* Maryknoll, NY: Maryknoll Sisters.

Galtung, Johan. 1993. *Buddhism, a Quest for Unity and Peace.* Ratmalana, Sri Lanka: Sarvodaya Book Pub. Services.

Kelsay, John and James Turner Johnson. eds. 1991. *Just War and Jihad: Historical and Theoretical Perspectives on War and Peace in Western and Islamic Traditions.* New York: Greenwood Press.

Klejment, Anne and Nancy L. Roberts. eds. 1996. *American Catholic Pacifism: The Influence of Dorothy Day and the Catholic Worker Movement.* Westport, Conn: Praeger.

Moen, Matthew C. and Lowell S. Gustafson. eds. 1992. *The Religious Challenge to the State*. Philadelphia: Temple University Press.

Polner, Murray and Naomi Goodman. eds. 1994. *The Challenge of Shalom: the Jewish Tradition of Peace and Justice*. Philadelphia: New Society Publishers.

Powers, Gerard F., Drew Christiansen, and Robert T. Hennemeyer. eds. 1994. *Peacemaking: Moral and Policy Challenges for a New World*. United States Catholic Conference: Washington, D.C.

Runyon, Theodore. 1989. ed. *Theology, Politics, and Peace*. Maryknoll, NY: Orbis Books.

Schlabach, Theron F. and Richard T Hughes. eds. 1997. *Proclaim Peace: Christian Pacifism from Unexpected Quarters*. Urbana: University of Illinois Press.

Sivaraksa, Sulak. 1992. *Seeds of Peace: a Buddhist Vision for Renewing Society*. Berkeley Calif: Parallax Press.

Stone, Ronald H. and Dana W. Wilbanks, eds. 1985. *The Peacemaking Struggle: Militarism and Resistance: Essays Prepared for the Advisory Council on Church and Society of the Presbyterian Church (U.S.A.)*. Lanham, MD: University Press of America.

Wallis, Jim. ed. 1983. *Peacemakers: Christian Voices from the New Abolitionist Movement*. San Francisco: Harper & Row.

6

~·~·~

Peace Movements, Transformation, and the Future

The Cold War generated much of the momentum for recent peace movements, in part because the simmering antagonism between the United States and the former Soviet Union gave rise to numerous "proxy wars," fueled by the U.S.–Soviet rivalry. (Of these, the Vietnam War is perhaps the most dramatic for Americans, although residents of the Korean peninsula, Cambodia, Angola, Mozambique, the Dominican Republic, Afghanistan, and others all have their own stories to tell.) In addition, Cold War fears contributed to a tendency for both sides to prop up dictatorial, unrepresentative governments, thereby foisting painful conditions of "structural violence" upon local populations. Notably, this applies to the role of the United States in supporting right-wing despotisms in Spain, Portugal, Cuba, most of Central and South America, Zaire, South Africa, Iran, Pakistan, South Korea, Indonesia, etc., and to the actions of the Soviet Union throughout communist Eastern Europe.

Most of all, perhaps, the Cold War threat of nuclear holocaust gave special energy and urgency to people deeply worried about personal survival as well as the prospect of global extinction. Along the way, numerous other concerns surfaced, for varying lengths of time and with varying intensity: for example, chemical and biological warfare, apartheid in South Africa, land reform in Central America, opposition to specific weapons, weapons testing, or the military draft generally.

A variety of other peace movements achieved successes, such as the independence of India and of other victims of colonialism, the progress of civil rights in the United States, treaties banning biological weapons and genocide, and so forth. The long-term effects of the Cold War's end remain to be seen, although one clear consequence has been a diminution in antinuclear activism. There has also been less opposition to specific weapons systems, even though new weapons are regularly developed and deployed, though the international arms trade continues in high gear, and within the United States at least, the military budget has declined only slightly.

Overall, there has been a decrease in warfare between states, but no decrease in wars generally, as most wars currently take place within a given country. Ethnic and nationalist passions are as intense as ever, sometimes erupting into genocide. Proliferation of nuclear weapons has been less rampant than had been feared during the 1960s and 1970s, but an increase may be imminent. At the same time, the United States and Russia have signed a series of nuclear arms reduction treaties, and a worldwide Comprehensive Test Ban regime, although shaky, is currently in place.

There has been a welcome increase in democratization, notably in South and Central America; although Africa, the Middle East, and much of mainland Asia retain governments that are substantially less representative than most citizens would prefer. Human rights—especially religious freedom—are under attack in many places, although over-all there seems to be progress. Women's rights and population policy are just beginning to receive their due. Economic fairness seems to be diminishing, as the gap between rich and poor continues to grow. Ecological issues are "all over the map." There have been improvements in air and water quality, for example, in certain parts of the "developed world," but if anything, air and water quality have generally gotten worse in most developing countries. Species extinction, global warming, and ozone depletion are, if anything, more severe than ever, while the earth's population continues to expand (albeit at a decreasing rate). On the positive side, there is more worldwide environmental awareness than ever before, an essential prerequisite for any significant and lasting progress.

In summary, movement toward a more peaceful world has been, at best, uneven and painfully slow. And yet, in some ways the world has changed remarkably: not just with the end of the Cold War, but because of the breakup of the former Soviet Union itself, the transition to capitalism and at least a semblance of democracy in many countries where such change had been unimaginable, the end of apartheid in South Africa and the dramatic success of black African rule there, and the end of numerous insurrections and government repressions in Central and South America. There is still abundant room for peace movements in the future, and indeed, immense need for them. It seems likely, however, that in many cases they will focus on issues different from those of the past.

Nonetheless, certain things still have not changed. Militarism, violence, and the misdirection of national resources call for opposition. Denial of human rights, of economic fairness, and of ecological sustainability all demand redress. There is need for creative and empathic efforts to envision and promote a peaceful world. People must strive for both negative and positive peace.

It is a cliche for graduation speakers to announce that we have reached a crossroads, and that the present time is uniquely consequential . . . not just for individuals making their personal life decisions, but for society in general, even the world. But in fact, there truly may be unique opportunities as well as risks at this time in world history, when it often seems that we have been, as Matthew Arnold put it, "Wandering between two worlds, one dead, the other powerless to be born."[1]

The special hope of peace movements is that they might serve as midwives for that newer world, providing it with the impetus and power to be born at last. Just as birth may be difficult, often painful, even dangerous, the course of peace movements has not run altogether smoothly, nor have peace movements been unidimensional or universally welcomed. But just as birth is natural and necessary if life is to continue, it seems

---

[1]Matthew Arnold. 1934. Stanzas from the Grande Chartreuse. *Essays and Poems of Matthew Arnold*. New York: Harcourt Brace Jovanovich.

equally certain that peace is necessary (whether or not it is "natural") and that peace movements may contribute mightily toward success. Pope John Paul II once said that "it is only through a conscious choice and through a deliberate policy that humanity can survive." Peace movements and peace studies both strive to help establish such a policy, and to represent such a choice.

Peace Movements in History

"Those who forget the past," wrote philosopher George Santayana, "are condemned to repeat it." With regard to peace movements, it is more accurate to say that anyone with hopes and goals for the future would be wise to consult the past, if only because in certain basic ways, all that has happened—mistakes as well as triumphs—is a valuable guide to what is likely to take place.

A single peace movement does not exist. Rather, there have always been many peace movements, each differing in its circumstances and time, in numbers of adherents, numbers of groups, as well as in goals. One observer of the European antinuclear movements during the 1980s suggested that peace movements are like breaching whales, which periodically break the surface then disappear under the waves. "When the whale disappears in a dive, those on the right believe the movement no longer exists. Supporters . . . on the other hand, see the leaping whale and claim it can fly."The truth is somewhere in between.

Introduction

The idea of peace is probably as old as humanity. But secular or political movements for peace—what we have called peace movements—are not more than two hundred years old, and have evolved largely in the western and northern countries. Those peace movements with religious orientations are older and have arisen in many different periods and in all parts of the globe. . . .

Before the first modern popular mass movements against war emerged in the late nineteenth century, there existed a myriad of peace sects and traditions (almost all religious) which included peace and the renunciation of war as a principle or goal. The history of anti-war sentiments or peace ideas, actively expressed in the resistance to war by various sects and groups from the early Christian period onward, is thus much older than even the first secular peace groups in Europe (circa 1815). In many countries, ethnic and other groups have opposed specific wars and conscriptions on political or cultural grounds without necessarily being "anti-war" per se, or without having any conscious orientation to peace or peace movements. Although such groups were widespread in the nineteenth and early twentieth centuries, they are not included in this survey as peace or "anti-war" *movements*. Equally, more broad religious movements and churches, such as Buddhism, have concepts of peace as part of their doctrines without as a whole ever becoming part of an active peace movement. They too are marginal to this discussion, except when a section self-consciously creates or becomes a peace or war-resisting church, such as the Unified Buddhist Church in Indo-China after 1960, or Hinduism, which clearly contributes elements to the Gandhian movement without ever itself being a "peace movement" or tradition. Furthermore, one has to distinguish between peace and anti-war *movements* as broad, amorphous, and somewhat ephemeral social phenomena, and the specific peace *traditions* expressed in often small but prophetic

From *"Peace Movements in History"* by Nigel Young. In S. Mendlovitz and R. B. J. Walker, eds. *Towards a Just World Peace*. 1987 London: Butterworths.

[2]Philip P. Everts. 1989. Where the peace movement goes when it disapears. *Bulletin of the Atomic Scientists* 45: 26–30.

groups providing ideas, initiatives and motivation for the entire peace movement.

Aims and Objectives

This paper deals with the peace movement as it has evolved for over two centuries in the industrial societies: a social formation fundamentally concerned with the problems of war, militarism, conscription, and mass violence, and the ideals of internationalism, globalism and non-violent relations between people. Therefore it does not incorporate the contemporary concerns of the South with hunger, development and related repressions, nor does it explore the linkages of peace, democracy and human rights. Yet the peace movement *has*, to varying degrees, incorporated these concerns and, it will be argued, as the movement becomes more global in its scope and appeal, and the threat of species-death more of a reality, these issues will become more explicitly part of the peace programme of peoples' struggles everywhere. . . .

There is no such thing as a single peace movement, but a variety of peace traditions: religious pacifism; liberal internationalism; the women's peace movement; anti-conscriptionism; conscientious objection; socialist anti-militarism; socialist internationalism; the peace fronts associated with the Comintern; radical, secular pacifism; anarcho-pacifism; Gandhian non-violent revolution; unilateral nuclear pacifism of parts of the nuclear disarmament movement; the transnational anti-war New Left of the 1960s; and the ecologically inspired movements of the seventies and the eighties. Each has made a contribution, sometimes in coalition, sometimes as separate sects or subgroups. Yet at times a peace movement has arisen that is more than the sum total of these traditions or the organizations that represent them. At such times it has attracted a mass base.

To be sure, there have been moments of popular activity on issues related to war and peace when various strands and traditions, immensely diverse in character and often contradictory in their stance, have joined with the politically mobilized. But these minority traditions which coexist within the broader peace movement for much of the period have distinct histories and successes and failures of their own. Their impact on the larger peace movement, accordingly, must be analysed separately; some, for example, *grew* during World War I when the peace movement generally receded. Prophetic minorities and peace sects are able to survive and even flourish in periods of war and movement decline. Yet at other times these diverse fragments have had little or no contact with society or one another, and have all but disappeared from the historical scene; they have fought bitter feuds or retreated into alternative strategies, or even emigrated and escaped. In other words, the history of peace movements, as with so many other social movements, is one of discontinuities and divisions. . . .

THE RELIGIOUS PEACE TRADITIONS

The religious tradition is certainly the oldest of the major peace strands and predates the growth of the concept of a peace movement, that is, as a largely secular and political force independent of churches or the representatives of states. Even before the fourth century the tradition of religious pacifism was associated with individual witness and principled war resistance of an absolute kind. Later, conscientious objection to military service was claimed as a right as conscription spread, usually invoking both a universalistic ethic and moral critique of war, and was often rooted in a communal religious base. In some cases these collective values led to a withdrawal of the group from the world into monastic contemplation or quietist and retreatist sects, and this continued to play a role even in the twentieth century. In other cases these groups were confronted by state and military authorities, rebellion, emigration, and persecuted and repressed to the point of extinction.

Peace ideas, if not absolute pacifism, in Christianity, as in other major religions, certainly predate the era of the European religious Reformation. They can be found in the less orthodox social undercurrents of the Catholic Church and monastic movements which precede both the Anabaptist revolt and the cosmopolitan humanism of Erasmus. But it was out of that crucible, and the extensive warfare of the seventeenth century, that one group emerged that has played a virtually continuous role in peace issues both in England and elsewhere, providing witness against war since the English civil war: the Quakers.

The Society of Friends, or "Quakers,"

merit analysis despite their small numbers. They have had an influence on the sustenance and growth of the peace movement for more than 300 years in English-speaking countries and beyond that is truly remarkable and quite out of proportion to their size. Their activities combine a number of root elements which remained a key part of the broader movement as it grew. The Quakers draw together a number of elements found in earlier religious peace traditions for their particular contribution to peace visions, symbols, strategy and social organization, both religious and secular.

The first element is the desire not merely to oppose but to actively resist war, both collectively and through individual witness or non-cooperation with military service. The second element is the belief in the ultimate possibility of the abolition of war through non-violent unarmed relations between peoples and groups as well as individuals. This utopian vision is based on non-violence or non-resistance as both an ethical principle and an ultimately practical basis of order. The third element is a religious notion of universalism—unity as people under God or in the spirit. It stresses the ultimate identity of all human beings, using it as the basis for a moral critique of war as a collective crime against the species itself. This leads to a transnational loyalty beyond states and national borders which characterizes most religions but has special meaning for peace churches. The fourth element is a belief in the necessity for social and structural change. Peace and human fairness and compassion are perceived to be linked; an unequal world or society leads to violent conflict and death. Intrinsic in this idea is that change in the individual and the community is possible. . . .

LIBERALISM AND INTERNATIONALISM:
PROPOSALS FOR REFORM

A second major tradition of peace activity tried to prevent war through the reformed behaviour of states: peace plans, treaties and proposals, negotiations, or international law and arbitration between all groups and peoples. This search was developed further through the concepts of civil disobedience, mediation, conflict resolution, and non-violence. In the 1890s, there was a great surge of support for such initiatives. Elite plans and proposals for peace and disarmament had emerged even before the Quakers took them up and became widespread

in European ruling circles during the carnage of the Thirty Years War (1618–48). The Quakers (for example, Penn) adopted some of these ideas in America and combined them with ideas of positive peace and a non-violent social order (Woolman), and international harmony to parallel the more cosmopolitan and visionary ideas of the Enlightenment humanists. . . .

The first peace societies were formed in the early nineteenth century. Preventing war though international organization was closely

1. Religious Peace Traditions	Religious Pacifism, Society of Friends (Quakers), International Fellowship of Reconciliation, Pax Christi, Unified Buddhist Church of Vietnam
2. Liberal Internationalism	League of Nations Associations, Peace Councils, Peace Society, World Disarmament Campaigns, Union of Democratic Control
3. Anti-conscriptionism	(Single issue lobbies) No Conscription Fellowship, War Resisters' International
4. Socialist War-resistance	War Resisters' International, CGT (France)
5. Socialist Internationalism	Second International
6. Feminist Anti-militarism	WILPF, Women's Peace Party, Women Strike for Peace, Women for Peace
7. Radical Pacifism	War Resisters' International, No More War Movement, Gandhi's Congress, Movement for a New Society
8. Cominter-nationalism	World Peace Council; Peace Committees, Mouvement de la Paix
9. Nuclear Disarmament	Campaigns for Nuclear Disarmament, SANE, "The Hibakusha", Freeze, END
10. The "new peace movement"	The Greens

These categories are neither exhaustive nor mutually exclusive.

linked to a concept that was to remain basic to peace movement activity and thought: universalism, the cosmopolitan ethic that sprang from both the Enlightenment and earlier religious ideals of a universal or transnational church. With the growth of socialism, a new form of this internationalist ethic emerged to complete a peace perspective based on the relativity of national boundaries and frontiers and the ultimate limitation of the sovereignty of states.

These developments did not provide a united strategy or ideology for the early modern peace movement, but they did lay the foundations for a simple lowest common denominator of action and aims: namely, the survival of the species, the eventual elimination of war, and the basic unity of human society. It was this common platform that spurred the long delayed but deeply rooted reaction to the arms race in the early twentieth century....

What hindered the liberal internationalist dream were the geopolitical developments which preceded the 1914–18 war. After the American and French revolutions, Europe witnessed the spread of nation-states, mass conscripted armies, and industrial bases for militarism and imperial expansion. One of the key intellectual debates in the peace movement was between a non-conformist, free-trade liberalism that saw global capitalism as creating a new war-less world, and socialism, which saw capitalism as the engine of a highly militarized, exploitative and centralized state system of enormous destructive capacity....

CONSCRIPTION AND WAR RESISTANCE

The peace movement's third major tradition, anti-conscriptionism, was often linked to liberal issues of civil rights or the liberty of the individual. But it also coincided with religious non-conformity, such as the Quaker's witness against war (conscientious objection), and with socialist resistance to war especially by left labour unions. But even before modern conscription began in France in 1793, war and military service had in many countries at different times been opposed by the poor and the illiterate: inarticulate peasants and crafts people; persecuted religious sects and communities; emigrants and immigrants....

From early Christian times, many religious communities have resisted war, or at least distanced the religious group and the individual

from the institution of war and the performance of military service.... By the twentieth century, conscientious objection was being claimed as a basic human right. During the 1914–18 war, this was to prove of crucial importance in sustaining the peace movement and anti-conscriptionism in wartime, and in building the new anti-war movements at the end of the war. However ... socialists were deeply divided over the progressive character of conscription and the justification of progressive war.

SOCIALISM AND THE PEACE MOVEMENT: MILITARISM AND ANTI-MILITARISM

The rise of socialism highlights the fourth element in the inspirational roots of the peace movement: the necessity for social and human change, given that war is linked to problems of economic injustice and political repression, to the selfishness of narrow élites and powerful ruling groups, and to national and imperial as well as racial chauvinism. Marxists and non-Marxists alike continue to be divided over the role of the nation-state as an apt vehicle for socialist change, on the necessity for revolutionary violence, and the desirability of socialist participation in existing capitalist governments. And by no means were all socialists anti-conscriptionist or internationalist (or even anti-militarist). It is no wonder then that all the debates and proclamations of the Second International came to nothing in 1914, despite the rhetoric of the Stuttgart Resolution of 1904.

The socialist peace tradition can be best broken down into two main dimensions: "socialist war resistance," ... and "socialist internationalism," that was largely co-opted by "communist internationalism" after 1917.

Socialist war resistance opposed ... militarist governments, conscription, and war preparations, which they perceived to be integral aspects of capitalism, imperialism and class rule.... If the organized producers, now numbering tens of millions in Europe, could strike in unison across national frontiers against war, then the militarists and nationalists, generals, emperors, tsars and capitalist-backed governments would be immobilized by mass non-cooperation. Anti-militarist strikes did take place before, and also after, 1914; the dream of a general strike of workers of all countries against war did not die with the August mobilizations, but led to other political action during the war and after....

Socialism was divided between its *anti-militarist* and *militarist* traditions. Since the Russian Civil War, the latter predominated. In the fifty years before that, a *heroic anti-militarist tradition had evolved*, and at the turn of the twentieth century appeared to be in the ascendant. Socialist anti-militarism preceded Marxism, and was often in tension with it during this crucial half-century. However, the national mobilizations of August 1914 and the military consolidation of the Russian state after 1918 reversed that relationship and made socialist militarism a key factor in world politics.

. . . On the other hand, socialist internationalism took the nation-state for granted and was largely wedded to advancing within that framework. In 1914, one socialist party after another succumbed to the call for national unity and voted war credits. Only a minority of socialist anti-militarists and internationalists defied this debacle. When the socialist movement might have become more fundamentally anti-militarist given the appalling experiences of 1914–18, it turned in the opposite direction because of the perceived need to defend the Russian revolution. The revolutionary tradition had become militarized as well as "state-" and nation-centred.

Emergence of the Modern Peace Movement

In the wake of the butchery of the Napoleonic wars, the religious, liberal and internationalist traditions jostled each other in a somewhat unresolved and kaleidoscopic scatter of peace societies and pressure groups. Whilst retaining its religious heritage, the peace movement became more influenced by the secular ideas of the *Auklärung*, the development of modern ideological formulae. The idea of a "workers' strike against war" was heard for the first time. With the French revolution and the *levée en masse*, the reality both of the "peoples' army" and the ambiguities of the French "wars of liberation" in Europe soon became apparent. The latent dilemmas of violent social change were answered in part by utopian and communitarian views of social change without violence, or at least without resort to arms. From now on the peace movement would be divided over the ethics and issues of "just wars," whether

by progressive states or progressive oppositional groups. In the 1860s members of the peace movement, and indeed pacifists such as the Quakers, found themselves divided over a war that could emancipate black slaves in 1863. Time and time again in the nineteenth and twentieth centuries, such divisions would be repeated. The peace movement split over whether a war was "just" or "progressive," whether the evil to be overcome was any greater than the injustice and violence needed to succeed and whether military service—the "democratization of the means of violence" by conscription—might itself be a progressive phenomenon. . . .

The Twentieth-Century Peace Movement: New Traditions

Two of the major peaks of the peace movement in terms of mass public support occurred before and after the first (1914–18) "Great" European war. From the late 1880s until 1914, and from the 1920s until the mid-1930s, one can talk of a mass peace movement certainly in Europe and the United States (as one can again in the late 1960s and 1980s). The western peace movement as it reached the first peak of support between 1890–1900 reflects, as we have shown, the traditions upon which it was based and the development of peace-related groups and organizations, some of which initiated this impressive growth and some that jumped on the bandwagon.

Both socialist internationalism and anti-militarism suffered near terminal defeat in 1914, but socialist war resistance continued (sometimes illegally) in many belligerent countries. In fact, certain new peace traditions emerged as an understanding of the nationalist mobilizations grew. . . .

A major new force was feminist anti-militarism. Even before 1900, a new transnational women's peace movement had begun to assert an identity of its own. It created groups and brought together Marxist, socialist, anarchist and liberal women, feminists and non-feminists, those involved in the suffrage movement and those from Christian backgrounds, all united by the ideal of a distinctive role for women on the issue of peace and female unity across national boundaries even in wartime. . . .

TWO PATHS OF EVOLUTION

The European and North American peace movements gathered strength during the arms race that led to the war of 1914–18. In its wake, a new mass movement based on revulsion at the nature of the conflict arose. But by the 1930s the peace movement was focused on the renewed arms race and the rise of fascism. However, two opposing tendencies were articulated after 1918. One was to organize public opinion to reform the world system of nation-states either through a League of Nations or through a global hegemony by an enlightened power or powers. The other was to stress increasing claims against the state system, using extra-parliamentarist strategies of social change: extension of the rights of conscience, resistance to conscription, civil disobedience, and anti-militarist direct action (radical non-violence and transnational and subcultural identification).

In the short-term both of these tendencies were doomed to failure, given the context of national rivalries and the nascent period of political autocracy.... The peace movement failed to halt the arms race after 1930, as it had after 1900, and failed in most of its other stated goals. In addition, several key peace traditions suffered dramatic discontinuities.

Still, ideas and organizations were created in these three decades which remained alive and active. They provided links to strategies for peace and disarmament in the later years of the twentieth century, when a broad coalition of peace constituencies—like that which grew in the years between 1900 and 1914—re-emerged to form the contemporary movement.

THE PEACE MOVEMENT AS A
GLOBAL MOVEMENT

The rise of fascism and the cataclysm of the 1939–45 war led to another profound disjunction in the peace movement. Peace organizations and ideas remained, but not a peace movement. Indeed, the period from the growing peace protests against civilian bombing in the 1940s until the rising tide of concern in the mid-fifties is the longest single caesura in the two hundred year history of the peace movement. It can best be explained by the partial relegitimization of war in the face of fascism, East and West, and by extending the defence of liberties against autocracy by force of arms.

In the period before and after the war of 1914–18, it is plausible to argue that the silent majority had become sceptical of war as an instrument of politics and that at best most nation-states were considered quasi-legitimate. Ironically the subsequent democratization or "self-determination" of a number of states and the establishment of socialism in one country led to a more widespread legitimization of war, disseminated by socialism and liberalism through an expanding communications network and increased global literacy. The anti-fascist fronts of the thirties laid the groundwork for the "just war" theory of World War II. The silent majorities before and after 1945 supported the war alliances: the "unjust" stereotype of war from 1918 was replaced by a grudging acceptance of big battalions, and apostasy from pacifism and anti-militarism lasted beyond 1945. This is the only way to explain the delayed reaction to nuclear weapons (except in Japan where there are some additional specific circumstances). The state system itself shared in the general legitimization of the peace of the victors despite the bloc bifurcation and the new arms race. This acceptance of a "just nuclear peace" was paralleled by the shift of liberation movements to anti-colonial wars in Asia and Africa.

During the hiatus, perhaps for the first time, events, movements and ideas outside the white western and industrial countries became significant in the peace movement. Gandhi's movement to liberate India came to fruition in 1947 through an overwhelming non-violent social movement that linked itself explicitly to peace. The first use of atomic weapons took place on an Asian country, Japan, whose earlier peace movement had been shattered by fascist militarism. A new peace movement arose that was partly inspired by the witness of the atomic victims, the "Hibakusha." In many countries peace became identified again with social justice, and the end of racial and colonial oppression. Many countries tried to follow India's example, some like Gandhi through non-violent or peaceful means. The repression of Indo-Chinese independence led to a global anti-war reaction. Nuclear testing in the Pacific was responded to by transnational peace voyages. There were international protests in the French Sahara....

So far the peace movement has largely been analysed as a phenomenon developing in the western or Christian countries, in the industrial democracies, or the English-speaking world. But it is also arguable that Gandhi's movement, the response to Hiroshima and Nagasaki, and the influence of socialism—first Russian, then Chinese and other more indigenous forms—on liberation movements such as the Indo-Chinese, began to shift the locus of the peace movement to a more global plane. Rising radiation levels throughout the world that were due to nuclear testing by several countries, especially in the Pacific, led to a global outcry. Certainly the emerging peace movements of the northern hemisphere were beginning to find new echoes and counterparts in the South. Also, human or civil rights came to be seen as integral to peace, as in the massive US movement for black social justice which was associated with Martin Luther King, Jr. and his advocacy of non-violence, and which linked itself to struggles for black Africa.... By 1965, US involvement in Indo-China and the repression of non-violent movements there led to the formation of an international coalition, and the birth of the contemporary peace movement.

The Contemporary Peace Movement

More than any other single event, the spontaneous yet co-ordinated mass demonstrations in twelve European capitals and several other major cities in 1981 ... galvanized political negotiators, both East and West, and gave new life to the global peace movement. With several million participants, the upsurge of anti-nuclear activity between October and December 1981 in Bonn, Brussels, Paris, Athens, London, Bucharest, Rome, Madrid, Amsterdam, Helsinki, Oslo, East and West Berlin, Stockholm and Copenhagen engendered a sense of transnational unity and a vision of success. These demonstrations revealed a common political purpose rarely seen before; some observers looking back as far as 1848 for a comparable trans-European movement.

The new peace movement fanned out from the Netherlands to Germany, Britain, Belgium and Italy; it elicited signs of an independent peace mood in Eastern Europe; it steadily expanded through Scandinavia and the Mediterranean; it reached Canada, New Zealand, Australia and the United States; and, almost last of all, touched France. In Europe, these campaigns, in the context of a new cold war, had their decisive catalyst in the December 1979 NATO decisions to deploy a new generation of missiles, and the abandonment of serious disarmament negotiation after SALT II was left unratified.

The churches were more intimately involved than they had been in the first mass nuclear disarmament campaigns in Europe twenty years earlier. Following the example of the *Dutch churches*, both congregations and religious leaders, East and West, took considerably more radical stances. In all, this was a more transnational and massive protest than anything in the sixties, involving a broader political coalition with new elements from the Vietnam war period and the women's ecological and anti-nuclear power movements....

The profile in this paper is based mainly on historical evidence from the northern and western movements and the English-speaking areas, and even so it cannot reflect all the variation, or depth and quality of participation accurately. For example, 6,000 conscientious objectors ("subjects") willing to face imprisonment *may* have more impact on a society than 600,000 organized but transitory demonstrators ("objects").... One can measure [their] effectiveness because in most cases the peace movements made explicit a particular objective or goal: some sought to abolish war (pacifism or pacificism); some opposed particular wars on liberal or socialist grounds; some aspired to limit or prevent war by negotiated disarmament, international law and peace treaties; and some opposed specific dimensions or armaments and war (such as conscription). In some cases, such as with the socialist movements, anti-war movements fused with movements for social change to abolish the war-making society and associated institutions. These and a number of later peace movements (for example, the Gandhian) had positive as well as negative objectives of peace; they wished not only to create a non-violent or more just, equitable and harmonious society, but also to link with utopian and communitarian movements.

With peace movements, as with other social movements, the results of public activity are always ambiguous. Like other great social change or social protest campaigns, they have both latent and manifest consequences.

They may actually prolong the wars they aim to stop. They may alienate public opinion. Their relative success or failure always depends on other independent or external factors, not just the degree or level of activity achieved. This has always been one of the weakening illusions of peace movements: the structural and historical context of the deeply humanist abolitionist movement against slavery, for example, was just as, or more, important than the efforts of the abolitionist campaigns themselves. Moreover, the abolition of slavery left or even produced *new* evils, and involved the injustices and carnage of a terrible civil war that split and virtually destroyed the American peace movement, whilst racist oppression soon grew in virulent forms.

A further variation of this critique is the theory of "cycles" or of political "generations." For each wave of the peace movement, commitment appears inevitably cyclical. A theory involving "cycles of protest" argues that movements have an inherent limit, such as the energy, time and resources people will devote to a single issue or movement unless institutionalization takes place. Generational explanations stress the span of youthful involvement from age 17 to 25, roughly the years of compulsory military service for males. These years may be relatively free of social ties and commitments and therefore can be spent in radical movements where risks may be taken in social protest. Youth involvement in peace politics is undoubtedly a generational experience, as transient as military service in most countries—a few intense years and it is over. A movement that can institutionalize youth involvement, however, can capture a generation....

Another factor often cited to explain failure has to do with social class. It has been typically argued that peace movements have drawn from too narrow a social base to succeed (for example, they have been "middle class"). The Marxist charge that much *individualist* pacifism was originally "petty bourgeois" has some truth. Equally, liberal internationalism or "pacifism" was overwhelmingly middle class and "respectable" or professional and also male, white, and middle-aged most of the time. Yet other peace traditions, like anti-conscriptionism, have appealed in *all* countries and to all classes. Socialist anti-militarism was overwhelmingly working class, and socialist inter-

nationalism represented both the labour aristocracy and the independent intellectuals. Equally, many fundamental peace sects have been found amongst the very poor, the peasantry, and ethnic minorities....

A general problem for social and political movements in opposition has been that of participation in government through individual cooptation or group incorporation. Individuals can be manipulated and bought off; protests can become ritualistic; an élitist leadership may not wish to lose its prestige, its organization, its money or its position. The elevation of leaders into any national establishment or parliament can weaken and discourage the grass-roots who feel betrayed; or raise false hopes that are quickly shattered as has happened wherever local peace movements have looked to established leaders and politicians within the structure of the state.

As a result, several of the peace traditions analysed have displayed a deep ambivalence or distrust about operating within the state system—or have attempted to transcend it. This was most marked before and after World War I, and again in the 1980s. Movements in this situation can become a safety valve, rather than a challenge to the war-making system. A clear case is where conscientious objection is drawn into the actual machinery of the war effort as in the United States during World War II; or where socialist MPs vote for war credits (World War I) or nuclear bases (after 1963 in Britain), having been previously pledged to oppose them.

Peace movements can of course also be repressed and severely harassed—leaders jailed, even killed. The American anti-war movement of 1917 was virtually destroyed physically by police raids, arrests and vigilante action (1917–20), and the leaders were given long terms in prison. The civil disobedience campaign in Britain was badly shaken by long-term imprisonment of a few of its leaders (1961–62). The South Vietnamese Buddhists were attacked, imprisoned and killed by both sides (1965–75). The independent peace movements in the Soviet Union and Eastern Europe, and the peace movement in Turkey ... suffered similar setbacks. In Nazi Germany and other fascist countries, a number of peace leaders were executed; likewise with some pacifists after the Russian Revolution, and in Japan before World War II. But this does not provide a general explanation of the failure of peace movements. Surveillance, the limitation of human rights and censorship *are* key issues for peace movements, but do not constitute a sufficient, only a contributory, cause of decline.

Of course the role of media suppression or opposition is equally crucial; adverse conditions can pre-empt the emergence of peace movements, as illustrated in many developing countries. However, the experiences of the last peace movement since the "conspiracy of silence" of the late fifties are that the movement can have an impact on the communications systems of some societies and that such media are not permanently monolithic. The censorship and bias attending the peace movement, and which culminated in the banning of a major anti-nuclear film in Britain in 1965, was countered especially in the Vietnam years by a number of alternative strategies. The movement first established its own media or was reported in an alternative media (reaching over two million people in the United States, for example). . . .

Finally, but not least importantly, is the sense of *impotence* or paralysis that sets into many movements. This is the feeling of social despair, that nothing can be done, that the problem of war is beyond human control. Despondency and cynicism, even suicide or other forms of self-destruction, are common responses to the weakness and sense of failure that accompany many peace and social change movements as they enter their "troughs" or suffer major defeats. Among other solutions, this has led to a self-conscious attempt at "empowerment" based on the therapeutic politics of group affinity and solidarity. . . .

Attempts to be realistic about the discontinuities and fragmented character of the historic peace movements need not lead to an entirely pessimistic prognosis in the present. If one denies the very possibility of success of such human endeavour, further study or action might have very little justification. But because as a species we cannot afford the luxury of a people's peace initiative which ebbs again in the coming years, it is essential that the peace movement use its collective intellect to forge an analysis of present strengths and past weaknesses that can enlighten strategic and programmatic debates and help deemphasize certain actions, policies and linkages as against others.

This does *not* mean evolving some monolithic, unitary or reductionist strategy or ideology, as sectarians would hold—the peace movement is as plural as it is international. Pluralism is a source of unity as well as fragmentation: the very diversity of the peace movement described here may be an expression of an inner strength. . . . Peace, women, environment, participation, economic well-being, the secular and the spiritual—the synthesis in people's movements is from the communal base.

Research on the history and social character of war resistance reveals that ordinary people are able to oppose and resist war, militarism and war mobilization on a sustained basis most typically when they have both a strong local communal base of organization *and* an identity, as well as certain social factors or orientations (ideology, religion, ethnic linkage) which *transcend* national boundaries and the sovereign edicts of the state. Within the peace movements themselves, as this essay has tried to illustrate, such vision and strategy linking localism and globalism, cosmopolitanism and communalism, has sometimes descended into a narrow parochialism or become a form of rootlessness. But in groups such as the Quakers (or, later, the War Resisters International) the idea of linking the local and the global has often given vision and practical support to peace groups over a period of more than three centuries.

Certain factors (the opposite of "transnational and communal" ones) have specifically contributed to the failure of the peace movements. The following two sets of ideal type forces are by no means exhaustive but constitute the main dimensions, both positive and negative, of the contemporary movement.

1. State centrism (chauvinistic nationalism, ethnocentrism).
2. Limited pressure-group concepts of politics (reformist, secular).
3. Alignment (to parties, states, or state-centred ideologies or blocs); for example, cooptation by the social democratic left.
4. Reactive and short-term character (lack of social programme resulting in despair).
5. Lack of social alternatives (no strategy for political change); disempowerment.
6. Gap between leadership (intellectual/political) and grass-roots base (élitism); this may be a generational gap.

7. Lack of a strong communal base (amorphous superficial coalition character). . . .

In the historic clash between state and civil society, it was those entities under attack, the smaller communities, the churches, smaller political units, intellectual sub-cultures and autonomous cultural and economic entities, which became the vessels of anti-militarist activity and perspective. These are now regaining their salience as a base for a popular world view. Indeed they are much more than ideas. They have been realized in specific public events and people's movements which are no longer obsessed with altered national policies alone, but grasp the necessity of activating the affinities across military borders, not least of all the East/West divide: mobilizing groups on the basis of personal exchange and grass-root reciprocity; linkages of activists as well as leaders: twinning communities, municipalities and nuclear free zones; and diplomacy between cities. . . .

This survey has indicated how more and more peace traditions have accumulated over the past 200 years—in that sense there has been continual growth. But it has also shown that the mass support of organized public opinion has regularly and dramatically declined: in most countries in the period after mobilization for war, such as 1914 and 1940. The relation between this public involvement and the small peace groups or sects is itself a problematic one, but in general one can state that as a ratio of population there has been no clear quantitative growth in peace movements since the late nineteenth century. In addition, there is in any case, no clear correlation between the numbers mobilized, and impact on society or the state.

Clearly the multiple stranded peace traditions described here have so far patently failed to do more than marginally affect the arms race spiral. If they follow the patterns of the past, they are likely to fail again. State policies and public attitudes have been significantly shifted on such issues as certain wars (for example, Vietnam) and types of weapons (e.g., nuclear), or specific actions (bomb-testing) or conscription. But no twentieth-century state of any size has shown any serious inclination to substantially demilitarize itself, and it is clear that increased pressure will have to be largely external to the state apparatus and the system of states.

The peace movement has been divided over aims, methods, analysis and strategy, but has occasionally been forged into a strong coalition by particularly atrocious wars (such as Vietnam) or weapons (nuclear). But its failure has been the central one of failing to achieve a visionary synthesis, a new model and strategy that is appropriate to a changing global society. It has not been able to effectively harness even those emerging social tendencies such as communal and transnational growth which favour it. . . . [But] the peace movement contains within its present character . . . the potentiality for . . . a "permanent and global peace movement." The question remains whether it has the time, the will, and the imagination to realize that potential.

ELISE BOULDING

Building Utopias in History

When it comes to utopias—idealized images of a perfect world society—there is a tendency to extremism: to be carried away oneself on glorious flights of fantasy or to disparage others who are. Peace advocates can marginalize themselves as seemingly unrealistic dreamers, holding out for perfect solutions, which turn out to be unworkable and,

From "Building Utopias in History" by Elise Boulding. In S. Mendlovitz and R. B. J. Walker, eds. Towards a Just World Peace. 1987. London: Butterworths.

thus, no solutions at all. The best, in short, can become the enemy of the good. On the other hand, it is also possible to be so jaded, pessimistic, even cynical, that all proposals for betterment appear unrealistic or unworkable, and self-proclaimed "hard-headed realists" find reasons to disparage any hope of amelioration. Or, giving up on the visionary approach altogether, one can become so willing to compromise that any measures ultimately adopted are inconsequential, or even counterproductive.

However there is a middle ground, one that recognizes the importance of goals and dreams, but without insisting that unless a specific reform directly equates with these dreams, it is not worth pursuing. To paraphrase Robert Browning: Peace workers' reach must exceed their grasp, or what's a heaven for? Peace movements need substance, not just goals and images, and yet, as Isaiah put it, "Without vision, the people perish." In this next selection, Elise Boulding, one of the founding mothers of peace studies, reviews some peaceful visions and efforts.

Historical Overview

The human capacity to visualize *The Other* as different and better than the experienced present is found in archetypal form in all civilizational traditions through visions of the Elysian Fields, the Isles of the Blessed, Zion, Valhalla, Paradise. However, these visions are more ancient than civilizational. Anthropologists report that blessed isles are part of the dreamworld of tribal peoples. Nor are they confined to the West. Utopian elements are found in Taoism, Theravada Buddhism, medieval Islam, and in Chinese, Japanese and Indian stories about imaginary havens of delight.

Under the pressure of social upheaval, the archetypal vision is transformed into concrete imagery that answers to specific social needs and dissatisfactions. Thus Plato's *Republic* was a response to the upheavals of the Peloponnesian Wars. The hundreds of desert communes established by Christian men and women in Egypt and Syria in the first few centuries of the Christian era were a response to the corruption of urban life in Imperial Rome, an affirmation of an alternative human potentiality that has continued as a viable monastic tradition for 2000 years. The millenialist crusades and utopian communities that erupted by the hundreds in the Middle Ages were a series of responses to plague, famine and the gradual breakdown of the feudal order.

It is ironic then that utopia ("no place," as Thomas More named his pattern-setting *Utopia* in 1516) has come to be synonymous with a flight from reality. All the great utopians have been masterful critics of their own time. Utopians have many forms and functions, but one enduring function is to satirize society as it exists; another is to describe a more desirable way of organizing human affairs. One key problem of utopia-writing is that all utopias have implicit political goals, but few utopianists are able to devise political strategies to achieve their utopia which do not destroy these very goals. Historically, the theoreticians of utopia and the practitioners have not been the same people, and when they have, the results have been disastrous. On the other hand, the theoreticians have to be in touch with the currents of the times in very special ways. . . .

The particular set of upheavals which ushered in modernism originated in Europe and provided the ingredients for the great utopias of the past three centuries, including: (1) the voyages of discovery, which brought news of many different lifestyles and cultures and produced a rash of literary island utopias; (2) a rapid rate of scientific discovery and technological invention, which gave a new sense of control over the environment to human beings; (3) urbanization and industrialization, which introduced the concept of class interests for new social groupings—industrial workers, and the bourgeoisie; and (4) the rise of the modern nation-state and the military expansion of the industrial order through colonization. All four of these factors contributed to the sense of social progress and control over the future. The four major ideologies of socialism, marxism, liberalism and anarchism, which developed in different contexts within different social formations, all worked to realize their respective utopias. . . .

Because Utopia is always *The Other*—something totally different from existing society, a radical restructuring of the existing order—the changes implied by utopia are in effect revolutionary whether based on a commitment to gradual evolutionary change or sudden restructuring. This is why revolutionary violence keeps appearing in many utopian efforts, even when there is a commitment to peaceableness as with the Anabaptists. If the goal is a total restructuring of how humans live, whether on the micro- or macrolevel, then the destruction of existing arrangements, including the physical destruction of the human beings who maintain it, may come to be seen as a necessary wiping clean of the slate. . . .

Violence has been particularly important in certain Third World settings. Frantz Fanon, speaking of the process of liberation in Algeria, writes that "for the native, life can only spring up again out of the rotting corpse of the settler." And again, ". . . violence is a cleansing force. It frees the native from his inferiority complex and from his despair and inaction; it makes him fearless and restores his self-respect." In the West, the very size of the challenge posed by the abstract globalism of a revolutionary commitment to free all humans everywhere would seem to necessitate violence to prepare the ground for change. During the crisis, when the time is ripe, anything goes. . . .

It is an oversimplification to say that the resort to violence has been the operative cause of utopian failures, since nonviolent utopias also fail. The same problems of human learning beset both types of utopia. It is true however that the visibility of revolutionary violence, and the pride and fear it engenders, affects deeply our assessment of radical change, and indeed the assessment of utopias in general. With rising tides of violence in industrial countries (to say nothing of the Third World), there is a loss of faith today in the capacity for peaceful change. . . .

Buber takes the position that no revolution can succeed unless it has already happened, that the taking of power by a new group can only be the formal legitimation of a process that has already taken place. He focuses on the pre-existing traditional structures in every case, and shows how the richness of those associational structures determines the capacity of a society to engage in participatory change that is responsive to local situations and local needs while fitting into a larger societal picture. . . . We will see how differently various experimental groups have dealt with the tension between the rage for order and the longing for the spontaneity of organic processes; between the desire for central control, and the recognition that locality has its own competence; between the desire to destroy all traces of oppressive structures and wipe the slate clean before beginning anew, and the impulse to nurture the seeds of the new within the shell of the old, trusting that gentleness, not violence, will free the goodness in humans; and finally the tension between structural redesign and trying to produce new kinds of human beings to achieve the new society. . . .

While the United States cannot be technically regarded as a utopian experiment, for many, historically, the United States *was* utopia. As indicated earlier, it was seen as the new Garden of Eden. It became the home of many utopian experiments that could not take place in Europe because there was not enough room, both physically and socially. If the United States is the home of many utopian experiments at the microlevel, it could be said that Europe has been a prime exporter of such experiments. The United States has always rejected socialism, but its values of individualism have enabled it to give space to socialist, anarchist and religious experiments of every kind. Europe has gone much further with socialism, but few states would conceive of themselves as utopian experiments. Sweden is an exception. The Swedish experiment is comprehensive in terms of providing a welfare state without parallel in Europe. At the state level it has been possible because Sweden has the richest associative structures of any country on the continent. Early in the nineteenth century, it had a country-wide adult education program at the village level, and village debating forums, which would be the envy of any western country today. It was those structures which enabled Sweden to develop the first effective, country-wide participatory population control policy of any country in the world. These local structures continue alive and well as Sweden moves into the twenty-first century.

MICROLEVEL UTOPIAN EXPERIMENTS

Microlevel utopian experiments are much easier to initiate than macrolevel ones, since the responsibility of the experimenters is only to a limited group of people operating on a small scale. Microlevel utopias are thought of as a western phenomenon, but in fact there are many village-level utopian experiments in the Third World. They have a special characteristic of reaching into the past to find traditional local structures which can be redeveloped to make a better life at the village level under contemporary conditions.

MICROLEVEL UTOPIAS
IN THE FIRST WORLD

When Charles Nordhoff did his survey of *Communistic Societies in the United States* in the early 1870s, he found there were eight societies for the promotion of communes and 72 communes which had developed between 1794 and 1852. . . . The culture was very limited, and no one had higher education. But they were all good farmers! Nordhoff pointed out that the commune members seemed to enjoy life, and find pleasure in amusements which looked tame to him.

What do such communes achieve? A demonstration of a more serene and humane way of life, with a higher level of altruism than in the outside world. These utopias do not set out to change the world, only to show that it is possible to live differently in it. Economic forces should not be ignored in considering the founding of this type of commune. Its members are working class people who frequently have a hard time making it alone. More new communes are founded during times of economic depression than at any other time. Many single women who could not find a place in the economy joined these communities and prospered. These religious communities were primarily agrarian. During this same period there were 47 socialist experiments, studied by John Humphrey Noyes, all of which failed in rather short order. Unlike the religious communities, the socialist utopians tried to develop a model which could change the world. Their founders were, as Noyes says, "high-minded, highly cultivated men and women, with sufficient means, one would think, to achieve success." Unlike their religious counterparts, the socialist utopians were rarely skilled farmers. Equally unlike their counterparts, they were highly individualistic. . . .

The last round of utopian experiments came with the so-called hippie communes in the 60s and 70s. Lacking the social disciplines which the religious and social communitarians

were able to establish, most of them disintegrated rapidly. However a few have survived, usually through the persistence of an articulate leader. . . . Secular communes which survive have achieved some minimal degree of work discipline, and a critical mass of altruistic members with some vision of a society for which they are willing to keep working. This vision includes the abolition not only of militarism, but also war itself, and (frequently) the end of the nation-state system as we now know it. It includes a sense of social justice, a strong environmental ethic, and (usually) a discerning attitude toward science and technology. Most communes are rural because it is easier to live simply and cheaply in such a setting, and not just because of a desire to escape the city. The longer-lived ones all have active urban-rural networks. The misuse of power is a major issue with communitarians. Most of them find that leadership is important, but insist on a highly participatory process, with strong checks against authoritarianism.

None of these communities, whether long- or short-lived, act as powerful social forces in contemporary society. Very few of them do overtly political work, and there seems to be a huge gulf between their very small-scale efforts at human betterment and state-level utopian designs. Are they therefore insignificant failures? Or are they laboratories functioning as laboratories do: providing a more or less controlled environment for discovery? . . .

Connecting the Micro and the Macro: The Future of Utopianism

One context in which the micro–macro linkage of utopian experiments should be seen is the rapid development of transnational nongovernmental organizations in this century. Over 4000 transnational nongovernmental networks bring diverse peoples together through common interests and concerns, and are today a major new set of actors in the international system. Compared to nation-states they have few resources and little power. Yet most of the world's intellectual resources and many of its craft and social skill resources are concentrated in these organizations, particularly in the scientific, cultural and social welfare associations. Research on major world problems, such as the threat of nuclear war, environmental deterioration, malnutrition, disease, and climatic change, is done by scientific NGOs with support from the United Nations and largely nongovernmental sources. Governments would be helpless without the policy recommendations NGOs are able to make, based on their research and experience, although the advisory process is nearly invisible to the general public. Most major policy initiatives at the international level of the UN and governments in recent decades have been based on the work of transnational nongovernmental organizations. Many of the most innovative community development projects at the local level are also NGO projects.

. . . If, as Kenneth Boulding says, our most significant learnings are from failure, not success, then each utopian experiment is successful to the extent that learning from its failures takes place. . . . Even very short-lived utopias represent thoughtfully chosen responses to upheaval and change, and presumably have enabled the experimenter to move on to other more sustained responses.

The message about the importance of associative richness as the basis for utopia-building on anything beyond the local scale has gotten across to the extent that "networking" is a word almost as common as Coca Cola. The message about the importance of a focus on learning has not had equal promotion. There is still a tendency to believe that designing the situation will produce the desired behaviors. People may denounce Skinnerian philosophy, but they prefer manipulation by design to venturing out on the uncharted seas of human learning. How does anyone learn a really new thing? Since utopias are by definition "new," "not-yet," "other," how will human beings be able to function in them in ways that do not throw us back to the old order if we do not pay more attention to learning? Wishful thinking about the desired transformation of consciousness as an inevitable historical process distracts us from studying the difficult disciplines that will make transformation possible.

The real test of whether we have learned from the failures of past utopias is whether we can develop a theory of utopia-building that solves the problem of scale in human organization in a new way. Weber's theory of bureaucracy carried us from feudalism to industrialism, but it cannot carry us to the post-industrial society. We are paralyzed by the centralist-decentralist dilemma, since efficiency appears to require lines of hierarchical authority, yet the need to match policy to local terrain requires local participation. Buber's theory of associative richness as the basis for effective responses to social change beyond the local level, and the phenomenon of an increasingly dense network of transnational nongovernmental associations on a global scale, suggest new solutions to the old dilemmas. The overall theory has, however, yet to be formulated.

Most writers on utopia focus on only one type. An examination of the whole range of utopian experiments in their highly diverse settings, going beyond the very broad generalizations I have made here in the interest of length, may lead to a more sophisticated theory of utopia-building. Such a theory will have to deal with the problematic fact that utopia is at once a vision, a way of life, and a tool.

On Humane Governance

Long before President George Bush spoke of a "new world order" in 1990, peace advocates were concerned with a world order that would be truly "new," in that it would involve remaking the world political system in a manner responsive to social justice, environmental protection, human rights, democratization, and the demilitarization of international relations. One of the leaders in this effort has been Richard Falk, an active participant in the decades-long World Order Models Project, affectionately known as WOMP. The following selection is from the last chapter of Falk's book, *On Humane Governance: Toward a New Global Politics*, a superb overall introduction to socially responsible, hard-headed, yet visionary futurism, informed by a deep commitment to all dimensions of peace.

> *What is most revealing in this world is not where we are, but where we are going.*
> —*Anonymous saying*

> *Every child is born with the message that God is not yet discouraged with humanity.*
> —*Rabindranath Tagore*

The contemporary quest for humane governance builds on kindred efforts in the past, while being rooted in an unfolding present, and above all aspiring to achieve an imagined future. The idea of humane governance is itself a way of expressing this process that is sensitive to the shortcomings, achievements, and gropings toward human betterment on this planet. What shapes the orientation and gives it substantive content in diverse settings is this normative underpinning, a blend of legal, moral, and spiritual perspectives.

To endow this underpinning with greater concreteness and sense of direction, this chapter briefly depicts ten dimensions of this world-encompassing normative project, acknowledg-ing its historical depth yet also identifying its inspirational and prophetic assumptions about the future. Such a depiction should not be regarded as a listing of attributes or an inventory, and far less as a program. Each aspect that is rendered as distinct touches and influences the others in countless ways. . . .

The normative project posits an imagined community for the whole of humanity which overcomes the most problematic aspects of the present world scene: the part (whether as individual, group, nation, religion, civilization) and the whole (species, world, universe) are connected; difference and uniformities across space and through time are subsumed beneath an overall commitment to world order values in the provisional shape of peace, economic well-being, social and political justice, and environmental sustainability. As such, the normative project partakes of shared values and aspirations, trends, fears and expectations about the future, rooted hopes, visions of the possible. The framing of this project acknowledges primarily the efforts of movements and peoples at the grassroots, but also takes note of the participation of prominent leaders, governments and other institutions, as well as the specificity of opportunities and challenges

From *On Humane Governance* by Richard Falk. 1995. University Park: Pennsylvania State University Press. Reprinted by permission of World Order Models Project.

arising in the aftermath of the Cold War. The normative project has ten dimensions.

Taming war The contemporary normative project has its roots in the reaction to the barbarity of warfare. It was Grotius's horrified response to the Thirty Years War in Europe that gave birth to international law in the seventeenth century and to the specific regulatory urge to put limits on what states could do in the midst of war. This impulse ripened through time, leading to the Hague Conferences of 1899 and 1907 which brought together the leaders of the dominant states of the day, purporting to be the managers of the global order. For the first time a series of international law treaties were drafted and adopted to regulate the tactics and weaponry of warfare to some degree, incorporating some customary principles of behavior embodied at high levels of abstraction in religion and morality: the requirement that tactics and weaponry distinguish between civilian and military targets, sparing the former; that force be used in a proportionate manner; that cruelty be avoided, including unnecessary suffering for those wounded or captured, even if part of the opposing military forces.

This endeavor to tame the conduct of war has persisted to the present. After World War II the Geneva Conventions of 1949 placed great stress on specific duties to protect the victims of war, including civilians and those military personnel wounded or captured in battle. These protections were later extended to the circumstances of intervention and civil war by the Geneva Protocols of 1977. Much current attention at the grassroots and governmental levels is being devoted to regimes of prohibition associated with weaponry of mass destruction: nuclear, chemical, and biological. At present, with respect to nuclear weaponry, the governmental emphasis has been on maintaining a partial regime (nonproliferation) as opposed to the efforts of transnational democratic initiatives to achieve a comprehensive regime of prohibition (delegitimizing nuclear weapons as such and arranging for their phased elimination from arsenals, thereby treating these weapons as chemical and biological weapons have been treated).

Whether this enterprise has been successful, on balance, remains controversial. Advocates claim that the suffering of war has been mitigated for millions of participants. Skeptics believe that the law of war is a hypocritical and deceptive misnomer which deflects reformist energy from war itself. At the root of the difficulty is the subordination of the principle of restraint to the achievement of victory in war by whatever means it takes. The supremacy of "military necessity" has tended to overwhelm the normative pressures of law, morality, and religion. This supremacy has been abetted by continuous innovation in the weaponry of war, the search by states for military superiority, and the development, reliance, and use of ultimate weapons and tactics in the course of winning World War II. Evidence of civilian devastation rarely inhibits tactics or weaponry. The current movement to prohibit landmines is illustrative. Despite the evidence of overwhelming civilian injury, much of it long after hostilities have ceased, governments seem reluctant to ban landmines, partly because of their cost-benefit advantages compared to other weapons. The debate itself confirms that nothing significant will happen until civil initiatives mount strong pressures.

Although the results are disappointing, the struggle to tame war continues alongside the wider, more dramatic series of efforts to abolish war itself as a hideous and outmoded social institution.

Abolishing war The more fundamental struggle, at the very center of the normative project, is to challenge war itself, the social and political process of mass, intentional killing in the name of the state, for the sake of wealth and power, in defense of ideology and a way of life, allegedly on behalf of security in self-defense, but also to satisfy expansionist ambitions. This challenge directed against war is often analogized to the struggle against slavery, the divine right of kings, colonialism, each a social institution that like war was once generally accepted, at least by elites, as necessary and inevitable. Arguably, all advances in the human condition have involved challenging institutions and practices treated as necessary and inevitable.

The real and imagined carnage of war has been the principal impetus to abolitionist efforts, as have certain pacifist traditions of religious and secular thought. After World War I, in particular, antiwar sentiments flourished, taking aim at the legality of so-called "aggressive war" and at "the merchants of death" (those who made profits from arms sales). Public pressures were so great that leading countries subscribed to the Kellogg-Briand Pact of 1928 (also known as the Pact of Paris) that renounced war as an instrument of national policy, authorizing war only as a response to aggression, in a posture of self-defense. This new ground rule was invoked after World War II as a principal basis for convicting German and Japanese leaders of crimes against the peace for their role in planning and waging aggressive warfare. This prohibition is reproduced in the UN Charter in the form of Article 2(4), which prohibits altogether the use of force, although it is qualified by Article 51 which preserves the "inherent right of self-defense." The Charter seeks to restrict the scope of self-defense by requiring that only in situations of "prior armed attack" is self-defense permitted, and even then the claimant state is required to seek immediate approval from the Security Council.

As with the efforts to tame war, those to abolish war remain controversial and are not implemented to any great extent. States interpret for themselves what self-defense means, and have ignored the requirement of armed attack. The mobilization of response against aggression has been inconsistent and often half-hearted. Preparation for war, the tactics, secrecy, and weaponry have made war an integral part of the global landscape, especially in the South where more than 125 wars have been fought in the last 50 years. In the North, fear of catastrophic war, reinforced by deterrence and containment, avoided direct war during the Cold War, but added to the frequency and intensity of warfare in the South.

With the Cold War over, there is at present no strategic rivalry of the sort likely to produce warfare, but the war system seems as rooted as ever in the operational code of statecraft, expressed by way of large military establishments, expensive weapons innovations, huge arms sales, and interventionary diplomacy. What is also discouraging, especially during this period of geopolitical moderation, is the absence of moves from above or below that challenge seriously the war system, or even move toward large reductions of spending and embark upon ambitious types of disarmament. Yet the abolition of war remains a centerpiece of the normative project, and its

political relevance is embedded in each and every dimension.

The intractability of war as a social institution suggests that unlike slavery and the other analogies relied upon by the new abolitionists, war is different: it presupposes shifts in the structures of power and authority, or at least in their normative foundations. Those who argue on the basis of structure generally regard world government as the precondition for disarmament; those who emphasize normative foundations tend either to insist upon democratizing the world (on the presumption that democracies don't go to war against one another and hence that if the foundations of authority in all states become democratic, there will be no political will to engage in war and the war system will wither away) or to disseminate the ethos of nonviolence throughout the whole gamut of social relations so widely that it undermines support for military approaches to conflict, displacing the war system in time by pacifism.

Making individuals accountable . . . One dimension of the normative project has been to make those in authority accountable for their transgressions, especially with respect to war and in relation to severe abuses of human rights. The essence of this approach has been to criminalize *aggressive* war, while not challenging rights of self-defense or military preparations. The Nuremberg and Tokyo War Crimes Tribunals at the end of World War II were the foundation of this struggle to impose individual accountability, and the decisions reached rejected defenses based on reason of state or superior orders. It was also notable that secondary trials were held to assess the individual responsibility of doctors, judges, business leaders, local military commanders, and local officials, expanding the reach of accountability to encompass those who variously implemented the policies of the regime or carried out independent atrocities of their own.

This Nuremberg experience, now being widely reassessed during the fiftieth anniversary year of the main judgment, has been criticized as "victors' justice." The crimes of the victorious powers, most notably the use of atomic bombs and the excesses of strategic bombing, were exempted from any scrutiny. The prosecutors at Nuremberg did pledge that the principles being laid down to judge the defendants would become binding international law that would henceforth be made applicable to the whole world and its leaders. Indeed, the UN General Assembly by unanimous vote endorsed the Nuremberg principles, seeking their authoritative formulation by the International Law Commission, the expert body at the UN, which in 1950 provided the text of these principles that is relied upon to this day to identify the nature of individual accountability.

Governments have not implemented the Nuremberg principles. Indeed, the victorious powers in World War II, the countries which provided the judges, have each engaged subsequently in aggressive war. Further, these leading states have opposed efforts to institutionalize Nuremberg through the creation of procedures and some sort of international criminal court. The Nuremberg idea has been kept alive by two major developments: first, by activists who relied on the Nuremberg idea to challenge the supremacy of the state in the war/peace area, validating the emergence of civil resistance as a step beyond what Thoreau and others had in mind by "civil disobedience"; secondly, after the Cold War, by moves toward convening war crimes tribunals to address allegations of genocidal behavior in Bosnia and Rwanda (even prior to this, issues of accountability emerged in various countries in South America as the transitions were made from the authoritarian rule of the 1960s to some sort of constitutional governance).

The importance of individual accountability to the establishment of global governance is evident. Crimes of states need to be deterred and, once committed, dealt with effectively if confidence in the emergence of wider regional communities of participation is to arise and if the formation of an eventual global community is to be encouraged. At this point, all the contradictions of world order are present: powerful states enjoy the full prerogatives of territorial supremacy and sovereignty, exempting leaders from accountability, especially if an authoritarian political order prevails; further, the diplomacy of reconciliation and peace often sharply conflicts with the impulse to impose individual responsibility—without surrender or defeat, the accused leadership is elusive and may well prolong its period of rule, fearing what the Argentinean human rights activist Jacopo Timmermann

referred to in the 1970s as "the ghosts of Nuremberg."

Collective security . . . One important strand of the normative project for a reformed world was to replace balance-of-power geopolitics with a rule-governed global security system that protected states threatened by aggressive war. Woodrow Wilson championed such an approach and advocated the creation of the League of Nations to achieve collective security. These efforts have persisted in various forms. The League was created but the United States refused to join, and when aggressive war occurred in Asia and Europe the response was ineffectual. Yet the idea of collective security persisted, and was embodied in a more detailed form in Chapter VII of the UN Charter. Again the experience of the Cold War confirmed the inadequacy of existing mechanisms of collective security, highlighted by the bipolarity of the period and the inability of the opposed blocs of states to agree upon the identity of an aggressor in most situations involving the outbreak of war. The defense of South Korea in 1950 was nominally a UN operation, but was substantively controlled by the United States, receiving a UN mandate only because the Soviet Union deprived itself of its veto by temporarily boycotting the Security Council in protest against the unrelated failure to seat representatives from the People's Republic of China.

The Gulf crisis of 1990 presented a renewed, neo-Wilsonian opportunity to establish collective security. The conditions were finally right: clear aggression against a UN member; a political consensus of the permanent members of the Security Council; a threat to the strategic interests of leading countries; and the political will to provide the capabilities to perform effectively. The Gulf War that resulted in 1991 has had an ambiguous impact. It certainly established the possibility of UN effectiveness since Kuwait's sovereignty was restored and aggression was reversed. Yet the undertaking was again essentially geopolitical in motivation and character, the decisions being made in Washington, not at the Security Council in New York. When the challenge of Serbian aggression and ethnic cleansing in Bosnia arose a year later, the old circumstance of ineffectuality was again evident. Without both political consensus and a strategic stake of magnitude, leading states are not willing to pay the price for maintaining collective security. It was clear that countries without strategic relevance were on their own; the case of East Timor is exemplary, with Indonesia's aggression and crimes against humanity being neglected almost totally in the setting of collective security.

Not only is geopolitical practice discouraging, but leading states oppose the creation of independent UN capabilities by way of a peace force of volunteers and a reliable means to finance collective security. Perhaps collective security will take hold on a regional level during the decade ahead. In any event, the time has come to rethink collective security within the UN setting, associating UN uses of force with ideas of policing and reconciliation, not as a species of war-making. Such a reorientation would also greatly constrain uses of force that could not be focused on the elite responsible for aggression or genocide. The Wilsonian impulse survives. Without collective security as an interim mechanism to deter and resist aggression, the prospects of abolishing war in the near future seem severely diminished.

Rule of law The legal mindset has exerted considerable influence on shaping the priorities of the normative project for a reformed world order. In particular, US reformist energies since the Wilsonian era have stressed the importance of judicial procedures for the settlement of disputes. The establishment of a World Court in The Hague, initially in 1920, has epitomized this logic of world peace through law, although isolationist tendencies within the United States have polarized opinion on the desirability of enhancing the role and prestige of the judicial arm of the UN.

This manifested itself strongly during the controversy with the Sandinista government in Nicaragua in the 1980s. The Court decided in favor of Nicaragua with respect to the basic contention as to whether the US was illegally sponsoring Contra violence against an established state. This outcome so angered the White House that it withdrew the US from full participation, limiting its role to ad hoc arrangements to appear before the Court if it specifically agreed to do so. Additionally, the US government refused to abide by the 1986 decision, and the Security Council did not fulfill its Charter responsibility to implement World Court decisions. Surprisingly perhaps, the Non-Aligned Movement picked up the dropped baton, impressed by the objectivity of the World Court and its willingness to decide in favor of Nicaragua. It is highlighting the importance of obliging all countries to resolve their disputes by recourse to the World Court if diplomacy fails, and setting as a goal the year 1999, the hundredth anniversary of the initial Hague peace conference.

So far the reliance on judicial solutions has not been very successful in relation to fundamental conflicts involving core interests of states. The World Court has effectively resolved potentially troubling, long-festering, marginal disputes, especially involving disputed frontiers and maritime boundaries, as well as other technical matters. The regional role of judicial institutions in Europe is suggestive of how far the rule of law can be carried in crucial matters of economic policy and the protection of human rights, according precedence to supranational authority and subordinating in the event of conflict the highest expressions of judicial and legislative authority at the level of the sovereign state. The structuring of global governance on the basis of enhanced judicial roles within the various regional settings and for the world as a whole would be a major step in averting both civil and international warfare, being expressive of the disposition of well-governed political communities to entrust even the most serious disputes to third party procedures.

Nonviolent revolutionary politics . . . The thrust of Mahatma Gandhi's courageous and brilliantly managed nonviolent anticolonial struggle against British rule in India introduced a radical new dimension into many subsequent political struggles for freedom, dignity, independence, and well-being that have been at the center of numerous historical narratives of the last half century. Martin Luther King imaginatively and powerfully carried a nonviolent orientation into the domain of race relations, specifically on behalf of civil rights for black Americans. Such victories were until recently viewed as special cases, and nonviolence was not widely regarded as capable of challenging major structures of oppression around the world. Then came a series of developments in the 1980s that gave a great potency to nonviolent political strategies, although with outcomes that were sometimes disappointing in various ways: the Khomeini-led revolutionary movement against the Shah in Iran; the People Power movement of Corazon Aquino in the Philippines; the various emancipatory struggles in East Europe against Communist rule; the *intifada* in occupied Palestine; the pro-democracy movement in China and other Asian countries, including Burma, Nepal, and South Korea; the negotiated settlements of long-lasting and seemingly perpetual armed struggles in South Africa, El Salvador, possibly Cambodia—and most recently even the struggle in Northern Ireland appears to be moving on to a political plane. (It has to be realized that these and other manifestations of nonviolence were never pure, and that recourse to nonviolent tactics often seemed to be for opportunistic and temporary reasons, and sometimes merely done as a clever adjustment to the lack of weaponry.)

This sense that nonviolence can challenge formidable power systems is indispensable in relation to the central struggles against war, militarism, and civic abuse of all types. It represents the countertradition to the persisting dominance of violence at all levels of social organization, and underpins the various approaches to the construction of a global civil society that both constitutes and is constituted by cosmopolitan democracy. Yet to achieve enduring results in relation to governance the commitment to nonviolence must be constantly deepened and extended to the most private spheres of human existence, including the socializing of the young, the reconceiving of "manhood," the aims of education, and the "pleasures" nurtured in the marketplace. The theory and practice of nonviolence involves the reconstruction of society, culture, and even consciousness, challenging many current practices, beliefs, and world-views in various civilizational spaces. Yet without the substantial displacement of violence in all its forms, humane governance is not attainable, especially given the global character of interaction that is becoming standard. Rwanda and Bosnia are neighborhood events for the entire world, and as such are not capable of being cordoned off even in a physical sense: refugees and dis-

ease flow across borders and reach distant shores by boat and plane.

Human rights . . . Sovereignty and democracy are profoundly affected by the realization of human rights. The European idea of past centuries that the governing authority of a territorial state is supreme and unaccountable is challenged to the extent that the standards of human rights are effectively superimposed by either citizen initiative or external intervention. Sovereignty is subverted from without and diluted from within, giving rise to interventionary and resistance claims and prerogatives on behalf of the victims of abuse. In particular, the citizenry is morally and legally empowered to the extent it appreciates that its leaders can be challenged when they transgress the restraints on power as contained in the international law of human rights. In these regards, the protection of human rights represents a radical tendency in our historical period, but the potency of this effort depends on education (human rights need to be far better understood as empowering by those most victimized if they are to function even more widely as a political instrument of resistance and transformation) and a focus of conviction (human rights must appear consistent with cultural values, or at least these values must themselves be reassessed from within).

Recourse to genocidal practice by any government is increasingly regarded as a forfeiture of its claim to sovereign authority within territory. Other breakdowns of authority in terms of minimal provision of food, shelter, and medicine are being perceived as calling for a response by the wider regional and global communities. The extension of human rights from their civil and political character in liberal democracies to the economic and social concerns of the poor is a crucial transition in thought. The socialist challenge to capitalism and the individualist ethic were responsible for the broad, earlier acceptance that every person has the material entitlement to the necessities of life, a ground rule for humane governance already present in the seminal document, the Universal Declaration of Human Rights in 1948. With the market ascendant since the late 1980s, international competitiveness has been elevated as a criterion for policy choice and socialist concerns have been discredited. As matters now stand, the unmet challenge of economic and social rights is greater than ever. Ground has been lost in recent years. The only hope now is that globalization from below, with the many initiatives of transnational democracy and the emergence of global civil society, will rearticulate human solidarity in a manner that gives political weight to a renewed movement to achieve social and economic rights.

In the end, the struggle for human rights is the struggle against all forms of abuse, neglect, humiliation, and vulnerability. As Upendra Baxi has so eloquently argued in the setting of India, human rights in the end is a matter of taking suffering seriously. Looking back on this century of world wars and weaponry of mass destruction, it may well be that the gradual development of a human rights framework will be the centerpiece of a more hopeful narration of the experience of the period. Of course, the evolution of human rights is itself a source of suspicion, emanating from the West, reeking of hypocrisy, selective application, and contradictory implications. A wider process of creation and application is unfolding, and is essential, bringing into the domain of human rights the interplay of diverse tendencies within and between cultures, combining the educative imperative to know with the religious imperative to listen, to be humble in the face of the claims of the other, and above all, to refrain from linking the right of self-determination to claims of ethnic exclusivity.

Stewardship of nature A recent addition to the normative agenda has been the rediscovery of human dependence on natural surroundings. Ancient peoples, of course, were acutely sensitive to their vulnerability to the severities of nature, especially cycles of drought and flooding. The modern scientific illusion supposed that technological ingenuity could enable human society to master nature, ignore limitations on resource availability, and expand indefinitely both resource-consuming lifestyles and the population of the planet. An emergent environmental consciousness over the last several decades, while still subordinate to market pressures and an ideology of growth, is emphasizing anew ideas of sustainability and limits. What these limits should be is a matter of fundamental political controversy, raising issues of conditions of survival at one end of the debate and matters of the conditions of human happiness and relations to the animal kingdom at the other end.

The distinctive challenge in the establishment of humane governance is to connect development with the stewardship of nature in a manner that realizes economic and social rights for all peoples, adjusting for unevenness of circumstance.... At the same time, the enjoyment of the beauty of nature is the foundation of spirituality and creativity, and thus stewardship cannot be conceived of merely in materialist terms.

Positive citizenship The foundations of community reflect the contours of individual and group identity, and more specifically in relation to governance, the quality of participation. In the West, positive participation has been associated with the shift from the status of "subject" (slave, vassal, serf) to "citizen." The modern media-shaped political life threatens individuals with a new type of postmodern serfdom, in which elections, political campaigns, and political parties provide rituals without substance, a politics of sound bytes and manipulative images, reducing the citizen to a mechanical object to be controlled, rather than being the legitimating source of legitimate authority.

What forms of political participation can combine rootedness in the circumstances of a given place (the grassroots test of integrity and relevance) with the connections and aspirations of an emergent global civil society is an essential, variable challenge. Empowerment from below as an alternative to the ritualization of politics at the level of the state and to subordination to those types of globalization that express market priorities is at the core of the evolving normative project. The projection of a global identity, without the conditions of community, and the claim now to be "world citizens" express striving for humane governance, but they also arouse serious suspicions that the necessary struggles associated with transformation are being evaded by the sentimental, New Age pretense that a reorientation of personal energy will suffice.

Positive citizenship, stressing this interplay between the concreteness of situation and the imagined community that represents humane governance, will mean various things in different societies. The idea of citizenship is being promoted, also, as extending beyond state/society relations and involving all relationships of a participatory nature, that is, institutions and practices that invoke authority. Positive citizenship also draws on nonviolence and human rights as inspirational sources. The greatest challenge, at present, is to reconcile the territorial dimensions of citizenship with the temporal dimensions: acting in the present for the sake of the future, establishing zones of humane governance as building blocks.

Cosmopolitan democracy This is the binding idea of democracy encompassing all relationships, providing the grounds of institutional legitimacy, and establishing the basis for procedures and practices linking individuals and groups with institutions. It is becoming the pervasive underpinning that has been evolving along several tracks for several centuries, and now, in tandem with technology and high finance, is necessarily operative across statist boundaries as well as within them. Of course, leadership styles based on hierarchy and soft authoritarianism remain potent realities, especially in the Asian/Pacific region and in Islamic countries; elsewhere, a democratic facade is fashioned to hide the persistence of authoritarian institutional controls. But what gives promise to the vision of cosmopolitan democracy is the legitimation of democratic ideas of governance on a universal basis, the embodiment of these ideas in human rights as specified in global instruments, the democratic implications of nonviolent approaches to resistance and reform, and most of all, the deeply democratic convictions of transnational initiatives that have begun to construct the alternative paradigm of a global civil society.

We can expect many ebbs and flows, many relapses and pitfalls, endless discussion about the failure and character of democracy, and yet the cumulative drift of the normative project has been and remains dedicated to the deepening and the expansion of democracy in relation to all fields of human endeavor. It is virtually impossible to imagine humane governance as a global phenomenon without presupposing the increasing influence and acceptance of participatory politics, whether or not called "democracy," resting on the dignity and worth of the individual, but also of the group. Democracy, in these senses, provides the indispensable organizing principle, with the aim that it can be eventually presupposed, possibly to such an extent that the label can and will be dropped.

These ten dimensions of the normative project, some of recent origin, but all with many antecedents throughout the world, suggest the contours of humane governance. Their emergence remains . . . generally subordinate to globalization from above, acutely uneven, provisional, precarious, at the margins, but yet undeniable. Whether the dynamics of emergence will create a toppling of "the Berlin wall" of militarist, market-driven, materialist globalism is far from assured. At the same time, such a shift in fundamental prospects for governance is a sufficiently plausible outcome as to make the struggle to achieve it the only responsible basis for positive citizenship at this stage of history. Whether ours is an axial moment of normative restructuring of collective and individual life cannot yet be determined, but such possibilities inherent in the present situation provide us with the best and most realistic basis of hope about how to work toward human betterment, as understood and applied in many separate ways around the world.

Sexism and the War System

Making peace, in the deepest sense, requires us to acknowledge that the personal is political, and vice versa. Among the most personal human traits is gender, which has numerous implications—just beginning to be recognized—for social behavior, including but not limited to violence and oppression. In the following selection, long-time peace educator, feminist, and activist Betty Reardon examines some of the connections between sexism and the war system, as well as some alternatives, including the importance of personal transformation.

The problems and issues to be explored in this examination of sexism and the war system are viewed through four major conceptual lenses: the war system, sexism, feminism, and world order. Each concept comprises a set of subconcepts and the underlying assumptions that determine the connotations carried by the conceptual terms. I offer the following definitions not as an assertion of the essential meaning of the concepts but rather to clarify the terms as they are used in this work. They are offered as well to expose my own underlying assumptions and to support the thesis that the two phenomena, sexism and the war system, arise from the same set of authoritarian constructs. . . .

The War System:
Enforcement of Patriarchy

My use of the term *war system* refers to our competitive social order, which is based on authoritarian principles, assumes unequal value among and between human beings, and is held in place by coercive force. The institutions through which this force is currently controlled and applied are dominated by a small minority, elites who run the global economy and conduct the affairs of state. These elites are men from industrial countries, primarily Western, and for the most part educated to think in Western, analytic terms. Although their relationship is competitive within the elite structures, there is a common objective that holds the elites together: the maintenance of their own control and dominance. This purpose accounts for the degree of accommodation and cooperation that can be found among all elites. Their primary competition is therefore with the nonelites, the majority of the world's people. Control is maintained by force in the form of threat, intimidation, and, when necessary, violent coercion. The control system requires that only intimidation and threat of force be used whenever possible, in part to save the cost of violent coercion but mainly to keep the majority at a sufficient level of wellbeing to maintain their productive capacity.

This latter, fundamental purpose of maintaining productive capacity necessitates a level of subelites within the general hierarchical structure. These subelites, for example, heads of client states, military officers, or favorite wives, carry out the day-to-day management of the productive functions of the majority of the population. Their lot is sufficiently better than the majority, from whose ranks they are usually drawn, to convince them that service to the elites and maintenance of the system is in their own best interest. They help keep the basic conflict between the elites and the majority submerged in cultural norms, traditional myths, and political ideologies. Their effectiveness depends on their remaining as removed as possible from the actual application of force, which is executed by more replaceable individuals. With the exception of those states so militarized

From *Sexism and the War System* (pp. 10–11, 14–17, 83–89) by Betty Reardon, 1985. Reprinted by permission of Syracuse University Press.

that state violence need not be obscured, a general characteristic of the system is that the higher the level of command, the farther away it is from the actual application of violent force or the conduct of warfare. . . .

Militarism—the belief system that upholds the legitimacy of military control of the state—is based on the assumption that military values and policies are conducive to a secure and orderly society. It has served to legitimate both warfare and civil use of coercive force (i.e., national guards and militia) in the interest of "national security." It is not surprising, given the relationship between patriarchy and the war system, that the more militarist a society tends to be the more sexist are its institutions and values. Feminists have noted this relationship in such cases as Nazi Germany and, more recently, Chile.

Militarization—the process of emphasizing military values, policies, and preparedness, often transferring civil functions to military authority—assumes that when a society is in crisis or threatened, the crisis or threat can best be weathered by strengthening the military. Two significant indicators of militarization are public expenditures, particularly the percentage of total expenditures allocated to military purposes, and the discussion or application of military measures as solutions to problems and conflicts that are basically political or economic. It should be noted that women take virtually no part in the decision making regarding such policies and that increasing military spending at the cost of social expenditures impacts most negatively on women. It contributes significantly to the feminization of poverty. Sivard indicates that the majority of the world's poor will soon be women.

The militarization of post-World War II Euro-American society has paralleled the women's movement. Given the chronological relationship of the two phenomena and some of the working assumptions shared by feminists and the peace movement, this relationship is likely to be more than coincidental. It was to be expected that Phyllis Schlafly, heroine of the New Right, would take on the nuclear freeze movement in the wake of the defeat of the Equal Rights Amendment. Much of contemporary feminism that is anathema to the New Right springs from conceptual roots totally antithetical to the concepts of war, warfare, militarism, and militarization, which

derive from negative masculine values. Militarism manifests the excesses of those characteristics generally referred to as *machismo*, a term that originally connoted the strength, bravery, and responsibility necessary to fulfill male social functions. Militarist concepts and values are upheld by patriarchy, the structures and practices of which have been embodied in the state, forming the basic paradigm for the nation-state system. Thus there is in all aspects of that system an inevitable sexist bias that is especially acute in matters related to security, the term all political units apply to self-preservation. Security is the impulse that produces the *military*—"structures of organized violence controlled by the state." . . .

The military, then, is the distilled embodiment of patriarchy; the militarization of society is the unchecked manifestation of patriarchy as the *overt* and *explicit* mode of governance. . . .

World Order Values: Indicators of Militarism and Sexism

World order studies inquire into the possibilities for abolishing war and developing a peaceful and human global order. This inquiry offers the greatest potential for the integration of feminism and feminist perspectives into both peace research and the political struggle for peace. The concept of world order studies . . . provides a normative approach to global problems. It projects and evaluates alternatives to the present system that could achieve world order values and open possibilities for the evolution of a more peaceful and just social order. Those who adopt a world order perspective view such evolution as progress toward the universal enjoyment of values that they see as fundamental criteria for the assessment of peace and justice and that they assert should be the basic norms upheld by the structures of a transformed global system. As I will explicate in a later section, these values are somewhat wanting from a feminist perspective in minimal standards for humane norms and global transformation. They do, however, provide us with some basic guidelines for assessing the degree of those antitheses of peace and justice, *violence* (that is, the unnecessary and avoidable harm to life and well-being) and *oppression* (the humanly devised barriers to the exercise of choice and self-determination), which characterize and bind together sexism and the war system. A brief review of world order values is offered here to illustrate this point and to support the case that substantive progress toward either peace or justice cannot be achieved without the elimination of sexism.

Each of the five world order values—economic equity, social justice, ecological balance, political participation, and peace—can be used to demonstrate that the present global order, the war system, is maintained by violence and oppression, and that women are more victimized by the system than are men. The current severe frustration of these values also suggests the possibility that both increased militarization and the male-chauvinist backlash are symptoms of an authoritarian system responding to a threat to its continuation.

The degree to which economic equity is frustrated by the war machine has been clearly documented each year by *World Military and Social Expenditures,* edited annually by Ruth Sivard. . . . It provides data that demonstrate that global poverty is greatly exacerbated as a result of military spending. It also documents an alarming increase in militarization, which is revealed by the number of governments that have fallen under military control, thereby verifying the assertion that public expenditures are an indicator of militarism.

Structural design certainly figures into my notion of transformation, but its role in the total change process is secondary to that of significant changes in human relations. The fundamental values of equity and mutuality, which I advocate as the norms to guide the changes, would of necessity also influence social and political structures. The structural changes, however, should emerge from the changing relations rather than coming prior to them. In other words, structures should facilitate human relations and give institutional form to the fundamental values rather than dictate and control relations and values as they have in male-dominated society. Thus a blueprint is not part of these reflections on the question of transformation. The emphasis here is more on the need for personal and relational change. If we cannot change ourselves, I doubt we can change the world.

In this context transition strategies are means by which personal and relational changes are translated into social movement and political action. The personal and the political are thoroughly intertwined in the present reality and therefore cannot be divided neatly into two distinct separate arenas for change in any transition plan that purports to be headed toward genuine transformation. This intertwining of the personal and the political makes education, viewed as the process by which we learn new ways of thinking and behaving, a very significant component of the transition-transformation processes. Education is that process through which we glimpse what might be and what we ourselves can become. It is also the process through which we articulate what might be and through which we strive to become what we choose to be. Through it we learn to choose and to pursue choices. Education is transformative when it produces visions to be pursued (that is, the goal of the *transformation*) and when it develops the capacities to achieve the goal (that is, *transition* skills, the strategies for struggle). . . .

It has long been my belief that authentic transformation of the global order is as much a matter of emotional maturity as of structural change. The crux of the argument set forth in this book, that neither sexism nor the war system can be overcome independently from the other, lies in the assumption that structural, even revolutionary, changes in the public order without significant inner psychic changes in human beings will be ineffective, old wine in new bottles. . . .

This indeed is the lesson we learn from a long history of revolutions. Authentic transformations have occurred only when people themselves have changed their world views, their values, and their behaviors as a basis for change in the social and political structures. Such changes usually involve the society coming to perceive itself as a manifestation of a new set of human, sometimes cosmic, relationships. This assumption about the interrelationship of personal and political change, which has been a major influence on my approach to peace education, began as an intuition but has evolved into a fundamental hypothesis, one that is shared by other feminists.

This hypothesis is what lies at the base of feminist insistence that the personal circumstances of women have political roots and political significance. It is central to what some have perceived as an inordinate feminist emphasis on specific details of personal relationships between men and women and preoccupation with domestic social and economic policies that affect the everyday quality of life for women. Child care, abortion rights, and payment for housework, although conceptualized and expressed in terms of improving women's lot, are at base as structural as the concerns with such issues as peace-keeping forces and adjudication procedures that world order models have emphasized.

Such feminist proposals integrated into our concepts of transformation and transition could introduce into world order studies notions of the human and quotidian, the everyday lived experience of ordinary people, to which most people can relate more readily. It is at least one approach to overcoming the commonly held perception that world order models and peace research proposals lack relevance to the real world. It is, in fact, this lack of human detail that gives the pejorative connotation to the criticism that such academic visions of a peaceful and just world system are utopian. Feminist utopias provide flesh and bone, human and quotidian dimensions that enable us to catch a glimpse of what human life might be like in a preferred future. As the phrase "think global, act local" has characterized futurist efforts to involve people where "they're at" (that is, geographically and socially), feminists might include the human element in the phrase "think futuristically, act daily," giving the movement a different kind of time dimension, making it more relevant to the present and the personal.

Feminists also see the task of future building as preserving and nurturing the positive elements and small-scale changes we all perceive and participate in. A positive future most likely will be made up of these elements of the preferred present that reflect the requisite values, behaviors, and world view changes that will constitute the larger transformation. Because of their more intimate physical connection to the life cycle, women understand that the future is not an abstract condition in a remote time. It is the process of becoming. Women know in their bones that the achievement of a preferred future requires us to act in the present on the basis of the norms and values we enshrine in our visions of transformation....

As individual human development is cyclical, and often regresses at stages rather than progresses, so too a feminist view of transition is not a step-by-step linear progression but rather an organic, flowing and eddying notion of change. It is, I believe, this very notion of organic change with its expectation and understanding of recurrent regression that keeps women from despairing of their failures and infuses their continued struggle for a better life and for peace. I am, in fact, convinced that linear, step-by-step concepts of transition not only are bound to lead to severe disappointments, but are more likely to result in the despair that engulfs so many as the militarist negative trends increase in volume and speed....

Masculine Mode, Feminine Mode: Separation and Connection

Gilligan points out how a masculine bias in the study of the different development emphases between men and women—men striving for separation and independence and women for connection and interdependence—has given us an unbalanced and inadequate notion of maturity. And, I would add, it has led to an overemphasis on individualism and the power to control, which so characterize the present dangerous stage of the war system, the arms race. These observations help us to see how the masculine bias actually has limited the conceptual repertoire and styles of problem resolution we bring to the arenas of politics and conflict. Individuation and separation have so determined our concepts of national interests that we are blinded to the many realities of interdependence that are the major determinants of our present world situation. That we are willing to risk our very survival to defend the national interest is not so surprising in a masculine-biased system when we understand that "the morality of rights differs from the morality of responsibility in its emphasis on separation rather than connection, in its consideration of the individual rather than the relationship as primary."...

This significant difference in the types of morality that are developed by men and women provides us with an important insight into the causes of our present crises. It also suggests that transformation, the realization of global change, and transition, the process of achieving it, may well depend on the integration of masculine and feminine perspectives and modes in the processes of designing new structures and the political and educational programs to achieve them.

Finally, it seems to me, Gilligan's work lends further support to the hypothesis of reciprocal causation and provides grounds for the assertion that the structures of violence that constitute the war system are as much imbedded in the human psyche as in social structure. They are undoubtedly influenced by the attributes we use to guide the development of masculine identity and by masculine modes of public decision making. These factors are revealed only when the whole truth about the human experience is no longer filtered through an exclusive masculine bias, for "in the different voice of women lies the truth of an ethic of care, the tie between relationships and responsibility and the origins of aggression in the failure of connection." . . .

The masculine mode approaches transformation and transition of the global order in the same analytic abstract fashion as it approaches other intellectual issues. The two concepts are perceived as a discrete set of end circumstances and a specific sequence of strategies to achieve them. The transformation, the end circumstances, generally are described in terms of *specific* structures and processes. These very often take the form of models that frequently appear to feminist and Third World eyes to be a rearrangement of traditional forms of power rather than a full and authentic transformation of the present reality.

Masculine models of transformation, frequently referred to as "system change," tend to be abstracted from everyday human conditions, to display a central concern with power arrangements, and to be preoccupied with the concept of sovereignty, an essentially patriarchal notion. Some focus much attention on determining which component of the revised structures will be endowed with the power and the right legitimately to use force, whether that force be armed or "nonviolent." Such models can be depicted by charts, diagrams, computer games, and institutional descriptions, but almost never do they have any explicit element of human relations or affective, emotional content, and few have displayed any cultural dimension.

The strategies set forth in the masculine mode for the transition process tend to be primarily political and economic. They are at their best in proposals for staged disarmament and plans for industrial conversion. They are conceived as steps to be taken in the public arena in a particular, incremental style (though of varying degrees of rapidity) and impacting primarily on public life. The value changes included in transition scenarios tend to be norms for social and public policies such as protection for human rights and procedures for conflict resolution. They are corporate rather than personal and conceived so as to have a direct impact on the public domain. The consequent effects of value changes on the private and personal spheres are given little if any more attention in world order transition strategies than in present public policy formation. This blindness to "secondary" consequences gives feminists, who do assess policy impact on women, cause for concern that the proposals are indeed more rearrangement than transformation. Indeed, it is this masculine preoccupation with the public and structural that has aborted the transformative potential of most twentieth-century revolutions. It kept them as just that: a revolution, a turning of the major power wheels that failed to produce changes in the fundamental global order. Such changes remove a particular group from political power but do not make connections to changes in the interpersonal realm nor to the nonmaterial sources of personal empowerment that feminism emphasizes. (It must be noted that some women researchers and futurists, myself included, have produced these same kinds of masculine scenarios.) The transition scenarios in the masculine mode have always been far weaker, less convincing, and less relevant either to the goal or the present reality than are their visions of transformed structures. In general there is a significant disjuncture between the transformative visions and the plans for the process to achieve them. Masculine models of transformation exhibit little or no consideration of the personal and individual changes that will be required. It is my opinion that this weakness in world order modeling results from the lack of the human, explicit, behavioral elements that are characteristic of the feminine mode. . . .

Most feminist visions or models of the future world order are found not in academic essays, computerized games, graphs, or charts but in novels, poetry, works of art, and specific behavioral changes that women are currently making in themselves and seeking to help others to make. Women are significantly active in initiating political movements, particularly movements related to peace and justice, but they have yet to be as concerned with political strategy design and the devising of structural changes for the institutionalization of the kind of human interrelationships they seek. Yet their current efforts and their visions of healing and wholeness are in some ways far more transformative than the precise structural designs and abstract political processes that male researchers have offered to date.

Transcending Polarization: Reconciliation as a World Order Value

To move toward a broader comprehension of the meaning of healing and wholeness in our fragmented world and to comprehend the full dimensions of the transformational task, we need to take note of the many damaging divisions and separations that are in large part a consequence of the masculine bias in science, politics, and social structures in general. We need to focus on the major separations and dichotomies in thought and social functions and the consequent inequity, conflict, and violence that this bias has produced. Among the deepest of these divisions that the feminine flow toward healing and wholeness call us to transcend are those between science and philosophy, fact and value, the individual and the community, the family and the state, the public and the private spheres, citizens and nurturers, and male and female social roles. For example, citizenship in a feminist future order would carry responsibility to nurture and enhance life as well as participate in politics and public affairs. . . .

What I am advocating here is a new world order value, reconciliation, and perhaps even forgiveness, not only of those who trespass against us, but primarily of ourselves. By understanding that no human being is totally incapable of the most reprehensible of human acts, or of the most selfless and noble, we open up the possibilities for change of cosmic dimensions. Essentially this realization is what lies at the base of the philosophy of nonviolence. If we are to move through a disarmed

world to a truly nonviolent one, to authentic peace and justice, we must come to terms with and accept the other in ourselves, be it our masculine or our feminine attributes or any of those traits and characteristics we have projected on enemies and criminals, or heroes and saints.

If we advocate the equal value and dignity of all persons, we need also accept their shortcomings as well as their gifts and talents, and understand that all (even ourselves) are capable of changing. The question is whether we will be motivated to do so. My own belief is that this motivation is primarily a task for education, particularly for peace education. Indeed, we have seen little evidence of motivation to change either in the bastions of male chauvinism or in the entrenched militaristic social system. But without the possibility of such change there is little hope of escaping from the war system trap. Education is an enterprise based on hope and the possibility of change.

At its best, education, like the struggle for peace, is motivated by love. The facts that men and women continue to love each other, and that some even struggle to understand each other despite the overwhelming dimensions of the system that separates and alienates us from each other, are a tremendous source of hope. So, too, is the growing bonding among women transcending a socialization that separated and alienated them from each other, setting them into competition to win the favor of men. As men have bonded in the hunt and on the battlefields and playing fields, women now bond in the feminist movement and in the peace movement, offering each other some of the love and support they have been socialized to lavish on husbands and children. They are supporting and nurturing each other through personal change and political challenge. Such sources of hope make it possible to believe we can change. It is this belief that feminists find empowering and from which we take a new definition of *power*: the capacity to change, to change ourselves and our environment.

Indeed, the empowerment of the powerless is the fundamental change required to transcend sexism and the war system. It would be the very antithesis of the present coercive use of power. It is one of the major motivations behind the feminist demand that women have control over their own bodies, the prime requisite of empowerment, and it clearly makes these women's issues world order issues. It means as well that world order must at last fully embrace that elusive fifth value, *participation*, as it moves toward the stronger, more transformative value of universal human empowerment. Only through this kind of process can we be liberated from the continued global dominance of the industrial male elites. Women's movements, anticolonial movements, and all forms of human rights movements are evidence that such a process is underway. All such movements begin with the refusal of the oppressed to continue to accept their inferior status as inevitable or deserved. Value of self, a primary value of feminism, is essential to the process of liberation and to the development of mature responsibility. . . . The most significant aspect of the process is recognizing the costs. Empowerment, self-respect, and authentic responsibility are not easily come by, not by individuals or societies. Nor do we have the specific strategies of empowerment at hand. However, given the commitment and the visions, feminist strategies are born out of specific contexts and conditions.

These examples hold forth the possibility of relating to others, and to the other, as full persons, not as enemies or objects. The focus was on both political objective, or social model, and on human relations. They seemed to combine the masculine abstract intellectual approach with the feminine concrete, practical approach. This, it seems to me, is what we need in transition strategies—a convergence of masculine and feminine styles of change.

There is a significant similarity between feminist peace strategists and male practitioners of nonviolence in their refusal to accede to the seemingly unchangeable, and their challenge to the authority of raw, coercive power. They have taken responsibility to ask the fundamental questions about the necessity of human suffering. Questioning, taking responsibility, empowerment and value of self are attributes of maturity and transformation. They are evidence, too, of the convergence of positive masculine and feminine values, modes of thought, and styles of action. These developments are cited as signs of the hoped-for convergence of feminism and the peace movement, and to indicate that the possibilities for truly transformatory movements can be greatly enhanced by encouraging and

widening this convergence. The possibility of a cultural transformation of unprecedented proportions is, indeed, emerging. The chances of making that possibility become a probability, of achieving a truly human future, will be enhanced by deeper study of the connections between sexism and the war system. The potential for transformation that I see in the knowledge such study would yield gives me hope at a time when ordinary politics and traditional scholarship offer none.

Conclusion: Reproducing the Future

Because one major purpose of this monograph has been to reflect on the life-enhancing possibilities of feminism and women's movements, the language of human reproduction provides an appropriate frame for the conclusion. The conception of a transformed society will be found in the actualizing of the central ideas that will give birth to that society. As male and female genetic material converge in the conception of an individual human life, so must masculine and feminine perceptions, modes, and participation merge into a conception of a truly human society. This conception can be politically symbolized by taking on as one goal the two major transformative tasks of our generation: achieving equality for women and complete disarmament. Achieving the first task would give social value to positive feminine human traits, and the accomplishment of the second would require denial of social value to the most negative masculine traits.

The gestation of the transformed society would be in the processes we devise to develop the basic conception into a living social order, capable of maturing into an entity no longer dependent on specific structures or controlled by the circumstances that led to its conception. Such processes are likely to be simultaneous and complementary behavioral and structural changes guided by the masculine values of justice and equality and the feminine values of care and equity. Transition strategies equal to this task can be designed only by men and women together working in a style of true mutuality.

The "cry of life" of the transformation might be the public articulation and institutionalization of the fundamental values derived from the parents. The birth would be symbolized, as have been the births of societies for centuries, by the inauguration of new governing structures. Such an inauguration might be the formal recognition of the institutional framework of a global peace system, derived as the result of the equal political participation of men and women in the maintenance and development of a disarmed and demilitarized world.

The maturity of such a peace system would be indicated by continuous reflection on and challenge to its rules and structures and by its capacity to change in response to new conditions leading to new stages of human maturation. Maturity is, in the last analysis, the capacity to transform, and to bring forth new life. Transformation is the continuous process by which human beings exercise choice, change reality, and find meaning. Transformation is life. Feminism chooses life.

VACLAV HAVEL

The Politics of Responsibility

Democracy is a bit like Mom and apple pie: everyone claims to be in favor of it. At its heart, however, the notion that countries should be governed according to the will of their people is radical indeed. Some of the most astounding and hopeful events of the late twentieth century involved democratization: in South Africa, South Korea, the Philippines, Haiti, much of Latin America, even, haltingly, in Russia and the former "Soviet bloc" states of Eastern Europe.

On the negative side, democracy is nearly always under siege. In 1941, sociologist Harold Lasswell warned in a now classic paper about the possible rise of "garrison states—a world in which the specialists on violence are the most powerful group in society."[3] Lasswell predicted that there would likely be "transitional forms, such as the party propaganda state, in which the dominant figure is the propagandist, and the party bureaucratic state, in which the organization men of the party make the vital decisions." It can be debated whether the United States has risen—or sunk—to any of these levels, and whether or to what extent other countries are in transition.

On the other hand, with the end of the Cold War and the apparent spread of democracy, peace researchers have been actively debating another of the more optimistic generalizations: that democracies do not go to war against other democracies. This gives added cogency to the question of "garrison states," incipient or hidden garrison states, and the relationship between militarism and democracy.

Another important—and sometimes troubling—aspect of democracy is that it invokes serious questions about responsibility: the responsibility of each citizen for his or her immediate social unit, larger community, and the world. These questions are increasingly cogent in a world that is becoming culturally homogenized. Vaclav Havel, former playwright, is the president of the Czech Republic, and a long-time prodemoc-

From "The Politics of Responsibility" by Vaclav Havel. 1995. World Policy Journal 12(3): 81–87. Reprinted by permission of World Policy Journal.

[3]Harold Lasswell. 1941. "The Garrison State." American Journal of Sociology 156: 455–68.

racy dissident. He offers a thought-provoking statement about some of democracy's burdens and opportunities, personal committment, and national involvement in the problems of a diverse, yet interconnected world.

One evening not long ago, I was sitting in an outdoor restaurant by the water. My chair was almost identical to the chairs they have in restaurants by the Vltava River in Prague. They were playing the same rock music they play in most Czech restaurants. I saw advertisements I'm familiar with back home. Above all, I was surrounded by young people who were similarly dressed, who drank familiar-looking drinks, and who behaved as casually as their contemporaries in Prague. Only their complexions and their facial features were different—for I was in Singapore.

I sat there thinking about this and again—for the umpteenth time—I realized an almost banal truth: that we now live in a single, global civilization. The identity of this civilization does not lie merely in similar forms of dress, or similar drinks, or in the constant buzz of the same commercial music all around the world, or even in international advertising. It lies in something deeper: thanks to the modern idea of constant progress, with its inherent expansionism, and to the rapid evolution of science that comes directly from it, our planet has, for the first time in the long history of the human race, been covered in the space of a very few decades by a single civilization—one that is essentially technological. The world is now enmeshed in webs of telecommunications networks consisting of millions of tiny threads or capillaries that not only transmit information of all kinds at lightning speed, but also convey integrated models of social, political, and economic behavior. . . .

Thanks to the accomplishments of this civilization, practically all of us know what checks, bonds, bills of exchange, and stocks are. We are familiar with CNN and Chernobyl, and we know who the Rolling Stones, and Nelson Mandela, and Salman Rushdie are. More than that, the capillaries that have so radically integrated this civilization also convey information about certain modes of human coexistence that have proven their worth, like democracy, respect for human rights, the rule of law, the laws of the marketplace. Such information flows around the world and, in varying degrees, takes root in different places.

In modern times, this global civilization emerged in the territory occupied by European and, ultimately, by Euro-American culture. Historically, it evolved from a combination of traditions—classical, Judaic, and Christian. In theory, at least, it gives people not only the capacity for worldwide communication but also a coordinated means of defending themselves against many common dangers. It can also, in an unprecedented way, make our lives on this earth easier and open up to us hitherto unexplored horizons in our knowledge of ourselves and the world we live in.

And yet there is something not quite right about it . . .

Civilization's Thin Veneer

Many of the great problems we face today, as far as I understand them, have their origin in the fact that this global civilization, though in evidence everywhere, is no more than a thin veneer over the sum total of human awareness, if I may put it that way. This civilization is immensely fresh, young, new, and fragile, and the human spirit has accepted it with dizzying alacrity, without itself changing in any essential way. Humanity has evolved over long millennia in all manner of civilizations and cultures that gradually, and in very diverse ways, shaped our habits of mind, our relationship to the world, our models of behavior, and the values we accept and recognize. In essence, this new single epidermis of world civilization merely covers or conceals the immense variety of cultures, of peoples, of religious worlds, of historical traditions and historically formed attitudes, all of which in a sense lie "beneath" it. At the same time, even as the veneer of world civilization expands, this "underside" of humanity, this hidden dimension of it, demands more and more clearly to be heard and to be granted a right to life.

And thus, while the world as a whole increasingly accepts the new habits of global civilization, another contradictory process is taking place: ancient traditions are reviving, different religions and cultures are awakening to new ways of being, seeking new room to exist, and struggling with growing fervor to realize what is unique to them and what makes them different from others. Ultimately, they seek to give their individuality a political expression.

It is often said that in our time, every valley cries out for its own independence or will even fight for it. Many nations, or parts of them at least, are struggling against modern civilization or its main proponents for the right to worship their ancient gods and obey the ancient divine injunctions. They carry on their struggle using weapons provided by the very civilization they oppose. They employ radar, computers, lasers, nerve gases, and, perhaps, in the future, even nuclear weapons—all products of the world they challenge—to help defend their ancient heritage against the erosions of modern civilization. In contrast with these technological inventions, other products of this civilization—like democracy or the idea of human rights—are not accepted in many places in the world because they are deemed to be hostile to local traditions.

In other words: the Euro-American world has equipped other parts of the globe with instruments that not only could effectively destroy the enlightened values that, among other things, made possible the invention of precisely these instruments, but that could well cripple the capacity of people to live together on this earth.

What follows from all of this?

It is my belief that this state of affairs contains a clear challenge not only to the Euro-American world but to our present-day civilization as a whole. It is a challenge to this civilization to start understanding itself as a multicultural and multipolar civilization, whose meaning lies not in undermining the individuality of different spheres of culture and civilization but in allowing them to be more completely themselves. This will only be possible, even conceivable, if we all accept a basic code of mutual coexistence, a kind of common minimum we can all share, one that will enable us to go on living side by side. . . .

A Utopian Idea?

But is humanity capable of such an undertaking? Is it not a hopelessly utopian idea? Haven't we so lost control of our destiny that we are con-

demned to gradual extinction in even harsher high-tech clashes between cultures, because of our fatal inability to cooperate in the face of impending catastrophes, be they ecological, social, or demographic, or because of dangers generated by the state of our civilization as such?

I don't know.

But I have not lost hope.

I have not lost hope because I am persuaded time and time again that, lying dormant in the deepest roots of most, if not all, cultures there is an essential similarity, something that could be made—if the will to do so existed—a genuinely unifying starting point for that new code of human coexistence that would be firmly anchored in the great diversity of human traditions.

Don't we find somewhere in the foundations of most religions and cultures, though they may take a thousand and one distinct forms, common elements, such as a respect for what transcends us, whether we mean the mystery of Being, or a moral order that stands above us; certain imperatives that come from heaven, or from nature, or from our own hearts; a belief that our deeds will live after us; respect for our neighbors, for our families, for certain natural authorities; respect for human dignity and for nature; a sense of solidarity and benevolence toward guests who come with good intentions?

Isn't the common, ancient origin or human roots of our diverse spiritualities, each of which is merely another kind of human understanding of the same reality, the thing that can genuinely bring people of different cultures together?

And aren't the basic commandments of this archetypical spirituality in harmony with what even an unreligious person—without knowing exactly why—may consider proper and meaningful?

Naturally, I am not suggesting that modern people be compelled to worship ancient deities and accept rituals they have long since abandoned. I am suggesting something quite different: we must come to understand the deep mutual connection of kinship between the various forms of our spirituality. We must recollect our original spiritual and moral substance, which grew out of the same essential experience of humanity. I believe that this is the only way to achieve a genuine renewal of our sense of responsibility for ourselves and for the world. At the same time, it is the only way to achieve a deeper understanding among cultures that will enable them to work together in a truly ecumenical way to create a new order for the world.

Spiritual Politics

The veneer of global civilization that envelops the modern world and the consciousness of humanity, as we all know, has a dual nature, bringing into question, at every step of the way, the very values it is based upon, or which it propagates. The thousands of marvelous achievements of this civilization that work for us so well and enrich us can equally impoverish, diminish, and destroy our lives, and so frequently do. Instead of serving people, many of these creations enslave them. Instead of helping people to develop their identities, they take them away. Almost every invention or discovery—from the splitting of the atom and the discovery of DNA to television and the computer—can be turned against us and used to our detriment. How much easier is it today than it was during the First World War to destroy an entire metropolis in a single air raid. And how much easier would it be today, in the era of television, for a madman like Hitler or Stalin to pervert the spirit of a whole nation. When have people ever had the power we now possess to alter the climate of the planet or deplete its mineral resources or the wealth of its fauna and flora in the space of a few short decades? And how much more destructive potential do terrorists have at their disposal today than at the beginning of this century?

In our era, it would seem that one part of the human brain, the rational part that has made all these morally neutral discoveries, has undergone exceptional development, while the other part, which should be alert to ensure that these discoveries really serve humanity and will not destroy it, has lagged behind catastrophically.

Yes, regardless of where I begin my thinking about the problems facing our civilization, I always return to the theme of human responsibility, which seems incapable of keeping pace with civilization and preventing it from turning against the human race. It's as though the world has simply become too much for us to deal with.

There is no way back. Only a dreamer can believe that the solution lies in curtailing the progress of civilization in some way or other. The main task in the coming era is something else: a radical renewal of our sense of responsibility. Our conscience must catch up to our reason, otherwise we are lost.

It is my profound belief that there is only one way to achieve this: we must divest ourselves of our egotistical anthropocentrism, our habit of seeing ourselves as masters of the universe who can do whatever occurs to us. We must discover a new respect for what transcends us: for the universe, for the earth, for nature, for life, and for reality. Our respect for other people, for other nations, and for other cultures, can only grow from a humble respect for the cosmic order and from an awareness that we are a part of it, that we share in it and that nothing of what we do is lost, but rather becomes part of the eternal memory of Being, where it is judged. . . .

It will certainly not be easy to awaken in people a new sense of responsibility for the world, an ability to conduct themselves as if they were to live on this earth forever, and to be held answerable for its conditions one day. Who knows how many horrific cataclysms humanity may have to go through before such a sense of responsibility is generally accepted. But this does not mean that those who wish to work for it cannot begin at once. It is a great task for teachers, educators, intellectuals, the clergy, artists, entrepreneurs, journalists, people active in all forms of public life.

Above all, it is a task for politicians. . . .

The main task of the present generation of politicians is not, I think, to ingratiate themselves with the public through the decisions they take or their smiles on television. It is not to go on winning elections and ensuring themselves a place in the sun till the end of their days. Their role is something quite different: to assume their share of responsibility for the long-range prospects of our world and thus to set an example for the public in whose sight they work. Their responsibility is to think ahead boldly, not to fear the disfavor of the crowd, to imbue their actions with a spiritual dimension (which of course is not the same thing as ostentatious attendance at religious services), to explain again and again—both to the public and to their colleagues—that politics must do far more than reflect the interests of particular groups and lobbies. After all, politics is a matter of serving the community, which means that it is morality in practice. And how better to serve the community, and practice morality, than by seeking in the midst of the global (and globally threatened) civilization their own global political responsibility: that is, their responsibility for the very survival of the human race? . . .

The American Engagement

It is obvious that those who have the greatest power and influence also bear the greatest responsibility. Like it or not, the United States of America now bears probably the greatest responsibility for the direction our world will take. The United States, therefore, should reflect most deeply on this responsibility. . . .

There is far more at stake here than simply standing up to those who would like once again to divide the world into spheres of interest, or subjugate others who are different from them and weaker. What is now at stake is saving the human race. In other words, it's a question of what I've already talked about: of understanding modern civilization as a multicultural and multipolar civilization, of turning our attention to the original spiritual sources of human culture, and above all, of our own culture, of drawing from these sources the strength for a courageous and magnanimous creation of a new order for the world.

The Banal Pride of the Powerful

Not long ago I was at a gala dinner to mark an important anniversary. There were 50 heads of state present, perhaps more, who came to honor the heroes and victims of the greatest war in human history. This was not a political conference, but the kind of social event that is meant principally to show hospitality and respect to the invited guests. When the seating plan was given out, I discovered to my surprise that those sitting at the table next to mine were not identified simply as representatives of a particular state, as was the case with all the other tables; they were referred to as "permanent members of the U.N. Security Council and the Group of Seven."

I had mixed feelings about this. On the one hand, I thought, how marvelous that the richest and most powerful of this world see each other often and, even at this dinner, can talk informally and get to know each other better. On the other hand, a slight chill went down my spine, for I could not help observing that one table had been singled out as being special and particularly important. It was a table for the big powers. Somewhat perversely, I began to imagine that those sitting at it were, along with their Russian caviar, dividing the rest of us up among themselves, without asking our opinions. Perhaps all this is merely the whimsy of a former and perhaps future playwright. But I wanted to express it here, for one simple reason: to emphasize the terrible gap that exists between the responsibility of the great powers and their hubris. The architect of that seating arrangement—I should think it was none of the attending presidents—was not guided by a sense of responsibility for the world, but by the banal pride of the powerful.

But pride is precisely what will lead the world to hell. I am suggesting an alternative: humbly accepting our responsibility for the world. . . .

Whether our world is to be saved from everything that threatens it today depends above all on whether human beings come to their senses, whether they understand the degree of their responsibility and discover a new relationship to the very miracle of Being. The world is in the hands of us all.

A Few Poetic Visions

We end with some poetic visions: tragic, ironic, idyllic, pessimistic, optimistic, corny, and profound . . . sometimes all of these at the same time. If such ambiguity is occasionally frustrating, it is at least consistent with the world situation, as we approach what might eventually be peace.

War Is Kind: Stephen Crane

Do not weep, maiden, for war is kind.
Because your lover threw wild hands
toward the sky
And the affrighted steed ran on alone.
Do not weep
War is kind.

Hoarse, booming drums of the regiment,
Little souls who thirst for fight,
These men were born to drill and die.
The unexplained glory flies above them,
Great is the Battle-God, great, and his
Kingdom—
A field where a thousand corpses lie.

Do not weep, babe, for war is kind.
Because your father tumbled in the yellow
trenches,
Raged at his breast, gulped and died,
Do not weep.
War is kind.

Swift blazing flag of the regiment,
Eagle with crest and red and gold,
These men were born to drill and die.
Point for them the virtue of slaughter,
Make plain to them the excellence of
killing
And a field where a thousand corpses lie.

Mother, whose heart hung humble as a
button
On the bright splendid shroud of your son,
Do not weep.
War is kind.

Anthem for Doomed Youth: Wilfred Owen

What passing-bells for these who die as
cattle?
—Only the monstrous anger of the guns.
Only the stuttering rifles' rapid rattle
Can patter out their hasty orisons.
No mockeries now for them: no prayers
nor bells;
Nor any voice of mourning save the
choirs,—
The shrill, demented choirs of wailing
shells;
And bugles calling for them from sad
shires.

What candles may be held to speed them
all?
Not in the hands of boys, but in their eyes
Shall shine the holy glimmers of good-
byes.
The pallor of girls' brows shall be their
pall;
Their flowers the tenderness of patient
minds,
And each slow dusk a drawing-down of
blinds.

Dulce Et Decorum Est: Wifred Owen

Bent double, like old beggars under
sacks,
Knock-kneed, coughing like hags, we
cursed through sludge,

Till on the haunting flares we turned our
backs
And towards our distant rest began to
trudge.
Men marched asleep. Many had lost their
boots
But limped on, blood-shod. All went lame;
all blind;
Drunk with fatigue; deaf even to the hoots
Of tired, outstripped Five-Nines that
dropped behind.

Gas! GAS! Quick, boys!—An ecstasy of
fumbling,
Fitting the clumsy helmets just in time;

But someone still was yelling out and stumbling,
And flound'ring like a man in fire or lime . . .
Dim, through the misty panes and thick green light,
As under a green sea, I saw him drowning.

In all my dreams, before my helpless sight,
He plunges at me, guttering, choking, drowning.

If in some smothering dreams you too could pace
Behind the wagon that we flung him in,
And watch the white eyes writhing in his face,
His hanging face, like a devil's sick of sin;
If you could hear, at every jolt, the blood
Come gargling from the froth-corrupted lungs,
Obscene as cancer, bitter as the cud
Of vile, incurable sores on innocent tongues,—
My friend, you would not tell with such high zest
To children ardent for some desperate glory,
The old Lie: Dulce et decorum est
Pro patria mori.

The Second Coming: W. B. Yeats

Turning and turning in the widening gyre
The falcon cannot hear the falconer;
Things fall apart; the centre cannot hold;
Mere anarchy is loosed upon the world,
The blood-dimmed tide is loosed, and everywhere
The ceremony of innocence is drowned;
The best lack all conviction, while the worst
Are full of passionate intensity.

Surely some revelation is at hand;
Surely the Second Coming is at hand.
The Second Coming! Hardly are those words out
When a vast image out of *Spiritus Mundi*
Troubles my sight somewhere in sands of the desert
A shape with lion body and the head of a man,
A gaze blank and pitiless as the sun,
Is moving its slow thighs, while all about it

Reel shadows of the indignant desert birds.
The darkness drops again; but now I know
That twenty centuries of stony sleep
Were vexed to nightmare by a rocking cradle,
And what rough beast, its hour come round at last,
Slouches towards Bethlehem to be born?

The Lake Isle of Innisfree: W. B. Yeats

I WILL arise and go now, and go to Innisfree,
And a small cabin build there, of clay and wattles made:
Nine bean-rows will I have there, a hive for the honey-bee,
And live alone in the bee-loud glade.

And I shall have some peace there, for peace comes dropping slow,
Dropping from the veils of the morning to where the cricket sings;
There midnight's all a glimmer, and noon a purple glow,
And evening full of the linnet's wings.

I will arise and go now, for always night and day
I hear lake water lapping with low sounds by the shore;
While I stand on the roadway, or on the pavements grey,
I hear it in the deep heart's core.

Abou Ben Adhem: Leigh Hunt

ABOU BEN ADHEM (may his tribe increase!)
Awoke one night from a deep dream of peace,
And saw, within the moonlight in his room,
Making it rich, and like a lily in bloom,
An Angel writing in a book of gold:
Exceeding peace had made Ben Adhem bold,
And to the Presence in the room he said,
"What writest thou?" The Vision raised its head,
And with a look made of all sweet accord
Answered, "The names of those who love the Lord."
"And is mine one?" said Abou. "Nay, not so,"

Replied the Angel. Abou spoke more
low,
    But cheerily still; and said, "I pray thee,
then,
    Write me as one that loves his fellow
men."

    The Angel wrote, and vanished. The
next night
    It came again with a great wakening
light,
    And showed the names whom love
of God had blessed,
    And, lo! Ben Adhem's name led all the
rest!

A Man Who Had Fallen Among Thieves: e. e. cummings

a man who had fallen among thieves
lay by the roadside on his back
dressed in fifteenthrate ideas
wearing a round jeer for a hat

fate per a somewhat more than less
emancipated evening
had in return for consciousness
endowed him with a changeless grin

whereon a dozen staunch and leal
citizens did graze at pause
then fired by hypercivic zeal
sought newer pastures or because

swaddled with a frozen brook
of pinkest vomit out of eyes
which noticed nobody he looked
as if he did not care to rise

one hand did nothing on the vest
its wideflung friend clenched weakly dirt
while the mute trouserfly confessed
a button solemnly inert.

Brushing from whom the stiffened puke
i put him all into my arms
and staggered banged with terror through
a million billion trillion stars

STUDY QUESTIONS

1. What are some important lessons to be learned from peace movements of the past, and how might they inform peace movements of the future?
2. What do you see as one or more likely scenarios for the world in the near future? The distant future?
3. What would you *like to see* as one or more likely scenarios for the world in the near future? The distant future?
4. Many people claim that "peace begins with me." Discuss some pros and cons of this attitude.
5. Suggest a classification of peace movements other than those presented in this chapter.
6. Develop some of your own criticisms of the field of peace studies.
7. Is it possible to have a world without violence? How about one without conflict?
8. If peace studies did not exist, perhaps it would be necessary to invent it. Try your hand at inventing peace studies, as though it did not exist; consider education, practical action, connections to other traditions, and so on.
9. Look deeply into one or more of the poems included in this chapter, and/or suggest some others. To what extent does the poetic imagery add to your intellectual grasp of the issue of peace? What are some "futuristic" novels that might also be appropriate to this chapter?
10. Have you been treating the material in this book as anything other than just one more text to be studied, learned from, tested and graded on, and then filed away somewhere? If so, why? If not, why not?

Suggestions for Further Reading

Alonso, Harriet Hyman. 1993. *Peace as a Women's Issue: A History of the U.S. Movement for World Peace and Women's Rights*. Syracuse, NY: Syracuse University Press.

Brock, Peter. 1991. *Studies in Peace History*. Syracuse, NY: Syracuse University Press.

Carter, April. 1992. *Peace Movements: International Protest and World Politics Since 1945*. New York: Longman.

Chatfield, Charles and Peter van den Dungen. eds. 1988. *Peace Movements and Political Cultures*. Knoxville: University of Tennessee Press.

Downton, James V. 1997. *The Persistent Activist: How Peace Commitment Develops and Survives*. Boulder, Colo: Westview Press.

Falk, Richard A. 1992. *Explorations at the Edge of Time: The Prospects for World Order*. Philadelphia: Temple University Press.

Foster, Carrie A. 1995. *The Women and the Warriors: The U.S. Section of the Women's International League for Peace and Freedom, 1915–1946*. Syracuse, NY: Syracuse University Press.

Heineman, Kenneth J. 1993. *Campus Wars: The Peace Movement at American State Universities in the Vietnam Era*. New York: New York University Press.

Lofland, John. 1993. *Polite Protesters: The American Peace Movement of the 1980s*. Syracuse, NY: Syracuse University Press.

Reardon, Betty. 1993. *Women and Peace: Feminist Visions of Global Security*. Albany: State University of New York Press.

Reardon, Betty and Eva Nordland. eds. 1994. *Learning Peace: The Promise of Ecological and Cooperative Education*. Albany: State University of New York Press.

Rochon, Thomas R. and David S. Meyer. eds. 1997. *Coalitions and Politial Movements: The Lessons of the Nuclear Freeze*. Boulder, Colo: L. Rienner.

Smith, Christian. 1996. *Resisting Reagan: The U.S. Central America Peace Movement*. Chicago: University of Chicago Press.

Wittner, Lawrence S. 1984. *Rebels Against War: The American Peace Movement, 1933–1983*. Philadelphia: Temple University Press.

Zisk, Betty H. 1992. *The Politics of Transformation: Local Activism in the Peace and Environmental Movements*. Westport, Conn: Praeger.

Index

~~~